T0214644

Lecture Notes in Computer Science 11636

More information about this series at http://www.springer.com/series/7407

Fabrizio Biondi · Thomas Given-Wilson ·
Axel Legay (Eds.)

Model Checking
Software

26th International Symposium, SPIN 2019
Beijing, China, July 15–16, 2019
Proceedings

 Springer

Editors
Fabrizio Biondi
Avast Software
Prague, Czech Republic

Thomas Given-Wilson
Université Catholique de Louvain
Louvain-la-Neuve, Belgium

Axel Legay
Université Catholique de Louvain
Louvain-la-Neuve, Belgium

ISSN 0302-9743   ISSN 1611-3349 (electronic)
Lecture Notes in Computer Science
ISBN 978-3-030-30922-0   ISBN 978-3-030-30923-7 (eBook)
https://doi.org/10.1007/978-3-030-30923-7

LNCS Sublibrary: SL1 – Theoretical Computer Science and General Issues

This Springer imprint is published by the registered company Springer Nature Switzerland AG
The registered company address is: Gewerbestrasse 11, 6330 Cham, Switzerland

Preface

This volume contains the proceedings of the 26th International Symposium on Model Checking Software, SPIN 2019, held in Beijing, China, July 15–16, 2019. SPIN is a well-recognized periodic event started in 1995 around the model checking tool SPIN. Since 1995, the event has evolved and has been consolidated as a reference symposium in the area of formal methods related to model checking. The previous edition of the SPIN symposium took place in Málaga (Spain) with a record number of submissions and participants.

The SPIN 2019 edition requested regular papers, short papers, and tool demos in the following areas: formal verification techniques for automated analysis of software; formal analysis for modeling languages, such as UML/state charts; formal specification languages, temporal logic, and design-by-contract; model checking, automated theorem proving, including SAT and SMT; verifying compilers; abstraction and symbolic execution techniques; static analysis and abstract interpretation; combination of verification techniques; modular and compositional verification techniques; verification of timed and probabilistic systems; automated testing using advanced analysis techniques; combination of static and dynamic analyses; derivation of specifications, test cases, or other useful material via formal analysis; case studies of interesting systems or with interesting results; engineering and implementation of software verification and analysis tools; benchmark and comparative studies for formal verification and analysis tools; formal methods education and training; and insightful surveys or historical accounts on topics of relevance to the symposium. The symposium attracted 29 submissions that were carefully reviewed by three Program Committee (PC) members. The selection process included further online discussion open to all PC members. As a result, 13 papers were selected for presentation at the symposium and publication in Springer's proceedings. The program consisted of 11 regular papers and 2 demo-tool papers. The program also included one invited talk.

We would like to thank all the authors who submitted papers, the Steering Committee, the PC, the additional reviewers, the invited speakers, the participants, and the local organizers for making SPIN 2019 a successful event. We also thank all the sponsors that provided logistics and financial support to make the symposium possible.

July 2019

Fabrizio Biondi
Thomas Given-Wilson
Axel Legay

Organization

Program Committee

Saddek Bensalem	VERIMAG, France
Fabrizio Biondi	Avast, Czech Republic
Dragan Bosnacki	Eindhoven University of Technology, The Netherlands
Gilles Geeraerts	Université libre de Bruxelles, Belgium
Thomas Given-Wilson	Universite Catholique de Louvain, Belgium
Patrice Godefroid	Microsoft, USA
Gregor Goessler	Inria, France
Radu Iosif	VERIMAG, CNRS, University of Grenoble Alpes, France
Axel Legay	UCLouvain, Belgium
Stefan Leue	University of Konstanz, Germany
Alberto Lluch Lafuente	Technical University of Denmark, Denmark
Alice Miller	University of Glasgow, UK
Corina Pasareanu	CMU, NASA Ames Research Center, USA
Charles Pecheur	Université catholique de Louvain, Belgium
Doron Peled	Bar Ilan University, Israel
Jiri Srba	Aalborg University, Denmark
Maurice H. ter Beek	ISTI-CNR, Italy
Antti Valmari	University of Jyväskylä, Finland
Jaco van de Pol	Aarhus University, Denmark
Farn Wang	National Taiwan University, Taiwan

Additional Reviewers

Bozga, Marius
Caltais, Georgiana
Dricot, Jean-Michel
Guha, Shibashis
Jensen, Peter Gjøl
Koelbl, Martin

Kölbl, Martin
Mariegaard, Anders
Mazzanti, Franco
Spoletini, Paola
Xu, Xiao

Contents

Model Verification Through Dependency Graphs

Søren Enevoldsen, Kim Guldstrand Larsen, and Jiří Srba[✉]

Department of Computer Science, Aalborg University,
Selma Lagerlofs Vej 300, 9220 Aalborg East, Denmark
srba@cs.aau.dk

Abstract. Dependency graphs, as introduced more than 20 years ago by Liu and Smolka, are oriented graphs with hyperedges that connect nodes with sets of target nodes in order to represent causal dependencies in the graph. Numerous verification problems can be reduced into the problem of computing a minimum or maximum fixed-point assignment on dependency graphs. In the original definition, assignments link each node with a Boolean value, however, in the recent work the assignment domains have been extended to more general setting, even including infinite domains. We present an overview of the recent results on extensions of dependency graphs in order to deal with verification of quantitative, probabilistic and timed systems.

Keywords: Dependency graphs · Verification ·
Fixed-point computation · On-the-fly algorithms

1 Model Verification

The scale of computational systems nowadays varies from simple toggle-buttons to various embedded systems and network routers up to complex multi-purpose computers. In safety critical applications, we need to provide guarantees about system behaviour in all situations/configurations that the system can encounter. Such guarantees are classically provided by first creating a *formal model* of the system (at an appropriate abstraction level) and then using formal methods such as model checking and equivalence checking to rigorously argue about the behaviour of the models. At the highest abstraction level, systems are usually modelled as labelled transition systems or Kripke structures (see [5] for an introduction). In labelled transition systems (LTS), a process changes its (unobservable) internal states by performing visible actions. Kripke structures on the other hand allow to observe the validity of a number of atomic predicates revealing some (partial) information about the current state of a given process, whereas the state changes are not labelled by any visible actions.

An example of LTS modelling a simple traffic light is given in Fig. 1a. Although the states have been named for convenience, they are considered opaque. Instead, this formalism uses the action-based perspective where the

© Springer Nature Switzerland AG 2019
F. Biondi et al. (Eds.): SPIN 2019, LNCS 11636, pp. 1–19, 2019.
https://doi.org/10.1007/978-3-030-30923-7_1

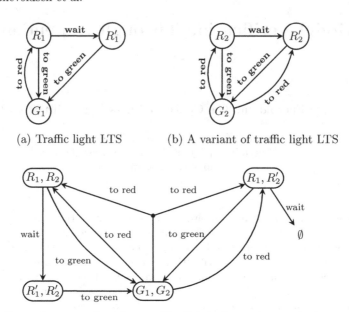

(a) Traffic light LTS   (b) A variant of traffic light LTS

(c) Dependency graph with root (R_1, R_2) for bisimulation checking

Iteration	$A(R_1, R_2)$	$A(R_1', R_2')$	$A(G_1, G_2)$	$A(R_1, R_2')$
0	0	0	0	0
1	0	0	0	1
2	0	0	1	1
3	1	1	1	1

(d) Iterative minimum fixed-point computation by using the global algorithm

Fig. 1. Traffic light LTS variants

actions of the transitions are considered visible. For example from R_1 there is a transition to R_1' labelled with a 'wait' action that allows to extend the duration of the red color, after which only the action 'to green' is available. A slight variant of the LTS is given in Fig. 1b where from G_2 it is possible to enter directly the state R_2' by performing the 'to red' action. We can now ask the (*equivalence checking*) question whether the two systems are equivalent up to some given notion of equivalence (see e.g. [22]), e.g. bisimilarity [36], which is not the case in our example.

The simple traffic light can also be modelled as a Kripke structure that is depicted in Fig. 2a. Here the transitions are not labelled by any actions while the states are labelled with the propositions 'red' and 'green' that indicate the status of the light in that state. We note that the states R and R' are indistinguishable as they are labelled by the same proposition 'red'. We can now ask the (*model checking*) question whether the initial state R satisfies the property that on any execution the proposition 'green' will eventually hold and until this happens the light is in 'red'. This can be e.g. expressed by the CTL property 'A red U green' and it indeed holds for R in the depicted Kripke structure.

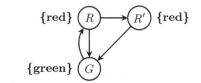

(a) Traffic light Kripke structure

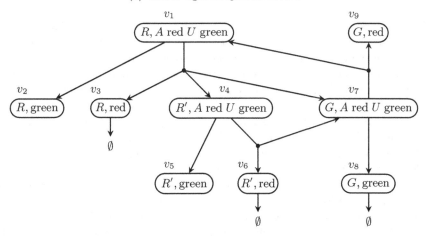

(b) Dependency graph with root v_1 encoding $R \models A$ red U green

Iteration	$A(v_1)$	$A(v_2)$	$A(v_3)$	$A(v_4)$	$A(v_5)$	$A(v_6)$	$A(v_7)$	$A(v_8)$	$A(v_9)$
0	0	0	0	0	0	0	0	0	0
1	0	0	1	0	0	1	0	1	0
2	0	0	1	0	0	1	1	1	0
3	0	0	1	1	0	1	1	1	0
4	1	0	1	1	0	1	1	1	0
5	1	0	1	1	0	1	1	1	0

(c) Interactive minimum fixed-point computation using the global algorithm

Fig. 2. Kripke structure of traffic light

1.1 On-the-Fly Verification

The challenge is how to decide the equivalence and model checking problems even for systems described in high level formalism such as automata networks or

Petri nets. These formalisms allow for a compact representation of the system behaviour, meaning that even though their configurations and transitions can still be given as a labelled transition system or a Kripke structure, the size of these can be exponential in the size of the input formalism. This phenomena is known as the *state-space explosion problem* and it makes (in many cases) the full enumeration of the state-space infeasible for practical applications. In order to deal with state-space explosion, *on-the-fly* verification algorithms are preferable as they construct the reachable state-space step by step and hence avoid the (expensive) a priory enumeration of all system configurations. In case a conclusive answer about the system behaviour can be drawn by exploring only a part of the state-space, this may grant a considerable speed up in the verification time.

The idea of local or on-the-fly model checking was discovered simultaneously and independently by various people in the end of the 80s all engaged in making model checking and equivalence checking tools for various process algebras, e.g. the Concurrency Workbench CWB [15]. Due to its high expressive power— as demonstrated in [16,37]—particular focus was on truly local model-checking algorithms for the modal mu-calculus [28]. Several discussions and exchanges of ideas between Henrik Reif Andersen, Kim G. Larsen, Colin Stirling and Glynn Winskel lead to the first local model-checking methods [3,10,29,30,38,40]. Besides the CWB these were implemented in the model checking tools TAV [9,23] for CCS and EPSILON [12] for timed CCS.

Simultaneously, in France a tool named VESAR was developed that combined the model checking idea (from the Sifakis team in Grenoble) and the simulation world (from Roland Groz at CNET Lannion and Claude Jard in Rennes, who were checking properties on-the-fly using observers). The VESAR tool was developed by a French company named Verilog and its technology was later reused for another tool named Object-Geode from the same company, which was heavily sold in the telecom sector [1].

As an alternative to encoding into the modal mu-calculus, it was realized that an even simpler formalism—Boolean equation systems (BES)—would provide a universal framework for recasting all model checking and equivalence checking problems. Whereas [31] introduces BES and first local algorithms, the work in [2] provides the first optimal (linear-time) local algorithm. Later extensions and adaptions of BES were implemented in the tools CADP [35] and muCRL [24].

1.2 Dependency Graphs Related Work

In this paper we survey the (extensions) of *dependency graphs* [33] (DG) introduced in 1998 Liu and Smolka. Similar to Boolean equation systems, DG serve as a universal tool for the representation of various model checking and equivalence checking problems, providing us with a universal method for on-the-fly exploration of DG. The elegant local (on-the-fly) algorithm presented in [33] runs in linear time with respect to the size of the DG and allows for an early termination in case the chosen search strategy manages to reveal a conclusive answer without necessarily exploring the whole graph.

Recently, the ideas of DG have been extended to various domains such as timed [11], weighted [25, 26] and probabilistic [34] systems. We shall account for some of the most notable extensions and further improvements to the local algorithm from [33] such as its parallelization. We shall start by defining the notion of dependency graphs as introduced by Liu and Smolka [33].

2   Dependency Graphs

Dependency graphs are a variant of directed graphs where each edge, also called a *hyperedge*, may have multiple target nodes [33]. The intuition is that a property of a given node in a dependency graph depends simultaneously on all the properties of the target nodes for a given hyperedge, while different outgoing hyperedges provide alternatives for deriving the desirable properties. Formally, a *dependency graph* (DG) is a pair $G = (V, E)$ where V is a set of nodes and $E \subseteq V \times 2^V$ is the set of hyperedges.

Figure 3a graphically depicts a dependency graph. For example the root node v_1 has two hyperedges: the first hyperedge has the target node v_2 and the second hyperedge has two targets v_3 and v_4. The node v_2 has no outgoing hyperedges, while the node v_3 has a single outgoing hyperedge with no targets (shown by the empty set).

As shown in Fig. 3b it is possible to interpret the dependencies among the nodes in dependency graph as a system of Boolean equations, using the general formula

$$v = \bigvee_{(v,T)\in E} \bigwedge_{u \in T} u$$

where by definition the conjunction of zero terms is true, and the disjunction of zero terms is false. We denote false by ff (or 0), and true by tt (or 1).

We can now ask the question whether there is an assignment of Boolean values to all nodes in the graph such that all constructed Boolean equations simultaneously hold. Formally, an *assignment* is a function $A : V \to \{0, 1\}$ and an assignment A is a *solution* if it satisfies the equality:

$$A(v) = \bigvee_{(v,T)\in E} \bigwedge_{u \in T} A(u).$$

In our case, there are three solutions as listed in Fig. 3c. The existence of several such possible assignments that solve the equations is caused by cyclic dependencies in the graph as e.g. v_5 depends on v_6 and at the same time v_6 also depends of v_5.

However, if we let the set of all possible assignments be $\mathcal{A}$ and define $A_1 \leq A_2$ if and only if $A_1(v) \leq A_2(v)$ for all $v \in V$ where $A_1, A_2 \in \mathcal{A}$, then we can observe that $(\mathcal{A}, \leq)$ is a complete lattice [4, 19] which guarantees the existence of the minimum and maximum assignment in the lattice.

There is a standard procedure how to compute such a minimum/maximum solution. For example for the minimum solution we can define a function $F : \mathcal{A} \to \mathcal{A}$ that transforms an assignment as follows:

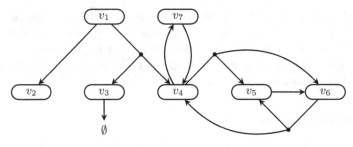

(a) Dependency graph

(b) Corresponding equation system

$$v_1 = v_2 \vee (v_3 \wedge v_4)$$
$$v_2 = f\!f$$
$$v_3 = tt$$
$$v_4 = (v_5 \wedge v_6) \vee v_7$$
$$v_5 = v_6$$
$$v_6 = v_4 \wedge v_5$$
$$v_7 = v_4$$

$v_1 = tt$	$v_1 = tt$	$v_1 = f\!f$
$v_2 = f\!f$	$v_2 = f\!f$	$v_2 = f\!f$
$v_3 = tt$	$v_3 = tt$	$v_3 = tt$
$v_4 = tt$	$v_4 = tt$	$v_4 = f\!f$
$v_5 = tt$	$v_5 = f\!f$	$v_5 = f\!f$
$v_6 = tt$	$v_6 = f\!f$	$v_6 = f\!f$
$v_7 = tt$	$v_7 = tt$	$v_7 = f\!f$

(c) Possible solutions

Iteration	v_1	v_2	v_3	v_4	v_5	v_6	v_7
0	0	0	0	0	0	0	0
1	0	0	1	0	0	0	0
2	0	0	1	0	0	0	0

(d) Iterative minimum fixed-point computation by using the global algorithm

Fig. 3. Example of dependency graph

$$F(A)(v) = \bigvee_{(v,T) \in E} \bigwedge_{u \in T} A(u).$$

Clearly, the function F is monotonic and an assignment A is a solution to a given dependency graph if and only if A is a fixed point of A, i.e. $F(A) = A$. From the Knaster-Tarski fixed-point theorem [39] we get that the monotonic function F on the complete lattice $(\mathcal{A}, \leq)$ has a unique minimum fixed point (solution).

By repeatedly applying F to the initial assignment A^0 where $A^0(v) = 0$ for all nodes v, we can iteratively find a minimum fixed point as formulated in the following theorem.

Theorem 1. *Let A_{min} denote the unique minimum fixed point of F. If there is an integer i such that $F^i(A^0) = F^{i+1}(A^0)$ then $F^i(A^0) = A_{min}$.*

Input: A dependency graph $G = (V, E)$.
Output: Minimum fixed point A_{min}.
1 $A := A^0$
2 **repeat**
3       $A' := A$
4   **forall** $v \in V$ **do**
5         $A(v) := \bigvee_{(v,T) \in E} \bigwedge_{u \in T} A'(u)$
6
7 **until** $A \neq A'$
8 **return** A

Algorithm 1. Global algorithm for minimum fixed point A_{min}

Clearly $F^i(A^0)$ is a fixed point as $F(F^i(A^0)) = F^i(A^0)$ by the assumption of the theorem. We notice that $A^0 \leq A_{min}$ and because F is monotonic and A_{min} is a fixed point, we also know that $F^j(A^0) \leq F^j(A_{min}) = A_{min}$ for an arbitrary j. Then in particular $F^i(A^0) \leq A_{min}$ and because A_{min} is the minimum fixed point and $F^i(A^0)$ is a fixed point, necessarily $F^i(A^0) = A_{min}$.

For any finite dependency graph, the iterative computation of A_{min} as summarized in Algorithm 1, also referred to as the *global algorithm*, is guaranteed to terminate after finitely many iterations and return the minimum fixed-point assignment. Dually, the iterative algorithm can be used to compute maximum fixed points on finite dependency graphs.

3 Encoding of Problems into Dependency Graphs

We shall now demonstrate how equivalence and model checking problems can be encoded into the question of finding a minimum fixed-point assignment on dependency graphs. Typically, the nodes in the dependency graph encode the configurations of the problem in question and the hyperedges create logical connections between the subproblems. We provide two examples showing how to encode strong bisimulation checking and CTL model checking into dependency graphs.

3.1 Encoding of Strong Bisimulation

Recall that two states s and t in a given LTS are strongly bisimilar [36], written $s \sim t$, if there is a binary relation R over the states such that $(s, t) \in R$ and

– whenever $s \xrightarrow{\alpha} s'$ then there is $t \xrightarrow{\alpha} t'$ such that $(s', t') \in R$, and
– whenever $t \xrightarrow{\alpha} t'$ then there is $s \xrightarrow{\alpha} s'$ such that $(s', t') \in R$.

We encode the question whether $s_0 \sim t_0$ for given two states s_0 and t_0 into a dependency graph where the nodes (configurations) are pairs of states of the form (s, t) and the hyperedges represent all possible 'attacks' on the claim that

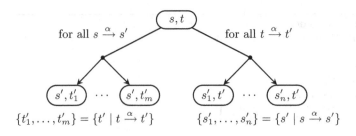

Fig. 4. Encoding rule for strong bisimulation checking

s and t are bisimilar. For example, if one of the two states can perform an action that is not enabled in the other state, we will introduce a hyperedge with the empty set of target nodes, meaning that the minimum fixed-point assignment of the node (s,t) will get the value 1 standing for the fact that $s \not\sim t$. In general the aim is to construct the DG in such a way that for any node (s,t) we have $A_{min}((s,t)) = 0$ if and only if $s \sim t$. The construction, as mentioned e.g. in [19], is given in Fig. 4. The rule says that if s can take an α-action to s', then the configuration (s,t) should have a hyperedge containing all target configurations (s',t') where t' are all possible α-successors of t. Symmetrically for the outgoing transitions for t that should be matched by transitions from s.

Let us consider again the transition systems from Fig. 1. The dependency graph to decide whether R_1 is bisimilar with R_2 is given in Fig. 1c where we can note that the configuration (R_1, R'_2) has a hyperedge with no target nodes. This is because R_1 can perform the 'wait' action that R'_2 can not match. If we now compute A_{min}, for example using the global algorithm in Fig. 1d, we notice that $A_{min}((R_1, R'_2)) = 1$ which means that R_1 and R'_2 are not bisimilar.

3.2   Encoding of CTL Model Checking

We shall now provide an example of encoding a model checking problem into dependency graphs. In particular, we demonstrate the encoding for CTL logic as described e.g. in [18]. We want to check whether a state s of a given LTS satisfies the CTL formula φ. We let the nodes of the dependency graph be of the form (s, φ) and these nodes will be decomposed into a number of subgoals depending of the structure of the formula φ. The encoding will ensure that $A_{min}((s, \varphi)) = 1$ if and only if $s \models \varphi$ for any node (s, φ) in the dependency graph [17]. Figure 5 shows the rules for constructing such a dependency graph.

Returning to our example from Fig. 2, we see in Fig. 2b the constructed dependency graph for the model checking question $R \models A\ red\ U\ green$. The fixed-point computation using the global algorithm is given in Fig. 2c and because $A_{min}(v_1) = 1$, we can conclude that the state R indeed satisfies the CTL formula $A\ red\ U\ green$. For simplicity, the encoding as shown in Fig. 5 does not include negation, but the construction can be extended to support negation [17].

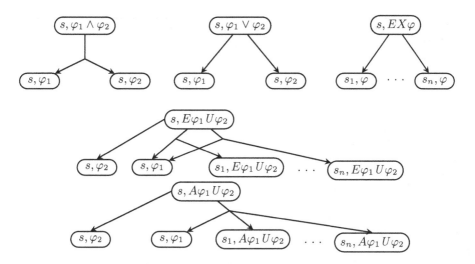

Fig. 5. Encoding to determine whether $s \models \varphi$ where $\{s_1, \ldots, s_n\} = \{s' \mid s \rightarrow s'\}$

4   Local Algorithm for Dependency Graphs

The encodings of verification problems into dependency graphs, as discussed in the previous section, construct a graph with a root node v_0 such that from the value of the minimum fixed-point assignment of the node v_0, we can deduce the answer to the verification problem in question.

In Algorithm 1 we have already seen a method for computing iteratively the minimum fixed point A_{min} for all nodes in the dependency graph. However, due to the state-space explosion problem, such a graph can be exponentially large (or even infinite) and hence it is infeasible to explore it completely. As we are often only interested in $A_{min}(v_0)$ for a given node v_0, we do not necessarily have to explore the whole dependency graph. This is shown in Fig. 7a, where we can see that $A_{min}(v_1) = 1$ due to the outgoing hyperedge from v_1 with empty set of targets, and this value can propagate directly to the node v_0 and we can also conclude that $A_{min}(v_0) = 1$; all this without the need to explore the (possibly large or even infinite) subtree with the root v_2. This idea is formalized in Liu and Smolka's *local algorithm* [33] that computes the value of $A_{min}(v_0)$ for a given node v_0 in an on-the-fly manner.

Algorithm 2 shows the pseudocode of the local algorithm. The algorithm maintains the waiting set W of hyperedges to be explored (initially all outgoing hyperedges from the root node v_0) as well as the list of dependencies D for every node v, such that $D(v)$ contains the list of all hyperedges that should be reentered into the waiting list in case the value of the node v changes from 0 to 1. Due to a small technical omission, the original algorithm of Liu and Smolka did not guarantee termination even for finite dependency graph. This is fixed in Algorithm 2 by inserting the if-test at line 10 that makes sure that we do not

---

Input: A dependency graph $G = (V, E)$ and a node $v_0 \in V$.
Output: $A_{min}(v_0)$

```
 1  forall v ∈ V do
 2  │   A(v) := ?
 3  A(v₀) := 0
 4  D(v₀) := ∅
 5  W := {(v₀, T) | (v₀, T) ∈ E}
 6  while W ≠ ∅ do
 7  │   e := (v, T) ∈ W
 8  │   W := W \ {e}
 9  │   if A(v') = 1 for all v' ∈ T then
10  │   │   if A(v) ≠ 1 then
11  │   │   │   A(v) := 1
12  │   │   │   W := W ∪ D(v)
13  │   else if ∃v' ∈ T such that A(v') = 0 then
14  │   │   D(v') := D(v') ∪ {e}
15  │   else if ∃v' ∈ T such that A(v') = ? then
16  │   │   A(v') := 0
17  │   │   D(v') := ∅
18  │   │   W := W ∪ {(v', U) | (v', U) ∈ E}
19  return A(v₀)
```

Algorithm 2. Liu and Smolka's local algorithm computing $A_{min}(v_0)$

reinsert the dependencies $D(v)$ of a node v in case that the value of v is already known to be 1.

In Fig. 6b we see the computation of the local algorithm on the dependency graph from Fig. 6a. Under the assumption that the algorithm makes optimal choices when picking among hyperedges from the waiting list (third column in the table), we can see that only a subset of nodes is ever visited and the value of $A_{min}(v_1)$ can be determined by exploring only the middle subtree of v_1 because once in the 6*th* iteration the value $A(v_1)$ is improved from 0 to 1, we terminate early and announce the answer.

4.1 Optimizations of the Local Algorithm

The local algorithm begins with all nodes being assigned ? such that whenever a new node is discovered during the forward search, it gets the value 0 and this value may be possibly increased to 1. Hence the assignment values grow as shown in Fig. 7b. As soon as the root receives the value 1, the local algorithm can terminate. If the root never receives the value 1, we need to explore the whole graph and wait until the waiting set is empty before we can terminate and return the value 0. Hence during the computation, the value 0 of a node is 'uncertain' as it can be possibly increased to 1 in the future.

Consider the dependency graph in Fig. 7c. In order to compute $A_{min}(v_0)$, the local algorithm computes first the minimum fixed-point assignment both for v_1

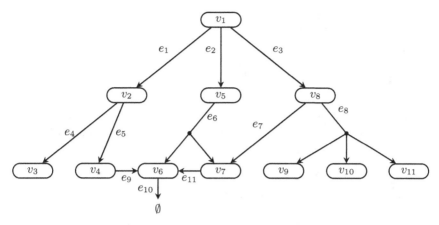

(a) Example of a dependency graph

Iteration	W	$(v,T) \in W$	$A(v_1)$	$A(v_{2...4})$	$A(v_5)$	$A(v_6)$	$A(v_7)$	$A(v_{8...11})$
0	$\{e_1, e_2, e_3\}$		0	?	?	?	?	?
1	$\{e_1, e_2, e_3\}$	e_2	0	?	0	?	?	?
2	$\{e_1, e_3, e_6\}$	e_6	0	?	0	?	0	?
3	$\{e_1, e_3, e_{11}\}$	e_{11}	0	?	0	0	0	?
4	$\{e_1, e_3, e_{10}\}$	e_{10}	0	?	0	1	0	?
5	$\{e_1, e_3, e_{11}\}$	e_{11}	0	?	0	1	1	?
6	$\{e_1, e_3, e_6\}$	e_6	0	?	1	1	1	?
7	$\{e_1, e_2, e_3\}$	e_2	1	?	1	1	1	?

(b) Execution of local algorithm for computing $A_{min}(v_1)$

Fig. 6. Demonstration of local algorithm for minimum fixed-point computation

and v_2 before it can terminate with the answer that the final value for the root is 0. However, we can actually conclude that $A_{min}(v_1) = 0$ as the final value of the node v_1 is clearly 0 and hence v_0 can never be upgraded to 1, irrelevant of the value of $A_{min}(v_2)$.

This fact was noticed in [18] where the authors suggest to extend the possible values of nodes with the notation of certain-zero (see Fig. 7d for the value ordering), i.e. once the assignment of a node becomes 0, its value can never be improved anymore to 1. The certain zero value can be back-propagated and once the root receives the certain-zero value, the algorithm can terminate early and hence speed up the computation of the fixed-point value for the root. The efficiency of the certain-zero optimization was demonstrated for example on the implementation of dependency graphs for CTL model checking of Petri nets [18] and for other verification problems in the more general setting of abstract dependency graphs [21].

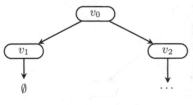

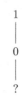

(a) Value of $A_{min}(v_2)$ is unnecessary for concluding that $A_{min}(v_0) = 1$

(b) Liu&Smolka value ordering

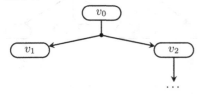

(c) Value of $A_{min}(v_2)$ is unnecessary for concluding that $A_{min}(v_0) = 0$

(d) Certain-zero value ordering

Fig. 7. Certain-zero optimization

4.2 Distributed Implementation of the Local Algorithm

State-space explosion problem means that the size of dependency graphs may become too large to fit into the memory of a single machine and/or the verification time may become infeasible. In [19] the authors describe a distributed fixed-point algorithm for dependency graphs that distributes the workload over several machines. The algorithm is based on message passing where the nodes of the dependency graphs are partitioned among the workers and each worker is responsible for computing the fixed-point values for the nodes it owns, sometimes requiring messages to be sent once the target nodes of an hyperedge are not own by the same worker as the root of the hyperedge. The experiments confirm an average speed up of around 25 times for 64 workers (CPUs) and 6 times for 8 workers. This is a satisfactory performance as the problem is P-complete (recall that we showed in Sect. 3 a polynomial time reduction from the P-complete problem of strong bisimulation checking [6] into fixed-point computation on dependency graphs), and hence inherently believed hard to parallelize. Moreover, the distributed algorithm can be used 'out-of-the-box' for a number for model verification problems (all those that can be encoded into dependency graphs), instead of designing single purpose distributed algorithms for each individual problem.

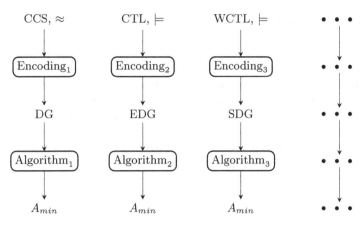

(a) Single-purpose algorithms for minimum fixed-point computation

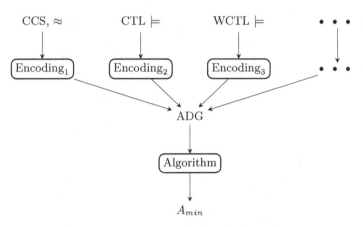

(b) Abstract Dependency Graph (ADG) solution

Fig. 8. Model verification without and with abstract dependency graphs

5   Abstract Dependency Graphs

Dependency graphs have recently been extended in several directions in order to reason about more complex problems. Extended dependency graphs, introduced in [18], add a new type of edge to dependency graphs to handle negation. Another extension with weights, called symbolic dependency graphs [26], extends the value annotation of nodes from the 0–1 domain into the set of natural numbers together with a new type of so-called cover-edges. Recently an extension presented in [14] considers as the value-assignment domain the set of piece-wise constant functions in order to be able to encode weighted PCTL model checking. Because the constructed dependency graphs in these extensions are different, for each problem that we consider we need to implement a single-purpose algorithm to compute the fixed points on such extended dependency graphs, as depicted in Fig. 8a.

In [21] *abstract dependency graphs* (ADG) are suggested that permit a more general, user-defined domain for the node assignments together with user-defined functions for evaluating the fixed-point assignments. As a result, a number of verification problems can be now encoded as ADG and a single (optimized) algorithm can be used for computing the minimum fixed point as depicted in Fig. 8b.

In ADG the values of node assignments have to form a *Noetherian Ordering Relation with least element* (NOR), which is a triple $\mathcal{D} = (D, \sqsubseteq, \bot)$ where $(D, \sqsubseteq)$ is a partial order, $\bot \in D$ is its least element, and $\sqsubseteq$ satisfies the ascending chain condition: for any infinite chain $d_1 \sqsubseteq d_2 \sqsubseteq d_3 \sqsubseteq \ldots$ there is an integer k such that $d_k = d_{k+j}$ for all $j > 0$. For algorithmic purposes, we assume that such a domain together with the ordering relation is effective (computable).

Instead of hyperedges, each node in an ADG has an ordered sequence of target nodes together with a monotonic function $f : D^n \to D$ of the same arity as the number of its target nodes. The function is used to evaluate the values of the node during an iterative, local fixed-point computation.

An assignment $A : V \to D$ is now a function that to each node assigns a value from the domain D and we define a function F as

$$F(A)(v) = \mathcal{E}(v)(A(v_1), A(v_2), \ldots, A(v_n))$$

where $\mathcal{E}(v)$ stands for the monotonic function assigned to node v and $v_1, v_2, \ldots v_n$ are all (ordered) target nodes of v.

The presence of the least element $\bot \in D$ means that the assignment $A_\bot$ where $A_\bot(v) = \bot$ for all $v \in V$ is the least of all assignments (when ordered component-wise). Moreover, the requirement that $(D, \sqsubseteq, \bot)$ satisfies the ascending chain condition ensures that assignments cannot increase indefinitely and guarantees that we eventually reach the minimum fixed-point assignment as formulated in the next theorem.

Theorem 2. *There exists a number i such that* $F^i(A_\bot) = F^{i+1}(A_\bot) = A_{min}$.

An example of ADG over the NOR $\mathcal{D} = (\{0, 1\}, \{(0, 1)\}, 0)$ that represents the classical Liu and Smolka dependency graph framework is shown in Fig. 9a. Here 0 (interpreted as false) is below the value 1 (interpreted as true) and the monotonic functions for nodes are displayed as node annotations. In Fig. 9b we demonstrate the fixed-point iterations computing the minimum fixed-point assignment.

A more interesting instance of ADG with an infinite value domain is given in Fig. 9c. The ADG encodes an example of a symbolic dependency graph (SDG) from [26] (with the added node E). The nodes are assigned nonnegative integer values (note that we use the ordering relation in the reverse order here) with the initial value being ∞ and the 'best' value (the one that cannot be improved anymore) being 0. The fixed-point computation is shown in Fig. 9d.

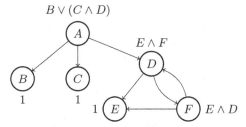

(a) Abstract dependency graph over NOR ($\{0, 1\}, \leq, 0$)

	A	B	C	D	E	F
$A_\perp$	0	0	0	0	0	0
$F(A_\perp)$	0	1	1	0	1	0
$F^2(A_\perp)$	1	1	1	0	1	0
$F^3(A_\perp)$	1	1	1	0	1	0

(b) Fixed-point computation of Figure 9a

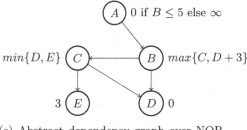

(c) Abstract dependency graph over NOR ($\mathbb{N} \cup \{\infty\}, \geq, \infty$)

	A	B	C	D	E
$A_\perp$	∞	∞	∞	∞	∞
$F(A_\perp)$	∞	∞	∞	0	3
$F^2(A_\perp)$	∞	∞	0	0	3
$F^3(A_\perp)$	∞	3	0	0	3
$F^4(A_\perp)$	0	3	0	0	3

(d) Fixed-point computation of Figure 9c

Fig. 9. Abstract dependency graphs

The authors in [21] devise an efficient local (on-the-fly) algorithm for ADGs and provide a publicly available implementation in a form of C++ library. The experimental results confirm that the general algorithm on ADGs is competitive with the single-purpose optimized algorithms for the particular instances of the framework.

6   Applications of Dependency Graphs

We shall finish our survey paper with an overview of selected applications of dependency graphs for various verification problems.

Timed Games: In [11] the zone-based on-the-fly reachability algorithm for timed automata implemented in UPPAAL [32] was extended with the synthesis of reachability strategies for timed games. In this application the nodes of the ADG are reachable symbolic states of the form (ℓ, Z) where ℓ is a location and Z is a zone, and the NOR D for such a node are all subsets $W \subseteq Z$ where W is a finite union of (sub-)zones such that $W \sqsubseteq W'$ if $W \subseteq W'$. Informally, the (increasing) set W contains information about the concrete states for which a winning strategy is already known to exist. The resulting on-the-fly algorithm is implemented in UPPAAL TIGA [7].

Weighted CTL: In [25,26] ADGs—called symbolic DGs at the time of writing of the papers—were used for efficient on-the-fly model checking for weighted Kripke structures with respect to weighted extensions of CTL. Here nodes of the ADG are pairs of the form (s, φ) where s a state of the weighted Kripke structure and φ is a WCTL formula. The NOR D for nodes (s, φ), where φ is a cost-bounded modality, is $(\mathbb{N} \cup \{\infty\}, \geq, \infty)$. Informally, the (decreasing) values for such nodes provide upper bounds for which the property is known to hold in the associated state s. The resulting on-the-fly algorithm has been implemented in the tool WKTool[1]. In [13], parametric model checking for WCTL has been considered. Here the outcome of the model checking effort is a direct description of the constraints on the parameters that will render the model checking problem true. In this case the NOR D is extended to $(P \to (\mathbb{N} \cup \{\infty\}), \geq, \infty)$, where P is the set of parameters and $\geq$ is the pointwise extension of $\geq$ to functions.

Probabilistic CTL: For model checking Markov reward models (MRM) with respect to probabilistic WCTL, the work in [14,34] provides an on-the-fly algorithm using ADG. Here nodes are of the form (s, φ) where s is a state of the MRM and φ is a property of PWCTL, and where modalities have upper cost-bounds and lower probability bounds. Semantically, the NOR D consists of monotonic functions of the type $p : \mathbb{R}_{\geq 0} \to [0, 1]$. Informally, assigning a function p to a node (s, φ) indicates that for any cost-bound c the property φ holds at least with probability $p(c)$. The Noetherian property of D is ensured by restricting D to piecewise constant functions.

Petri Nets and Games: The CTL model checking engine of the award-winning tool TAPAAL [20] applies dependency graphs with certain-zero optimization [17,18]. Also for various game engines dependency graphs have been applied. In [27] synthesis for safety games for timed-arc Petri net games have been given demonstrating (and exploiting) equivalence between continuous-time and discrete-time setting. Finally in [8] partial order reduction for synthesis of reachability games on Petri nets has been obtained based on dependency graph framework.

CAAL: Finally we want to point to the educational tool CAAL [4][2], which—using dependency graphs— supports a variety of equivalence checking techniques as well as model checking for recursive Hennessy-Milner logic for CCS and timed CCS.

Acknowledgments. We would like to thank to Hubert Garavel and Radu Mateescu for sharing the French history of on-the-fly model checking with us. The last author is partially affiliated with FI MU. The work of the second author has taken place in the context of the ERC Advanced Grant LASSO.

---

[1] http://wktool.jonasfj.dk/.
[2] http://caal.cs.aau.dk/.

References

1. Algayres, B., Coelho, V., Doldi, L., Garavel, H., Lejeune, Y., Rodríguez, C.: VESAR: a pragmatic approach to formal specification and verification. Comput. Netw. ISDN Syst. **25**(7), 779–790 (1993). https://doi.org/10.1016/0169-7552(93)90048-9

2. Andersen, H.R.: Model checking and boolean graphs. In: Krieg-Brückner, B. (ed.) ESOP 1992. LNCS, vol. 582, pp. 1–19. Springer, Heidelberg (1992). https://doi.org/10.1007/3-540-55253-7_1

3. Andersen, H.R., Winskel, G.: Compositional checking of satisfaction. In: Larsen, K.G., Skou, A. (eds.) CAV 1991. LNCS, vol. 575, pp. 24–36. Springer, Heidelberg (1992). https://doi.org/10.1007/3-540-55179-4_4

4. Andersen, J.R., et al.: CAAL: concurrency workbench, Aalborg edition. In: Leucker, M., Rueda, C., Valencia, F.D. (eds.) ICTAC 2015. LNCS, vol. 9399, pp. 573–582. Springer, Cham (2015). https://doi.org/10.1007/978-3-319-25150-9_33

5. Baier, C., Katoen, J.P.: Principles of Model Checking (Representation and Mind Series). The MIT Press (2008)

6. Balcázar, J.L., Gabarró, J., Santha, M.: Deciding bisimilarity is P-complete. Formal Asp. Comput. **4**(6A), 638–648 (1992)

7. Behrmann, G., Cougnard, A., David, A., Fleury, E., Larsen, K.G., Lime, D.: UPPAAL-tiga: time for playing games!. In: Damm, W., Hermanns, H. (eds.) CAV 2007. LNCS, vol. 4590, pp. 121–125. Springer, Heidelberg (2007). https://doi.org/10.1007/978-3-540-73368-3_14

8. Bønneland, F.M., Jensen, P.G., Larsen, K.G., Muñiz, M., Srba, J.: Partial order reduction for reachability games. In: CONCUR 2019 (2019, to appear)

9. Børjesson, A., Larsen, K.G., Skou, A.: Generality in design and compositional verification using TAV. In: Diaz, M., Groz, R. (eds.) Formal Description Techniques, V, Proceedings of the IFIP TC6/WG6.1 Fifth International Conference on Formal Description Techniques for Distributed Systems and Communication Protocols, FORTE 1992, Perros-Guirec, France, 13–16 October 1992. IFIP Transactions, vol. C-10, pp. 449–464. North-Holland (1992)

10. Bradfield, J.C., Stirling, C.: Local model checking for infinite state spaces. Theor. Comput. Sci. **96**(1), 157–174 (1992). https://doi.org/10.1016/0304-3975(92)90183-G

11. Cassez, F., David, A., Fleury, E., Larsen, K.G., Lime, D.: Efficient on-the-fly algorithms for the analysis of timed games. In: Abadi, M., de Alfaro, L. (eds.) CONCUR 2005. LNCS, vol. 3653, pp. 66–80. Springer, Heidelberg (2005). https://doi.org/10.1007/11539452_9

12. Čerāns, K., Godskesen, J.C., Larsen, K.G.: Timed modal specification—theory and tools. In: Courcoubetis, C. (ed.) CAV 1993. LNCS, vol. 697, pp. 253–267. Springer, Heidelberg (1993). https://doi.org/10.1007/3-540-56922-7_21

13. Christoffersen, P., Hansen, M., Mariegaard, A., Ringsmose, J.T., Larsen, K.G., Mardare, R.: Parametric verification of weighted systems. In: André, É., Frehse, G. (eds.) 2nd International Workshop on Synthesis of Complex Parameters (SynCoP 2015). OpenAccess Series in Informatics (OASIcs), vol. 44, pp. 77–90. Schloss Dagstuhl-Leibniz-Zentrum fuer Informatik, Dagstuhl, Germany (2015). https://doi.org/10.4230/OASIcs.SynCoP.2015.77. http://drops.dagstuhl.de/opus/volltexte/2015/5611

14. Claus Jensen, M., Mariegaard, A., Guldstrand Larsen, K.: Symbolic model checking of weighted PCTL using dependency graphs. In: Badger, J.M., Rozier, K.Y. (eds.)

NFM 2019. LNCS, vol. 11460, pp. 298–315. Springer, Cham (2019). https://doi.org/10.1007/978-3-030-20652-9_20

15. Cleaveland, R., Parrow, J., Steffen, B.: The concurrency workbench. In: Sifakis, J. (ed.) CAV 1989. LNCS, vol. 407, pp. 24–37. Springer, Heidelberg (1990). https://doi.org/10.1007/3-540-52148-8_3

16. Cleaveland, R., Steffen, B.: Computing behavioural relations, logically. In: Albert, J.L., Monien, B., Artalejo, M.R. (eds.) ICALP 1991. LNCS, vol. 510, pp. 127–138. Springer, Heidelberg (1991). https://doi.org/10.1007/3-540-54233-7_129

17. Dalsgaard, A., et al.: A distributed fixed-point algorithm for extended dependency graphs. Fundamenta Informaticae **161**(4), 351–381 (2018). https://doi.org/10.3233/FI-2018-1707

18. Dalsgaard, A.E., et al.: Extended dependency graphs and efficient distributed fixed-point computation. In: van der Aalst, W., Best, E. (eds.) PETRI NETS 2017. LNCS, vol. 10258, pp. 139–158. Springer, Cham (2017). https://doi.org/10.1007/978-3-319-57861-3_10

19. Dalsgaard, A.E., Enevoldsen, S., Larsen, K.G., Srba, J.: Distributed computation of fixed points on dependency graphs. In: Fränzle, M., Kapur, D., Zhan, N. (eds.) SETTA 2016. LNCS, vol. 9984, pp. 197–212. Springer, Cham (2016). https://doi.org/10.1007/978-3-319-47677-3_13

20. David, A., Jacobsen, L., Jacobsen, M., Jørgensen, K.Y., Møller, M.H., Srba, J.: TAPAAL 2.0: integrated development environment for timed-arc Petri nets. In: Flanagan, C., König, B. (eds.) TACAS 2012. LNCS, vol. 7214, pp. 492–497. Springer, Heidelberg (2012). https://doi.org/10.1007/978-3-642-28756-5_36

21. Enevoldsen, S., Guldstrand Larsen, K., Srba, J.: Abstract dependency graphs and their application to model checking. In: Vojnar, T., Zhang, L. (eds.) TACAS 2019. LNCS, vol. 11427, pp. 316–333. Springer, Cham (2019). https://doi.org/10.1007/978-3-030-17462-0_18

22. Glabbeek, R.J.: The linear time - branching time spectrum. In: Baeten, J.C.M., Klop, J.W. (eds.) CONCUR 1990. LNCS, vol. 458, pp. 278–297. Springer, Heidelberg (1990). https://doi.org/10.1007/BFb0039066

23. Godskesen, J., Larsen, K., Zeeberg, M.: TAV (tools for automatic verification) - user manual. Aalborg University, Technical report (1989)

24. Groote, J.F., Willemse, T.: Parameterised Boolean equation systems. In: Gardner, P., Yoshida, N. (eds.) CONCUR 2004. LNCS, vol. 3170, pp. 308–324. Springer, Heidelberg (2004). https://doi.org/10.1007/978-3-540-28644-8_20

25. Jensen, J., Larsen, K., Srba, J., Oestergaard, L.: Efficient model checking of weighted CTL with upper-bound constraints. Int. J. Softw. Tools Technol. Transfer (STTT) **18**(4), 409–426 (2016). https://doi.org/10.1007/s10009-014-0359-5

26. Jensen, J.F., Larsen, K.G., Srba, J., Oestergaard, L.K.: Local model checking of weighted CTL with upper-bound constraints. In: Bartocci, E., Ramakrishnan, C.R. (eds.) SPIN 2013. LNCS, vol. 7976, pp. 178–195. Springer, Heidelberg (2013). https://doi.org/10.1007/978-3-642-39176-7_12

27. Jensen, P.G., Larsen, K.G., Srba, J.: Discrete and continuous strategies for timed-arc petri net games. Int. J. Softw. Tools Technol. Transfer **20**(5), 529–546 (2018). https://doi.org/10.1007/s10009-017-0473-2

28. Kozen, D.: Results on the propositional μ-calculus. In: Nielsen, M., Schmidt, E.M. (eds.) ICALP 1982. LNCS, vol. 140, pp. 348–359. Springer, Heidelberg (1982). https://doi.org/10.1007/BFb0012782

29. Larsen, K.G.: Proof systems for Hennessy-Milner Logic with recursion. In: Dauchet, M., Nivat, M. (eds.) CAAP 1988. LNCS, vol. 299, pp. 215–230. Springer, Heidelberg (1988). https://doi.org/10.1007/BFb0026106

30. Larsen, K.G.: Proof systems for satisfiability in hennessy-milner logic with recursion. Theor. Comput. Sci. **72**(2&3), 265–288 (1990). https://doi.org/10.1016/0304-3975(90)90038-J
31. Larsen, K.G.: Efficient local correctness checking. In: von Bochmann, G., Probst, D.K. (eds.) CAV 1992. LNCS, vol. 663, pp. 30–43. Springer, Heidelberg (1993). https://doi.org/10.1007/3-540-56496-9_4
32. Larsen, K.G., Pettersson, P., Yi, W.: UPPAAL in a nutshell. STTT **1**(1–2), 134–152 (1997). https://doi.org/10.1007/s100090050010
33. Liu, X., Smolka, S.A.: Simple linear-time algorithms for minimal fixed points. In: Larsen, K.G., Skyum, S., Winskel, G. (eds.) ICALP 1998. LNCS, vol. 1443, pp. 53–66. Springer, Heidelberg (1998). https://doi.org/10.1007/BFb0055040
34. Mariegaard, A., Larsen, K.G.: Symbolic dependency graphs for $PCTL^{\geq}_{\leq}$ model-checking. In: Abate, A., Geeraerts, G. (eds.) FORMATS 2017. LNCS, vol. 10419, pp. 153–169. Springer, Cham (2017). https://doi.org/10.1007/978-3-319-65765-3_9
35. Mateescu, R.: Efficient diagnostic generation for Boolean equation systems. In: Graf, S., Schwartzbach, M. (eds.) TACAS 2000. LNCS, vol. 1785, pp. 251–265. Springer, Heidelberg (2000). https://doi.org/10.1007/3-540-46419-0_18
36. Milner, R.: A Calculus of Communicating Systems. LNCS, vol. 92. Springer, Heidelberg (1980). https://doi.org/10.1007/3-540-10235-3
37. Steffen, B.: Characteristic formulae. In: Ausiello, G., Dezani-Ciancaglini, M., Della Rocca, S.R. (eds.) ICALP 1989. LNCS, vol. 372, pp. 723–732. Springer, Heidelberg (1989). https://doi.org/10.1007/BFb0035794
38. Stirling, C., Walker, D.: Local model checking in the modal mu-calculus. Theor. Comput. Sci. **89**(1), 161–177 (1991). https://doi.org/10.1016/0304-3975(90)90110-4
39. Tarski, A.: A lattice-theoretical fixpoint theorem and its applications. Pac. J. Math. **5**(2), 285–309 (1955)
40. Winskel, G.: A note on model checking the modal ν-calculus. Theor. Comput. Sci. **83**(1), 157–167 (1991). https://doi.org/10.1016/0304-3975(91)90043-2

Model Checking Branching Time Properties for Incomplete Markov Chains

Shiraj Arora[(✉)][iD] and M. V. Panduranga Rao[iD]

Indian Institute of Technology Hyderabad, Kandi, India
{cs14resch11010,mvp}@iith.ac.in

Abstract. In this work, we discuss a numerical model checking algorithm for analyzing incompletely specified models of stochastic systems, specifically, Discrete Time Markov Chains (DTMC). Models of a system could be incompletely specified for several reasons. For example, they could still be under development or, there could be some doubt about the correctness of some components. We restrict ourselves to cases where incompleteness can be captured by expanding the logic of atomic propositions to a three valued logic that includes an *unknown* truth value. We seek to answer meaningful model checking queries even in such circumstances.

The approach we adopt in this paper is to develop the model checking algorithm from first principles. We develop a tool based on the algorithm and compare the performance of this approach with the indirect approach of invoking a binary model checker.

Keywords: Probabilistic model checking ·
Discrete Time Markov Chains · Probabilistic computational tree logic ·
Three valued logic · Incomplete models

1 Introduction

Probabilistic models are widely used to represent real-world systems that exhibit stochastic behaviour, like cyber-physical systems, biological processes, network and security protocols. Examples of such probabilistic models are Markov chains like Discrete and Continuous Time Markov Chains (DTMC and CTMC respectively) [3], Markov Decision Processes (MDP), Constrained Markov Chains [8] and Probabilistic Automata [13]. Verification of these types of probabilistic models involves asserting whether or not the system design exhibits the required behavior. The required behavior or property is formally specified as statements in logics like Probabilistic Computation Tree Logic (PCTL) [16] and Continuous Stochastic Language (CSL) [4].

Probabilistic Model Checking is a formal technique to analyze and verify the required behaviour of stochastic systems. Given a probabilistic model that describes a stochastic system, and a formal specification of the required behaviour of the system, the goal of probabilistic model checking is to decide

© Springer Nature Switzerland AG 2019
F. Biondi et al. (Eds.): SPIN 2019, LNCS 11636, pp. 20–37, 2019.
https://doi.org/10.1007/978-3-030-30923-7_2

whether the system exhibits the required behaviour or not. Probabilistic model checking has been explored in the literature using either numerical [4,12,16] or statistical algorithms [22,23,25].

Traditionally, systems are analyzed through model checking once the entire information about a model is available, at least in principle. An interesting question is if this analysis can be done when the model has incomplete information. The incompleteness may arise because of either (i) nonavailability of input information about either state space or transitions between states, (ii) if the correctness of some module is in doubt or (iii) loss of information due to abstraction of models, or some combination of the three. To capture incomplete information, a natural choice is to expand binary logic to include a third *unknown* truth value. We denote this by the question mark "?". Depending upon the type of incompleteness, different techniques have been reported to verify both stochastic as well as non stochastic incomplete models.

There exists a significant body of work on model checking with three valued logics. Bruns and Godefroid [6,7] use three valued modal logic to represent models with partial state space. These models are then verified by using model checking algorithms for binary truth values. Similarly, Chechik et al. [11] used multi-valued logic to represent incomplete and inconsistent information in a model. They verified such a model using a symbolic multi-valued CTL model checker. Abstraction is often used to deal with problems of state space explosion in model checking. However, such an approach may cause loss of information in the model. This incompleteness in the abstracted model can be represented using a third truth value. Godefroid et al. [15] and Chechik [10] discussed the verification of abstracted models using three valued LTL and CTL model checkers, respectively. Abstraction is also commonly used in verification of stochastic models like Markov chains, to overcome the problem of state-space explosion [14,17,19]. Besides abstraction, incompleteness in stochastic systems may arise from imprecise transition probabilities obtained from statistical experiments. For example, discrete-time Markov chains have been defined wherein transition probabilities are intervals instead of exact values to handle imprecision [18,20]. Verification of such interval based discrete-time Markov chains works by either reducing it to a class of discrete-time Markov chains or to a Markov decision process [5,9,24].

Another way of capturing incomplete information, the one on which this paper is based, is to allow some atomic propositions to assume the "?" truth value in some states [2]. An interesting question is to determine which properties of the system can be verified in the absence of complete information–is there sufficient information in the model to evaluate a particular property to either True or False? It is possible to answer this question by invoking PCTL model checking algorithms twice [2]. We refer to this approach as *2MC*.

In this paper, we adopt a direct approach that solves the numerical model checking problem from first principles as exposited in [4,21]. We call this approach *1MC*. While this approach is an adaptation of the standard numerical model checking algorithm, the fact that true and false are no longer complementary to each other raises some complications, which we address. We also show examples to illustrate the approach and practical applications of the problem formulation and the solution.

Intuitively, one expects the *1MC* algorithm to perform better in cases when the *2MC* algorithm has to invoke the model checker twice and *2MC* to perform better when it needs to invoke it only once. We back this intuition up with experimental evidence.

The rest of the paper is arranged as follows. Section 2 discusses the syntax and semantics of the modeling and specification formalism for incomplete models. Section 3 discusses the model checking algorithm. Implementation details, results and comparison with *2MC* are discussed in Sect. 4. Section 5 concludes the paper with a brief discussion on future directions.

2   qDTMC and qPCTL

2.1   Discrete Time Markov Chain with Question Marks (qDTMC)

A Discrete Time Markov Chain with question marks (qDTMC) extends the traditional DTMC to account for incomplete information in a model.

Definition 1. *A qDTMC is a tuple* $\mathcal{M} = (S, i_{init}, \mathbb{P}, AP, L)$ *where*

- S *is a finite non-empty set of states,*
- $i_{init} : S \to [0, 1]$ *is the initial distribution, such that* $\sum\limits_{s \in S} i_{init}(s) = 1$,
- $\mathbb{P} : S \times S \to [0, 1]$ *gives the transition probability between two states in S such that:*

$$\forall s \in S : \sum_{s' \in S} \mathbb{P}(s, s') = 1,$$

- AP *is a set of atomic propositions, and*
- $L : S \times AP \to \{T, F, ?\}$ *assigns a truth value from the set $\{T, F, ?\}$ to each atomic proposition $a \in AP$ in a state $s \in S$.*

A qDTMC differs from a DTMC only in terms of its labelling function. The truth values T and F correspond that an atomic proposition being true and false respectively in the state s. If it is not known whether an atomic proposition is true or false in s, then the truth value $?$ is assigned to the atomic proposition.

Figure 1 illustrates an example qDTMC $\mathcal{M}$ wherein the state s_0 is the initial state with probability 1 in the state space $S = \{s_0, s_1, ..., s_6\}$. The weight on each transition between the states denotes the probability of the transition. $AP = \{p, q\}$ is a set of atomic propositions in $\mathcal{M}$. The truth value of each atomic proposition in a state is also represented in the qDTMC. For instance, $\neg pq?$ denotes p is false and q is unknown in the state s_0 and pq denotes both p and q are true in the state s_2. We consider qDTMC $\mathcal{M}$ as a running example in the paper.

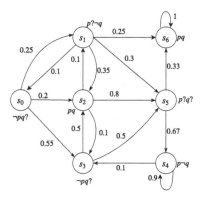

Fig. 1. Example of a qDTMC

Definition 2. *A path π in a qDTMC $\mathcal{M}$ is a sequence of states $s_0, s_1, s_2, \ldots$ such that for all $i = 0, 1, 2, \ldots$ $s_i \in S$ and $\mathbb{P}(s_i, s_{i+1}) > 0$. The $i + 1^{th}$ state in a path π is denoted by $\pi[i]$. The set $Path(s)$ is the set of all infinite paths starting from state s in $\mathcal{M}$.*

Definition 3. *A cylinder set $C(\omega)$ is the set of all infinite paths with a common finite prefix $\omega = s_0, s_1, \ldots, s_n$. The probability measure μ of $C(\omega)$ in the qDTMC $\mathcal{M}$ can be defined as*

$$\mu(C(\omega)) = \prod_{i=0}^{n-1} \mathbb{P}(s_i, s_{i+1})$$

2.2   qPCTL

Probabilistic Computation Tree Logic with question marks (qPCTL) is an extension of PCTL [16], defined to formally express a property required of a qDTMC model. In what follows, our notational convention will be similar to that of [2]. The syntax of qPCTL is the same as that of PCTL:

Syntax:

$$\Phi ::= \top \mid a \mid \Phi_1 \wedge \Phi_2 \mid \neg\Phi \mid Pr_{\bowtie\theta}[\psi]$$
$$\psi ::= X\Phi \mid \Phi_1 U\Phi_2 \mid \Phi_1 \ U^{\leq k} \ \Phi_2$$

where Φ, Φ_1, and Φ_2 are state formulas, ψ is a path formula, a is an atomic proposition, $\theta \in [0,1]$ defines the probability constraint, $\bowtie \in \{ <, >, \leq, \geq \}$ represents the set of comparison operators, and $k \in \mathbb{N}$ is the time bound. The X, U, and $U^{\leq k}$ operators are called *Next, Until* and *Bounded Until* respectively.

Recall that an atomic proposition a can have one of the three truth values $\{T, F, ?\}$ in a qPCTL formula. Thus, in addition to verifying a property as true (T) or false (F), a qPCTL formula can also be evaluated to "unknown" $(?)$. The conditions for which the logic returns $?$ are incorporated into the semantics of qPCTL.

For the truth values $(T, F, ?)$ in qPCTL, the logical operations $(\wedge, \vee, \neg)$ are as defined in Tables 1, 2 and 3.

Table 1. The AND operator

$\wedge$	T	?	F
T	T	?	F
?	?	?	F
F	F	F	F

Table 2. The OR operator

$\vee$	T	?	F
T	T	T	T
?	T	?	?
F	T	?	F

Table 3. The NOT operator

$\neg$	
T	F
?	?
F	T

Semantics:

Each state formula Φ in qPCTL is verified to either T, F, or $?$ in a state $s \in S$ that is $(s, \Phi) = \{T, F, ?\}$ as:

1. The qPCTL formula Φ can trivially be T.

$$(s, T) = T; \qquad (s, \neg T) = \neg(s, T) = F.$$

2. An atomic proposition a in a qDTMC can have three possible truth values $\{T, F, ?\}$. Thus, a qPCTL formula $\Phi = a$ in a state s is evaluated to $\{T, F, ?\}$ if

$$(s, a) = \begin{cases} T \text{ iff } L(s, a) = T \\ F \text{ iff } L(s, a) = F \\ ? \text{ iff } L(s, a) = ? \end{cases}$$

3. Using the *NOT* and *AND* operator from Tables 3 and 1 respectively, we have:

$$(s, \neg\Phi) = \begin{cases} T \text{ iff } (s, \Phi) = F \\ F \text{ iff } (s, \Phi) = T \\ ? \text{ iff } (s, \Phi) = ? \end{cases} \text{ and } (s, \Phi_1 \wedge \Phi_2) = \begin{cases} T \text{ iff } (s, \Phi_1) = T \wedge (s, \Phi_2) = T \\ F \text{ iff } (s, \Phi_1) = F \vee (s, \Phi_2) = F \\ ? \text{ otherwise} \end{cases}$$

4. If a qPCTL formula contains a probabilistic operator that is $\Phi = Pr_{\bowtie\theta}[\psi]$, then the probability measure of paths starting from state s that evaluate path formula ψ to true or false is calculated separately. The formula Φ is then verified as follows:

$$(s, Pr_{\bowtie\theta}[\psi]) = \begin{cases} T \text{ if } \mu\{\pi \in Path(s) : (\pi, \psi) = T\} \bowtie \theta \\ F \text{ if } \mu\{\pi \in Path(s) : (\pi, \psi) = F\} \bowtie 1 - \theta \\ ? \text{ otherwise} \end{cases}$$

A path formula ψ for a path $\pi \in Path(s)$ has the following semantics:

1. *Next operator*: A path formula of form $\psi = X\Phi$ is verified to $\{T, F, ?\}$ for a path π if the state formula Φ is evaluated to $\{T, F, ?\}$, respectively, in the second state of π.

$$(\pi, X\Phi) = \begin{cases} T \text{ if } (\pi[1], \Phi) = T \\ F \text{ if } (\pi[1], \Phi) = F \\ ? \text{ if } (\pi[1], \Phi) = ? \end{cases}$$

2. *Until operator*:

$$(\pi, \Phi_1 U \Phi_2) = \begin{cases} T \text{ if } \exists i : (\pi[i], \Phi_2) = T \ \wedge \ \forall i' < i : (\pi[i'], \Phi_1) = T \\ F \text{ if } (\forall i : (\pi[i], \Phi_2) = F) \\ \quad \vee \ [\exists i : (\pi[i], \Phi_2) = T \ \wedge \ \exists i' < i : (\pi[i'], \Phi_1) = F] \\ ? \text{ otherwise.} \end{cases}$$

Thus, ψ evaluates to ? if one of the following occurs:
- Φ_2 is ? for all the states in π.
- Φ_2 is ? for at least one state in π and is never T in any of the states along the path and Φ_1 is never F.
- Φ_2 is T for some state $\pi[i]$ and Φ_1 is ? for at least one state $\pi[k]$ with $k < i$ but never F in any of the states upto $\pi[i]$.

3. *Bounded Until*: A path formula of the form $\psi = \Phi_1 U^{\leq k} \Phi_2$ is verified to $\{T, F, ?\}$ same as that for *until* operator, but only for paths of finite length k.

$$(\pi, \Phi_1 U^{\leq k} \Phi_2) = \begin{cases} T \text{ if } \exists i \leq k : (\pi[i], \Phi_2) = T \ \wedge \ \forall i' < i : (\pi[i'], \Phi_1) = T \\ F \text{ if } (\forall i \leq k : (\pi[i], \Phi_2) = F) \\ \quad \vee \ [\exists i \leq k : (\pi[i], \Phi_2) = T \ \wedge \exists i' < i : (\pi[i'], \Phi_1) = F] \\ ? \text{ otherwise.} \end{cases}$$

3   qPCTL Model Checking

For a qDTMC $\mathcal{M} = (S, \mathbb{P}, i_{init}, AP, L)$, a state $s \in S$ and a qPCTL state formula Φ, we want to determine if $(s, \Phi) = T$. We note that if $(s, \Phi) \neq T$, then Φ need not be false in the state s. Unlike for DTMCs, the two statements are not complementary for qDTMCs. Hence we define three satisfaction sets $Sat_T(\Phi)$, $Sat_F(\Phi)$, and $Sat_?(\Phi)$.

Definition 4. *A state $s \in Sat_T(\Phi)$ if and only if $(s, \Phi) = T$. A state $s \in Sat_F(\Phi)$ if and only if $(s, \Phi) = F$. Finally, $s \in Sat_?(\Phi)$ if and only if $(s, \Phi) = ?$.*

We now describe an algorithm 1MC, to compute these satisfaction sets $Sat_T(\Phi)$ and $Sat_F(\Phi)$ by performing a bottom-up traversal of the syntax tree of Φ. The remaining satisfaction set $Sat_?(\Phi)$ can be computed as $Sat_?(\Phi) = S \setminus [Sat_T(\Phi) \cup Sat_F(\Phi)]$. For a given state formula Φ, these satisfaction sets will partition the state space S. We now discuss the 1MC algorithm in detail. Algorithm 1 lists the pseudocode.

Non-probabilistic Operators: The satisfaction sets for each of the non-probabilistic operators in the qPCTL is based on the logical operations described in Tables 1, 2 and 3. Cases 1 through 4 of the 1MC algorithm compute the satisfaction sets for non-probabilistic operators. It is easy to see that:

Lemma 1. *For the non-probabilistic state formulas, the 1MC Algorithm (cases 1 through 4) is correct.*

Probabilistic Operators: Construction of the satisfaction sets for probabilistic operators is somewhat more complicated. We need a few definitions first.

Definition 5. *True satisfaction probability for a state s is defined as the probability measure of paths starting from s which evaluate the path formula ψ as T. It is denoted by $Pr((s, \psi) = T)$.*

Definition 6. *False satisfaction probability for a state s is defined as the probability measure of paths starting from s which evaluate the path formula ψ as F, and is denoted by $Pr((s, \psi) = F)$.*

Now, the satisfaction sets can be defined as:

$$
\begin{aligned}
Sat_T(Pr_{\bowtie\theta}[\psi]) &= \quad \{s \in S \,|\, Pr((s,\psi) = T) \bowtie \theta\} \\
Sat_F(Pr_{\bowtie\theta}[\psi]) &= \quad \{s \in S \,|\, Pr((s,\psi) = F) \bowtie 1 - \theta\} \\
Sat_?(Pr_{\bowtie\theta}[\psi]) &= S \setminus [Sat_T(Pr_{\bowtie\theta}[\psi]) \cup Sat_F(Pr_{\bowtie\theta}[\psi])]
\end{aligned}
$$

To construct these sets, we have to calculate $Pr((s, \psi) = T/F/?)$ for path formula ψ. There are three path formulas in qPCTL–*Next*, *Until* and *Bounded Until*. We now discuss the algorithms for computing the satisfaction probabilities for these path formulas:

1. **Next operator** – $[X\Phi]$: The satisfaction probabilities for *next* operator are calculated by adding transition probabilities of the state s to the states which

---

Algorithm 1. Algorithm 1MC

Function: ComputeSat(Φ)
switch (Φ)
case $\top$:
    $Sat_T(\Phi) \leftarrow S$; $Sat_F(\Phi) \leftarrow \emptyset$; $Sat_?(\Phi) \leftarrow \emptyset$
case a:
    for all $s \in S$ **do**
        if $L(s, a) = T$ **then**
            $Sat_T(\Phi) \leftarrow Sat_T(\Phi) \cup \{s\}$
        else if $L(s, a) = F$ **then**
            $Sat_F(\Phi) \leftarrow Sat_F(\Phi) \cup \{s\}$
        else
            $Sat_?(\Phi) \leftarrow Sat_?(\Phi) \cup \{s\}$
        end if
    end for
case $\neg\Phi_1$
    ComputeSat(Φ_1)
    $Sat_T(\Phi) \leftarrow Sat_F(\Phi_1)$; $Sat_F(\Phi) \leftarrow Sat_T(\Phi_1)$; $Sat_?(\Phi) \leftarrow Sat_?(\Phi_1)$
case $\Phi_1 \wedge \Phi_2$
    ComputeSat(Φ_1); ComputeSat(Φ_2)
    $Sat_T(\Phi) \leftarrow Sat_T(\Phi_1) \cap Sat_T(\Phi_2)$
    $Sat_F(\Phi) \leftarrow Sat_F(\Phi_1) \cup Sat_F(\Phi_2)$
    $Sat_?(\Phi) \leftarrow S \setminus [Sat_T(\Phi) \cup Sat_F(\Phi)]$

---

case $Pr_{\bowtie\theta}[\psi]$
      switch (ψ)
      case $X\Phi_1$
          $\mathrm{ComputeSat}(\Phi_1)$
          for all $s, s' \in S$ **do**
            if $s' \in Sat_T(\Phi_1)$ **then**
              $Pr_T(s, \psi) \leftarrow Pr_T(s, \psi) + \mathbb{P}(s, s')$
            else if $s' \in Sat_F(\Phi_1)$ **then**
              $Pr_F(s, \psi) \leftarrow Pr_F(s, \psi) + \mathbb{P}(s, s')$
            else
              $Pr_?(s, \psi) \leftarrow Pr_?(s, \psi) + \mathbb{P}(s, s')$
            end if
          end for
      case $[\Phi_1 U \Phi_2]$
          $ComputeSat(\Phi_1); ComputeSat(\Phi_2)$
          $S_{=0} \leftarrow Compute\_Until\_S_{=0}$
          $S_{=?} \leftarrow Compute\_Until\_S_{=?}$
          $S_{=1} \leftarrow Compute\_Until\_S_{=1}$
          $S_{find} \leftarrow S \setminus [S_{=0} \cup S_{=1} \cup S_{=?}]$
          for all $s \in S$ **do**
            $Pr_T(s, \psi) \leftarrow Compute\_Until\_Pr_T(s)$
                  ▷ Computes true satisfaction probability using equation 1.
            $Pr_F(s, \psi) \leftarrow Compute\_Until\_Pr_F(s)$
                  ▷ Computes false satisfaction probability using equation 2.
          end for
      case $[\Phi_1 U^{\leq k} \Phi_2]$
          $ComputeSat(\Phi_1); ComputeSat(\Phi_2)$
          $S_{=0} \leftarrow Sat_F(\Phi_2) \cap Sat_F(\Phi_1)$
          $S_{=?} \leftarrow [(Sat_?(\Phi_1) \setminus Sat_?(\Phi_2)) \cup (Sat_?(\Phi_2) \setminus Sat_T(\Phi_1))]$
          $S_{=1} \leftarrow Sat_T(\Phi_2)$
          $S_{find} \leftarrow Sat_T(\Phi_1) \setminus Sat_T(\Phi_2)$
          for all $s \in S$ **do**
            $Pr_T(s, \psi) \leftarrow Compute\_BUntil\_Pr_T(s, k)$
                   ▷ Computes true satisfaction probability using equation 4
            $Pr_F(s, \psi) \leftarrow Compute\_BUntil\_Pr_F(s, k)$
                   ▷ Compute false satisfaction probability using equation 5
          end for
      end switch
      for all $s \in S$ **do**
          if $Pr_T(s, \psi) \bowtie \theta$ **then**
            $Sat_T(\Phi) \leftarrow Sat_T(\Phi) \cup \{s\}$
          else if $Pr_F(s, \psi) \bowtie 1 - \theta$ **then**
            $Sat_F(\Phi) \leftarrow Sat_F(\Phi) \cup \{s\}$
          else
            $Sat_?(\Phi) \leftarrow Sat_?(\Phi) \cup \{s\}$
          end if
      end for
end switch
return $Sat_T(\Phi), Sat_F(\Phi), Sat_?(\Phi)$

satisfy Φ as T, F or ?.

$$Pr((s, X\Phi) = T) = \sum_{s' \in Sat_T(\Phi)} \mathbb{P}(s, s')$$

$$Pr((s, X\Phi) = F) = \sum_{s' \in Sat_F(\Phi)} \mathbb{P}(s, s')$$

$$Pr((s, X\Phi) = ?) = \sum_{s' \in Sat_?(\Phi)} \mathbb{P}(s, s')$$

Based on satisfaction probabilities, each state s in S belongs to only one of the three satisfaction sets $Sat_T(Pr_{\bowtie\theta}[X\Phi])$, $Sat_F(Pr_{\bowtie\theta}[X\Phi])$ or $Sat_?(Pr_{\bowtie\theta}[X\Phi])$. If $Pr((s, X\Phi) = T) \bowtie \theta$ then $s \in Sat_T(Pr_{\bowtie\theta}[X\Phi])$. Else if $Pr((s, X\Phi) = F) \bowtie 1-\theta$ then $s \in Sat_F(Pr_{\bowtie\theta}[X\Phi])$. Otherwise, s belongs to the set $Sat_?(Pr_{\bowtie\theta}[X\Phi])$.

Example 1. In Fig. 1, a qDTMC $\mathcal{M}_1$ with state space $S = \{s_0, s_1, \ldots, s_6\}$ with an initial state s_0 is given. If we want to verify a qPCTL state formula $\Phi = Pr_{\geq 0.5}[Xq]$ for $\mathcal{M}_1$, then the satisfaction sets will be: $Sat_T(\Phi_1) = \{s_1, s_3, s_6\}$, $Sat_F(\Phi_1) = \{s_4, s_5\}$ and $Sat_?(\Phi_1) = \{s_0, s_2\}$. Thus for the initial state s_0, the qPCTL state formula Φ_1 will be evaluated to ?.

2. **Until operator** – $[\Phi_1 U \Phi_2]$: Identifying B with the set of states where Φ_2 is true and C as the set of states where Φ_1 is true, a graph theoretic notion of constrained reachability is useful:

Definition 7. *Constrained reachability in a qDTMC $(s, C\ U\ B)$ is defined as an event of reaching the destination set $B \subseteq S$ from the state s such that all the preceding states in the path belong to a constraint set $C \subseteq S$.*

Thus the true satisfaction probability $Pr((s, \Phi_1 U \Phi_2) = T)$ can be calculated as the probability of constrained reachability being true for paths starting from state s. We can also denote this probability as $Pr((s, C\ U\ B) = T)$. Similarly, the false satisfaction probability $Pr((s, \Phi_1 U \Phi_2) = F) = Pr((s, C\ U\ B) = F)$ is the probability of constrained reachability being false.

Notably, it is possible that constrained reachability for a path in a qDTMC is neither true nor false. For such paths, constrained reachability is evaluated to *unknown* (?). This requires us to calculate all the reachability probabilities separately for each state in $\mathcal{M}$. For each state s, the probability that the constrained reachability is $T/F/?$ is denoted by $x_s^{(T/F/?)}$ respectively, and is defined as:

$$x_s^{(T/F/?)} = Pr((s, C\ U\ B) = T/F/?) = Pr((s, \Phi_1 U \Phi_2) = T/F/?).$$

To calculate these constrained reachability probabilities, we first partition the state space S into $\{S_{=0}, S_{=1}, S_{=?}$ and $S_{find}\}$. We now define each of these partition sets and discuss how to construct these sets later.

$$S_{=0} = \{s \in S \mid Pr((s, C\ U\ B) = F) = 1\}$$

$$B \subseteq S_{=1} \subseteq \{s \in S \mid Pr((s, C\ U\ B) = T) = 1\}$$

$$S_{=?} = \{s \in S \mid Pr((s, C\ U\ B) = ?) = 1\}$$

The remaining states in S form the set S_{find}:

$$S_{find} = S \setminus [S_{=0} \cup S_{=1} \cup S_{=?}]$$

Thus, for states $s \in S_{=1}$, $x_s^{(T)} = 1$, $x_s^{(F)} = 0$ and $x_s^{(?)} = 0$. Similarly for states $s \in S_{=0}$, $x_s^{(F)} = 1$, $x_s^{(T)} = 0$ and $x_s^{(?)} = 0$ and for states $s \in S_{=?}$, $x_s^{(?)} = 1$, $x_s^{(T)} = 0$ and $x_s^{(F)} = 0$.

For a state s in the set S_{find}, the constrained reachability probabilities are neither exactly 1 nor 0. We now identify the paths starting from s that eventually reach the set $S_{=1}$ such that all the preceding states are from set S_{find}. These paths will evaluate $C \ U \ B$ (or $\Phi_1 U \Phi_2$) to T and the probability measure of these paths gives $x_s^{(T)}$. Similarly, $x_s^{(F)}$ is the probability measure of paths from s that reach $S_{=0}$ through the states from S_{find} and hence evaluate $C \ U \ B$ (or $\Phi_1 U \Phi_2$) to F.

The satisfaction probabilities for the path formula $[\Phi_1 U \Phi_2]$ is then calculated using the following sets of linear equations.

$$x_s^{(T)} = \begin{cases} 1 & \text{if } s \in S_{=1} \\ 0 & \text{if } s \in S_{=0} \\ 0 & \text{if } s \in S_{=?} \\ \sum_{t \in S} \mathbb{P}(s,t).x_t^{(T)} & \text{if } s \in S_{find} \end{cases} \tag{1}$$

$$x_s^{(F)} = \begin{cases} 0 & \text{if } s \in S_{=1} \\ 1 & \text{if } s \in S_{=0} \\ 0 & \text{if } s \in S_{=?} \\ \sum_{t \in S} \mathbb{P}(s,t).x_t^{(F)} & \text{if } s \in S_{find} \end{cases} \tag{2}$$

$$Pr((s, \Phi_1 U \Phi_2) =?) = x_s^{(?)} = 1 - [x_s^{(T)} + x_s^{(F)}] \tag{3}$$

We now discuss how to construct $S_{=0}$, $S_{=?}$ and $S_{=1}$. Pseudocode listing for these subroutines is provided in the Algorithms 2, 3 and 4. Then, the set $S_{find} = S \setminus [S_{=0} \cup S_{=1} \cup S_{=?}]$ is computed.

We first compute $S_{=0}$, the set of states that have the false satisfaction probability $Pr((s, \Phi_1 U \Phi_2) = F) = 1$. We identify the states that have false satisfaction probability less than 1. To do this, we first identify the set R of states for which Φ_2 is either T or ?. Then we do a backward search on the paths leading to R, to find states where Φ_1 is not F. We add these states to R. When no more states can be added to R, we remove R from the state space to get the set $S_{=0}$.

Example 2. For the qDTMC $\mathcal{M}_1$ in Fig. 1 and a qPCTL state formula $\Phi = Pr_{\geq 0.5}[\neg p \ U \ q]$, we first identify the satisfaction sets for the state formulas $\Phi_1 = \neg p$ and $\Phi_2 = q$:
$Sat_T(\Phi_1) = \{s_0, s_3\}$, $Sat_T(\Phi_2) = \{s_2, s_6\}$,
$Sat_F(\Phi_1) = \{s_2, s_4, s_6\}$, $Sat_F(\Phi_2) = \{s_1, s_4\}$
$Sat_?(\Phi_1) = \{s_1, s_5\}$ and $Sat_?(\Phi_2) = \{s_0, s_3, s_5\}$.

We can now compute the set $R = \{s_0, s_1, s_2, s_3, s_5, s_6\}$. Thus the partition set $S_{=0}$ will be $\{s_4\}$.

We follow a similar procedure to identify the set of states for which the probability $Pr((s, \Phi_1 U \Phi_2) =?)$ will be 1. We start with the states that belong to either $S_{=0}$ or $Sat_T(\Phi_2)$ and then identify the paths leading to these states. The probability $Pr((s, \Phi_1 U \Phi_2) =?)$ for such paths will always be less than 1. We thus exclude these states from the set $S_{=?}$.

Example 3. In continuation of Example 2, the set R is now computed as $R = \{s_4, s_2, s_6\} \cup \{s_0, s_3\} = \{s_0, s_2, s_3, s_4, s_6\}$. Thus the set $S_{=?}$ is computes to $\{s_1, s_5\}$.

The set $S_{=1}$ consists of states that have the true satisfaction probability $Pr((s, \Phi_1 U \Phi_2) = T) = 1$. As before, we first identify the set of states that have true satisfaction probability less than 1, and then remove them from the state space to compute $S_{=1}$.

Example 4. The set R in Algorithm 4 for $\mathcal{M}_1$ is now computed as $R = \{s_4, s_1, s_5\} \cup \{s_0, s_3\} = \{s_0, s_1, s_3, s_4, s_5\}$. Thus the set $S_{=1}$ will be $\{s_2, s_6\}$. Also, the set S_{find} can now be computed as $S_{find} = \{s_0, s_3\}$.

Algorithm 2. Algorithm to compute $S_{=0}$ for until operator

---

Function: $Compute\_Until\_S_{=0}$
$R \leftarrow Sat_T(\Phi_2) \cup Sat_?(\Phi_2)$
while true **do**
    $R' \leftarrow R \cup \{s \in S \setminus Sat_F(\Phi_1) \mid \exists s' \in R, \mathbb{P}(s, s') > 0\}$
    if $R' = R$ **then**
        break
    else
        $R \leftarrow R'$
    end if
end while
$S_{=0} \leftarrow S \setminus R$ **return** $S_{=0}$

Algorithm 3. Algorithm to compute $S_{=?}$ for until operator

---

Function: $Compute\_Until\_S_{=?}$
$R \leftarrow S_{=0} \cup Sat_T(\Phi_2)$
while true **do**
    $R' \leftarrow R \cup \{s \in Sat_T(\Phi_1) \setminus Sat_T(\Phi_2) \mid \exists s' \in R, \mathbb{P}(s, s') > 0\}$
    if $R' = R$ **then**
        break
    else
        $R \leftarrow R'$
    end if
end while
$S_{=?} \leftarrow S \setminus R$ **return** $S_{=?}$

Algorithm 4. Algorithm to compute $S_{=1}$ for until operator

---

Function: $Compute\_Until\_S_{=1}$
$R \leftarrow S_{=0} \cup S_{=?}$
while true **do**
    $R' \leftarrow R \cup \{s \in Sat_T(\Phi_1) \setminus Sat_T(\Phi_2) | \exists s' \in R, \mathbb{P}(s, s') > 0\}$
    if $R' = R$ **then**
        break
    else
        $R \leftarrow R'$
    end if
end while
$S_{=1} \leftarrow S \setminus R$

Example 5. Now for $\mathcal{M}_1$ and the qPCTL formula $\Phi = Pr_{\geq 0.5}[\neg p \ U \ q]$, we can compute the satisfaction sets using the true and false satisfaction probabilities: $Sat_T(\Phi) = \{s_2, s_3, s_6\}$, $Sat_F(\Phi) = \{s_4\}$ and $Sat_?(\Phi) = \{s_0, s_1, s_5\}$. Thus, for the initial state s_0, Φ will be evaluated to ?.

3. **Bounded Until operator** – $[\Phi_1 U^{\leq k} \Phi_2]$: The satisfaction probabilities for $[\Phi_1 U^{\leq k} \Phi_2]$ can be directly computed by evaluating k transitions of the qDTMC. Depending on the truth values of Φ_1 and Φ_2 in a state, the state space S is partitioned into sets $S_{=0}$, $S_{=1}$, $S_{=?}$ and S_{find} in the 1MC algorithm. This partition is illustrated in Fig. 2.

$$
\begin{aligned}
S_{=0} &= Sat_F(\Phi_2) \cap Sat_F(\Phi_1), \\
S_{=?} &= [\, (Sat_?(\Phi_1) \setminus Sat_T(\Phi_2)) \, \cup \, (Sat_?(\Phi_2) \setminus Sat_T(\Phi_1)) \,], \\
S_{=1} &= Sat_T(\Phi_2), \\
S_{find} &= S \setminus [S_{=0} \cup S_{=1} \cup S_{find}] \, = \, Sat_T(\Phi_1) \setminus Sat_T(\Phi_2)
\end{aligned}
$$

A state $s \in S_{=1}$ if the truth value of Φ_2 is T in s. Now irrespective of the truth value of Φ_1, the path formula $\Phi_1 U^{\leq k} \Phi_2$ will be evaluated as T for all paths starting from this state s, because Φ_2 is T in the initial state of the path. Thus, the true (false) satisfaction probability for states in $S_{=1}$ will be 1 (0).

A state belonging to set $S_{=0}$ will have truth values of both Φ_1 and Φ_2 as F. All paths starting from such a state $s \in S_{=0}$ will have both Φ_1 and Φ_2 false in the initial state itself and will evaluate $\Phi_1 U^{\leq k} \Phi_2$ to F. Thus, the true (false) satisfaction probabilities for states in $S_{=0}$ will be 0 (1).

A state s belongs to the set $S_{=?}$ if the truth value of at least one of Φ_1 or Φ_2 is ? in s and the other is not T. No path starting from such a state $s \in S_{=?}$ can evaluate $\Phi_1 U^{\leq k} \Phi_2$ to either T or F–the truth or falsehood of $\Phi_1 U^{\leq k} \Phi_2$ for a path starting in s is cannot be determined if (i) Φ_1 is ? in s and Φ_2 is not T or (ii) Φ_1 is not T and Φ_2 is ?. For such states, both true and false satisfaction probabilities are 0.

Now, the remaining states in the state space will have Φ_1 as T, but Φ_2 is either F or ?. Since Φ_2 is not T in starting state s of the path, we need to find the value of Φ_1 and Φ_2 in the subsequent states. Thus, these states form the set S_{find}.

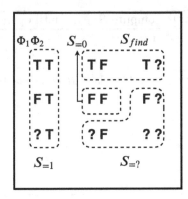

Fig. 2. A table illustrating possible combinations of truth values for Φ_1 and Φ_2 at a state s and corresponding partition set

Example 6. Given a qDTMC $\mathcal{M}_1$ and qPCTL formula $\Phi = Pr_{\geq 0.5}[\neg p \ U^{\leq 3} \ q]$, we can compute the partition sets of the state space S as: $S_{=0} = \{s_4\}$, $S_{=?} = \{s_1, s_5\}$, $S_{=1} = \{s_2, s_6\}$ and $S_{find} = \{s_0, s_3\}$.

We now calculate the satisfaction probabilities of the path formula $[\Phi_1 U^{\leq k} \ \Phi_2]$ for the paths starting at a state s using the 1MC algorithm. We denote the true satisfaction probability for state s as $Pr((s, \Phi_1 U^{\leq k} \ \Phi_2) = T)$ or $x_s^{(T),k}$. We know that the true satisfaction probability for states in $S_{=1}$ is 1. Also for states in $S_{=0}$ and $S_{=?}$, the true satisfaction probability is 0.

To evaluate the path formula $\Phi_1 U^{\leq k} \Phi_2$, a path with initial state $s \in S_{find}$ is traversed until either a state in one of $S_{=0}$, $S_{=1}$ or $S_{=?}$, or the bound k is reached. If a state $s \in S_{find}$ when bound k is reached, then the probability of $[\Phi_1 U^{\leq k} \ \Phi_2]$ being evaluated to T is 0. The 1MC algorithm thus computes the true satisfaction probability as follows.

$$
x_s^{(T),k} = \begin{cases}
1 & \text{if} & s \in S_{=1} \\
0 & \text{if} & s \in S_{=0} \\
0 & \text{if} & s \in S_{=?} \\
0 & \text{if } s \in S_{find} \wedge k = 0 \\
\sum_{t \in S} \mathbb{P}(s,t).x_t^{(T),k-1} & \text{if } s \in S_{find} \wedge k > 0
\end{cases}
\tag{4}
$$

Similarly, we now calculate the false satisfaction probability and denote it as $Pr((s, \Phi_1 U^{\leq k} \ \Phi_2) = F)$ or $x_s^{(F),k}$. Recall that the path formula $[\Phi_1 U^{\leq k} \ \Phi_2]$ evaluates to F if either the formula Φ_2 is F at all states of k-length path, or if at some state Φ_2 evaluates to T but at some preceding state, Φ_1 evaluated to F.

We know that the false satisfaction probability for states in $S_{=0}$ is 1 and is 0 for states in $S_{=1}$ and $S_{=?}$. We also know that the states in set S_{find} will have Φ_1 as T and Φ_2 is either F or ?. Now no path starting from a state that has Φ_1 as T and Φ_2 as ? ($S_{find} \cap Sat_?(\Phi_2)$) will evaluate $\Phi_1 U^{\leq k} \Phi_2$ as F. Thus, false satisfaction probability for such states will be 0.

We now traverse paths with initial state $s \in S_{find} \cap Sat_F(\Phi_2)$ until either a state in one of $S_{=0}$, $S_{=1}$, $S_{=?}$ or $S_{find} \cap Sat_?(\Phi_2)$, or the bound k is reached. If a state $s \in S_{find} \cap Sat_F(\Phi_2)$ when bound k is reached, then the probability of $[\Phi_1 U^{\leq k} \Phi_2]$ being evaluated to F is 1. This correlates to Φ_2 evaluating to F at all states in the path, and thus path formula $[\Phi_1 U^{\leq k} \Phi_2]$ being evaluated to F.

$$
x_s^{(F),k} = \begin{cases}
0 & \text{if} & s \in S_{=1} \\
1 & \text{if} & s \in S_{=0} \\
0 & \text{if} & s \in S_{=?} \\
0 & \text{if} & s \in (S_{find} \cap Sat_?(\Phi_2)) \\
1 & \text{if } s \in (S_{find} \cap Sat_F(\Phi_2)) \wedge k = 0 \\
\sum_{t \in S} \mathbb{P}(s,t).x_t^{(F),k} & \text{if } s \in (S_{find} \cap Sat_F(\Phi_2)) \wedge k > 0
\end{cases}
\tag{5}
$$

$$
x_s^{(?),k} = 1 - [x_s^{(T),k} + x_s^{(F),k}]
\tag{6}
$$

Example 7. For the given qDTMC $\mathcal{M}_1$ and qPCTL formula $\Phi = Pr_{\geq 0.5} [\neg p\, U^{\leq 3}\, q]$, the true satisfaction probability for state s_0, $Pr((s_0, \neg p\, U^{\leq 3}\, q) = T)$ is 0.475. Also, the false satisfaction probability $Pr((s_0, \neg p\, U^{\leq 3}\, q) = F)$ is 0. Thus, the initial state $s_0 \in Sat_?(\Phi)$ and the formula Φ is evaluated to ? at state s_0.

From the above arguments, we conclude that:

Lemma 2. *For the path formulas $X\Phi$, $\Phi_1 U^{\leq k}\Phi_2$ and $\Phi_1 U\Phi_2$, Algorithm 1 is correct for the corresponding probabilistic state formulas:*

- *$1MC(s, Pr_{\bowtie\theta}[X\Phi]) = T$ (alt., F or ?) iff $(s, Pr_{\bowtie\theta}[X\Phi]) = T$ (resp., F or ?)*
- *$1MC(s, Pr_{\bowtie\theta}[\Phi_1 U\Phi_2]) = T$ (alt., F or ?) iff $(s, Pr_{\bowtie\theta}[\Phi_1 U\Phi_2]) = T$ (resp., F or ?)*
- *$1MC(s, Pr_{\bowtie\theta}[\Phi_1 U^{\leq k}\Phi_2]) = T$ (alt., F or ?) iff $(s, Pr_{\bowtie\theta}[\Phi_1 U^{\leq k}\Phi_2]) = T$ (resp., F or ?)*

From lemmas 1 and 2, we have:

Theorem 1. *$1MC(s, \Phi) = T$ (alt., F or ?) iff $(s, \Phi) = T$ (resp., F or ?)*

Complexity of qPCTL Model Checking: Unlike for the standard PCTL model checking algorithm [4], the 1MC algorithm for qPCTL model checking computes an additional partition set $S_{=?}$ before solving the system of linear equations for the states in the set S_{find}. The computation of set $S_{=?}$ is done in $\Theta(|S|)$ time. Other than that, the asymptotic time complexity is polynomial with respect to the size of the model $\mathcal{M}$ and linear in terms of the size of the query Φ. Thus, the time complexity of the 1MC qPCTL model checking algorithm is the same as that of the PCTL algorithm and the 2MC algorithm for qPCTL–$\mathcal{O}(poly(size(M)).n_{max}.|\Phi|)$, where n_{max} is the maximum step bound for bounded *until* and 1 if the formula does not contain a bounded *until*. However, in many cases, a drop in the number of runs results in a significant performance improvement over the 2MC algorithm. This is more pronounced for larger models. We validate this with extensive experimentation in the next section.

4   Implementation and Results

We have implemented the 1MC algorithm as a Java tool. The tool takes as an input the qDTMC model and the qPCTL query. The tool supports both qualitative and quantitative qPCTL queries. A qualitative query only checks if the required probability threshold is met, and results in T, F or ?. A quantitative query on the other hand computes the exact probability of the query being T, F and ?.

We will begin by mentioning that the 1MC approach discussed in this paper yields matching results for the case studies reported in [1] and [2]– (i) a model representing an incomplete program code, and (ii) a network model that has incomplete information about its nodes respectively.

We now compare the performance of the proposed 1MC algorithm with the 2MC algorithm in [2] for model checking different qDTMCs. For the sake of fairness, we also implemented the standard PCTL model checker from scratch. The 2MC algorithm calls this bare-bones model checker as a subroutine.

For a fixed size of state space, we randomly generate 50 qDTMCs with different transition probability matrices and labeling functions. We study the variation in time taken to verify models with different structures for different qPCTL queries, and record the minimum and maximum time taken.

We repeat this for different sizes of state spaces starting from qDTMCs with 5 states, and up to 1500 states. Thus the algorithms were compared in terms of the time taken to verify the models of varying sizes.

Figure 3 plots the minimum and maximum times taken by the 1MC and 2MC algorithms to verify the properties $\Phi_1 = Pr_{\geq 0.8}[p_0 \ U \ p_1]$, $\Phi_2 = Pr_{\geq 0.7}[\ p_0 \ U \ Pr_{\geq 0.6}[X \ p_1]]$ and $\Phi_3 = Pr_{\geq 0.7}[\ p_0 \ U \ Pr_{\geq 0.6}[\ p_1 \ U \ p_2]]$ where p_0, p_1 and p_2 are atomic propositions in the incomplete models.

It can be seen from the results that the minimum time curve for 1MC algorithm is higher than that for the 2MC algorithm. This is due to the fact that the 2MC algorithm need not compute both its steps in all cases. For instance, if the probability of a property being true meets the required threshold in the first step itself, the model checker need not calculate the probability of a property being false. However, the 1MC algorithm calculates both true as well as false probability in single step, which increases the computation overhead. In many cases, however, both steps of 2MC algorithm are needed; thus making it very expensive for models with large state space. The proposed 1MC algorithm generates results faster for such models and has a lower maximum time curve than that for 2MC algorithm.

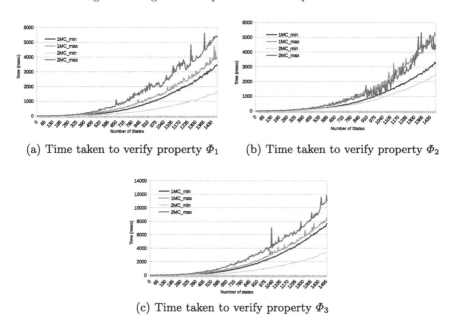

(a) Time taken to verify property Φ_1 (b) Time taken to verify property Φ_2

(c) Time taken to verify property Φ_3

Fig. 3. Minimum and maximum time taken by the algorithms to verify properties Φ_1, Φ_2 and Φ_3 for models of varying sizes and topology.

5   Conclusion and Future Work

We believe that model checking for incomplete models will be of immense practical use. While it is possible to design algorithms that use existing techniques designed for binary logic, it is useful to have algorithms designed exclusively for three-valued logics. We discussed an algorithm and its application for model checking PCTL queries against incomplete DTMCs that accommodate a three-valued logic.

Future efforts in this direction would be (i) applying these algorithms for interim analysis of incomplete models in practice and (ii) designing similar algorithms and tools for other models and systems of logic.

References

1. Arora, S., Legay, A., Richmond, T., Traonouez, L.-M.: Statistical model checking of incomplete stochastic systems. In: Margaria, T., Steffen, B. (eds.) ISoLA 2018. LNCS, vol. 11245, pp. 354–371. Springer, Cham (2018). https://doi.org/10.1007/978-3-030-03421-4_23
2. Arora, S., Rao, M.V.P.: Probabilistic model checking of incomplete models. CoRR (2017). http://arxiv.org/abs/1706.05082
3. Baier, C., Haverkort, B., Hermanns, H., Katoen, J.P.: Model-checking algorithms for continuous-time Markov chains. IEEE Trans. Softw. Eng. **29**(6), 524–541 (2003). https://doi.org/10.1109/TSE.2003.1205180

4. Baier, C., Katoen, J.P.: Principles of Model Checking (Representation and Mind Series). The MIT Press (2008)
5. Benedikt, M., Lenhardt, R., Worrell, J.: LTL model checking of interval Markov chains. In: Piterman, N., Smolka, S.A. (eds.) TACAS 2013. LNCS, vol. 7795, pp. 32–46. Springer, Heidelberg (2013). https://doi.org/10.1007/978-3-642-36742-7_3
6. Bruns, G., Godefroid, P.: Model checking partial state spaces with 3-valued temporal logics. In: Halbwachs, N., Peled, D. (eds.) CAV 1999. LNCS, vol. 1633, pp. 274–287. Springer, Heidelberg (1999). https://doi.org/10.1007/3-540-48683-6_25
7. Bruns, G., Godefroid, P.: Generalized model checking: reasoning about partial state spaces. In: Palamidessi, C. (ed.) CONCUR 2000. LNCS, vol. 1877, pp. 168–182. Springer, Heidelberg (2000). https://doi.org/10.1007/3-540-44618-4_14
8. Caillaud, B., Delahaye, B., Larsen, K.G., Legay, A., Pedersen, M.L., Wąsowski, A.: Constraint Markov chains. Theor. Comput. Sci. 412(34), 4373–4404 (2011). https://doi.org/10.1016/j.tcs.2011.05.010
9. Chakraborty, S., Katoen, J.-P.: Model checking of open interval Markov chains. In: Gribaudo, M., Manini, D., Remke, A. (eds.) ASMTA 2015. LNCS, vol. 9081, pp. 30–42. Springer, Cham (2015). https://doi.org/10.1007/978-3-319-18579-8_3
10. Chechik, M.: On interpreting results of model-checking with abstraction. University of Toronto, Technical report (2000)
11. Chechik, M., Easterbrook, S., Petrovykh, V.: Model-checking over multi-valued logics. In: Oliveira, J.N., Zave, P. (eds.) FME 2001. LNCS, vol. 2021, pp. 72–98. Springer, Heidelberg (2001). https://doi.org/10.1007/3-540-45251-6_5
12. Courcoubetis, C., Yannakakis, M.: Verifying temporal properties of finite-state probabilistic programs. In: 29th Annual Symposium on Foundations of Computer Science, pp. 338–345. IEEE (1988)
13. Delahaye, B., et al.: Abstract probabilistic automata. Inf. Comput. 232, 66–116 (2013). https://doi.org/10.1016/j.ic.2013.10.002
14. Fecher, H., Leucker, M., Wolf, V.: Don't Know in probabilistic systems. In: Valmari, A. (ed.) SPIN 2006. LNCS, vol. 3925, pp. 71–88. Springer, Heidelberg (2006). https://doi.org/10.1007/11691617_5
15. Godefroid, P., Piterman, N.: LTL generalized model checking revisited. Int. J. Softw. Tools Technol. Transfer 13(6), 571–584 (2011)
16. Hansson, H., Jonsson, B.: A logic for reasoning about time and reliability. Formal Asp. Comput. 6(5), 512–535 (1994). https://doi.org/10.1007/BF01211866
17. Huth, M., Piterman, N., Wagner, D.: Three-valued abstractions of Markov chains: completeness for a sizeable fragment of PCTL. In: Kutyłowski, M., Charatonik, W., Gębala, M. (eds.) FCT 2009. LNCS, vol. 5699, pp. 205–216. Springer, Heidelberg (2009). https://doi.org/10.1007/978-3-642-03409-1_19
18. Jonsson, B., Larsen, K.G.: Specification and refinement of probabilistic processes. In: Proceedings 1991 Sixth Annual IEEE Symposium on Logic in Computer Science, pp. 266–277. IEEE (1991)
19. Klink, D.: Three-valued abstraction for stochastic systems. Verlag Dr, Hut (2010)
20. Kozine, I.O., Utkin, L.V.: Interval-valued finite Markov chains. Reliable Comput. 8(2), 97–113 (2002)
21. Kwiatkowska, M., Norman, G., Parker, D.: Stochastic model checking. In: Bernardo, M., Hillston, J. (eds.) SFM 2007. LNCS, vol. 4486, pp. 220–270. Springer, Heidelberg (2007). https://doi.org/10.1007/978-3-540-72522-0_6
22. Sen, K., Viswanathan, M., Agha, G.: Statistical model checking of black-box probabilistic systems. In: Alur, R., Peled, D.A. (eds.) CAV 2004. LNCS, vol. 3114, pp. 202–215. Springer, Heidelberg (2004). https://doi.org/10.1007/978-3-540-27813-9_16

23. Sen, K., Viswanathan, M., Agha, G.: On statistical model checking of stochastic systems. In: Etessami, K., Rajamani, S.K. (eds.) CAV 2005. LNCS, vol. 3576, pp. 266–280. Springer, Heidelberg (2005). https://doi.org/10.1007/11513988_26
24. Sen, K., Viswanathan, M., Agha, G.: Model-checking Markov chains in the presence of uncertainties. In: Hermanns, H., Palsberg, J. (eds.) TACAS 2006. LNCS, vol. 3920, pp. 394–410. Springer, Heidelberg (2006). https://doi.org/10.1007/11691372_26
25. Younes, H.L.S., Simmons, R.G.: Probabilistic verification of discrete event systems using acceptance sampling. In: Brinksma, E., Larsen, K.G. (eds.) CAV 2002. LNCS, vol. 2404, pp. 223–235. Springer, Heidelberg (2002). https://doi.org/10.1007/3-540-45657-0_17

A Novel Decentralized LTL Monitoring Framework Using Formula Progression Table

Omar Bataineh[1][(⊠)], David S. Rosenblum[2], and Mark Reynolds[3]

[1] Nanyang Technological University, Singapore, Singapore
`omar.ibrahim@ntu.edu.sg`
[2] National University of Singapore, Singapore, Singapore
[3] University of Western Australia, Perth, Australia

Abstract. This paper presents a new technique for optimizing formal analysis of Boolean formulas and Linear Temporal Logic (LTL) formulas, namely the formula simplification tables. A formula simplification table is a mathematical table that shows all possible simplifications of the formula under different truth assignments of its variables. The simplification table is constructed using a three-valued logic: besides true and false, the variable can take an unknown value. The advantages of constructing a simplification table of a formula are two-fold. First, it can be used to compute the logical influence weight of each variable in the formula, which is a quantitative score that shows the importance of the variable in affecting the outcome of the formula. Second, it can be used to identify variables that have the highest logical influences on the outcome of the formula. We demonstrate the effectiveness of formula simplification table in the context of software verification by developing an efficient framework for the well-known decentralized monitoring problem.

1 Introduction

This paper describes a new technique to improve formal analysis of both Boolean formulas and Linear temporal logic formulas (LTL). The new presented improvement technique is mainly based on the notion of *formula simplification tables*. A formula simplification table is a mathematical table that shows all possible simplified forms of the formula under different truth assignments of its variables. The simplification table is constructed using a three-valued logic: besides true and false, the variable can take an unknown value. Constructing a simplification table of a formula has several advantages. First, it can be used to compute a logical influence weight (i.e., a quantitative score) of each variable in the formula, which is a metric that shows the importance of the variable to the outcome of the formula. Second, it can be used to identify variables in the specification that have the highest logical influence on its outcome.

However, the scalability of formula simplification tables requires controlling the size of the formula (i.e., the number of variables in the formula), as the

© Springer Nature Switzerland AG 2019
F. Biondi et al. (Eds.): SPIN 2019, LNCS 11636, pp. 38–55, 2019.
https://doi.org/10.1007/978-3-030-30923-7_3

size of the table grows exponentially with respect to the number of variables. To address this issue we present an algorithm for reducing large formulas to a simplified form by detecting and contracting variables whose logical influences on the outcome of the formula are equivalent. The simplifications we perform in this paper cannot be obtained using traditional techniques by detecting duplicates, syntactic contradictions or tautologies.

The presented simplifications are mainly based on the observation that large formulas contain variables with equivalent logical influences, and therefore one needs not consider all the variables in the formula when constructing a formula simplification table. It is possible then to construct a much smaller formula sufficient to prove the original property. In particular, given an input formula φ, our simplification technique produces a simplified formula φ' while reducing and contracting variables whose logical influences on the outcome of the formula are equivalent. Then some sound logical extension rules are applied to draw valid conclusions about the original formula.

We demonstrate the effectiveness of formula simplification tables in the context of software verification by developing an efficient solution to the well-known decentralized LTL monitoring problem. In the decentralized LTL monitoring problem, a group of processes cooperate with each other in order to monitor a global LTL formula, where each process observes only a subset of the variables of the main formula. The goal is then to develop a solution that allows processes to detect violation of the global formula as early as possible and with least communication overhead. We develop a solution to the problem by synthesizing an efficient communication strategy for processes that allows them to propagate their observations in an optimal way.

2   The Decentralized LTL Monitoring Problem

A distributed program $\mathcal{P} = \{p_1, p_2, \ldots, p_n\}$ is a set of n processes which cooperate with each other in order to achieve a certain task. Distributed monitoring is less developed and more challenging than local monitoring: they involve designing a distributed algorithm that monitors another distributed algorithm. In this work, we assume that no two processes share a common variable. Each process of the distributed system emits events at discrete time instances. Each event σ is a set of actions denoted by some atomic propositions from the set AP. We denote 2^{AP} by Σ and call it the alphabet of the system. We assume that the distributed system operates under the perfect synchrony hypothesis, and that each process sends and receives messages at *discrete* instances of time, which are represented using an identifier $t \in \mathbb{N}^{\geq 0}$. An event in a process p_i, where $1 \leq i \leq n$, is either

- internal event (i.e. an assignment statement),
- message sent, where the local state of p_i remains unchanged, or
- message received, where the local state of p_i remains unchanged.

Since each process sees only a projection of an event to its locally observable set of actions, we use a projection function Π_i to restrict atomic propositions to the local view of monitor $\mathcal{M}_i$ attached to process p_i, which can only observe those of process p_i. For atomic propositions (local to process p_i), $\Pi_i : 2^{AP} \to 2^{AP}$, and we denote $AP_i = \Pi_i(AP)$, for all $i = 1 \ldots n$. For events, $\Pi_i : 2^{\Sigma} \to 2^{\Sigma}$ and we denote $\Sigma_i = \Pi_i(\Sigma)$ for all $i = 1 \ldots n$. We assume that $\forall_{i,j \leq n, i \neq j} \Rightarrow AP_i \cap AP_j = \emptyset$ and consequently $\forall_{i,j \leq n, i \neq j} \Rightarrow \Sigma_i \cap \Sigma_j = \emptyset$. That is, events are local to the processes where they are monitored. The system's global trace, $g = (g_1, g_2, \ldots, g_n)$ can now be described as a sequence of pair-wise unions of the local events of each process's traces. We denote the set of all possible events in p_i by E_i and hence the set of all events of P by $E_P = \bigcup_{i=1}^{n} E_i$. Finite traces over an alphabet Σ are denoted by Σ^*, while infinite traces are denoted by Σ^{∞}.

Definition 1 (LTL formulas [16]). *The set of LTL formulas is inductively defined by the grammar*

$$\varphi ::= true \mid p \mid \neg\varphi \mid \varphi \vee \varphi \mid X\varphi \mid F\varphi \mid G\varphi \mid \varphi U \varphi$$

where X is read as next, F as eventually (in the future), G as always (globally), U as until, and $p \in AP$ is an atomic proposition.

Definition 2 (LTL Semantics [16]). *Let $w = a_0 a_1 \ldots \in \Sigma^{\infty}$ be an infinite word with $i \in \mathbb{N}$ being a position. Then we define the semantics of LTL formulas inductively as follows*

- $w, i \models true$
- $w, i \models \neg\varphi$ *iff* $w, i \not\models \varphi$
- $w, i \models p$ *iff* $p \in a_i$
- $w, i \models \varphi_1 \vee \varphi_2$ *iff* $w, i \models \varphi_1$ *or* $w, i \models \varphi_2$
- $w, i \models F\varphi$ *iff* $w, j \models \varphi$ *for some* $j \geq i$
- $w, i \models G\varphi$ *iff* $w, j \models \varphi$ *for all* $j \geq i$
- $w, i \models \varphi_1 U \varphi_2$ *iff* $\exists_{k \geq i}$ *with* $w, k \models \varphi_2$ *and* $\forall_{i \leq l < k}$ *with* $w, l \models \varphi_1$ *and* $k, l \in \mathbb{N}$
- $w, i \models X\varphi$ *iff* $w, i+1 \models \varphi$.

We now review the definition of three-valued semantics LTL_3 that is used to interpret common LTL formulas, as defined in [5]. The semantics of LTL_3 is defined on finite prefixes to obtain a truth value from the set $\mathbb{B}_3 = \{\top, \bot, ?\}$.

Definition 3 (LTL₃ semantics). *Let $u \in \Sigma^*$ denote a finite word. The truth value of a LTL_3 formula φ with respect to u, denoted by $[u \models \varphi]$, is an element of $\mathbb{B}_3$ defined as follows:*

$$[u \models \varphi] = \begin{cases} \top & \text{if } \forall \sigma \in \Sigma^{\infty} : u\sigma \models \varphi \\ \bot & \text{if } \forall \sigma \in \Sigma^{\infty} : u\sigma \not\models \varphi \\ ? & \text{otherwise} \end{cases}$$

According to the semantics of LTL_3 the outcome of the evaluation of φ can be inconclusive (?). This happens if the so far observed prefix u itself is insufficient to determine how φ evaluates in any possible future continuation of u.

Problem 1 (**The decentralized monitoring problem** [6]). Given a distributed program $\mathcal{P} = \{p_1, p_2, \ldots, p_n\}$, a finite global-state trace $\alpha \in \Sigma^*$, an LTL property φ, and a set of monitor processes $\mathcal{M} = \{M_1, M_2, \ldots, M_n\}$ such that

- each process p_i has a local set of propositions AP_i, and
- each process p_i has a local monitor M_i, and
- monitor M_i can read truth values of AP_i, and
- monitor M_i can communicate with other monitors.

The main constraint that decentralised LTL monitoring addresses is the lack of a global sensor or monitor and a central decision making point asserting whether the system's global trace α has violated or satisfied the property φ. The decentralised monitoring problem aims then to design an algorithm for distributing and monitoring φ, such that satisfaction or violation of φ can be detected by local monitors alone.

3   Simplification Tables for Boolean Formulas

In this section, we discuss techniques that can be used to detect variables in a Boolean formula or in an LTL formula whose logical influences on the outcome of the formula are equivalent. Given a formula φ with a set of atomic propositions $prop(\varphi) = \{a_1, \ldots, a_n\}$, we ask the following questions:

1. Does φ contain variables whose logical influences on the outcome of the formula are equivalent?
2. Can we develop tests to extract variables with equivalent logical influences?
3. Can we assign a value (a quantitative score) to every variable in φ, corresponding to its importance in affecting the outcome of the formula?
4. Can we identify the variables that have the highest logical influence on the outcome of the formula φ?

Consider the Boolean formula $\varphi = (a \vee (b \wedge c))$. Do variables a and b have equivalent logical influence? Which variable has the highest logical influence on the outcome of φ? The answers to these questions depend on how the formula φ is simplified under different truth assignments of its variables. To answer the questions we introduce what we call a *formula simplification table*.

Definition 4 *(**Formula simplification table**). A simplification table is a mathematical table that shows all possible simplified forms of a given formula that result from different truth assignment of its variables. A simplification table has one column for each input variable, and one final column showing the simplified formula under the given combination of truth assignments. The variables take their truth values from the truth domain $\mathbb{B}_3 = \{\bot, \top, ?\}$. Each row of the table contains one possible configuration of the variables and the formula that results from substituting truth values of the variables in the main formula.*

Table 1. A simplification table for the formula $\varphi = (a \vee (b \wedge c))$

a	b	c	Simplified formula	a	b	c	Simplified formula	a	b	c	Simplified formula
?	?	?	$(a \vee (b \wedge c))$	⊤	?	?	⊤	⊥	?	?	$(b \wedge c)$
?	⊥	?	a	⊤	?	⊤	⊤	⊥	?	⊥	⊥
?	⊥	⊥	a	⊤	?	⊥	⊤	⊥	?	⊤	b
?	⊥	⊤	a	⊤	⊥	?	⊤	⊥	⊥	?	⊥
?	?	⊤	$(a \vee b)$	⊤	⊥	⊥	⊤	⊥	⊥	⊥	⊥
?	?	⊥	a	⊤	⊥	⊤	⊤	⊥	⊥	⊤	⊥
?	⊤	?	$(a \vee c)$	⊤	⊤	?	⊤	⊥	⊤	?	c
?	⊤	⊥	a	⊤	⊤	⊤	⊤	⊥	⊤	⊤	⊤
?	⊤	⊤	⊤	⊤	⊤	⊥	⊤	⊥	⊤	⊥	⊥

Definition 5 (Variables with equivalent logical influences). *Two variables in a formula are said to be equivalent in their logical influences on the outcome of the formula if under the same truth assignment they yield formulas with identical syntactic structure. Let φ be a formula with the set of atomic propositions φ. We say that the two variables $a, b \in prop(\varphi)$ have equivalent logical influences on φ (denoted as $a \equiv b$) if the following condition holds*

$$prog(\varphi, a = \bot) = prog(\varphi, b = \bot)[b/a] \wedge$$
$$prog(\varphi, a = \top) = prog(\varphi, b = \top)[b/a]$$

where $prog(\varphi, a = v)$ is a function that returns a new formula of φ after substituting the truth value of a in φ. We write $prog(\varphi, b = \bot)[b/a]$ to indicate that the variable a will be renamed by b in the resulting formula $prog(\varphi, b = \bot)$.

From the simplification table of the formula $\varphi = (a \vee (b \wedge c))$ (Table 1) we note that the two variables b and c have equivalent logical influence on the outcome of φ as $prog(\varphi, b = \bot) = prog(\varphi, c = \bot)[b/c]$ and $prog(\varphi, b = \top) = prog(\varphi, c = \top)[b/c]$, while the variables a and b have inequivalent logical influence on the outcome of the formula as $prog(\varphi, a = \top) \neq prog(\varphi, b = \top)[a/b]$.

We now introduce a new notion that can be used to improve the efficiency of decentralized LTL monitoring, namely the notion of influence weights of variables in a formula. We show then how to measure the influence weights of variables in a given formula by constructing a simplification table for the formula.

Definition 6 (Influence weights of variables). *The influence weight of a variable in a given formula is a quantitative score that shows the importance of the variable in affecting the outcome of the formula. It can be computed from the simplification table of the formula. Let φ be a formula and $prop(\varphi)$ be the set of atomic propositions of φ and $a \in prop(\varphi)$. The influence weight of the variable a (denoted as $IW_\varphi(a)$) can be computed by taking the ratio of the number of formulas in the simplification table that a appears in to the number of configurations in which a has unknown truth value ($a =?$).*

From Table 1 we note that $IW_\varphi(a) = \dfrac{8}{9}$, $IW_\varphi(b) = \dfrac{4}{9}$, and $IW_\varphi(c) = \dfrac{4}{9}$. We conclude that the variable a has higher logical influence on the outcome of the formula than both b and c. This can be shown from the value of the influence weight of a which is larger than the weights of both b and c.

Observation 1 (Properties of influence weights of variables). *Let φ be an LTL formula with atomic propositions $prop(\varphi) = \{a_1, \ldots, a_n\}$. The basic properties of logical influence weights of $\{a_1, \ldots, a_n\}$ can be summarized as follows*

1. for any variable $a_i \in prop(\varphi)$ we have $0 \leq IW_\varphi(a_i) \leq 1$.
2. when $a_i \equiv a_j$ then $IW_\varphi(a_i) = IW_\varphi(a_j)$ but the converse in not true.

Definition 7 (Equivalent configurations). *Let φ be a formula with a set of propositional variables $\{a_1, \ldots, a_n\}$. We say that the two configurations $O = (a_1 = v_1, \ldots, a_n = v_n)$ and $O' = (a_1 = v'_1, \ldots, a_n = v'_n)$ are equivalent if they lead to the same simplified formula, where $v_1, \ldots, v_n \in \mathbb{B}_3$. Formally, we say that the two configurations O and O' are equivalent if*

$$prog(...(prog(\varphi, a_1 = v_1), a_2 = v_2), \ldots, a_n = v_n) =$$
$$prog(...(prog(\varphi, a_1 = v'_1), a_2 = v'_2), \ldots, a_n = v'_n)$$

The simplification table of a formula can also be used to derive Boolean formulas characterizing the conditions under which the main formula can be simplified into some specific formulas. Deriving such Boolean formulas can be very useful for certain problems such as the decentralized LTL monitoring problem, where processes can use such formulas to determine the minimal set of variables whose truth values need to be propagated. For example, for the formula $\varphi = (a \vee (b \wedge c))$ one can see from the simplification table of φ that there are multiple configurations that lead to the same simplified formula. For instance, there are five different configurations that simplify the formula to the atomic formula $\phi = a$. One can then derive a Boolean formula $\mathbb{B}_\phi$ characterizing the cases under which φ can be simplified to ϕ, which will be in this case $\mathbb{B}_\phi = (\bar{b} + \bar{c})$ (i.e., we write $\bar{b}$ to refer to the logical complement of the variable b).

4 Progression Tables for LTL Formulas

The technique described at the previous section can be used also for LTL formulas to compute the influence weights of variables in a given LTL formula. Note that for propositional logic formulas, we call the table as simplification table since the formula gets simplified when we substitute a truth value of a variable in the formula (i.e., the size of the formula is reduced). This is not always the case for temporal formulas, as the formula may be expanded at each state of the trace to express sets of obligations (requirements) that the system should fulfill for the remaining part of the trace. We therefore call the table as progression table rather than simplification table when dealing with LTL formulas.

The notion of influence weights of variables in temporal formulas is very similar to the one introduced for the Boolean formulas with some slight modification, where we define the influence weight of a variable in a temporal formula to be the ratio of the number of formulas in the progression table in which the variable appears in where its truth value is unknown to the total number of configurations in which the variable has unknown truth value.

Let us construct a progression table for the temporal formula $\varphi = F(a \wedge b) \vee G(c \wedge d)$. Since we mainly use the progression table to measure the influence weights of the variables to the outcome of the formula, we choose to restrict the temporal operators to specific time step $t \geq 0$ and use the classical expansion rules to express the semantics of the operators (i.e., $F(a) \equiv a \vee XF(a)$). It is interesting to note that restricting temporal operators to specific time step does not harm the analysis, it just simplifies it. From the definition of influence weights (see Definition 6) it is sufficient then to consider the temporal operators at a single step to compute the logical influence weights of variables to the outcome of the formula.

Table 2. A partial progression table for the formula $F(a \wedge b) \vee G(c \wedge d)$

$a^{(t)}$	$b^{(t)}$	$c^{(t)}$	$d^{(t)}$	Progressive formula	$a^{(t)}$	$b^{(t)}$	$c^{(t)}$	$d^{(t)}$	Progressive formula
?	?	?	?	$((a^{(t)} \wedge b^{(t)}) \vee XF(a \wedge b)) \vee (c^{(t)} \wedge d^{(t)} \wedge XG(c \wedge d))$	$\bot$	?	?	?	$XF(a \wedge b) \vee ((c^{(t)} \wedge d^{(t)}) \wedge XG(c \wedge d))$
?	?	$\bot$	?	$(a^{(t)} \wedge b^{(t)}) \vee XF(a \wedge b)$	$\bot$	?	?	$\top$	$XF(a \wedge b) \vee (d^{(t)} \wedge XG(c \wedge d))$
?	?	$\bot$	$\bot$	$(a^{(t)} \wedge b^{(t)}) \vee XF(a \wedge b)$	$\bot$	$\bot$	?	?	$XF(a \wedge b) \vee ((c^{(t)} \wedge d^{(t)}) \wedge XG(c \wedge d))$
?	?	$\top$	$\bot$	$(a^{(t)} \wedge b^{(t)}) \vee XF(a \wedge b)$	$\bot$	$\top$	?	?	$XF(a \wedge b) \vee ((c^{(t)} \wedge d^{(t)}) \wedge XG(c \wedge d))$
?	?	$\bot$	$\top$	$(a^{(t)} \wedge b^{(t)}) \vee XF(a \wedge b)$	$\bot$	$\top$	?	$\bot$	$XF(a \wedge b)$
?	?	?	$\bot$	$(a^{(t)} \wedge b^{(t)}) \vee XF(a \wedge b)$	$\bot$	?	?	$\bot$	$XF(a \wedge b)$
?	?	$\top$	?	$(a^{(t)} \wedge b^{(t)}) \vee XF(a \wedge b) \vee (d^{(t)} \wedge XG(c \wedge d))$	$\bot$	?	?	$\top$	$XF(a \wedge b) \vee (d^{(t)} \wedge XG(c \wedge d))$
?	?	?	$\top$	$(a^{(t)} \wedge b^{(t)}) \vee XF(a \wedge b) \vee (c^{(t)} \wedge XG(c \wedge d))$	$\bot$	$\bot$	?	$\bot$	$XF(a \wedge b)$
?	?	$\top$	$\top$	$(a^{(t)} \wedge b^{(t)}) \vee XF(a \wedge b) \vee XG(c \wedge d)$	$\bot$	$\bot$	?	$\top$	$XF(a \wedge b) \vee (d^{(t)} \wedge XG(c \wedge d))$
?	$\bot$	?	?	$XF(a \wedge b) \vee ((c^{(t)} \wedge d^{(t)}) \wedge XG(c \wedge d))$	$\top$	?	?	?	$b^{(t)} \vee XF(a \wedge b) \vee (c^{(t)} \wedge d^{(t)} \wedge XG(c \wedge d))$
?	$\bot$	?	$\bot$	$XF(a \wedge b)$	$\top$	?	?	$\bot$	$b^{(t)} \vee XF(a \wedge b)$
?	$\bot$	$\bot$	?	$XF(a \wedge b)$	$\top$	?	?	$\top$	$b^{(t)} \vee XF(a \wedge b) \vee (d^{(t)} \wedge XG(c \wedge d))$
?	$\bot$	$\bot$	$\bot$	$XF(a \wedge b)$	$\top$	$\top$	?	$\top$	$\top$
?	$\bot$	$\top$	$\bot$	$XF(a \wedge b)$	$\top$	$\top$	?	?	$\top$
?	$\bot$	$\top$	$\top$	$XF(a \wedge b) \vee XG(c \wedge d)$	$\top$	$\top$	?	$\bot$	$\top$
?	$\bot$	$\top$	?	$XF(a \wedge b) \vee (d^{(t)} \wedge XG(c \wedge d))$	$\top$	$\bot$	?	?	$XF(a \wedge b) \vee ((c^{(t)} \wedge d^{(t)}) \wedge XG(c \wedge d))$
?	$\bot$	?	$\top$	$XF(a \wedge b) \vee (c^{(t)} \wedge XG(c \wedge d))$	$\top$	$\bot$	?	$\bot$	$XF(a \wedge b)$
?	$\top$	$\bot$	$\bot$	$a^{(t)} \vee XF(a \wedge b)$	$\top$	$\bot$	?	$\top$	$XF(a \wedge b) \vee ((c^{(t)} \wedge XG(c \wedge d))$
?	$\top$	$\bot$	?	$a^{(t)} \vee XF(a \wedge b)$	?	$\top$	?	$\bot$	$a^{(t)} \vee XF(a \wedge b)$
?	$\top$	?	$\top$	$(a^{(t)} \vee XF(a \wedge b)) \vee (c^{(t)} \wedge XG(c \wedge d))$	?	$\top$	?	?	$(a^{(t)} \vee XF(a \wedge b)) \vee ((c^{(t)} \wedge d^{(t)}) \wedge XG(c \wedge d))$
?	$\top$	$\top$	$\top$	$a^{(t)} \vee XF(a \wedge b) \vee XG(c \wedge d)$	?	$\top$	$\top$	?	$(a^{(t)} \vee XF(a \wedge b)) \vee (d^{(t)} \wedge XG(c \wedge d))$
?	$\top$	$\bot$	$\top$	$a^{(t)} \vee XF(a \wedge b)$	?	$\top$	$\top$	$\bot$	$a^{(t)} \vee XF(a \wedge b)$

However, before constructing a progression table for the formula we use Definition 5 to detect variables in the formula whose logical influences on the outcome of the formula are equivalent. This would help to reduce the size of the table. Using Definition 5 we conclude that $a \equiv b$ and $c \equiv d$ but $a \not\equiv c$. We therefore have two sets of variables whose logical influences are equivalent: $E_1 = \{a, b\}$ and $E_2 = \{c, d\}$. In this case we do not need to construct a full progression table for the formula as $IW_\varphi(a) = IW_\varphi(b)$ and $IW_\varphi(c) = IW_\varphi(d)$. From the constructed (partial) progression table of the formula $\varphi = F(a \wedge b) \vee G(c \wedge d)$ (Table 2) we can see that the variables a and b have higher logical influences on the outcome of the formula than the variables c and d, where $IW_\varphi(a) = IW_\varphi(b) = \dfrac{27}{27} = 1$ and $IW_\varphi(c) = IW_\varphi(d) = \dfrac{16}{27} \approx 0.60$. This is mainly due to the semantics of the operators F and G and that the subformulas $F(a \wedge b)$ and $G(c \wedge d)$ are connected using the logical connective $\vee$. This leads to the conclusion that the set of logical and temporal operators used in the formula affect the weights of the variables.

In general, when computing influence weights (quantitative scores) of variables in a given formula φ using progression tables, we construct partial progression tables of size $(3^n - 2^n)$ where we skip the configurations in which all the variables have definite truth values. Recall that an influence weight of a variable in a given formula is computed by taking the ration of the number of simplified formulas in the table in which the variable appears in to the number of configurations in which the variable is assigned an unknown truth value. We distinguish here two cases when constructing a progression table for a formula:

1. if the formula does not contain variables with equivalent logical influences then we construct a partial progression table of the size $(3^n - 2^n)$. We skip here the set of configurations in which all the variables have definite (known) truth values as such configurations will not considered when computing influence weights of variables.
2. if the formula contains variables whose logical influences on the outcome of the formula are equivalent then we construct a partial progression table of the size $(k \times 3^{n-1} - 3^{n-2})$. Suppose that the given formula has c sets of variables with equivalent logical influences $E_1, \ldots, E_c$ then the variable k can be computed as follows $k = (n - \sum_{i=1}^{c} |E_i|) + c$. For example, for the formula $\varphi = F(a \wedge b) \vee G(c \wedge d)$ considered above the progression table (Table 2) consists of 45 entries instead of 81 entries as the formula contains two sets of variables whose logical influences are equivalent $E_1 = \{a, b\}$ and $E_2 = \{c, d\}$. In this case $k = 2$ and the minimum size of the table that can be constructed to compute influence weights of variables will be 45 as variables with equivalent logical influences have the same influence weights.

5   Simplifications

When some variables are shown to be equivalent in their logical influences w.r.t. the outcome of a formula, then some of these variables can be replaced by one representative. We now describe the basic steps that can be followed to simplify a formula that contains variables with equivalent logical influences.

1. Detect sets of variables in the formula whose logical influences on the outcome of the formula are equivalent. This can be performed using Definition 5.
2. Fix the names of two variables in each derived set while replacing the names of the other variables to one of the fixed names. The reason for maintaining two variables from each set is to detect the influence of each variable on the other and their joint influence on the variables from the other sets.

```
1: Input: φ
2: int k := 1
3: Bool Equiv := false
4: for each aᵢ ∈ Varφ do
5:     for each aⱼ ∈ (Varφ \ aᵢ) do
6:         if prog(φ, aᵢ = ⊤) = prog(φ, aⱼ = ⊤)[aᵢ/aⱼ] ∧
7:            prog(φ, aᵢ = ⊥) = prog(φ, aⱼ = ⊥)[aᵢ/aⱼ] then
8:             Eₖ := ∅
9:             add aⱼ to Eₖ
10:            remove aⱼ from Varφ
11:            Equiv := true
12:        end if
13:        if Equiv = true then
14:            add aᵢ to Eₖ
15:            Equiv := false
16:            k + +
17:        end if
18:    end for
19: end for
```

Algorithm 1. Algorithm for detecting variables with equivalent logical influence

3. Reconstruct the formula using the new set of variable names. This yields a formula with redundant variables.
4. Simplify the resulting formula by eliminating redundant variables.

The resulting simplified LTL formula has the same syntactic structure as the original formula but in a reduced form, as the number of variables in the simplified formula is less than that of the original formula.

Example 1. Consider the following LTL formula

$$\varphi = G(a_1 \wedge a_2 \wedge \ldots \wedge a_{n_1}) \vee F(b_1 \wedge b_2 \wedge \ldots \wedge b_{n_2}).$$

According to Definition 5 the formula φ has two sets of variables with equivalent logical influences: $E_1 = \{a_1, \ldots, a_{n_1}\}$ and $E_2 = \{b_1, \ldots, b_{n_2}\}$. Suppose that we choose to maintain the variables a_1 and a_2 from E_1 and replace the names of the other variables in E_1 by a_1 and b_1 and b_2 from E_2 and replace the names of the other variables in E_2 by b_1. This yields the following formula

$$\varphi' = G(a_1 \wedge a_2 \wedge a_1 \wedge \ldots \wedge a_1) \vee F(b_1 \wedge b_2 \wedge b_1 \wedge \ldots \wedge b_1).$$

The formula φ' contains redundant variables and hence can be simplified to

$$\varphi_R = G(a_1 \wedge a_2) \vee F(b_1 \wedge b_2).$$

6   From Simplified Formula to Original Formula

We now describe the steps that can be followed to draw correct logical conclusions about the original formula from the results obtained of the analysis of the simplified formula. Given an LTL formula φ we simplify φ to φ_R by contracting variables with equivalent logical influences as described in Sect. 5.

1. Construct a progression table for the simplified formula φ_R.
2. Compute influence weights of the variables in the simplified formula φ_R.
3. Synthesize Boolean formulas for sets of configurations in the progression table of the formula φ_R that yield the same LTL formula.
4. Extend influence weights of the variables to the original formula φ.
5. Extend sets of synthesized Boolean formulas to the original formula φ.

Note that steps (1–3) of the above procedure can be performed as described in the previous section. We now describe how steps (4–5) can be implemented by developing rules for extending logical conclusions derived from the simplified formula. Let $\mathbb{B}_\phi^{\varphi_R}$ be a Boolean formula synthesized from the progression table of the formula φ_R for sets of configurations that yield the LTL formula ϕ. The general form of the Boolean formula $\mathbb{B}_\phi^{\varphi_R}$ can be expressed as follows

$$\mathbb{B}_\phi^{\varphi_R} = (T_0 + T_1 + \ldots + T_n)$$

where each term T_i has the form $\prod(V)$ (a product of a set of variables), where V is a set of propositional variables from $prop(\varphi)$. Let $\{E_1, \ldots, E_k\}$ be the sets of variables with equivalent logical influence extracted from the formula φ. Note that for each set E_i we maintain only two variables in the simplified formula. Let us denote the variables maintained from the set E_1 by a_1 and a_2 which we will use to formalize the extension rules given below. Extending sets of Boolean formulas from the simplified formula to the original formula can take one of the following forms: (i) extending $\mathbb{B}_\phi^{\varphi_R}$ by adding new variables to some terms in $\mathbb{B}_\phi^{\varphi_R}$, and (ii) extending $\mathbb{B}_\phi^{\varphi_R}$ by adding new terms to $\mathbb{B}_\phi^{\varphi_R}$.

1. When none of the variables in the equivalent set E_1 appears in the formula ϕ. That is, for all $a_i \in E_1$ we have $a_i \notin prop(\phi)$. We have three cases here:
   (a) if there exists a term T in $\mathbb{B}_\phi^{\varphi_R}$ such that $(|T.V| \geq 1 \wedge (T.V \cap E_1) = 1)$ then for each variable in E_1 that is not in the short formula φ_R add a new term to $\mathbb{B}_\phi$ that is identical to T while replacing the variable $(T.V \cap E_1)$ by one from the set E_1 that is not in the short formula.
   (b) if there exists a term T in $\mathbb{B}_\phi^{\varphi_R}$ such that $(|T.V| > 1 \wedge (T.V \cap E_1) = 2)$ then add all variables in E_1 that is not in the short formula φ_R to V.
   (c) if none of the variables in E_1 appears in the terms of $\mathbb{B}_\phi^{\varphi_R}$ then the formula $\mathbb{B}_\phi^{\varphi_R}$ needs not to be extended with respect to the set E_1.
2. When variables a_1 and a_2 appear in the formula ϕ. We have two case here
   (a) if variables a_1 and a_2 appear in the formula ϕ but none of them appears in the terms of the formula $\mathbb{B}_\phi^{\varphi_R}$. In this case, we need to extend the formula ϕ by adding all variables in E_1 that are not in φ_R to ϕ.
   (b) if variables a_1 and a_2 appear in the formula ϕ and in the formula $\mathbb{B}_\phi^{\varphi_R}$. Then the formula $\mathbb{B}_\phi^{\varphi_R}$ will be extended in two steps (i) add all variables in E_1 that are not in φ_R to ϕ, and (ii) use extension rules 1(a)-1(b) to extend the formula $\mathbb{B}_\phi^{\varphi_R}$.

We now discuss some useful results that can be used to simplify the computation of influence weights of variables.

Lemma 1. *Let φ be an LTL formula with propositional variables $prop(\varphi) = \{a_1, \ldots, a_n\}$. Let φ_R be a simplified version of φ computed as described in Sect. 5. Then when $IW_{\varphi_R}(a_i) = 1$ (the weight of a_i in the short formula) we have $IW_{\varphi}(a_i) = 1$ (the weight of a_i in the long formula).*

Theorem 1. *Let φ be an LTL formula with a set of propositional variables $prop(\varphi) = \{a_1, \ldots, a_n\}$. Let φ_R be a simplified formula of φ computed as described in Sect. 5. Then when all variables in φ have equivalent logical influence on the outcome of φ and that $IW_{\varphi_R}(a_1) = \frac{N}{D}$ then $IW_{\varphi}(a_1) = \frac{N^{n-1}}{D^{n-1}}$.*

Lemma 1 states that variables of weight one do not get influenced by adding more variables to the formula as long as the semantics of the formula is preserved. On the other hand, Theorem 1 states that for formulas whose variables are equivalent in their logical influences then the influence weights of these variables can be computed in a straightforward way using the formula $IW_{\varphi}(a_i) = \frac{N^{n-1}}{3^{n-1}}$, where a_i is a variable in φ and n is the number of variables in the formula φ.

Example 2. Consider the following LTL formula

$$\varphi = F(a_1 \wedge a_2 \wedge a_3 \wedge a_4 \wedge a_5) \vee G(b_1 \wedge b_2 \wedge b_3 \wedge b_4)$$

Note that φ has two sets of variables with equivalent logical behavior: $E_1 = \{a_1, a_2, a_3, a_4, a_5\}$ and $E_2 = \{b_1, b_2, b_3, b_4\}$. Using the simplification rules described in Sect. 5 we can simplify φ to $\varphi_R = F(a_1 \wedge a_2) \vee G(b_1 \vee b_2)$. The progression table of the reduced formula is given in Table 2. We consider here the Boolean formulas for the the cases of configurations that lead to the simplified formulas $XF(a_1 \wedge a_2)$ and $\top$. The expressions can be given as follows

$$\mathbb{B}^{\varphi_R}_{(XF(a_1 \wedge a_2))} = \sum_{i=1..2, j=1..2} (\overline{a_i}.\overline{b_j}) \qquad \mathbb{B}^{\varphi_R}_{\top} = \prod_{i=1..2} (a_i)$$

Extending the Boolean expression $\mathbb{B}^{\varphi_R}_{(XF(a_1 \wedge a_2))}$ to the original formula can be performed using rule 2(b), while extending the expression $\mathbb{B}^{\varphi_R}_{\top}$ to the original formula can be performed using rule 1(b) which yield the following formulas

$$\mathbb{B}^{\varphi}_{(XF(a_1 \wedge a_2 \wedge a_3 \wedge a_4 \wedge a_5))} = \sum_{i=1..5, j=1..4} (\overline{a_i}.\overline{b_j}) \qquad \mathbb{B}^{\varphi}_{\top} = \prod_{i=1..5} (a_i)$$

Note that the influence weights of the variables a_1, a_2, a_3, a_4, and a_5 will be the same since their logical influences on the outcome of the formula are equivalent. From the progression table of the simplified formula we note that $IW_{\varphi_R}(a_1) = IW_{\varphi_R}(a_2) = 1$ and $IW_{\varphi_R}(b_1) = IW_{\varphi_R}(b_2) = 0.66$. From Lemma 1 we conclude that $IW_{\varphi}(a_1) = IW_{\varphi}(a_2) = 1$ and from Theorem 1 we conclude that $IW_{\varphi}(b_1) = IW_{\varphi}(b_2) \approx 0.039$.

7   Using Progression Tables in Decentralized Monitoring

The information extracted from the progression table of the monitored formula can be used for two purposes: (i) to synthesize efficient communication strategy for processes, and (ii) to propagate observations of processes in an efficient way. However, for each process, we associate what we call *influence logical power*. Such power can be computed according to the observation power of the process (i.e., the set of variables in the formula that are locally observed by the process).

Definition 8 *(Influence power of processes).* *Let P be a distributed system with n processes $\{q_1, .., q_n\}$ and φ be an LTL property of P that we seek to monitor in a decentralized fashion. Let $q_i \in P$ be a process with a set of atomic propositions $AP_i = \{a_1, \ldots, a_k\}$ and that $AP_i \subseteq prop(\varphi)$. The influence power of process p_i (denoted as $IP_\varphi(q_i)$) can be computed as follows*

$$IP_\varphi(q_i) = \sum_{j=1}^{k}(IW_\varphi(a_j)).$$

That is, the influence logical power of a process can be computed by taking the sum of the logical weights of the variables observable by that process.

In our setting, processes with higher influence power will receive higher priority in the order of communication. This is mainly because processes with higher influence power they either observe larger number of variables of the monitored formula or variables with higher influence weights and hence their ability to simplify the formula are higher than those with lower influence power.

Example 3. Suppose that we would like to monitor a formula $\varphi = F(b \vee (a_1 \wedge a_2 \wedge c))$ and that we have three processes: process A with $AP_A = \{a_1, a_2\}$, process B with $AP_B = \{b\}$, and process C with $AP_C = \{c\}$. To synthesize an efficient round-robin communication policy for processes we use Definition 8 to compute their influence power. We first need to compute the logical influence weight of each variable in the formula. This can be computed by constructing a progression table for the formula φ. From the progression table of the formula we find that $IW_\varphi(a_1) = IW_\varphi(a_2) = IW_\varphi(c) = \frac{8}{27}$ and $IW_\varphi(b) = \frac{26}{27}$. From these values we can see that the influence power of processes are: $IP_\varphi(A) = \frac{16}{27}$, $IP_\varphi(B) = \frac{26}{27}$, and $IP_\varphi(C) = \frac{8}{27}$. However, since $IP_\varphi(B) > IP_\varphi(A) > IP_\varphi(C)$ then the round-robin policy will be of the form $(B \to A \to C \to B)$, where the direction of the arrows represents the order of communication.

Instead of allowing processes to propagate their entire observations to their neighbor processes, they can take advantage of the constructed progression table of the formula to compute the minimal set of variables whose truth values need to be propagated. Note that in some situations it is sufficient for processes to propagate only a subset of their observations while allowing the receiving process to draw the same conclusion about the truth value of the monitored formula. Suppose for example that processes A and B monitor an LTL formula $\varphi =$

$F(a_1 \wedge a_2 \wedge b_1 \wedge b_2)$ and that process A observes a_1 and a_2. Suppose that at some state s process A observes that $a_1 = \bot \wedge a_2 = \top$. Then A needs only to propagate the truth value of a_1 to B as this would be sufficient to allow B to know that $(a_1 \wedge a_2 \wedge b_1 \wedge b_2) = \bot$ and hence $F(a_1 \wedge a_2 \wedge b_1 \wedge b_2) =?$.

As mentioned earlier, a Boolean formula is given as sums of products of the form $B_\phi = (T_0 + T_1 + \ldots + T_k)$, where each term T_i represents a condition under which the formula φ can be simplified to ϕ and has the form $\prod(V)$ where V is a set of variables. Suppose that at some step s of the trace being monitored process A simplifies the monitored formula φ to formula ϕ using its observations. The question is then what A should communicate to its neighbor process? A simple procedure can be used to compute the minimal set of variables whose truth values need to be propagated as described below.

1. Find all terms in the formula B_ϕ which hold to *true* when replacing the variables in B_ϕ by their definite truth values. Let us denote the set containing all the terms that hold to *true* in the formula B_ϕ by L.
2. Find the term in L with the smallest corresponding V set, let us denote that set by V_{min}. In this case, the variables in the set V_{min} represent the minimal set of variables whose truth values need to be propagated.

Our decentralized monitoring algorithm consists of two phases: setup and monitor. The setup phase consists of the five steps described in Sect. 5. We now summarize the actual monitoring steps in the form of an explicit algorithm that describes how local monitors operate and make decisions:

1. [Read next event]. Read next $\sigma_i \in \Sigma_i$ (initially each process reads σ_0).
2. [Compute minimal set of variables to be transmitted]. Examine the set of Boolean formulas derived from the progression table to compute the minimal set of variables whose truth values need to be propagated.
3. [Compute the receiving process]. For our communication strategy, the receiving process of some process p is fixed between states and computed according to some round-robin communication policy, as described in Sect. 7.
4. [Propagate truth values of variables in V_{min}]. Propagate the truth values of variables in the minimal set in V_{min} to the receiving process.
5. [Evaluate the formula φ and return]. If a definite verdict of φ is found return it. That is, if $\varphi = \top$ return $\top$, if $\varphi = \bot$ return $\bot$.
6. [Go to step 1]. If the trace has not been finished or a decision has not been made then go to step 1.

We now turn to discuss the basic properties of our decentralized monitoring framework. Let $\models_D$ be the satisfaction relation on finite traces in the decentralized setting and $\models_C$ be the satisfaction relation on finite traces in the centralized setting, where both $\models_D$ and $\models_C$ yield values from the same truth domain. Note that in a centralized monitoring algorithm we assume that there is a central process that observes the entire global trace of the system being monitored, while in our decentralized monitoring algorithm processes observe part of the trace, perform remote observation, and use the progression table of the monitored formula in order to setup an efficient communication strategy.

Theorem 2 (Soundness). *Let* $\varphi \in LTL$ *and* $\alpha \in \Sigma^*$. *Then* $\alpha \models_D \varphi = \top/\bot \Rightarrow \alpha \models_C \varphi = \top/\bot$.

Soundness means that all verdicts (truth values taken from a truth-domain) found by the decentralized monitoring algorithm for a global trace α with respect to the property φ are actual verdicts that would be found by a centralized monitoring algorithm that have access to the trace α.

Theorem 3 (Completeness). *Let* $\varphi \in LTL$ *and* $\alpha \in \Sigma^*$. *Then* $\alpha \models_C \varphi :$ $B \Rightarrow \exists \alpha' \in \Sigma^*.|\alpha'| \leq n \wedge \alpha.\alpha' \models_D \varphi : B$, *where* n *is the number of processes in the distributed system and* $B \in \{\top, \bot\}$.

Completeness means that all verdicts found by the centralized monitoring algorithm will be found by the decentralized monitoring algorithm but not necessarily at the same time (i.e., after consuming the same number of events). That is, the decentralized algorithm reaches the same verdict as the centralized algorithm but with some bounded delay $\sigma \leq n$. This is mainly due to the distribution of information and communications. We refer the reader to the full version at http://arxiv.org/abs/1810.13129 for the missing proofs.

8   Experiments

We have evaluated our monitoring approach against the LTL decentralized monitoring approach of Bauer and Falcone [6], in which the authors developed a monitoring algorithm for LTL based on the formula-progression technique [4]. The formula progression technique takes a temporal formula ϕ and a current assignment I over the literals of ϕ as inputs and returns a new formula after acting I on ϕ. The idea is to rewrite a temporal formula when an event e is observed or received to a formula which represents the new requirement that the monitored system should fulfill for the remaining part of the trace. We also use the tool DECENTMON3 (http://decentmon3.forge.imag.fr/) in our evaluation, which is a tool dedicated to decentralized monitoring. The tool takes as input multiple traces, corresponding to the behavior of a distributed system, and an LTL formula. The reason for choosing DECENTMON3 in our evaluation is that it makes similar assumptions to our presented approach. Furthermore, DecentMon3 improves the original DecentMon tool developed in [6] by limiting the growth of the size of local obligations and hence it may reduce the size of propagated messages. We believe that by choosing the tool DECENTMON3 as baseline for comparison we make the evaluation much fairer.

We denote by BF the monitoring approach of Bauer and Falcone, and PDM our presented approach in which processes construct a progression table for the monitored formula which will be used to synthesize efficient round robin policy for processes and to propagate observations in an optimal way. We compare the approaches against benchmark for patterns of formulas [2] (see Table 3). In Table 3, the following metrics are used: $\#msg$, the total number of exchanged messages; $|msg|$, the total size of exchanged messages (in bits); $|trace|$, the average length of the traces needed to reach a verdict; and $|mem|$, the memory in bits needed for the structures (i.e., formulas plus state for our algorithm). For example, the first line in Table 3 says on average, traces were of length 4.65 when one of the local monitors in approach BF came to a verdict, and of length 5.26 when one of the monitors in PDM came to a verdict.

Table 3. Benchmarks for 1000 generated LTL pattern formulas (Averages)

$|\varphi|$	$|trace|$		$\#msg.$		$|msg.|$		$|mem|$	
	BF	PDM	BF	PDM	BF	PDM	BF	PDM
abs	4.65	5.10	4.46	5.15	1,150	102	496.4	11.9
exis	27.9	29.5	19.7	20.8	1,100	411	376	19.8
bexis	43.6	41.3	31.6	31.9	55,000	25415	28,200	20.6
univ	5.86	6.2	5.92	5.82	2,758	138	498	22.5
prec	54.8	54.5	25.4	26.9	8,625	755	663	34.9
resp	622	622	425	515	22,000	1211	1,540	17.5
precc	4.11	5.2	4.81	5.95	5,184	356	1,200	15.7
respc	427	444	381	409	9,000	2799	4,650	22.1
consc	325	324	201	234	7,200	1223	2,720	15.8

8.1 Benchmarks for Patterns of Formulas

We compared the two approaches with realistic specifications obtained from specification patterns [9]. Table 3 reports the verification results for different kinds of patterns (absence, existence, bounded existence, universal, precedence, response, precedence chain, response chain, constrained chain). The specification formulas are available at [2]. We generated 1000 formulas monitored over the same setting (processes are synchronous and reliable). For these benchmarks we generated formulas as follows. For each pattern, we randomly select one of its associated formulas. Such a formula is "parametrized" by some atomic propositions from the alphabet of the distributed system which are randomly instantiated. For this benchmark (see Table 3), the presented approach leads to significant reduction on both the size of messages and the amount of memory consumption compared to the optimized version of the BF algorithm (DECENTMON3).

9 Related Work

Finding redundancies in formulas has been studied in the form of vacuity detection in temporal logic formulas [3,14]. Here, the goal is to identify vacuously valid subparts of formulas, indicating, for example, a specification error. In contrast, our focus is to reduce the complexity of the formula by detecting variables whose logical influences on the outcome of the formula are equivalent and then reduce the complexity of the formula by reducing the number of variables.

Various simplification rules have also been successfully applied as a preprocessing step for solving, usually for bit-vector arithmetic [12,13]. These rules are syntactic and theory-specific. In contrast, the technique described in this paper is not meant as a preprocessing step for solving and guarantees non-redundancy, it is rather a simplification technique for detecting and contracting variables with equivalent logical influences for the purpose of optimizing formal analysis of formulas by constructing simpler forms sufficient to prove the original property.

The literature on decentralized monitoring problem is a rich literature, where several monitoring algorithms have been developed for verifying distributed systems at runtime [6,7,11,15,17,18]. We discuss here some interesting works on the problem and refer the reader to [1,10] for a more comprehensive survey.

Bauer and Falcone [6] propose a decentralized framework for runtime monitoring of LTL. The framework is constructed from local monitors which can only observe the truth value of a predefined subset of propositional variables. The local monitors can communicate their observations in the form of a (rewritten) LTL formula towards its neighbors. Mostafa and Bonakdarpour [15] propose similar decentralized LTL monitoring framework, but truth value of propositional variables rather than rewritten formulas are shared.

The work of Falcone et al. [11] proposes a general decentralized monitoring algorithm in which the input specification is given as a deterministic finite-state automaton rather than an LTL formula. Their algorithm takes advantage of the semantics of finite-word automata, and hence they avoid the monitorability issues induced by the infinite-words semantics of LTL. They show that their implementation outperforms the Bauer and Falcone decentralized LTL algorithm [6] using several monitoring metrics.

Colombo and Falcone [8] propose a new way of organizing monitors called choreography, where monitors are organized as a tree across the distributed system, and each child feeds intermediate results to its parent. The proposed approach tries to minimize the communication induced by the distributed nature of the system and focuses on how to automatically split an LTL formula according to the architecture of the system.

El-Hokayem and Falcone [10] propose a new framework for decentralized monitoring with new data structure for symbolic representation and manipulation of monitoring information in decentralized monitoring. In their framework, the formula is modelled as an automaton where transitions of the automaton are labelled with Boolean expressions over atomic propositions of the system.

10 Conclusion and Future Work

We presented a novel framework for decentralized monitoring of LTL formulas based on the notion of formula progression tables. The progression tables can be used to extract useful information about the analysed formula including logical influence weights of the variables in the formula. We showed how formula progression tables can be used to optimize decentralized monitoring solutions of LTL formulas by synthesizing efficient communication strategies for processes and propagating information in an optimal way. In future work, we aim to employ some decomposition techniques to split the global LTL formula into local LTL expressions. This would help to avoid the memory-explosion problem.

References

1. Al-Bataineh, O.I., Rosenblum, D.: Efficient decentralized LTL monitoring framework using tableau approach. CoRR, abs/1803.02051 (2018)
2. Alavi, H., Avrunin, J.G., Corbett, L.D., Dwyer, M., Pasareanu, C.: Specification patterns website (2011). http://patterns.projects.cis.ksu.edu/
3. Armoni, R., et al.: Enhanced vacuity detection in linear temporal logic. In: Hunt, W.A., Somenzi, F. (eds.) CAV 2003. LNCS, vol. 2725, pp. 368–380. Springer, Heidelberg (2003). https://doi.org/10.1007/978-3-540-45069-6_35
4. Bacchus, F., Kabanza, F.: Planning for temporally extended goals. In: Proceedings of the Thirteenth National Conference on Artificial Intelligence, pp. 1215–1222 (1996)
5. Bauer, A., Leucker, M., Schallhart, C.: Runtime verification for LTL and TLTL. ACM Trans. Softw. Eng. Methodol. (TOSEM) **20**, 14:1–14:64 (2011)
6. Bauer, A., Falcone, Y.: Decentralised LTL monitoring. In: Giannakopoulou, D., Méry, D. (eds.) FM 2012. LNCS, vol. 7436, pp. 85–100. Springer, Heidelberg (2012). https://doi.org/10.1007/978-3-642-32759-9_10
7. Colombo, C., Falcone, Y.: Organising LTL monitors over distributed systems with a global clock. In: Bonakdarpour, B., Smolka, S.A. (eds.) RV 2014. LNCS, vol. 8734, pp. 140–155. Springer, Cham (2014). https://doi.org/10.1007/978-3-319-11164-3_12
8. Colombo, C., Falcone, Y.: Organising LTL monitors over distributed systems with a global clock. Formal Methods Syst. Des. **49**(1–2), 109–158 (2016)
9. Dwyer, M.B., Avrunin, G.S., Corbett, J.C.: Patterns in property specifications for finite-state verification. In: Proceedings of the 21st International Conference on Software Engineering, pp. 411–420 (1999)
10. El-Hokayem, A., Falcone, Y.: Monitoring decentralized specifications. In: Proceedings of the 26th ACM SIGSOFT International Symposium on Software Testing and Analysis (ISTA), pp. 125–135 (2017)
11. Falcone, Y., Cornebize, T., Fernandez, J.-C.: Efficient and generalized decentralized monitoring of regular languages. In: Ábrahám, E., Palamidessi, C. (eds.) FORTE 2014. LNCS, vol. 8461, pp. 66–83. Springer, Heidelberg (2014). https://doi.org/10.1007/978-3-662-43613-4_5
12. Ganesh, V., Dill, D.L.: A decision procedure for bit-vectors and arrays. In: Damm, W., Hermanns, H. (eds.) CAV 2007. LNCS, vol. 4590, pp. 519–531. Springer, Heidelberg (2007). https://doi.org/10.1007/978-3-540-73368-3_52
13. Jha, S., Limaye, R., Seshia, S.A.: Beaver: engineering an efficient SMT solver for bit-vector arithmetic. In: Bouajjani, A., Maler, O. (eds.) CAV 2009. LNCS, vol. 5643, pp. 668–674. Springer, Heidelberg (2009). https://doi.org/10.1007/978-3-642-02658-4_53
14. Kupferman, O., Vardi, M.Y.: Vacuity detection in temporal model checking. In: Pierre, L., Kropf, T. (eds.) CHARME 1999. LNCS, vol. 1703, pp. 82–98. Springer, Heidelberg (1999). https://doi.org/10.1007/3-540-48153-2_8
15. Mostafa, M., Bonakdarpour, B.: Decentralized runtime verification of LTL specifications in distributed systems. In: 2015 IEEE International Parallel and Distributed Processing Symposium, pp. 494–503 (2015)

16. Pnueli, A.: The temporal logic of programs. In: Proceedings of the 18th Annual Symposium on Foundations of Computer Science, SFCS 1977, pp. 46–57. IEEE Computer Society (1977)
17. Scheffel, T., Schmitz, M.: Three-valued asynchronous distributed runtime verification. In: International Conference on Formal Methods and Models for System Design (MEMOCODE), vol. 12. IEEE (2014)
18. Sen, K., Vardhan, A., Agha, G., Rosu, G.: Efficient decentralized monitoring of safety in distributed systems. In: Proceedings of the 26th International Conference on Software Engineering, ICSE 2004, pp. 418–427. IEEE Computer Society (2004)

From Dynamic State Machines
to Promela

Massimo Benerecetti[1](✉), Ugo Gentile[2], Stefano Marrone[3], Roberto Nardone[4],
Adriano Peron[1], Luigi L. L. Starace[1], and Valeria Vittorini[1]

[1] University of Naples Federico II, Naples, Italy
{massimo.benerecetti,adriano.peron2,valeria.vittorini}@unina.it,
luigi.starace@gmail.com
[2] CERN, Geneva, Switzerland
ugo.gentile@cern.ch
[3] Università della Campania "Luigi Vanvitelli", Caserta, Italy
stefano.marrone@unicampania.it
[4] University Mediterranea of Reggio Calabria, Reggio Calabria, Italy
roberto.nardone@unirc.it

Abstract. Dynamic State Machines (DSTM) is an extension of Hierarchical State Machines recently introduced to answer some concerns raised by model-based validation of railway control systems. However, DSTM can be used to model a wide class of systems for design, verification and validation purposes. Its main characteristics are the dynamic instantiation of parametric machines and the definition of complex data types. In addition, DSTM allows for recursion and preemptive termination. In this paper we present a translation of DSTM models in Promela that can enable automatic test case generation via model checking and, at least in principle, system verification. We illustrate the main steps of the translation process and the obtained Promela encoding.

1 Introduction

Dynamic STate Machine (DSTM) is a recently-developed modelling language [1], developed in the context of the ARTEMIS Joint Undertaking project CRYSTAL (CRitical sYSTem engineering AcceLeration) [10]. DSTM has been devised to explicitly meet industrial requirements in design, verification and validation of complex control systems, and includes in its formal framework both complex control flow constructs (such as asynchronous forks, preemptive termination, recursive execution) and complex data flow constructs (such as custom complex type definition, parametric machines, and inter-process communication). DSTM borrows many syntactic elements from UML Statecharts, and extends them with the notion of module and with the possibility of recursion and dynamic instantiation. The possibility of modelling both complex behaviours and data enables the usage of DSTM at different levels of abstraction and for different purposes, for example property verification and model-based testing.

The ultimate objective of ongoing work on DSTM is to enable its usage within model-driven tool chains for application or product life-cycle management. In this direction, this paper presents a transformation from DSTM to

© Springer Nature Switzerland AG 2019
F. Biondi et al. (Eds.): SPIN 2019, LNCS 11636, pp. 56–73, 2019.
https://doi.org/10.1007/978-3-030-30923-7_4

PROMELA in order to provide the necessary support for the automatic integration of verification and validation methodologies based on DSTM into industrial verification and validation processes. Previous work [1, 8, 9] provides the motivation for the introduction of DSTM, the formal definition of the syntax semantics, and its application to the validation of railway control systems. In those papers the encoding of DSTM models to PROMELA models was merely sketched. Here a complete translation is presented, emphasizing how the the hierarchical structure of DSTM models can be encoded into the modular features of PROMELA embodied in the notion of process types. Even though, due to space constraints, a precise formal account of the equivalence between the DSTM semantics presented in [1] and the resulting PROMELA encoding is not provided here, the correctness can be stated in terms of a suitable correspondence between executions of a DSTM and of its PROMELA encoding, based on the step semantics. Such a correspondence would allow for formal verification of linear time properties of DSTM with SPIN.

Many works introducing transformations from high level specification languages to formal languages are discussed in the literature. Among them transformations from AADL, MARTE and MARTE-DAM UML profiles are of special interest for the analysis of critical systems (e.g., in [2, 3, 11]). In particular, a transformation from SysML to the specification languages of Spin, Prism and NuSMV model checkers is presented in [5]. The implementation of Statecharts in PROMELA has been studied since 1998 [7]. In [4] an algorithm to automatically encode an ASM specification in PROMELA is presented with the aim of automated generation of test sequences. The novelty of our work is the source formalism and its peculiarities, in particular recursion and dynamic instantiation that are not allowed in other state-based languages.

The paper is organized as follows. Section 2 provides the basics on DSTM and describes some original modelling examples. The translation from DSTM models to PROMELA models is introduced in Sect. 3, where the key issues to be addressed and the adopted solutions are discussed. Section 4 contains some closing remarks and suggestions for future work.

2   Dynamic State Machines

In this section we provide an overview of DSTM through some examples, in order to introduce the main notions used in the rest of the paper. For a complete account of the formal syntax and semantics of DSTM we refer to [1].

A Dynamic STate Machine (DSTM) model is a sequence of machines $M_1, M_2, \ldots, M_n$ communicating over a set X of global variables and a set C of global communication channels. Machine M_1 is the *initial machine*, namely the highest level of the hierarchical system. Each machine M_i, with $i \in \{2, \ldots, n\}$, may be parametric over a set of parameters $P_i \subseteq P$. Parameters are aliases for channels and variables names and are actualized at runtime, when the machine is instantiated, allowing multiple instantiations of the same machine with different parameter values. When a parametric machine is instantiated, each parameter is mapped to its actual value by means of a *parameter-substitution function*, which associates the parameters with actual ground values. A machine M_i represents a module in a DSTM specification and is defined as a state-transition diagram, whose possible kinds of vertices are:

node: basic control state of a machine;
entering node: initial pseudo-node of a machine. A machine may specify multiple entering nodes, corresponding to different initial conditions;
initial node: default entering pseudo-node of a machine, to be used when no entering node is explicitly specified;
exit node: final (or exiting) node of a machine corresponding to different termination conditions;
box: node modelling the parallel activation of machines associated with itself. A transition entering a box represents the parallel activation of the corresponding machines, while a transition exiting a box corresponds to a return;
fork: control pseudo-node modelling the activation of new processes. Such activation may be either *synchronous* (the forking process is suspended and waits for the activated processes to terminate) or *asynchronous* (the forking process continues its activity along the newly-activated processes);
join: control pseudo-node used to synchronize the termination of concurrently executing processes or to force their termination (*preemptive* join).

The vertices corresponding to stable, meaningful control points are called *nodes*, as opposed to *pseudo-nodes*, which are only transient points. Transitions represent changes in the control state of a machine. A transition is labelled with a name and decorated with a *trigger* (an input event originating from the external environment or from other machines, e.g. the presence of messages on a given channel), a *guard* (a Boolean condition on the current contents of variables and channels) and an *action* (one or more statements on variables and channels). For a transition to be fired its trigger must be fulfilled and its guard satisfied. When a transition fires, its action is executed with possible side-effects. In the following τ denotes the trivial trigger (no external event is required), *True* denotes the trivial guard (always satisfied), and ε denotes the empty action (no side effects).

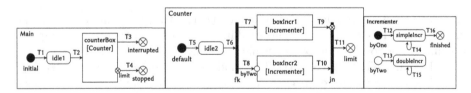

Fig. 1. The *Counting* DSTM specification

Example 1 (The Counting *DSTM).* Consider the *Counting* DSTM consisting of the machines *Main* (the initial machine), *Counter* and *Incrementer* represented in Fig. 1. Default entering pseudo-nodes are depicted as black circles, entering pseudo-nodes as white circles, final nodes as crossed-out white circles. Boxes are represented by rectangles and decorated with a comma-separated list of associated machines enclosed in square brackets. Nodes are drawn as rounded rectangles and fork and join pseudo-nodes are represented by black bars. Each node and pseudo-node is decorated with its name. Transitions are directed edges from source to target vertices, and are detailed in Table 1, where *Src* and *Trg* are the source and target of the transition, *Dec* is the associated decoration and *Inst* the parameter substitution function. Transitions T1, T5, T12, T13 are *implicit* transitions; T14 and T15, T16 are *internal* transitions; transitions T6 and T11 are, respectively, *entering fork* and *exiting join* transitions; T2 and T7 are *call by default* transitions, while T8 is a *call by entering*. T2, T7 and T8 are transitions with a non-empty substitution function since they enter boxes instantiating parametric machines. T9 and T10 are *return by default*, with the first being a preemptive transition (marked by $\otimes$). T3, with its non-trivial trigger signal?, is a *return by interrupt* while T4 is a well-formed *return by exiting* since its source is (counterBox, limit) and counterBox instantiates exactly one *Counter* machine and limit is an exiting state of such instantiated machine.

A DSTM is *well-formed* if it satisfies a set of syntactical constraints (formally defined in [1]) in order to guarantee that: (a) parameter substitution functions and *call by entering/exiting* transitions are consistent; (b) at each time, the control state of a machine can be located in at most one node; (c) for each *join* pseudonode, there exists a corresponding *fork*. Additionally, *exiting fork* and *entering join* transitions can only be labelled with a trivial trigger, guard and action, while boxes instantiated by a fork can only be refined by a single machine.

Table 1. Transitions of the *Counting* DSTM

T	Src	Trg	Dec	$Inst$
T1	initial	idle1	$\langle \tau, True, \varepsilon \rangle$	∅
T2	idle1	counterBox	$\langle \tau, True, \varepsilon \rangle$	P_to=100
T3	counterBox	interrupted	$\langle signal?, True, \varepsilon \rangle$	∅
T4	(counterBox, limit)	stopped	$\langle \tau, True, \varepsilon \rangle$	∅
T5	default	idle2	$\langle \tau, True, \varepsilon \rangle$	∅
T6	idle2	fk	$\langle \tau, True, \varepsilon \rangle$	∅
T7	fk	boxIncr1	$\langle \tau, True, \varepsilon \rangle$	P_limit=P_to
T8	fk	(boxIncr2, byTwo)	$\langle \tau, True, \varepsilon \rangle$	P_limit=P_to
T9	boxIncr1	(jn, $\otimes$)	$\langle \tau, True, \varepsilon \rangle$	∅
T10	boxIncr2	jn	$\langle \tau, True, \varepsilon \rangle$	∅
T11	jn	limit	$\langle \tau, True, \varepsilon \rangle$	∅
T12	byOne	simpleIncr	$\langle \tau, True, \varepsilon \rangle$	∅
T13	byTwo	doubleIncr	$\langle \tau, True, \varepsilon \rangle$	∅
T14	simpleIncr	simpleIncr	$\langle \tau, x<P\_limit, x++ \rangle$	∅
T15	doubleIncr	doubleIncr	$\langle \tau, True, x+=2 \rangle$	∅
T16	simpleIncr	finished	$\langle \tau, x \geq P\_limit, \varepsilon \rangle$	∅

Example 2. To illustrate the dynamic instantiation capabilities of DSTM and *asynchronous fork* transitions, consider the *Dynamic* DSTM detailed in Fig. 2 and in Table 2. Transition T4 is an *asynchronous fork*, T2 is triggered by the reception of any message on the channel req and T3 enters boxIncr instantiating an *Incrementer* machine, specified as in Example 1. T6 is an *entering join* transition. Notice that the *Dynamic* DSTM is able to instantiate an unbounded number of concurrent *Incrementer* machines by repeatedly firing transition T2 and

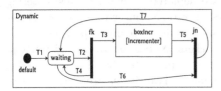

Fig. 2. The *Dynamic* DSTM

Table 2. Transitions of the *Dynamic* DSTM

T	Src	Trg	Dec	$Inst$
T1	default	waiting	$\langle \tau, True, \varepsilon \rangle$	$\varnothing$
T2	waiting	fk	$\langle \texttt{req?}, True, \varepsilon \rangle$	$\varnothing$
T3	fk	boxIncr	$\langle \tau, True, \varepsilon \rangle$	P_limit=10
T4	(fk, $\downarrow$)	waiting	$\langle \tau, True, \varepsilon \rangle$	$\varnothing$
T5	boxIncr	jn	$\langle \tau, True, \varepsilon \rangle$	$\varnothing$
T6	waiting	jn	$\langle \tau, True, \varepsilon \rangle$	$\varnothing$
T7	jn	waiting	$\langle \tau, True, \texttt{served++} \rangle$	$\varnothing$

performing the asynchronous fork T4. Indeed, T4 creates a loop with transition T2, involving the node *waiting* and the fork pseudo-node. When the *Dynamic* machine performs the asynchronous fork T4, it continues its execution in parallel with the activated *Incrementer* machine. Being still active, the process *Dynamic* might fire the transition T2 again, and a second activation of machine *Incrementer* occurs. Hence, this new instance would run in parallel with both the process *Dynamic* and the previously activated instance of *Incrementer*.

The types system in DSTM is based on the one of PROMELA, with the addiction of multi-types. Types in DSTM can either be *basic types*, *compound types* or *multi-types*. The *basic types* BT includes the Int type for integers, the Chn type for channel names and a set of user-defined enumeration types $BT_1, \ldots, BT_k$. *Compound types* are tuples of *basic types*, e.g., the compound type $CT = \langle BT_{j_1}, \ldots, BT_{j_k} \rangle$ is a tuple of basic types with $BT_{j_i} \in$ BT. *Simple types* contains both *basic types* and *compound types*. A *multi-type* MT is a composition of *simple types*: $MT = \{ST_1, \ldots, ST_k\}$. T denotes the set of all types.

Channels allow for communication with the external environment and between internal components via bounded *first-in first-out* buffers. Furthermore, channels are partitioned into the two sets of *internal* and *external* channels. Internal channels, whose names belong to $C_I \subseteq C$, are used for communications between components and are restricted to simple types, whereas external ones, whose names belong to $C_E \subseteq C$, are used for communications with the external environment and are restricted to having bounded buffers of length 1.

2.1 DSTM Semantics

The evolution of a DSTM consists in a sequence of instantaneous reactions called *steps*. A step is a maximal set of transitions that are triggered by the current system state and by the current value of channels. The firing of a transition can have side effects on the available channels and variables. The content sent during a step on an external channel, unlike for internal ones, can only be observed in the next step. DSTM semantics is defined over *ground machines*, namely machines in which actions, triggers and guards contain no parameters (parameters do not hold any value during execution, they serve only as placeholders and are substituted with actual values before instantiation). Ground machines are obtained from parametric machines by suitably applying parameter-substitution functions. The semantics of transition decorations is defined w.r.t. an evaluation context $\langle \rho, \chi, \eta \rangle$, where ρ associates variables with values, χ evaluates channels content in the current state, while η associates with each external channel its content in the next step. The formal semantics for DSTM is provided by defining a Labelled Transition System (LTS) [1]. The main intuition behind this formalization is that each state s of the LTS model represents a complete configuration (*state*) of the DSTM in a given instant, including the current control locations and the current evaluation context, while a *step* in the DSTM will correspond to a suitably-defined sequence of LTS transitions, each capturing DSTM transition firings. The global control state stores information about the current control state of each active process (ground machine). Since a machine may instantiate multiple machines, the control state can be represented by a tree, called the *control tree*. Each vertex of such a tree is labelled with either a machine, a box or a node. According to the intuition that pseudo-nodes represent only transient non-stable control points, control tree vertices cannot be labelled by pseudonodes. The root of a control tree, labelled by a machine, represents the main (initial) process, having the highest level in the hierarchy. Leaves represent control states in which each currently-active process is in and are labelled by nodes. Internal vertices represent the call hierarchy and cannot be labelled by nodes. Whenever a vertex is labelled by a machine M, it either is the root or is the child of a node labelled by a box instantiating M. If a node is labelled by either a box or a node, then its parent is labelled by the machine the box or the node belongs to.

Definition 1. *The state of a DSTM D is a tuple $\langle CT, Fr, \theta \rangle$ where:*

- *CT is a control tree over D, describing the current state of the control flow;*
- *Fr is the frontier of CT, containing those vertices of CT that can be the source of a transition in the current step;*
- *$\theta = \langle \rho, \chi, \eta \rangle$ is an evaluation context.*

Example 1 (Continued). Consider the *Counting* DSTM depicted in Fig. 1. Some of the *Counting* DSTM's possible control trees are represented in Fig. 3. In the figure, each machine-labelled (resp. box-labelled, node-labelled) vertex is depicted as a diamond $\diamond$ (resp. a square $\square$, a circle $\circ$ - possibly crossed-out $\otimes$ if labelled by an exiting state). Moreover, each node is decorated with the name of the corresponding machine/box/state.

Tree (a) encodes the control state in which only the *Main* machine is running and is in the idle1 state. Tree (b) encodes the control state in which the *Main* machine has entered the box counterBox, thus instantiating an instance of the *Counter* machine in its state idle2. Tree (c) is the control state in which the *Counter* machine, instantiated by *Main* by entering the box counter-Box, in turn instantiates two dis-

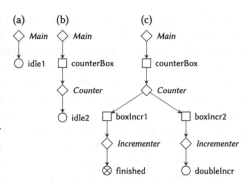

Fig. 3. Control trees of the *Counting* DSTM

tinct instances of the *Incrementer* machine. by entering the boxes boxIncr1 and boxIncr2. The first instance is in the finished end state, while the other one is in the doubleIncr state.

DSTM transitions may have source or target in pseudo-nodes which, as said, correspond to transient, unstable control points. Therefore, a transition involving pseudo-nodes may be seen as part of a *super-transition* connecting proper control points. For example, a fork (resp., a join) can be seen as a super-transition connecting one source with multiple targets (resp., multiple sources with one target). *Compound transitions* are able to capture this intuition and allow us to consider only transitions having source(s) and target(s) in proper control points. Hence, there exist three types of *compound transitions*: *simple* (non-implicit transition such that neither its source nor its target are fork or join nodes), *fork* and *join*. The notion of *enabledness* of a transition w.r.t. a DSTM state is as follows. A compound transition of a machine M is enabled in a DSTM state s if: (a) the guards and triggers of the transition are satisfied in the execution context of s; (b) the sources of the compound transition are contained in the frontier of s; and (c) no transition of an ancestor of M in the hierarchy is enabled. The targets of an executed transition cannot belong to the frontier of the resulting DSTM state, so as to prevent the sequential firing of transitions within the same step. Once the maximality of the current step has been reached (no other transition can be executed in the current step), an implicit *next step* transition occurs. Such transition updates: (a) the frontier with the vertices of the current control tree; and (b) the external channels with new messages, either those produced in the previous step or, if no message was produced for that channel, with non-deterministically generated messages.

Example 2 (Continued). Consider the *Dynamic* DSTM of Fig. 2. Figure 4 shows steps in one of its possible computations. In its initial state s_0, the DSTM has a control state encoded by tree (S_0). Suppose that the external environment generates a message on the external **req** channel, thus enabling transition T2.

The compound asynchronous fork $ct_1 = \langle\langle T2\rangle, \langle T3, T4\rangle\rangle$ is enabled in the waiting-labelled node. No other compound transitions are enabled, so the first step consists only in ct_1 and in the *next step* transition. When ct_1 fires, the node 1 (labelled by waiting) is replaced by two sub-

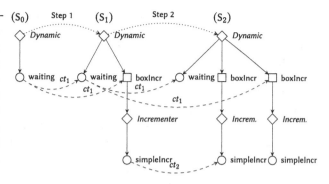

Fig. 4. Steps in a *Dynamic* DSTM computation

trees obtaining tree (S_1). Suppose that another message is available on the external channel **req**. Compound transition ct_1 is again enabled in node 1. This time also T14 from the *Incrementer* machine is enabled, and so is the simple compound transition $ct_2 = \langle\langle T14\rangle, \langle T14\rangle\rangle$. The second step consists of two compound transitions ct_1 and ct_2, which may be executed in any order, followed by the *next step* initialization transition. Execution of step 2 results in the control tree (S_2), where two instances of the *Incrementer* machine are executing concurrently along with the *Dynamic* machine, which is waiting for new requests in its waiting state.

3 From DSTM to Promela

Translating a DSTM to PROMELA presents several challenges, due to the substantial differences between the two specification languages. The translation we propose is a two-step process. The first step encodes the vertical hierarchical structure of a DSTM model (boxes) into the PROMELA *proctype* system. The second step transforms the resulting ordinary state machines into an actual PROMELA specification which also takes care of enforcing the step semantics and modelling a possibly non-deterministic environment.

3.1 Encoding the DSTM Vertical Hierarchy

This step transforms each machine of a hierarchical DSTM specification into an ordinary (flat) state machine, by removing all boxes, forks and joins and by substituting them with suitably defined nodes and transitions. Such transitions are also used to model the activation of other flat machines (by means of the PROMELA **run** command) and to ensure a correct handling of machine termination. Each such machine can then be encoded into a PROMELA **proctype**. Note that this transformation does not affect the size of the specification, indeed the size of the resulting model is linear in the size of the original DSTM.

For each machine M a type M_ex is introduced that enumerates all the exiting states of M. Recall that the execution of a PROMELA **run** command associates a pid to the activated process. The handling of termination is achieved by adding, for each machine M instantiated by a box B, two new channels: a channel of type M_ex, named chT_B_M_ex, and a channel of type {term,interrupt}, called chT_B_M. The first channel is used by the called machine to communicate the reaching of an exiting state to the caller, while the second is used by the caller to issue a termination message to the callee, signalling whether the termination is synchronous or preemptive (i.e., an interrupt).

Each machine activation action has the form run MachineName(params), where params is a list containing the following parameters:

- parent: the pid of its parent process in the hierarchy;
- initialState: the initial state for the instance being instantiated;
- ch_T_ex and ch_T: the channels required to handle termination.

When removing a box, three different situations may arise, depending on the structure of the DSTM, each dealt with a specific translation schema:

simple box: all the transitions entering the box have as source boxes or nodes;
synchronous fork: the source of the transition entering the box is a fork pseudo-node and no asynchronous fork transition exiting the fork exists;
asynchronous fork: the source of the transition entering the box is a fork pseudo-node and there is an asynchronous fork transition exiting the fork.

Simple Box Schema. In this case the box is substituted by a node having the same name. All transitions whose source (resp. target) is the box are replaced by transitions exiting (resp. entering) the newly-created node, as shown in Fig. 5. The decoration of this transition extends the one of the original transition, in order to model the instantiation of the other machines associated with the box and to handle their termination. As shown in Fig. 5, the triggers and guards of an entering transition are unchanged. A run action is added for each machine instantiated by the box, with the parent parameter set to the pid of the calling process.

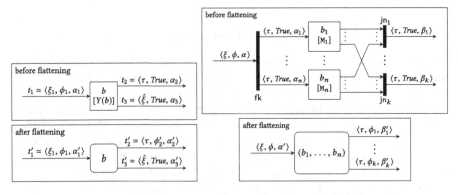

Fig. 5. Simple box flattening   **Fig. 6.** Synchronous fork flattening

As for the transitions exiting the box, we distinguish the following cases. If the original transition is a *return by exiting*, the guard needs to be enriched with a condition checking for termination of the instantiated machine in the required exit state. Hence, a guard of the form `chT_b_M_ex[?<ex>]` is conjoined with the original guard. If the original transition is a *return by default*, the guard needs to be conjoined with a check for the termination of each of the called machines. To check for a machine termination, regardless of the exiting state, we use a condition of the form `chT_b_M_ex[?<_>]`. If the original transition is a *return by interrupt*, the transition guard need not be enriched. In either case, when a return transition fires, all the called processes must terminate. This is achieved by adding, for each called process, two actions. One of the form `chT_b_M!<msg>`, where `msg` is either `interrupt` or `term`, which sends a termination message to the called process. The second action `chT_b_M_ex?<_>` is used, instead, to clean the corresponding channel used by the terminating machine to signal its termination.

Synchronous Fork Schema. In the synchronous fork case, the calling process suspends itself and waits for the termination of the called processes. In this case, the fork pseudo-node, the boxes called by the fork and the associated (non-preemptive) joins are considered as a single block. The entire block is replaced by a new node and suitably defined transitions to and from that node. The transition modelling the fork operation leads from the source node of the *entering fork* to the newly-introduced node. This transition instantiates the necessary processes by means of appropriate `run` actions, as in the *simple box* case. Each corresponding join operation is modelled by adding a transition from the new node to the target of the original exiting join transition. This transition is decorated with a trivial trigger, a guard requiring the appropriate termination of each machine instantiated by the involved boxes, and an action that takes care of issuing a termination message to each of the instantiated machines and removing messages from the exit-signalling channels.

In the general schema depicted in Fig. 6, the decoration of the transitions modelling the fork are of the form $\langle \xi, \phi, \alpha' \rangle$, where ξ and ϕ are the original trigger and guard of the corresponding *entering fork* transition, and $\alpha' = \alpha \cdot \overline{\alpha}$, with $\overline{\alpha}$ the sequence of `run` actions that activates the processes associated with the called boxes. Each one of the joins jn_i is modelled by a single transition of the form $\langle \tau, \phi_i, \beta_i' \rangle$, where: *(i)* ϕ_i is the conjunction of the appropriate termination conditions (either by exiting or by default) for each machine instantiated by the fork, as in the case of the *simple box* and *(ii)* $\beta_i' = \beta_i \cdot \overline{\beta}$, with $\overline{\beta}$ containing the appropriate termination-synchronization actions `chT_B_M!<term>` · `chT_B_M_ex?<_>` for each machine M in the box B instantiated by the fork.

Asynchronous Fork Schema. After performing an asynchronous fork the calling process continues to run concurrently with the newly instantiated processes. In this case the fork, the boxes entered by the fork and each associated join are considered as a single block and replaced by suitable transitions. The first transition models the fork operation and leads from the source node of the entering fork to the target node of the *asynchronous fork* transition, which is a node of the current machine. This transition must also instantiate, by means of appropriate

run actions, the necessary processes that model the called boxes. Note that, in this case the **parent** parameter corresponds to the parent of the calling process, as the new processes being instantiated become siblings of the calling process in the hierarchy tree. In order to model the join operations we add a transition for each join associated with the current fork. Each of these transitions leads from the source node of the *entering join* to the target of the exiting join.

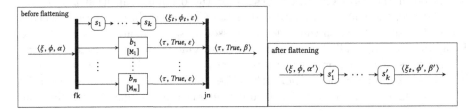

Fig. 7. Asynchronous fork flattening schema

Figure 7 depicts the case of a single fork/join pair, where $s'_i = (s_i, b_1, \ldots, b_n)$, with $i \in \{1, \ldots, k\}$, to keep track of the concurrently instantiated boxes as well. The decoration of the transition modelling the fork operation is defined exactly as in the case of a *synchronous* fork. The one modelling the join operation is decorated with $\langle \xi_t, \phi', \beta' \rangle$, where: ξ_t is the trigger associated with the *entering join*; the guard $\phi' = \phi_t \wedge \overline{\phi}$ conjoins the original guard ϕ_t in the entering join with the termination conditions for the instantiated machine; the action $\beta' = \beta \cdot \overline{\beta}$ concatenates the original action of the exiting join with the sequence of termination synchronization actions for the involved boxes.

Handling Preemptive Joins. The fork schemata described above need to be suitably extended in the case the corresponding join is preemptive. In a preemptive join, one or more entering join transitions may be qualified as preemptive. For each such entering join, a distinct transition inheriting the same trigger and guard as the corresponding original preemptive entering join is introduced. Moreover, if the original preemptive entering join is a *return* (either by default or by exiting) with source a box b, the guard is enriched with appropriate conditions requiring the termination of the machine associated with b, as in the previous cases. The action is defined as in the non-preemptive case, the only difference being that termination message issued to the terminating machine is an interrupt and has the form **chT_B_M!<interrupt>**.

3.2   From Flat DSTM to Promela

The PROMELA encoding we propose for a DSTM model is structured as follows:

1. an initial section for global declarations of datatypes, variables, and channels;

2. an `active proctype` named `Engine`, which is the root of the process hierarchy. Its purpose is to start the process modelling the initial machine, manage the proper initialization of external channels before each step, and orchestrate processes in order to simulate the step semantics of DSTM;

3. a `proctype` declaration for each of the n machines $M_1, \ldots, M_n$ of the DSTM.

In order to translate a flattened model into a PROMELA specification we need to address the following key points: (1) translation of data-flow elements; (2) orchestration of the concurrent flat machines and correct realization of the steps semantics; (3) encoding of each flat machine into a `proctype`.

Translation of Data-Flow Elements. The mapping of DSTM types and variables to their PROMELA equivalent is rather straightforward, with the DSTM types naturally mapped to the PROMELA types (`mtype` and datatypes declared by means of `typedef`). Internal DSTM channels are mapped to PROMELA channels with buffer size equal to the bound of the DSTM channel. If the DSTM channel is a multi-type channel, it is modelled by a set of PROMELA channels, one for each simple type constituting the multi-type. These channels are managed in a way that guarantees that, in each position, at most one of them contains a valid message. This can be achieved by adding a validity `bit` field to each message in the channels. External channels are encoded by channels with buffer size equal to two, with the first position containing the message for the current step and the second position containing the message for the next step possibly produced during the current one. External channels are managed in such a way that the first position in the channel is always filled. This ensures that messages produced in each step are always stored in the second position and that these messages cannot trigger transitions in the current step, as required by the step semantics. To this purpose, an additional validity `bit` field is introduced in every message, so that an empty external channels can be modelled by inserting in the first position a bogus message containing an invalid message.

To comply with the DSTM specification, additional operations on external channels are managed by the `Engine` process. At the beginning of the first step a, possibly-bogus, message for each external channel is non-deterministically generated and placed in the first position. At the beginning of any new step, instead, the messages in the first positions of the external channels, corresponding to the external inputs of the previous step, are removed. For all the channels that remain empty (i.e., no message was generated during the previous step) a, possibly-bogus, message is non-deterministically generated.

Enforcing the Step Semantics. From a global system state $s = \langle CT, Fr, \theta \rangle$, a machine M_i is allowed to execute a compound transition ct if such transition is enabled in state s of the control tree. Due to the encoding of the vertical hierarchy described in the previous section, there are no compound transitions anymore and the above condition can be simplified. An instance of a machine M_i is allowed to execute a transition if:

1. it has never executed during the current step (sequential firing of transitions in the same step is forbidden);

2. none of its descendants in the process hierarchy has executed;
3. none of its ancestors can execute a transition.

In order to simulate the step semantics, we exploit a token-passing mechanism. Each PROMELA process that models an instance of a DSTM machine is required to own a token in order to fire a transition. When a process holding a token is scheduled, it first checks if one of its transitions can be fired. In this case, it performs an enabled transition and consumes the token. If, on the other hand, no transition is executable, the process passes its token to all of its children. A complete top-down propagation of the token in the process hierarchy, starting from the **Engine** process, is called *phase*.

Since a transition fired during a *phase* may enable transitions that were not previously enabled (e.g., by sending messages or modifying the content of shared variables), the token-passing phase needs to be iterated so as to guarantee the maximality of each step. When a phase is concluded without any transition firing, a maximal step is reached.

Recall that sequential firing by the same process and the execution of both an ancestor and a descendant must be avoided during a single step. To this end, during each phase, processes who fire a transition propagate this information upwards in the process hierarchy so as to prevent ancestors from executing transitions (*back-propagation* mode). To implement this mechanism, the following global data structures are used:

- symbolic constants that refer to states of the machines, with an additional **backProp** label;
- a Boolean variable **HasFired**, used to keep track of the fact that at least one transition fired during the last concluded phase;
- an array **HasToken** of **MAX_PROC** bits, used to model token-ownership by active process instances; an array **dyingPid** of **MAX_PROC** bits used to keep track of the **pids** of terminated processes;
- an array **HasExecuted** (resp. **descendantExecuted**) of **MAX_PROC** bits, used to keep track of the fact that a given process (resp. one of its descendants including the process itself) fired a transition during the current step;
- a square matrix **ChildrenMatrix** of bits of size **MAX_PROC**, which encodes the active process hierarchy (**ChildrenMatrix[A].children[B]** is set if the process with pid **B** is a child of the process with pid **A**).

Information about the current state of every machine instance is stored in a **mtype** variable **DSTMstate** local to each PROMELA process. An additional variable **state**, assuming values in {**ready,backProp**}, is used to record whether a given **proctype** is ready to simulate the corresponding machine or is in the back-propagation mode. The step-semantics-enforcing mechanism is detailed as follows:

1. at the beginning of a step, after performing the required management operations for external channels, *Engine* passes the token to the main process and to its siblings. At this point, the global flag **HasFired** and the **DescendantExecuted** flag of every process are set to false;

2. every process owning the token and not having the DescendantExecuted flag set, tries to execute a transition. If a transition is executed, the global flag HasFired is set to true and a local variable DSTMstate is assigned to the machine next state. If no transition is executable, the process passes its token on to its children. In either case, state is set to backProp and the process enters the back-propagation mode in step 3. If a process is in the back-propagation mode and receives the token, then it is allowed to return to its simulation-ready state, without consuming the token;

3. every process in the back-propagation mode can execute if its Descendant-Executed flag is set but its parent flag is not. In this case, the process sets the DescendantExecuted flag for its parent as well. When no transition is enabled and the back-propagation is complete (i.e., a deadlock state is reached), the execution moves to step 4;

4. process *Engine* activates and
   (a) if flag HasFired is set, Engine starts a new phase. The hasFired flag is unset, Engine passes the token to its children once again, and the execution continues at step 2;
   (b) if HasFired is unset, then the current phase ended with no transitions fired and the current step is concluded. Execution continues by starting a new semantic step.

This mechanism is implemented in PROMELA by the proctypes schemas reported in Figs. 8 and 9, which are described in detail in the following section.

3.3   Promela Encoding

The complete PROMELA encoding of a DSTM D is as follows. The specification contains n proctypes, one for each machine M of the DSTM. The general schema of such proctypes is reported in Fig. 8. The generic M proctype has the same parameters as the corresponding flat machine, and starts with the declaration of local variables and channels required to handle communication of the termination requirements with its children, if any.

Then, the process enters the main iteration statement (line 4), which terminates in one of the following cases:

– an exiting state of M is reached and a termination request on the channel chT is received (line 30);
– it receives an interrupting termination request on the channel chT (line 37);
– its parent pid is marked as "dying" in the array dyingPid (line 37).

The main iteration statement features an option sequence for each machine state $S \in N \cup En$ guarded by the condition (state == S && HasToken[_pid]==1) && state==ready. Each of these option sequences immediately consumes the token (line 8) and, then, enters a selection statement that non-deterministically chooses an enabled transition to execute. This selection construct (line 9) contains an option sequence for each transition t with source state S. Each option sequence is guarded by a condition of the form (ξ && ϕ && !DescendantExecuted), with ξ

```
1  proctype M(pid parent;mtype initial;chan chT;chan chT_ex){
2    // declare channels for termination synch. with children here
3    byte i; mtype state=ready, DSTMstate=inital;
4    do
5    // for each state S ∈ Nᵢ ∪ Enᵢ
6    :: (DSTMstate==S && HasToken[_pid] && state==ready) ->
7       atomic {
8         HasToken[_pid]=0;
9         if
10        // for each transition t with Src(t) = S, Trg(t) = T, Dec(t) = ⟨ξ, φ, α⟩
11        :: (ξ && φ && !descendantExecuted[_pid]) ->
12           α; DSTMstate = T; HasFired=1;
13           HasExecuted[_pid]=1; descendantExecuted[_pid]=1;
14        :: else -> // no transition is executable
15           if
16           :: (!HasExecuted[_pid]) -> // did not exec. in this step
17              for (i:0..MAX_PROC-1) { // pass token to children
18                 if
19                 ::(ChildrenMatrix[_pid].children[i]) ->
20                    HasToken[i]=1;
21                 ::else->skip;
22                 fi;
23              }
24           ::else->skip;
25           fi;
26        fi;
27        state = backProp;
28      }
29    // for each exiting state ex ∈ Exᵢ
30    ::(DSTMstate==ex && chT?[term])->{chT?term; goto die}
31    // handle upwards propagation of descendantExecuted
32    ::(state==backProp && descendantExecuted[_pid] &&
33       !descendantExecuted[parent]) ->
34       { descendantExecuted[parent] = 1 }
35    // handle original state restoring after backProp
36    ::(state==backProp && HasToken[_pid])->{state=ready}
37    od unless (dyingPid[parent] || chT?[interrupt]) -> {
38       if
39       :: (chT?[_]) -> chT?<_>
40       :: else->skip
41       fi
42       goto die
43    }
44    die: dyingPid[_pid]=1
45 }
```

Fig. 8. Flat machine to proctype

```
1  active proctype Engine() {
2    pid PidMain; byte i;
3    chan chT_Main = [1] of {bit};
4    chan chT_Main_ex = [1] of {bit};
5    PidMain = run Main(_pid,initial,chT_Main,chT_Main_ex);
6    ChildrenMatrix[_pid].children[PidMain]=1;
7
8    nextStep: // starts a new step
9      atomic {
10        // handle external channels management
11        HasFired=0;
12        for (i : 0 .. MAX_PROC-1){
13           HasExecuted[i]=0; descendantExecuted[i]=0;
14           HasToken[i] = ChildrenMatrix[_pid].children[i];
15        }
16      }
17      goto waitTimeout;
18
19    nextPhase: // starts a new phase in the current step
20      atomic {
21        HasFired=0;
22        for ( i : 0 .. MAX_PROC - 1){ // give token to children
23           HasToken[i] = ChildrenMatrix[_pid].children[i];
24        }
25      }
26      goto waitTimeout;
27
28    waitTimeout:
29      do
30      :: timeout -> // deadlock
31         if
32         :: (!HasFired) -> goto nextStep;
33         :: (HasFired) -> goto nextPhase;
34         fi;
35      od unless (chT_Main_ex?[_]) -> {chT_Main!<term>}
36 }
```

Fig. 9. The Engine proctype

and ϕ being the trigger and the guard associated with transition t, respectively (line 11). When executed, it performs the actions specified in the transition decoration (line 12). For each run operator occurring within the actions (of the form run P(X,init,chT,chT_ex), where X is either _pid or parent, in case of asynchronous forks) the pid of the newly-instantiated process is stored in a local variable (pidTemp = run P(...)). An assignment statement of the form ChildrenMatrix[X].children[pidTemp]=1 takes care of updating the process hierarchy accordingly. The token is then given to the newly-instantiated process.

Each option sequence updates the DSTMstate variable to the corresponding transition target and sets the flags HasFired, HasExecuted, and DescendantExecuted to *true* (lines 12–13). An additional option sequence, executable only when no transitions are enabled, takes care of passing the token to the process children (line 14–25). After the selection statement, state is set to backProp (line 27) and the process moves into the back-propagation mode. Lines 30–36 take care of handling process termination, the back-propagation within the current phase, and the restoration of the state after the back-propagation. Specifically, for each exiting state, an option sequence of the form shown in line 30 is present. The `DescendantExecuted` back-propagation is handled by the option sequence in lines 32–34. These lines are executable when `state == backProp`, and `DescendantExecuted` is set for the proctype and not for its parent. In this case, the `DescendantExecuted` flag for its parent is set to *true*. The option sequence in line 36 resets the simulation-ready state after the back-propagation.

To conclude the specification, Fig. 9 shows a PROMELA encoding for the process `Engine`. Process `Engine`, after declaring local variables and channels required for handling termination of the initial machine (lines 2–4), starts an instance of the `Main` process (line 5) for that machine and records it as one of its children (line 6). Lines 8–16 are responsible for starting a new semantic step, by executing the statement labelled `nextStep`. This statement manages the initialization of the external channels for the new step, resets the `hasFired` flag and passes the token onto its children (line 14). The `nextPhase` statement (lines 19–25) takes care of starting a new phase, by reinitializing `hasFired` flag and passing the token again to the children. Finally, the `waitTimeout` statement (lines 28–35) forces `Engine` to wait for the current phase to complete. If the phase completes with no transition fired (i.e., `hasFired` is not set), then a new step is initiated, otherwise a new phase starts.

Table 3. Generated PROMELA code statistics

Proctype	Lines of code	Local channels	Options in the main loop
Main (Fig. 1)	164	2	7
Counter (Fig. 1)	140	4	6
Incrementer (Fig. 1)	160	0	7
Dynamic (Fig. 2)	92	2	4
Engine (model in Fig. 1)	57	2	–
Engine (model in Fig. 2)	56	1	–

The application of the transformation rules to the models in Figs. 1 and 2 generates four proctypes for the first model and three proctypes for the second model. Table 3 reports, for each proctype, the number of lines of code, channels and options in the main loop of each process in the PROMELA encoding of the two DSTMs. The prototypical environment for DSTM specification we have implemented is available at https://github.com/stefanomarrone/dstm. The repository includes the source code of: (a) a textual editor for DSTM producing DSTM specifications in xml format; (b) the compiler translating a DSTM specification (in xml format) into a PROMELA program (.pml). The textual specifications and the .pml programs for Counter (Fig. 1) and Dynamic (Fig. 2) can be found in the same repository.

Correctness of the Translation. We briefly discuss the correspondence between the DSTM specification and its encoding into PROMELA. In the first phase, boxes are replaced by machine states, whose labels keep track of the actual boxes they represent. Each DSTM machine is, then, encoded with a single proctype, which records the current state of the machine in the local variable `DSTMstate`. Data types, on the other hand, have a direct correspondence with PROMELA types. According the these observations, each global state of DSTM can easily be mapped into a PROMELA state. Indeed, the hierarchical structure of a DSTM state is encoded in the `ChildrenMatrix` global variable, which connects process instances corresponding to box instances. In other words, all the semantic information encoded in a DSTM state is present in a PROMELA state as well. Moreover, every PROMELA state can be mapped into a DSTM state by abstracting away the additional elements (variables and channels) introduced to simulate the semantics. A DSTM step corresponds to a sequence of PROMELA transitions connecting two PROMELA states in which the control of the process `Engine` is located at the `nextStep` label. With this correspondence in place, it is, then, possible to define a relation between DSTM executions and executions of the PROMELA encoding. Such a relation can be formalized by a *weak bisimulation relation*, where the implementation details, such as the token passing, the back-propagation and the termination mechanisms, are considered non-observable internal actions.

4   Conclusions

In this paper the translation from Dynamic STate Machines to PROMELA is presented. DSTM is a concise formalism expressive enough to easily capture peculiar features of multi-process control systems. The automated translation to PROMELA eases the implementation and the integration of tool chains exploiting the usage of formal methods into industrial verification and validation processes. Future work include the study of suitable tunings of the translation in PROMELA in order to mitigate unnecessary state explosion phenomena during the model analysis phase. On the applicative side, we plan to investigate instrumentation methods of the resulting PROMELA code, in particular to support automatic test case generation via model checking with respect to different coverage criteria on the original DSTM model that can take into account the intrinsic hierarchy and modularity of the formalism (e.g., coverage of state/transition of a machine in a specific instantiation context). Finally, the correspondence between executions of a DSTM and of its encoding, as discussed at the end of the previous section, enables model checking of linear time properties with the SPIN engine. To this end, we plan to investigate a suitable extension of LTL, in the same vain of [6], able to contextualize properties within the structure of a DSTM. The extended logic can, then, be translated into classic LTL, by exploiting the correspondence above, and verified with SPIN.

References

1. Benerecetti, M., et al.: Dynamic state machines for modelling railway control systems. Sci. Comput. Program. **133**, 116–153 (2017). https://doi.org/10.1016/j.scico.2016.09.002
2. Bernardi, S., et al.: Enabling the usage of UML in the verification of railway systems: the DAM-rail approach. Reliab. Eng. Syst. Saf. **120**, 112–126 (2013). https://doi.org/10.1016/j.ress.2013.06.032. http://www.sciencedirect.com/science/article/pii/S095183201300197X
3. Bernardi, S., Merseguer, J., Petriu, D.C.: A dependability profile within marte. Softw. Syst. Model. **10**(3), 313–336 (2011). https://doi.org/10.1007/s10270-009-0128-1
4. Gargantini, A., Riccobene, E., Rinzivillo, S.: Using spin to generate tests from ASM specifications. In: Börger, E., Gargantini, A., Riccobene, E. (eds.) ASM 2003. LNCS, vol. 2589, pp. 263–277. Springer, Heidelberg (2003). https://doi.org/10.1007/3-540-36498-6_15
5. Kölbl, M., Leue, S., Singh, H.: From SysML to model checkers via model transformation. In: Gallardo, M.M., Merino, P. (eds.) SPIN 2018. LNCS, vol. 10869, pp. 255–274. Springer, Cham (2018). https://doi.org/10.1007/978-3-319-94111-0_15
6. Lanotte, R., Maggiolo-Schettini, A., Peron, A.: Structural model checking for communicating hierarchical machines. In: Fiala, J., Koubek, V., Kratochvíl, J. (eds.) MFCS 2004. LNCS, vol. 3153, pp. 525–536. Springer, Heidelberg (2004). https://doi.org/10.1007/978-3-540-28629-5_40
7. Mikk, E., Lakhnech, Y., Siegel, M., Holzmann, G.J.: Implementing statecharts in promela/spin. In: Proceedings. 2nd IEEE Workshop on Industrial Strength Formal Specification Techniques, pp. 90–101. IEEE, October 1998. https://doi.org/10.1109/WIFT.1998.766303
8. Nardone, R., et al.: Modeling railway control systems in promela. In: Artho, C., Ölveczky, P.C. (eds.) FTSCS 2015. CCIS, vol. 596, pp. 121–136. Springer, Cham (2016). https://doi.org/10.1007/978-3-319-29510-7_7
9. Nardone, R., et al.: Dynamic state machines for formalizing railway control system specifications. In: Artho, C., Ölveczky, P.C. (eds.) FTSCS 2014. CCIS, vol. 476, pp. 93–109. Springer, Cham (2015). https://doi.org/10.1007/978-3-319-17581-2_7
10. Pflügl, H., El-Salloum, C., Kundner, I.: CRYSTAL, critical system engineering acceleration, a truly European dimension. ARTEMIS Mag. **14**, 12–15 (2013)
11. Rugina, A.E., Kanoun, K., Kaâniche, M.: The ADAPT tool: from AADL architectural models to stochastic Petri nets through model transformation. In: 2008 Seventh European Dependable Computing Conference, pp. 85–90. IEEE (2008)

String Abstraction for Model Checking of C Programs

Agostino Cortesi[1], Henrich Lauko[2(✉)], Martina Olliaro[1], and Petr Ročkai[2]

[1] Ca' Foscari University, Via Torino 155, Venezia, Mestre, Italy
{cortesi,martina.olliaro}@unive.it
[2] Faculty of Informatics, Masaryk University, Brno, Czech Republic
xlauko@mail.muni.cz, xrockai@fi.muni.cz

Abstract. Automatic abstraction is a powerful software verification technique. In this paper, we elaborate an abstract domain for C strings, that is, null-terminated arrays of characters. We describe the abstract semantics of basic string operations and prove their soundness with regards to previously established concrete semantics of those operations. In addition to a selection of string functions from the standard C library, we provide semantics for character access and update, enabling automatic lifting of arbitrary string-manipulating code into the domain.

The domain we present (called M-String) has two other abstract domains as its parameters: an index (bound) domain and a character domain. Picking different constituent domains allows M-String to be tailored for specific verification tasks, balancing precision against complexity.

In addition to describing the domain theoretically, we also provide an executable implementation of the abstract operations. Using a tool which automatically lifts existing programs into the M-String domain along with an explicit-state model checker, we have evaluated the proposed domain experimentally on a few simple but realistic test programs.

1 Introduction

The C programming language is still very relevant [3]: a large number of systems of critical importance are written in C, including server software and embedded systems. Unfortunately, due to the way C programs are laid out in memory, they often contain bugs that can be exploited by malicious parties to mount security attacks. Guaranteeing correctness of such software is of great concern. In particular, we are interested in ensuring correctness of C programs that manipulate strings. Incorrect string manipulation can cause a number of catastrophic events, ranging from crashes in critical software components to loss or exposure of sensitive data.

In the C programming language, strings are not a basic data type and operations on them are provided as library functions [7]. Indeed strings are represented as zero-terminated arrays of characters – due to the possible discrepancy

This work has been partially supported by the Czech Science Foundation grant No. 18-02177S.

F. Biondi et al. (Eds.): SPIN 2019, LNCS 11636, pp. 74–93, 2019.
https://doi.org/10.1007/978-3-030-30923-7_5

between string size and array (buffer) size, C programs which manipulate strings can suffer from buffer overflows and related issues. A buffer overflow is a bug that affects C code which incorrectly tries to access a buffer outside its bounds – an out-of-bounds write (a related bug – an out-of-bounds read – is also a problem, even though not as immediately dangerous as a buffer overflow). Moreover, buffer overflows are usually exploitable and often can easily lead to arbitrary code execution [25]. In the light of these facts, it is clearly important to investigate methods to automatically reason about correctness of string manipulation code in C programs. Automated code analysis tools can identify existing bugs, reduce the risk of introducing new bugs and therefore help prevent costly security incidents.

In this paper, we present a sound approach for conducting string analysis in C programs. In particular, we consider the M-String segmentation abstract domain [10]. We use it to perform abstraction-based model checking [9] of C programs, with focus on string manipulation. The model checker is split into two parts, as proposed in [23]: a program transformation which changes the program to execute in the abstract domain, and a standard, explicit-state model checker which exhaustively explores the abstract state space.

1.1 Related Work

Static methods with the ability to automatically detect buffer overflows have been widely studied in the literature and many different inference techniques were proposed and implemented: constraint solvers for various theories (including string theories) and techniques based on them (e.g. symbolic execution), tainted data-flow analysis, string pattern matching analysis or annotation analysis [27]. Additionally, a large number of bug hunting tools based on static analysis and the above mentioned techniques have been implemented [1,14,16,17,29,30].

For instance, in [19] authors introduced a performant backward compatible method of bounds checking of C program, i.e., the representation of pointers is left unchanged (thus differentiating the proposed schema from previously existing techniques), allowing inter-operation between checked and unchecked code, with recompilation confined to the modules where problems might occur. In [14], a static verifier of C strings has been presented, namely CSSV. Contracts are supplied to the tool, which acts in 4 stages, reducing the problem of checking code that manipulates string to checking code that manipulates integers. Finally, Splat, described in [31], is a tool that automatically generates test inputs, symbolically reasoning about lengths of input buffers.

Briefly, static code analysis attempts to quickly approximate possible behaviours of a program, without examining its actual executions. This way, static analysis reasons about many of the possible runs of a program and provides a degree of assurance that the property of interest holds (or that it is violated). However, with static analysis, neither positive nor negative results are guaranteed to be correct [2].

To obtain a higher degree of confidence, a number of more expensive methods are available in the software verification toolbox [15]. Model checking with abstraction and refinement is one such high-assurance, high-precision method [9], though of course both the precision and reliability come at a price in terms of computational complexity.

Various researchers have shown how the framework of abstract interpretation [12] can be used to approximate semantics of string operations. The basic, well-known domains are a *string set* domain, which simply keeps track of a set of strings – this is specific instance of the general (bounded) set domain. Another is the *character inclusion* domain (which keeps track of which characters appear in a string, but not in what order or how many times), the *prefix-suffix* domain (which keeps track of the first and the last letter) and their various products. Another general-purpose string domain is the *string hash* domain proposed in [24], based on a distributive hash function. A more complete review of general-purpose string domains is readily available in the literature, e.g. [5,11].

Such general-purpose domains focus on the generic aspects of strings, without accounting for the specifics of string handling in different programming languages. It is, however, often beneficial to consider such specific aspects of string representation when designing abstract domains for program analysis: indeed, M-String is a domain tailored specifically for the representation of strings used in C programs. A number of abstract string domains (and their combinations) for analysis of JavaScript programs have been evaluated in [5]. Another domain that was conceived for JavaScript analysis is the simplified regular expression domain defined in [26]. While dynamic languages heavily rely on strings and their analysis benefits greatly from tailored abstract domains, the specifics of the C approach to strings also deserves attention: the M-String domain, tailored for modeling zero-terminated strings stored in character buffers in C programs has first been described in [10]. In addition to theoretical work, a number of tools based on the abovementioned abstract domains and their combinations have been designed and implemented [18,20,26,28].

Finally, combining many domains in a single analysis can often substantially improve precision over either of the individual domains. However, combining domains naively requires a quadratic number of translation functions. A solution to this problem, with special focus on string domains, has been proposed in [4]. Moreover, analysis of strings based on abstract interpretation is not limited to designing abstract string domains – an analysis for programs which process structured text, based on grammar inference, was proposed in [21]. A related approach based on over-approximation of string expressions using regular grammars (widened from context-free grammars constructed via static analysis) is described in [8].

1.2   Paper Contribution

In this paper we define the semantics of the M-String abstract domain, based on the concrete semantics presented in [10], both in human-readable and in executable form. Additionally, we have extended LART [23], a tool which can perform automatic abstraction on programs, with support for more complicated (non-scalar) domains, which allowed us to also integrate the M-String domain.

By using the extended version of LART along with DIVINE 4 [6], an explicit state model checker based on LLVM, we can automatically verify correctness of string operations in C programs. We demonstrate this capability by analysing a number of C programs, ranging from quite simple to moderately complex, including parsers generated by bison, a tool which translates context-free grammars into C parsers. The main contribution of this paper is in demonstrating the actual impact of an ad-hoc segmentation-based abstract domain on model checking of C programs.

2   M-String

M-String (**M**) [10] is an ad hoc segmentation-based abstract domain designed for string analysis in C programs, based on a refinement of the segmentation approach to array representation proposed in [13]. In [13], the array's content is abstracted by consecutive, non-overlapping segments covering all array elements. In [10] the authors took advantage of this representation and defined a domain that abstracts C-like strings, distinguishing the so-called *string of interest*[1] of a character array from the rest of its content.

The goal of the domain is to infer the presence of common string manipulation errors that may result in buffer overflows or, more generally, that may lead to undefined behaviours. Additionally, keeping track of the content of the char array after the first null character allows us to reduce false positives: in particular, rewriting the first null character in the string is not always a bug, since further null characters may follow. Finally, M-String, like the array segmentation-based representation defined in [13], is parametric with respect to the abstraction of the array elements value, and the representation of array indices.

2.1   Concrete Domain

Let A be a finite set of characters representable by the character encoding in use and let $\mathbb{C} = A^*$ be the set of all the possible character arrays. Then, the operational semantics of character array variables ($c \in \mathbb{C}$) are concrete array environments $\mu \in \mathcal{R}_m$ mapping character array names $c \in \mathbb{C}$ to their values $\mu(c) \in \mathcal{M} \triangleq \mathcal{R}_v \times \mathbb{E} \times \mathbb{E} \times M \times \mathbb{Z}$, where:

- $\mathcal{R}_v \triangleq \mathbb{X} \to \mathcal{X}$ is the environment which maps names $x \in \mathbb{X}$ to values $\rho(x) \in \mathcal{X}$,
- $\mathbb{E}$ is the expressions domain,
- $M : \mathbb{Z} \to \mathbb{Z} \times A$, and $\mathbb{Z}$ is the integers domain.

---

[1] The *string of interest* of a character array is the sequence of characters up to the first null one (included). In the case in which the null character occurs at the first index of a character array, then its *string of interest* is defined as "null". If the null character does not occur in the array, then its *string of interest* is defined as "undefined". Otherwise, the *string of interest* is considered to be "well-defined".

For more details we invite the reader to refer to [10,13]. Moreover, we highlight the fact that the concrete domain we present is used as a framework that helps us in constructing the abstract representation, and it is not how the (concrete) values are actually represented in programs. That said, let c be an array of characters. Its concrete value is a quintuple $\mu(\mathtt{c}) = (\rho, \mathtt{c.low}, \mathtt{c.high}, M_\mathtt{c}, N_\mathtt{c}) \in \mathcal{M}$ where $\rho \in \mathcal{R}_v$ and:

- $\mathtt{c.low}, \mathtt{c.high} \in \mathbb{E}$ are expressions whose values $[\![\mathtt{c.low}]\!]\rho$ and $[\![\mathtt{c.high}]\!]\rho$ respectively represent the integer lower bound and the integer upper bound of c,
- $M_\mathtt{c}$ is a function that maps an index i to a pair $M_\mathtt{c}(\mathtt{i}) = \langle \mathtt{i}, v \rangle$ of the index i and the corresponding character array element value v, i.e. $M_\mathtt{c} : \mathtt{I}_\mathtt{c} \to \mathtt{P}_\mathtt{c}$ such that:

$$\mathtt{I}_\mathtt{c} = \{\mathtt{i} : \mathtt{i} \in [\![\mathtt{c.low}]\!]\rho, [\![\mathtt{c.high}]\!]\rho)\}$$
$$\mathtt{P}_\mathtt{c} = \{\langle \mathtt{i}, v \rangle : \mathtt{i} \in [\![\mathtt{c.low}]\!]\rho, [\![\mathtt{c.high}]\!]\rho \wedge \mathtt{c}[\mathtt{i}] = {'}v{'}\}$$

- $N_\mathtt{c}$ is the set of indexes which map to the string terminating characters, i.e. $N_\mathtt{c} = \{\mathtt{i} \in [\![\mathtt{c.low}]\!]\rho, [\![\mathtt{c.high}]\!]\rho) \mid M_\mathtt{c} = \langle \mathtt{i}, {'}\backslash 0{'} \rangle\}$.

Example 1. Let $\mathtt{s}$ = "Hello\0" be a character array then, its concrete value is given by $\mu(\mathtt{s})$ = $(\rho, 0, 6, M_\mathtt{s}, N_\mathtt{s})$, where $\mathtt{P}_\mathtt{s}$ is the set $\{(0, {'}\mathtt{H}{'}), (1, {'}\mathtt{e}{'}), (2, {'}\mathtt{l}{'}), (3, {'}\mathtt{l}{'}), (4, {'}\mathtt{o}{'}), (5, {'}\backslash 0{'})\}$ and $N_\mathtt{s}$ corresponds to the singleton $\{5\}$.

2.2   Abstract Domain

The M-String (**M**) abstract domain approximates sets of character arrays with a pair of segmentations that highlight the nature of their *strings of interest*. The elements of the domain are split segmentation abstract predicates. Segments capture sequences of identical abstract values, and are delimited by so-called segment bounds. More precisely, the M-String abstract domain is given by **M(B, C, R)**. **R** denotes the abstraction of scalar variable environments. **C** is the abstraction of the character array elements, and it is equipped with is_null, a special monotonic function lifting abstract elements in **C** to a value in the set {true, false, maybe}. **B** denotes the abstraction of segment bounds, equipped with the following operations: equality ($=_\mathbf{B}$), ordering ($\leqslant_\mathbf{B}$), least upper bound between subsequent segment bounds ($\sqcup_\mathbf{B}[b_i, b_{i+1})$), addition ($+_\mathbf{B}$), and subtraction ($-_\mathbf{B}$). The M-String abstract domain is the complete lattice $(\mathcal{M}, \leqslant_\mathbf{M}, \perp_\mathbf{M}, \top_\mathbf{M}, \sqcap_\mathbf{M}, \sqcup_\mathbf{M})$ where:

- $\overline{\mathcal{M}} \triangleq (\overline{\mathcal{M}}_s, \overline{\mathcal{M}}_{ns}) \cup \{\perp_\mathbf{M}, \top_\mathbf{M}\}$
  - $\overline{\mathcal{M}}_s$ corresponds to $\bigcup \{\overline{\mathcal{S}}_{sb} \times \overline{\mathcal{S}}_{sm}^k \times \overline{\mathcal{S}}_{se} \mid k \geqslant 0\} \cup \overline{\mathcal{S}}_{se} \cup \{\emptyset\}$, and it represents the segmentation of the *string of interest* of a given character array, where,
    $$[\overline{\mathcal{S}}_{sb} = \{\overline{\mathcal{B}} \times \overline{\mathcal{C}}\}, \overline{\mathcal{S}}_{sm} = \{\overline{\mathcal{B}} \times \overline{\mathcal{C}} \times \{\_, ?\}\}, \overline{\mathcal{S}}_{se} = \{\overline{\mathcal{B}} \times \{\_\}\}]$$

- $\overline{\mathcal{M}}_{ns}$ corresponds to $\bigcup\{\overline{S}_{nsb} \times \overline{S}_{nsm}^{k} \times \overline{S}_{nse} \mid k \geqslant 0\} \cup \{\emptyset\}$, and it represents the segmentation of the content of a given character array after its *string of interest*, or character arrays that do not contain the null terminating character. Here,

$$[\overline{S}_{nsb} = \overline{S}_{sb}, \overline{S}_{nsm} = \overline{S}_{sm}, \overline{S}_{nse} = \{\overline{B} \times \{\_, ?\}\}]$$

In particular:

1. $b_i \in \overline{B}$ denotes the segment bounds, such that $i = 1, \ldots, n$ and $n > 1$ (notice that b_1 and b_n respectively represent the array lower bound and the array upper bound),
2. $p_i \in \overline{C}$ are abstract predicates, chosen in an abstract domain **C**, denoting possible values of pairs $\langle i, v \rangle$ in a segment (i.e. $\mathbf{C}[\![\langle i, v \rangle]\!]\overline{p}$),
3. the question mark ? indicates the preceding segment might be empty, while $\_$ indicates a non-empty segment

The elements in $\overline{\mathcal{M}}$ are $\overline{m} = (s, ns)$ (i.e. split segmentation abstract predicates). Let $\mathbf{c} \in \mathbb{C}$ be an array of characters, and $\mu(\mathbf{c})$ be its concrete value; for instance, if the *string of interest* of $\mathbf{c}$ is null (i.e. $min(N_c) = 0$) then: $\overline{m}$ is equal to $(b_{1\_}, \emptyset)$ if the size of $\mathbf{c}$ is equal to 1, $(b_{1\_}, b_2 p_2 b_3 ?^3 p_3 b_4 ?^4 \ldots b_n ?^n)$ otherwise. In the rest of the paper we will refer to the s and to the ns parameters of a given abstract string $\overline{m}$ by $\overline{m}.s$ and $\overline{m}.ns$ respectively.

- Let $\overline{m}_1$ and $\overline{m}_2$ be two abstract values in the M-String domain then: $\overline{m}_1 \leqslant_M \overline{m}_2 \Leftrightarrow \overline{m}_1 = \bot_M \vee \overline{m}_1 \equiv \overline{m}_2 \vee \text{unify}(\overline{m}_1, \overline{m}_2) = \overline{m}_2$. Notice that $\overline{m}_1$ and $\overline{m}_2$ are equivalent when they represent the same set of character arrays. Here, "unify" is a sound upper bound operator (originally defined in [13] and tweaked in [10] to modify two split segmentations so that they coincide).
  Take $\overline{m}_1$ and $\overline{m}_2$ to be compatible if their parameters have common lower and upper bounds of s and ns. Then, $\text{unify}(\overline{m}_1, \overline{m}_2) = (\text{unify}(s_1, s_2), \text{unify}(ns_1, ns_2))$ if $\overline{m}_1$ and $\overline{m}_2$ are compatible, $\top_M$ otherwise.
- $\bot_M$, $\top_M$ are special elements denoting the bottom/top element of the lattice.
- $\sqcup_M$ represents the join operator, that defines the least upper bound between two abstract elements, such that: $\overline{m}_1 \sqcup_M \overline{m}_2 = \text{unify}(\overline{m}_1, \overline{m}_2)$ if $\overline{m}_1$ and $\overline{m}_2$ are compatible, $\top_M$ otherwise. Then the character abstract domain join is applied segment-wise.

Abstraction. Let X be a set of concrete character array values. The abstraction function on the M-String abstract domain α_M maps X to $\bot_M$ in the case in which X is empty, otherwise to the pair of segmentations that best over-approximate values in X.

Concretization. The concretization function on the M-String abstract domain γ_M maps an abstract element to a set of character arrays values as follows: $\gamma_M(\bot_M) = \emptyset$, otherwise $\gamma_M(\overline{m})$ is the set of all possible character arrays values represented by a split segmentation abstract predicate $\overline{m}$. The formalization is quite complex, and the reader may refer to Appendix A.1.

Example 2. Let $S = \{s_1, s_2, s_3\}$ be a set of character arrays, such that: $s_1 =$ "car\0xx", $s_2 =$ "bay\0xx", and $s_3 =$ "day\0xx". The abstract value of S in **M**, instantiated with the standard constant propagation domain ($\mathcal{CP}$), is given by $\bar{s} = \alpha_M(\{\mu(x) \mid x \in S\}) = (\{0\} \top_{\mathcal{CP}} \{1\} \text{ 'a' } \{2\} \top_{\mathcal{CP}} \{3\}, \{4\} \text{ 'x' } \{6\})$. The concretization function of $\bar{s}$, i.e. $\gamma_M(\bar{s})$ maps $\bar{s}$ to the set of all possible character arrays values of length 6 that contain a *string of interest* of length 4, and having the character 'a' at position 1 and the character 'x' at position 4 and 5.

2.3   Abstract Semantics

In [10] authors restricted their focus on a small representative set of operators which are part of the `string.h` library of the C programming language (i.e. `strcpy`, `strcat`, `strlen`, `strchr`, `strcmp` and the "assignment to an array element" operator), and they defined the concrete semantics of those operators. We recall the character arrays concrete semantics (slightly modified from the one presented in [10]). In particular, $\mathfrak{S}$ is the semantics that, given a statement and eventually some concrete character arrays values in $\mathcal{M}$, returns a concrete character array resulting from that operation, i.e. $\mathfrak{S} : Stm \times \mathcal{M} \to \mathcal{M} \cup \{\text{null}\}$ where, null denotes unknown values. Moreover, for `strlen` and `strcmp` we give the semantics $\mathfrak{L} : Stm \times \mathcal{M} \to \mathbb{Z} \cup \{\top_{\mathbb{Z}}\}$.

Below we present the abstract semantics of the `strcat`, `strlen` and `strchr` operators, and we prove their soundness (the reader interested in the definitions of the abstract semantics and of the proofs of soundness of the complete set of operators introduced above may refer to Appendix A.4). We denote by $\mathfrak{S}_M$ and $\mathfrak{L}_M$ the abstract counterparts of $\mathfrak{S}$ and $\mathfrak{L}$ respectively, such that: $\mathfrak{S}_M : Stm \times \mathbf{M} \to \mathbf{M}$ and $\mathfrak{L}_M : Stm \times \mathbf{M} \to \mathbf{B}$.

Additional Operators. We present some additional abstract operators useful to define the abstract semantics. Their complete algorithms are defined in Appendix A.3.

Length Operators (minLen, maxLen, Len). We introduce the notions of minimum and maximum length of a split segmentation abstract predicate, and the length of the *strings of interest* that it represents. Precisely, we define: $\text{minLen}(\overline{m}) = min\{len(x) \mid x \in \gamma_M(\overline{m})\}$, $\text{maxLen}(\overline{m}) = max\{len(x) \mid x \in \gamma_M(\overline{m})\}$, and $\text{Len}_{\overline{m}.s} = max\{len(x) \mid x \in \gamma_M^\star(\overline{m}.s)\}$ (see Appendix A.1 for the definition of $\gamma_M^\star$), where $len(x)$ denotes the size of a concrete character array value.

Segment concatenation ($\oplus$). Let bpb' and uru' be two segments ($b, b', u, u' \in \overline{\mathcal{B}}$ and $p, r \in \overline{\mathcal{C}}$) then, their concatenation is defined as follows: $bpb' \oplus uru'$ such that $bpb' \oplus uru' = bpb'ru^*$ where $u^* = b' + (u' - u)$. In the case in which the right hand side operand is a segmentation, then all the segment bounds belonging to it are modified accordingly. Question marks, if present, are left unchanged.

Abstract Semantics of `strcat`: If the input ($\overline{m}_1$ and $\overline{m}_2$ respectively) approximate character arrays that contain a well-defined or null *string of interest*, and if the minLen of $\overline{m}_1$ is greater than or equal to the the sum of $\text{Len}_{\overline{m}_1.s}$ and $\text{Len}_{\overline{m}_2.s}$ minus one then the `strcat` returns $\overline{m}_1'$ where $\overline{m}_2.s$ has been appended to $\overline{m}_1.s$ and the following segments are modified accordingly. Otherwise it returns $\top_{\mathbf{M}}$.

Let $\overline{m}.s[b_i]^s$ ($\overline{m}.ns[b_i]^s$) be the left hand side parameter (the right hand side parameter) of $\overline{m}$ starting from the i-th segment bound. Conversely, $\overline{m}.s[b_i]_{\mathrm{u}}$ ($\overline{m}.ns[b_i]_{\mathrm{u}}$) is the left hand side parameter (the right hand side parameter) of $\overline{m}$ up to the i-th segment bound.

Then $\mathfrak{S}_{\mathbf{M}}[\![\texttt{strcat}]\!](\overline{m}_1, \overline{m}_2)$ is equal to:

- $\overline{m}_1'$ if $\overline{m}_1 \neq (\emptyset, ns)$, $\overline{m}_2 \neq (\emptyset, ns)$ and $\text{minLen}(\overline{m}_1) \geqslant (\text{Len}_{\overline{m}_1.s} + \text{Len}_{\overline{m}_2.s} - 1)$;
- $\top_{\mathbf{M}}$ otherwise, where:

1. If $\overline{m}_1 = (b_1 p_1 ... b_{i\llcorner}, ns) \wedge \overline{m}_2 = (b_{1\llcorner}, ns) \Rightarrow \overline{m}_1' = (\overline{m}_1.s[b_i]_{\mathrm{u}} \oplus \overline{m}_2.s, \overline{m}_1.ns)$
2. If $\overline{m}_1 = (b_1 p_1 ... b_{i\llcorner}, ns) \wedge \overline{m}_2 = (b_1 p_1 ... b_{i\llcorner}, ns) \Rightarrow \overline{m}_1' = (\overline{m}_1.s[b_i]_{\mathrm{u}} \oplus \overline{m}_2.s, \overline{m}_1.ns[b^*]^s)$, where $b^* = (b_{i_{\overline{m}_2}} -_{\mathbf{B}} b_{1_{\overline{m}_2}}) +_{\mathbf{B}} b_{i_{\overline{m}_1}} +_{\mathbf{B}} 1$

Notice that, question marks, if present, are left unchanged.

Abstract Semantics of `strlen`: If the input split segmentation abstract predicate ($\overline{m}$) approximates character arrays that contain a well-defined or null *string of interest* then the `strlen` operator returns the least upper bound between the segment bounds which limit a certainly or maybe `is_null` segment abstract predicate. Otherwise it returns $\top_{\mathbf{B}}$.

Let $\overline{\mathrm{x}}$ be an abstract character value (i.e. $\mathbf{C}[\![v]\!]\overline{p}$) appearing in a generic segment abstract predicate p. Formally, $\mathfrak{L}_{\mathbf{M}}[\![\texttt{strlen}]\!](\overline{m})$ is equal to:

- $\bigsqcup_{\mathbf{B}} \atop \forall b_i \in \overline{m}.s} \{\bigsqcup_{\mathbf{B}} [b_i, b_{i+1}) \mid \overline{\mathrm{x}} \text{ occurs in } p_i \wedge \overline{\mathrm{x}} \text{ may be null}\}$ if $\overline{m} \neq (\emptyset, ns)$;
- $\top_{\mathbf{B}}$ otherwise, where $\bigsqcup_{\mathbf{B}} [b_i, b_{i+1})$ is a shorthand for $b_i \sqcup_{\mathbf{B}} b_i + 1 \sqcup_{\mathbf{B}} b_i + 2 \sqcup_{\mathbf{B}}$ ... $\sqcup_{\mathbf{B}} b_{i+1} - 1$, and it returns the set of elements in the interval $[b_i, b_{i+1})$.

Abstract Semantic of `strchr`: If the input split segmentation abstract predicate ($\overline{m}$) approximates character arrays that contain a well-defined or null *string of interest*, and if the abstract character we are looking for ($\overline{\mathrm{x}} \in \mathbf{C}$) appears in $\overline{m}.s$ then the $\texttt{strchr}_{\overline{\mathrm{x}}}$ operator returns a split segmentation abstract predicate denoting the sub-segmentation of its left hand side input parameter starting from the first occurrence of $\overline{\mathrm{x}}$. Otherwise it returns $\top_{\mathbf{M}}$. Formally, $\mathfrak{S}[\![\texttt{strchr}_{\overline{\mathrm{x}}}]\!](\overline{m})$ is equal to:

- $(b_{1\llcorner}, \emptyset)$ if $\overline{m} = (b_{1\llcorner}, ns)$ and $\overline{\mathrm{x}}$ is *null*;
- $(b_{i\llcorner}, \emptyset)$ if $\overline{m} = (b_1 p_1 ... b_{i\llcorner}, ns)$ and $\overline{\mathrm{x}}$ is *null*;
- $(s[b_k]^s, \emptyset)$ if $\overline{m} = (b_1 p_1 ... b_{i\llcorner}, ns)$, $\overline{\mathrm{x}}$ may be not *null* and $\exists k : k = min\{z \in [1, i) : \overline{\mathrm{x}} \text{ appears in } p_z\}$;
- $\top_{\mathbf{M}}$ otherwise.

Theorem 1 (Soundness of the abstract semantics). $\mathfrak{S}_M$ and $\mathfrak{L}_M$ are sound over-approximations of $\mathfrak{S}$ and $\mathfrak{L}$ respectively. Formally,

$$\gamma_M(\mathfrak{S}_M[\![stm]\!](\overline{m})) \supseteq \{\mathfrak{S}[\![stm]\!](c) : c \in \gamma_M(\overline{m})\}$$
$$\gamma_B(\mathfrak{L}_M[\![stm]\!](\overline{m})) \supseteq \{\mathfrak{L}[\![stm]\!](c) : c \in \gamma_M(\overline{m})\}$$

where $c = \mu(\mathsf{c})$ denotes the concrete value of c.

Proof. We prove the soundness separately for each operator.

- See Appendix A.4 (Theorem 2) for the `strcat` proof of soundness.
- Consider the unary operator `strlen`, and let $\overline{m}$ be a split segmentation abstract predicate. We have to prove that $\gamma_B(\mathfrak{L}_M[\![\mathtt{strlen}]\!](\overline{m})) \supseteq \{\mathfrak{L}[\![\mathtt{strlen}]\!](c) : c \in \gamma_M(\overline{m})\}$. The `strlen` of c, if c contains a well-formed string, returns an integer value n denoting the length of the sequence of characters before the first null one, $\top_\mathbb{Z}$ otherwise, by definition of $\mathfrak{L}$. Then n belongs to $\gamma_B(\mathfrak{L}_M[\![\mathtt{strlen}]\!](\overline{m}))$ because $\mathfrak{L}_M[\![\mathtt{st\text{-}rlen}]\!](\overline{m})$ is equal to the least upper bound of all the segment bounds in $\overline{m}.s$ (included their inner values) in which a certainly or maybe *null* value is contained, if $\overline{m}$ highlights the presence of well-formed strings; otherwise, the abstract operator returns $\top_B$, by definition of $\mathfrak{L}_M$.
- Consider the unary operator `strchr`$_{\overline{x}}$, and let $\overline{m}$ be a split segmentation abstract predicate. We have to prove that $\gamma_M(\mathfrak{S}_M[\![\mathtt{strchr}_{\overline{x}}]\!](\overline{m})) \supseteq \{\mathfrak{S}[\![\mathtt{strchr}_x]\!](c) : c \in \gamma_M(\overline{m})\}$. The `strchr`$_x$ of c returns, if x is present in c, a sub-array of c (i.e. *sub.c*) that goes from the first occurrence of x in c to the first occurrence of the null-terminating character included, null otherwise, by definition of $\mathfrak{S}$. Then *sub.c* belongs to $\gamma_M(\mathfrak{S}_M[\![\mathtt{strchr}_{\overline{x}}]\!](\overline{m}))$ because $\mathfrak{S}_M[\![\mathtt{strchr}_{\overline{x}}]\!](\overline{m})$, if $\overline{m}$ highlights the presence of well-formed strings and $\overline{x}$ appears in $\overline{m}.s$, is equal to a sub-segmentation of $\overline{m}.s$ that goes from the first appearance of $\overline{x}$ in $\overline{m}.s$ to the end of $\overline{m}.s$, and $\alpha_C(x) = \overline{x}$; otherwise, the abstract operator returns $\top_M$, by definition of $\mathfrak{S}_M$. □

3 Program Abstraction

Adapting M-String to the analysis of real-world C programs requires, first of all, a procedure that identifies string operations automatically. A subset of such operations then needs to be performed using abstract operations, carried out on a suitable abstract representation. The technique that captures this approach is known as abstract interpretation. A typical implementation is based on an interpreter in the programming language sense: it executes the program by directly performing the operations written down in the source code. However, instead of using concrete values and concrete operations on those values, part (or the entirety) of the computation is performed in an *abstract domain*, which over-approximates the semantics of the concrete program.

Since in this paper, we focus on string abstraction, we would like to be able to perform the remainder of the program (i.e. the portions that do not work with

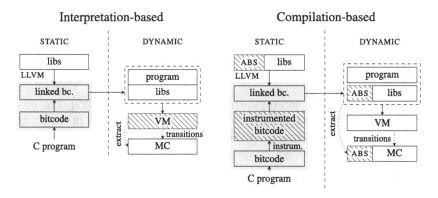

Fig. 1. The figure depicts a comparison of interpretation/compilation-based approaches. In interpretation-based approach, entire abstract interpretation is performed during runtime. A virtual machine (VM) interprets bitcode operations abstractly and maintain an abstract state. Consequently, it generates an abstract state-space for a model-checking algorithm (MC). On the other hand, compilation-based approach instruments abstract operations into the compiled program and provides their implementation as a library. A virtual machine then executes the instrumented program as regular bitcode.

strings) concretely. In fact, we only want to abstract some of the strings and string operations in the program, since the domain at hand is an approximation: in cases, where the program works with strings that exhibit minimal variation, e.g. string literals, using the M-String representation would not offer any benefit, and could actually hurt performance or introduce spurious counterexamples.

These considerations lead us to conclude that it would be beneficial to re-use, or rather re-purpose, existing tools which work with explicit programs to implement abstract interpretation in a modular fashion. A design in this style (compilation-based abstract interpretation) was proposed and implemented in [23].

However, as presented, the approach was limited to abstracting scalar values. In this paper, we extend this approach to work with strings and other domains that represent more complex objects.

3.1 Compilation-Based Approach

To perform abstraction, instead of (re-)interpreting instructions abstractly, we transform abstract instructions into equivalent explicit code, which implements the abstract computation. The transformation occurs before model checking (or other dynamical analysis), during the compilation process.

The transformed program can be further analyzed or processed without special knowledge of the abstract domains in use, because those are now encoded directly in the program. Comparison of this compilation-based approach and the approach of more traditional abstract interpreters (an interpretation-based approach) is shown in Fig. 1. In compilation-based approach, we consider two levels of abstraction:

1. *static*, concerning the syntax and the type system,
2. *dynamic*, or semantic, concerning execution and values.

LART performs syntactic (*static*) abstraction on LLVM bitcode [22]. The goal of syntactic abstraction is to replace some of the LLVM instructions in the program with their abstract counterparts. We illustrate syntactic abstraction in Fig. 2.

3.2 Syntactic Abstraction

During syntactic abstraction, LART performs a data flow analysis, starting from annotated abstract values (`abstract`) as the roots. The result of this analysis is the set of all operations that may come into contact with an abstract value. These are then substituted by their abstract counterparts (`a_strcat`, `a_strlen`). An abstract instruction takes abstract values as its inputs and produces an abstract value as its result. The specific meaning of those abstract instructions and abstract values then defines the semantic abstraction.

To formulate syntactic abstraction unambiguously, we take advantage of the static type system of LLVM. By assigning types to program variables, we can maintain a precise boundary between concrete and abstract values in our program.

We recognize a set of *concrete scalar types* S. We give a map Γ that inductively defines finite (non-recursive) algebraic types over the set of given scalars. To be specific, the set of all types $\Gamma(T)$ derived from a set of scalars T is defined as follows:

1. $T \subseteq \Gamma(T)$, meaning each scalar type is included in $\Gamma(T)$,
2. if $t_1, \ldots, t_n \in \Gamma(T)$ then also the *product type* is in $\Gamma(T)$: $(t_1, \ldots, t_n) \in \Gamma(T), n \in \mathbb{N}$,
3. if $t_1, \ldots, t_n \in \Gamma(T)$ then also *disjoint union* is in $\Gamma(T)$: $t_1 \mid t_2 \mid \cdots \mid t_n \in \Gamma(T), n \in \mathbb{N}$,
4. if $t \in \Gamma(T)$ then $t^* \in \Gamma(T)$, where t^* denotes pointer type.

In syntactic abstraction, we extend the concrete set of types by abstract types. From these, we generate admissible types using Γ. Depending on the level of abstraction, we define a different set of basic abstract types. In the case of scalar abstraction, a set of basic abstract types contains abstract scalar types A. Correspondence between abstract and concrete scalars is given by a bijective map $\Lambda : S \to A$. Finally, each value, which exists in the abstracted program, has an assigned type of $\Gamma(S \cup A)$. In particular, this means that the abstraction works

Concrete program:

```
a:str ← abstract()
b:str ← string()
c:str ← strcat(a,b)
l:int ← strlen(c)
```

Transformed program:

```
a:a_str ← a_string()
b:str   ← string()
c:a_str ← a_strcat(a,b)
l:a_int ← a_strlen(c)
```

Fig. 2. Syntactic abstraction.

with *mixed types* – products and unions with both concrete and abstract fields. Likewise, it is possible to form pointers to both abstract values and to mixed aggregates.

3.3   Aggregate Domains

Scalars in a program are simple values which cannot be further decomposed into meaningful constituent parts. A typical example would be an integer, or a pointer. However, programs typically also work with more complex data, that we can think of as compositions – aggregates – of multiple scalar values. Depending on the nature of such aggregates, we can classify them as arrays, which contain a variable number of items which all belong to a single type, records (structures), which contain a fixed number of items in a fixed layout, but each of these can be of a different type. The items in such aggregates can be (and often are) scalars, but more complicated aggregates are also possible: arrays of records, records which in turn contain other records, and so on.

In contrast to scalar domains, which deal with scalar values, an *aggregate domain* represents composite data, in the spirit of the above definition. An *abstract* aggregate domain approximates (concrete) aggregate values by keeping track of certain properties of the aggregate, for instance the length of an array, or a set of scalars that appear in the array. In the case of M-String, the information it tracks is a segmentation, where segments are represented using their bounds and a single value abstracting their content.

Aggregate domains could be equipped with quite arbitrary operations, though there are two that stand out, because they are in some sense universal, and those are byte-wise access and modification (update) of the content of the aggregate. The universality of those operations stems from the fact that in a low-level representation of a program, all operations with aggregate values take this form. In LLVM, it is possible (though not guaranteed), that access to the aggregate is encoded at a slightly higher level: as extraction and modification of entire scalars (as opposed to individual bytes). For M-String, though, this distinction is not important: the scalars stored in C strings are individual bytes. It should be also noted that the *access* and *update* form the interface between scalars and aggregates (even in the case of byte-oriented access, since bytes are also scalars). Therefore, the types of those two operations contain a single aggregate and (at least) a single scalar domain. Some (or all) of those domains may be abstract domains.

Syntactic abstraction has to handle aggregate domains differently from scalar domains. In LLVM, aggregate values are usually represented using pointers of a specific (aggregate) type. For this reason, aggregate abstraction starts from the types that represent its objects. In the case of arrays, those are concrete pointers into those arrays: let us call them P^*, where $P \subseteq \Gamma(S)$. We use the set of abstract pointers A^* to represent the types of abstract values in an aggregate domain. Thus the set of admissible types in the abstract program is generated by $\Gamma(S \cup A^*)$. Like in scalar domains, we define a natural correspondence between pointers to concrete values P^* as a bijective map $\Lambda : P^* \to A^*$.

Please note that pointers in general contain two pieces of information: they determine the *object* and an *offset* into that object. In explicit programs, this distinction is not very important, since those two parts are represented uniformly and often cannot be distinguished at all. The distinction, however, becomes important when we deal with abstract aggregate values. In this case, the *object* portion of the pointer is concrete, since it determines a single specific abstract object. However, the *offset* may or may not be concrete – depending on the specific abstract aggregate domain, it may be more advantageous to represent the offset abstractly. In either case, however, all memory access through such a pointer needs to be treated as an abstract *access* or *update* operation.

In LLVM, there are two basic memory access operations – *load* and *store*, which correspond to the *access* and *update* operations. Rather importantly, memory access is always explicit – memory is never directly used in a computation. We use this fact in the design of aggregate abstraction, where we can assume that access to the content of an aggregate will always go through a pointer associated with the abstract object.

3.4   Semantic Abstraction

Where syntactic abstraction was concerned with the syntax of operations, their types and the types of values and variables, semantic abstraction is concerned with the runtime values that appear during the computation performed by a program. While syntactic abstraction introduced the maps Λ and Λ^{-1} to transfer between concrete and abstract *types*, semantic abstraction introduces *lift* and *lower*: operations (instructions) which convert between concrete and abstract *values*. They represent a realization of the abstraction (α) and concretization (γ) functions.

While *lift* and *lower* form a boundary between concrete and abstract scalar computation, the *access* and *update* operations of an aggregate domain form a boundary between scalar and aggregate domains. We kindly refer to [23], where a reader may find how LART transforms an abstract program into an executable form.

3.5   Abstract Operations

After syntactic abstraction, the program temporarily contains abstract instructions. Abstract instructions take abstract values as operands and give back abstract values as their results. However, after transformation, we require that the resulting program is semantically valid LLVM bitcode. Hence, it is crucial that each abstract instruction can be realized as a suitable sequence of concrete instructions. This makes it possible to obtain an abstract program that does not actually contain any abstract instructions and execute it using standard (concrete, explicit) methods.

In detail, syntactic abstraction replaces concrete instructions with their abstract counterparts: an instruction with type $(t_1, \ldots, t_n) \to t_r$ is substituted by an abstract instruction of type $(\Lambda(t_1), \ldots, \Lambda(t_n)) \to \Lambda(t_r)$. Moreover, *lift* and *lower* are inserted as needed. The implementation is free to decide which instructions to abstract and where to insert value lifting and lowering, so long as it obeys type constraints.

Additionally, in string abstraction, we also want to abstract function calls such as `strcat`, `strcpy` etc. From the perspective of abstraction, we treat these functions as single operations that take abstract values and produce results. Therefore, we can process them in the same way as instructions. For example, by transforming `strcat` of type $(str, str) \rightarrow str$ we obtain $strcat_a$ of type $(\Lambda(str), \Lambda(str)) \rightarrow \Lambda(str)$. Afterwards, all abstract operations are realized using concrete subroutines [23].

We could have also transformed standard library functions (`strcat`, `strcmp`, etc.) instruction by instruction using only abstract access and update of a content, but in this way we would lose a certain degree of precision in the abstraction, the exact amount depending on the operation.

4   Instantiating M-String

M-String, as a content domain, enables a parametrization of string abstraction. To be specific, it supports the parametrization of string segmentation representation in which we can substitute different domains of bounds and characters. As a representation of string values, we can use a scalar domain equipped with the correct operations, and the same holds for bounds of segments as described in Sect. 2.

An implementation of a particular M-String instance can be automatically derived from a parametric description, given well-defined abstract domains **C** for characters and **B** to represent segment bounds. M-String also requires that both **C** and **B** support certain operations that appear in the generic implementation of the abstract operations. These are mainly basic arithmetic and relational operators. For further details of the implementation, see the appendix of this paper.

4.1   Symbolic Scalar Values

In program verification, it is common practice to represent certain values symbolically (for instance inputs from the environment). This type of representation enables a verification procedure to consider all the possible values with a reasonably small overhead. computation is implemented using abstraction of the same type as described here: computations on scalar values are lifted into the term domain, which simply keeps track of values using terms (expressions) in form of abstract syntax trees. Those trees contain atoms (unconstrained values) and operators of the bitvector logic. The term domain additionally keeps track of any constraints derived from the control flow of the program (a *path condition*). A more detailed description is presented in [23].

Paired with a constraint solver for the requisite theory,[2] the term domain coincides with symbolic computation. The solver makes it possible to detect

---

[2] For scalars in C programs, we use the bitvector theory.

computations that have reached the bottom of the term domain (those are the infeasible paths through the program) and also to check for equality or subsumption of program states. With those provisions, the bitvector theory is completely precise (i.e. it is not an approximation, but rather models the program state faithfully).

4.2 Concrete Characters, Symbolic Bounds

For evaluation purposes, we have instantiated the M-String domain by setting **C**, the domain of the individual characters, to be the concrete domain (i.e. characters are represented by themselves) and **B**, the domain of segment bounds, to be symbolic 64b integers. The main motivation for this instantiation is a balance between simplicity on one hand (both the domains we used for parameters were already available in the tools we used) and the ability to describe strings with undetermined length and structure.

At the implementation level (as explained in more detail in the following section), the domain continues to be parametric: the specific domains we picked could be easily swapped for other domains (an immediate candidate would be using both symbolic characters and symbolic bounds). Compared to the theoretical description of M-String, the implementation uses a slightly simplified representation using a pair of arrays (cf. Fig. 3), where the specific type of characters and bounds is given by the parameter domains **C** and **B** respectively.

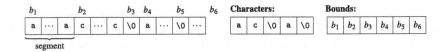

Fig. 3. M-String value with symbolic bounds, where string of interest is from b_1 to b_3.

Table 1. Benchmarks of abstract operations were evaluated on three types of M-Strings (*Word*, *Sequence*, and *Alternation*) – see Sect. 5 for description. The table depicts the number of states in the state space of the verified program, verification time in seconds for the different length of inputs and an average time of a transformation (LART).

	Word						Sequence						Alternation					
	States	verification(s)				LART (s)	States	verification (s)				LART (s)	States	verification (s)				LART (s)
		8	64	1024	4096			8	64	1024	4096			8	64	1024	4096	
strcmp	163	12.8	14.7	17.1	27.2	0.85	12	0.55	0.67	1.15	1.79	0.65	744	63.4	110	129	141	0.77
strcpy	36	1.67	1.63	2.18	2.48	0.51	9	0.36	0.27	0.51	0.83	0.88	74	3.62	4.9	5.3	4.36	0.46
strcat	477	32.2	33.4	31.9	33.4	0.92	25	2.28	2.5	2.79	3.19	0.93	2406	208	218	220	205	0.95
strchr	24	0.28	0.35	0.53	1.14	0.88	6	0.03	0.08	0.13	0.26	0.56	45	0.54	0.54	0.92	1.89	0.83
strlen	26	0.45	0.46	0.69	1.31	0.86	6	0.09	0.11	0.17	0.33	0.86	53	1.01	1.21	1.94	2.33	0.82

M-String, when instantiated like this, is particularly suitable for representing strings with runs of a single character of variable length, i.e. the strings of the form $a^k b^l c^m \ldots$ where relationships between $k, l, m, \ldots$ can be specified using standard arithmetic and relational operators and each of a, b, c is a specific letter. This in turn allows M-String to be used for checking program behaviour on broad classes of input strings described this way. A more detailed account of this approach can be found in Sect. 5.

4.3   Implementation

We have implemented the abstract semantics of operations in the M-String domain as a C++ library, in a form that allows programs to be automatically lifted into this domain by LART and later model-checked with DIVINE. An abstract domain definition in LART consists of a C++ class that describes both the representation (in terms of data) and the operations (in terms of code) of the abstract domain.

The abstract domain is equipped with a set of essential operations, which appear in all programs that work with strings: these are *lift*, *update* and *access*. All other operations which involve strings can be, in principle, derived automatically using the same procedure that is applied to user programs. However, abstracting only *access* and *update* causes either a loss of precision or a blowup in complexity. For this reason, we also include hand-crafted implementations of the following abstract operations: `strcmp`, `strcpy`, `strcat`, `strchr`, and `strlen`. These are all based on the abstract semantics of the respective operations as described in Sect. 2 and in the Appendix A.4.

A more complete description of the implementation of LART and DIVINE, their source code, and the Appendices A.1–A.4 which describe the technical details of the MString domain can be found online.[3]

5   Experimental Evaluation

For evaluation purposes, we have picked three scenarios. In first of those, we show that the provided implementation of basic string functions is more efficient than lifting them automatically based on the *access* and *update* operations. In the second scenario, we analyse various implementations of the same string functions by lifting them automatically and checking that their outputs match the ones we expect based on the concrete semantics of those operations – in this case, the inputs are provided in the form of specific abstract (M-String) values. In the last scenario, we have picked a few real-world programs to demonstrate that M-String can be successfully used in analysis of moderately complex C code. To this end, we have chosen two context-free grammars and used them to generate C parsers using the `bison` and `flex` tools, again providing abstract strings as inputs to the generated parsers. All experiments were performed with an identical set of resource constraints: 1 h of CPU time, 80 GB of RAM and 4 CPU cores.[4]

---

[3] https://divine.fi.muni.cz/2019/mstring.

[4] The processor used to run the benchmarks was Intel Xeon E5-2630 clocked at 2.60 GHz. To make reproduction of the benchmarks easier, we provide instructions and scripts in the online supplementary material.

Table 2. The table depicts the verification results of functions from `pdclib`. For each type of input M-String of a given length, we present duration of verification and the size of the state space. T denotes a timeout of the verification.

Length	Word 4		8		16		Sequence 4		8		16		Alternation 4		8		16	
strcmp	18.5s	90	597s	1228	2410s	11416	3.82s	14	12s	32	32.2s	68	70.7s	348	T	–	T	–
strcpy	8.4s	45	99s	438	775s	4410	5.7s	14	17.5s	24	71.8s	44	11.6s	80	168s	928	3230s	19234
strcat	75.5s	303	T	–	T	–	23.7s	35	117s	149	769s	737	249s	1085	T	–	T	–
strchr	12.4s	39	166s	245	934s	1265	4.34s	8	16.5s	12	158s	20	13.4s	57	316s	815	T	–
strlen	0.5s	27	7.9s	169	811s	1365	0.27s	8	0.6s	14	1.7s	20	1.8s	48	69s	357	3250s	5307

Abstract Operations: The first set of benchmarks covers resource usage measurements of M-String operations. Results are presented in Table 1. We run each operation separately on three different M-String inputs with a single parameter, *length*:

- *Word* is a string of the form $a^i b^j c^k$, $i + j + k \leq length$,
- *Sequence* has the form a^{length}, and
- *Alternation* is $a^i b^j a^k b^l$, $i + j + k + l \leq length$.

We have measured how much time we spend in the abstract operations which are part of the M-String domain and compare them to the same programs, but with the functions abstracted automatically, using only the M-String definitions of *access* and *update*.

One of the results is that the size of the state space does not depend on the length of the string when using the operations from M-String. This is because the number of segments does not change and the operations perform the same amount of work. In comparison, analysis of automatically lifted implementations of the same functions[5] does not terminate in a 1-hour time limit for strings of length 64 and more. This is caused by the fact that the concrete implementations need to iterate over each character individually, while the M-String implementation directly works with segments.

C Standard Library: The second scenario deals with correctness of various concrete implementations of the same set of standard library functions. Namely, we used 3 sources: `pdclib`, `musl-libc` and μCLibc. The results are very similar, hence we only present results for `pdclib` (Table 2) – data for the remaining 2 are part of the supplementary material.

In these benchmarks, we compare the results of the abstract implementation with the result of the automatically abstracted (originally concrete) implementation of each function and check that they give identical results.

Results show that analysis of strings with alternating characters is more expensive. This is because a segment might disappear and two segments are

---

[5] The implementations were taken from `pdclib`, a public-domain `libc` implementation.

Table 3. Evaluation on parsers of mathematical expressions (ME) and simple programs (BP). Inputs for ME were of 3 forms: *Addition* is a string with two numbers with + between them, *Ones* is a sequence of ones, and *Alternation* represent a number with multiple digits. Inputs for BP were of the form: *Value* constructs a constant, while *Loop* is a program with a single bounded loop and *Wrong* is a program with a syntax error.

	Numeric Expression Grammar							
length	10		20		25		35	
Add.	40.2s	416	319s	3548	622s	13k	T	–
Ones	5.5s	62	8.1s	196	29.7s	402	189s	2186
Alter.	708s	105	582s	11k	T	–	T	–

	BP Grammar							
length	10		50		100		1000	
Value	6.58s	38	44.4s	238	90.4s	488	1100s	4988
Loop	1.53s	23	3.28s	23	4.88s	23	33.3s	23
Wrong	7.34s	82	27.9	442	67.7s	892	311s	8992

merged into one: the SMT queries arising from those events are hard to solve, because of the large number of possible overlaps in the segment bounds.

The library implementations access and update the string one character at a time, resulting in large SMT formulas – this causes the blowup in analysis time and hence timeouts with longer strings.

Bison Grammar: In the last scenario, we analyse two parsers generated by bison. First is a parser for numerical expressions which consist of binary operators and numbers (see Table 3). The second example is a parser for a simple programming language.

Like with the previous scenarios, inputs which contain long sequences of the same character perform the best, especially when contrasted with a similar task performed on an input with alternating digits.

6   Conclusion

We have presented a segmentation-based abstract domain for approximating C strings. The main novelty of the domain lies in its focus on string buffers, which consist of two parts: the string of interest itself, and a tail of allocated and possibly initialized but unused memory. This paradigm allows for precise modeling of string functions from the standard C library, including their often fragile handling of terminating zeroes and buffer bounds. In principle, this allows the M-String domain to identify string manipulation errors with security consequences, such as buffer overflows.

In addition to presenting the domain theoretically, we have implemented the abstract semantics in executable form (as C++ code) and combined them with a tool that automatically lifts string-manipulating code in existing C programs to the M-String domain. Since M-String is a parametric domain – the domains for both segment content and segment bounds can be freely chosen – we have instantiated M-String (for evaluation purposes) with concrete characters and with symbolic (bitvector) bounds.

References

1. Polyspace, MathWorks (2001)
2. Static Code Analysis, OWASP (2017)
3. Interactive: the top programming languages 2018. IEEE Spectrum Magazine (2018)
4. Amadini, R., et al.: Reference abstract domains and applications to string analysis. Fundam. Inform. **158**(4), 297–326 (2018)
5. Amadini, R., et al.: Combining string abstract domains for JavaScript analysis: an evaluation. In: Legay, A., Margaria, T. (eds.) TACAS 2017. LNCS, vol. 10205, pp. 41–57. Springer, Heidelberg (2017). https://doi.org/10.1007/978-3-662-54577-5_3
6. Baranová, Z., et al.: Model checking of C and C++ with DIVINE 4. In: D'Souza, D., Narayan Kumar, K. (eds.) ATVA 2017. LNCS, vol. 10482, pp. 201–207. Springer, Cham (2017). https://doi.org/10.1007/978-3-319-68167-2_14
7. Bultan, T., Yu, F., Alkhalaf, M., Aydin, A.: String Analysis for Software Verification and Security. Springer, Cham (2017). https://doi.org/10.1007/978-3-319-68670-7
8. Christensen, A.S., Møller, A., Schwartzbach, M.I.: Precise analysis of string expressions. In: Cousot, R. (ed.) SAS 2003. LNCS, vol. 2694, pp. 1–18. Springer, Heidelberg (2003). https://doi.org/10.1007/3-540-44898-5_1
9. Clarke, E.M., Grumberg, O., Long, D.E.: Model checking and abstraction. ACM Trans. Program. Lang. Syst. **16**(5), 1512–1542 (1994)
10. Cortesi, A., Olliaro, M.: M-string segmentation: a refined abstract domain for string analysis in C programs. In: Proceedings of the 12th International Symposium on Theoretical Aspects of Software Engineering, TASE 2018, Guangzhou, China, 29–31 August 2018 (2018)
11. Costantini, G., Ferrara, P., Cortesi, A.: A suite of abstract domains for static analysis of string values. Softw. Pract. Exp. **45**(2), 245–287 (2015)
12. Cousot, P., Cousot, R.: Abstract interpretation: a unified lattice model for static analysis of programs by construction or approximation of fixpoints. In: Conference Record of the Fourth ACM Symposium on Principles of Programming Languages, Los Angeles, California, USA, January 1977, pp. 238–252 (1977)
13. Cousot, P., Cousot, R., Logozzo, F.: A parametric segmentation functor for fully automatic and scalable array content analysis. In: Proceedings of the 38th ACM SIGPLAN-SIGACT Symposium on Principles of Programming Languages, POPL 2011, Austin, TX, USA, 26–28 January 2011, pp. 105–118 (2011)
14. Dor, N., Rodeh, M., Sagiv, S.: CSSV: towards a realistic tool for statically detecting all buffer overflows in C. In: Proceedings of the ACM SIGPLAN 2003 Conference on Programming Language Design and Implementation 2003, San Diego, California, USA, 9–11 June 2003, pp. 155–167 (2003)
15. D'Silva, V., Kroening, D., Weissenbacher, G.: A survey of automated techniques for formal software verification. IEEE Trans. CAD Integr. Circ. Syst. **27**(7), 1165–1178 (2008)
16. Evans, D., Larochelle, D.: Improving security using extensible lightweight static analysis. IEEE Softw. **19**(1), 42–51 (2002)
17. Holzmann, G.J.: Static source code checking for user-defined properties. In: Integrated Design and Process Technology, IDPT 2002. Society for Design and Process Science, Pasadena (2002)
18. Jensen, S.H., Møller, A., Thiemann, P.: Type analysis for JavaScript. In: Palsberg, J., Su, Z. (eds.) SAS 2009. LNCS, vol. 5673, pp. 238–255. Springer, Heidelberg (2009). https://doi.org/10.1007/978-3-642-03237-0_17

19. Jones, R.W.M., Kelly, P.H.J.: Backwards-compatible bounds checking for arrays and pointers in C programs. In: AADEBUG, pp. 13–26 (1997)

20. Kashyap, V., et al.: JSAI: a static analysis platform for JavaScript. In: Proceedings of the 22nd ACM SIGSOFT International Symposium on Foundations of Software Engineering, (FSE-22), Hong Kong, China, 16–22 November 2014, pp. 121–132 (2014)

21. Kim, S.-W., Chin, W., Park, J., Kim, J., Ryu, S.: Inferring grammatical summaries of string values. In: Garrigue, J. (ed.) APLAS 2014. LNCS, vol. 8858, pp. 372–391. Springer, Cham (2014). https://doi.org/10.1007/978-3-319-12736-1_20

22. Lattner, C., Adve, V.: LLVM: a compilation framework for lifelong program analysis & transformation. In: International Symposium on Code Generation and Optimization (CGO 2004), Palo Alto, California, March 2004

23. Lauko, H., Ročkai, P., Barnat, J.: Symbolic computation via program transformation. In: Fischer, B., Uustalu, T. (eds.) ICTAC 2018. LNCS, vol. 11187, pp. 313–332. Springer, Cham (2018). https://doi.org/10.1007/978-3-030-02508-3_17

24. Madsen, M., Andreasen, E.: String analysis for dynamic field access. In: Cohen, A. (ed.) CC 2014. LNCS, vol. 8409, pp. 197–217. Springer, Heidelberg (2014). https://doi.org/10.1007/978-3-642-54807-9_12

25. One, A.: Smashing the stack for fun and profit. Phrack **7**(49) (1996). http://www.phrack.com/issues.html?issue=49&id=14

26. Park, C., Im, H., Ryu, S.: Precise and scalable static analysis of jQuery using a regular expression domain. In: Proceedings of the 12th Symposium on Dynamic Languages, DLS 2016, Amsterdam, The Netherlands, 1 November 2016, pp. 25–36 (2016)

27. Shahriar, H., Zulkernine, M.: Classification of static analysis-based buffer overflow detectors. In: Fourth International Conference on Secure Software Integration and Reliability Improvement, SSIRI 2010, Singapore, 9–11 June 2010, Companion Volume, pp. 94–101 (2010)

28. Spoto, F.: The julia static analyzer for Java. In: Rival, X. (ed.) SAS 2016. LNCS, vol. 9837, pp. 39–57. Springer, Heidelberg (2016). https://doi.org/10.1007/978-3-662-53413-7_3

29. Wagner, D.A., Foster, J.S., Brewer, E.A., Aiken, A.: A first step towards automated detection of buffer overrun vulnerabilities. In: Proceedings of the Network and Distributed System Security Symposium, NDSS, San Diego, California, USA, p. 2000 (2000)

30. Xie, Y., Chou, A., Engler, D.R.: ARCHER: using symbolic, path-sensitive analysis to detect memory access errors. In: Proceedings of the 11th ACM SIGSOFT Symposium on Foundations of Software Engineering 2003 Held Jointly with 9th European Software Engineering Conference, ESEC/FSE 2003, Helsinki, Finland, 1–5 September 2003, pp. 327–336 (2003)

31. Xu, R-G., Godefroid, P., Majumdar, R.: Testing for buffer overflows with length abstraction. In: Proceedings of the ACM/SIGSOFT International Symposium on Software Testing and Analysis, ISSTA 2008, Seattle, WA, USA, 20–24 July 2008, pp. 27–38 (2008)

Swarm Model Checking on the GPU

Richard DeFrancisco$^{(\boxtimes)}$, Shenghsun Cho, Michael Ferdman,
and Scott A. Smolka

Stony Brook University, Stony Brook, NY 11794-2424, USA
rdefrancisco@cs.stonybrook.edu

Abstract. We present *Grapple*, a new and powerful framework for explicit-state model checking on GPUs. Grapple is based on *swarm verification* (SV), a model-checking technique wherein a collection or *swarm* of small, memory- and time-bounded *verification tests* (VTs) are run in parallel to perform state-space exploration. SV achieves high state-space coverage via diversification of the search strategies used by constituent VTs. Grapple represents a swarm implementation for the GPU. In particular, it runs a parallel swarm of internally-parallel VTs, which are implemented in a manner that specifically targets the GPU architecture and the SIMD parallelism its computing cores offer. Grapple also makes effective use of the GPU shared memory, eliminating costly inter-block communication overhead. We conducted a comprehensive performance analysis of Grapple focused on the various design parameters, including the size of the queue structure, implementation of guard statements, and nondeterministic exploration order. Tests are run with multiple hardware configurations, including on the Amazon cloud. Our results show that Grapple performs favorably compared to the SPIN swarm and a prior non-swarm GPU implementation. Although a recently debuted FPGA swarm is faster, the deployment process to the FPGA is much more complex than Grapple's.

Keywords: GPU · Model checking · Swarm verification · Grapple

1 Introduction

Modern computing exists in a space that is increasingly parallel, distributed, and heterogeneous. High-performance co-processors such as GPUs (Graphics Processing Units) are utilized in many super-computing applications due to their high computational throughput, energy efficiency, and low cost [5]. GPGPU (General-Purpose Computing on a GPU) is achieved through the use of GPU programming languages such as the Open Computing Language (OpenCL) [6] and the Compute Unified Device Architecture (CUDA) [1].

In 2014, we adapted the multicore SPIN model checking (MC) algorithm of [24] to the GPU [12]. While our approach achieved speedups up to 7.26x over traditional SPIN, and 1.26x over multicore SPIN, it was severely limited by the

© Springer Nature Switzerland AG 2019
F. Biondi et al. (Eds.): SPIN 2019, LNCS 11636, pp. 94–113, 2019.
https://doi.org/10.1007/978-3-030-30923-7_6

memory footprint of the GPU, and by an explicit limit on state-vector size set by the hash function [8].

The introduction of *Swarm Verification* (SV) in [27] represented an entirely new approach to parallel MC. In SV, a large number of MC instances are executed in parallel, each with a restricted memory footprint and a different search path. Each instance is called a *verification test* (VT), because it does not seek to cover the full state space as a model checker would. Through the use of *diversification techniques*, VTs are independent of one other in terms of the portions of the model's state space they cover. By executing a sufficiently large number of VTs, one is therefore statistically guaranteed to achieve nearly complete, if not complete coverage of the entire state space.

In this paper, we present *Grapple*, bringing the light-weight yet powerful nature of SV to the massively parallel GPU architecture. While other swarm implementations run internally sequential VTs in parallel, Grapple VTs are internally parallel and evolved from our previous GPU-based MC design [12]. Each VT runs on a single block of the GPU, with a bitstate hash table in shared memory, compacting per-state storage *by a factor of 64* compared to the cuckoo tables used in [12]. These tables use the hash function of [29], eliminating the hard 64-bit state vector limit of our previous model checker.

Grapple VTs run in parallel on all available GPU streaming multiprocessors (SMs), and make efficient use of the GPU scheduler to quickly replace jobs the instant an SM becomes available. As VTs are independent of each other and each one is tightly bound to a single chip on hardware, there is no need for inter-block communication or additional synchronization primitives.

To assess Grapple's performance, we used a benchmark specifically designed for SV-based model checkers [16,27]: a model that can randomly generate more than 4 billion states. Exploration progress in the benchmark is captured by the visitation of 100 randomly distributed states, or *waypoints*, with 100 waypoints approaching complete state-space exploration. Our experiments, which we ran on multiple hardware configurations, including the Amazon cloud [2], evaluate the impact of variations in queue size, guard-statement implementation, and nondeterministic exploration order.

We also compared Grapple's performance with the FPGA swarm implementation of [16], the CPU swarm of [27], and the original (non-swarm) GPU implementation of [12]. Grapple easily outperforms the GPU implementation and the CPU swarm, and reaches all waypoints in a number of VTs comparable to that required by the FPGA implementation. While it cannot compete in raw speed with the hardware-level FPGA implementation, it offers much easier deployment, with VTs that complete in under a second. We additionally evaluated Grapple using multiple configurations of the Dining Philosophers problem, a small model with a known state-space size and deadlock violation.

In summary, our main contributions are as follows. (i) We introduce Grapple, a GPU-based swarm verification model checker with internally parallel verification tasks. (ii) We analyze structural elements of VTs (e.g., search strategy, queue size, guard logic, number of threads per VT) to determine how they impact the rate of exploration. (iii) We compare Grapple's performance to previous SV implementations on the CPU [27] and FPGA [16], as well as to our non-swarm GPU-based model checker [12].

The rest of the paper is organized as follows. Section 2 provides background on GPU hardware, the CUDA programming model, the SPIN model checker, and swarm verification. Section 3 presents our Grapple model checker. Section 4 presents our various experimental results. Section 5 considers related work. Section 6 interprets our findings and offers directions for future work.

2   Background

To motivate our design decisions for Grapple, we first explain the intricacies of GPU hardware and the associated CUDA programming model, and provide an overview of the SPIN model checker [7], on which Grapple is based. Further details on the GPU hardware and CUDA are available in the CUDA C Programming Guide [4].

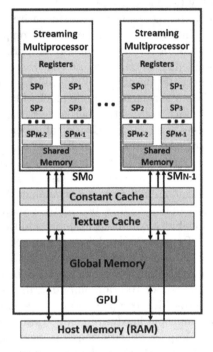

Fig. 1.   GPU   hardware   model. SP = Stream Processor

2.1   GPU Hardware Model

The GPU is a high-performance co-processor designed to efficiently render 3D graphics in real time. GPUs are well-suited for linear algebra, matrix arithmetic, and other computations frequently used in graphical applications. As illustrated in Fig. 1, the GPU architecture consists of a scalable array of N multithreaded *Streaming Multiprocessors* (SMs), each of which is made up of M *Stream Processor* (SP) cores. Each core is equipped with a fully pipelined integer-arithmetic logic unit (ALU) and a floating-point unit (FPU) that execute one integer or floating-point instruction per clock cycle. Each SM controls a *warp* of 32 threads, executing the same instructions in lock-step for all threads.

The GPU features a number of memory types, differing in access speed, capacity, and read/write availability. Global memory is large (order of gigabytes), available device-wide, but relatively slow. Constant memory is a cached, read-only memory intended for storing constant values that are not updated during execution. Finally, each SM has a shared memory region (16–48 KB). In practice, accessing shared memory can be *up to 100 times faster* than using global memory for the same transaction.

Devices connect to the host machine using the PCIe bus. Communication between the host and device are extremely costly compared to on-board memory accesses, including those that use global memory.

2.2 CUDA Programming Model

CUDA is the proprietary NVIDIA programming model for general-purpose computing on their GPU architecture. While the alternative model, OpenCL, is universally compatible with all GPU architectures, the high-performance of CUDA has led to wide adoption. We decided to write Grapple in CUDA for this reason, but an OpenCL implementation would be very similar.

The CUDA parallel computing model uses tens of thousands of lightweight *threads* assembled into one- to three-dimensional *thread blocks*. A thread executes a function called a *kernel*, which contains the computations to be run in parallel. Each thread uses different parameters. Threads located in the same thread block can work together in several ways. They can insert a synchronization point into the kernel, which requires all threads in the block to reach that point before execution can continue. They can also share data during execution. In contrast, threads located in different thread blocks cannot communicate in such ways and essentially operate independently.

Shared-memory transactions are typically parallel to some number n distinct banks, but if two or more address requests fall in the same bank, the collision causes a serialization of the access. It is therefore important to understand addressing patterns when utilizing shared memory. Register management is also critically important. Use of registers is partitioned among all threads and, as such, using a large number of registers within a CUDA kernel will limit the number of threads that can run concurrently. Double and long variables, use of shared memory, and unoptimized block/warp geometry all lead to increased register use. If available registers are exhausted, the contents will spill over into local memory- a special type of device memory with the same high-latency and low-bandwidth as global memory.

The SIMD nature of warps on SPs has a great impact on code structure for the GPU. As warps act in lock-step, any *branching logic* encountered by a warp must have all branches explored by all threads. The data created during the additional branch exploration is simply discarded. This phenomena is referred to as *branch divergence* and is warp-local; other warps continue to perform independently of the divergent warp. This can lead to scheduling conflicts where non-branching warps must wait for the divergent warps to complete. It is also generally a performance loss within a warp, especially for cases where one or more branches is long but uncommonly taken.

Finally, kernels can be launched in parallel on a single device, as long as that device has the capacity to do so. Streams are command sequences that execute in order internally, but can be concurrent with each other. The number of concurrent streams is device dependent, and additional streams will queue until the device has availability. Streams are unnecessary to run parallel commands on multiple devices, and are not needed for pipelining data transfers with kernel execution. Two commands from multiple streams cannot run concurrently if the host specifies memory manipulation or kernel launches on stream 0 (default) between them. Synchronization, where necessary, can be invoked within a stream or across streams with provided CUDA sync statements.

2.3 SPIN Model Checker

SPIN [7] is a widely used model checker designed to verify multi-threaded software. SPIN has an ever-growing list of features and options, including optimization techniques, property specification types, and hardware support. State spaces can be pruned using partial order reduction, speed can be increased by changing search strategies or disabling certain checks, and memory footprint can be reduced through bitstate hashing. SPIN can handle safety and liveness properties, any LTL specification, Büchi automata, never claims, and invariant assertions. Multicore support was added in 2007 [23], improved in 2012 [24], and extended to liveness properties in 2015 [20].

A central feature of the 2012 algorithm is the structure holding the frontier of newly discovered states. In order to assign these states to the N worker threads, SPIN uses two sets of $N \times N$ queues. By splitting each frontier queue into an $N \times N$ structure all threads can communicate without the need for mutex locks. Of these two queue sets, one (output) fills with a new frontier as the other (input) empties the current frontier. When the input queue is empty, all threads synchronize and the two swap labels. This process continues until both the input and output are empty or a violation is found. We adopt this structure for Grapple.

2.4 Swarm Verification

Recently, support for large-scale parallel model checking on CPU-based systems was added to SPIN in the form of swarm verification (SV) [25–27]. SV is a technique wherein a large number of small *verification tasks* (VTs) are run in parallel on many independent processors, including multiple CPUs, multicore CPUs, and distributed systems [25]. The term verification test is used in place of model checker or verifier because these tests are not guaranteed to complete. Instead, each test is given a set amount of time and memory to explore whatever portion of the state space it can. VTs can be as small as a number of KBs.

Each VT is independent, and the state space it covers is differentiated through the use of various *diversification techniques*. These techniques include reversing search direction or search order, randomizing nondeterministic choice order of transitions, and other perturbations of the original search algorithm. VTs do not share resources nor need to live on the same physical machine. Given enough parallel hardware, all VTs can run concurrently. When these resources are more limited, VTs will be scheduled like any other batch of independent programs.

The most potent diversification technique is the use of *statistically independent hash functions*. With up to 10^8 suitable unique 32-bit hash polynomials, in addition to other search diversification methods, the potential number of distinct concurrent searches is easily in the billions [25]. Hash functions reduce the state space graph via collisions; as each hash table is much smaller than the total number of states, collisions are frequent. If we treat each collision as valid (consider them the same state, even if that is not the case), the state space will be quickly, and naturally pruned.

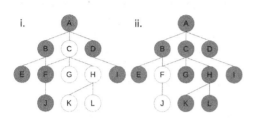

Fig. 2. Pruning states via hash collision. (i) Hash collision $\{B, C\}$ on trace $ABEFJDI$. (ii) Hash collision $\{E, F\}$ on trace $ABECGHKLDI$.

Figure 2 depicts state-space pruning via collision. In both searches, a left-favoring Depth-First Search strategy is used, but their hash tables use different hash polynomials to store states. In the left graph, nodes B and C have the same hashed value, so C appears to be the same state and will not be expanded. In the right graph, E and F have the same value, preventing the expansion of F. While this method of pruning all but assures that individual VT will not reach all states in the state space, with a sufficient number of diverse VTs, the swarm as a whole will achieve full coverage.

3   Swarm Verification via the Grapple Model Checker

The Grapple model checker brings the power of GPU computing to the model-checking problem via swarm verification. For simplicity of presentation, we discuss Grapple's design in terms of a *Waypoints* (WPs) benchmark specifically designed for SV-based model checkers [16,27]. The WP benchmark involves a model that can randomly generate more than 4 billion states. Said model is comprised of 8 processes each in control of 4 bits. At successor generation, the current process will nondeterministically set one of its bits to 1. Exploration progress in the benchmark is captured by the visitation of 100 randomly distributed states, or *waypoints*, with 100 waypoints suggesting a nearly complete state-space exploration. This style of presentation does not in any way imply that Grapple is limited to this one benchmark; it is still a general-purpose model checker. And indeed, we present results from an additional model in Sect. 4.

Although traditionally each VT is a small, sequential version of SPIN, this is not the case for Grapple VTs, which run on the GPU. As discussed in Sect. 2.1, the GPU has a SIMD/SIMT programming model: a single instruction or set of instructions is given to a group of threads operating on different data. Warps of 32 threads execute in lock-step, and all branches in logic must be fully explored by the entire warp. Mimicking SPIN by running a completely sequential VT on an entire warp would waste massive amounts of resources. Instead, we use a modified version of the 2014 GPU MC algorithm [12] to run a single, internally-parallel VT per warp. VTs execute independently in parallel outside of the warp, but internally (i.e., within a given VT), all data structures are shared among the threads and there is a single state space to explore.

While the queue structure and general search algorithm remain the same as the 2014 MC, there are a number of alterations made to the GPU VT to take advantage of the new swarm environment. First and foremost, the hash table is a bitstate implementation moved to shared memory. This hash table is only shared among threads within a VT and not between VTs. Factors typically considered weaknesses of a shared-memory approach are its locality to an SM and its small size (48 KB maximum). With each SIMD-parallel VT limited to a single warp, all threads within the VT are guaranteed to be on the same SP within the same SM, and therefore all have access to this structure. The 48 KB limit is not an issue for VTs utilizing bitstate hashing, as such a table can hold nearly 400,000 entries. This is on the low end of the scale for a VT compared to those in other SV implementations [25,27], but VTs of this size were shown to work well in a recent FPGA implementation [16].

Also as in the FPGA implementation, cuckoo hashing [8] has been replaced with an AB mix function based on the Jenkins Linear Feedback Shift Register (LFSR) [29]. For this purpose, two random integers, A and B, are generated on the host machine for each VT and included as parameters in the VT's kernel launch. This hash function change is motivated by a desire to better align with the FPGA implementation, as well as the elimination of the multiple-function schema used in the cuckoo algorithm. The random variables are reused on the GPU in some search strategies as quick random-digit generators, as on-device random generation tends to be convoluted and this method is more efficient. Since each VT is relegated to a single warp, the fast-barrier synchronization [41] used in the previous GPU MC implementation has also been removed. Instead, the on-board CUDA _syncthreads() function is used at the required synchronization points.

Grapple, like the FPGA swarm [16], runs multiple VTs within a single program, with additional copies of that program launched by script if necessary. In contrast, the SPIN swarm [27] is coordinated by a script that simply launches every VT as an independent thread. A Grapple program running on the GPU initiates multiple VTs, each a CUDA kernel, and utilizes streams to run these kernels in parallel whenever possible. The number of VTs that a core program can launch is dependent upon the hardware of the device(s) available, the memory footprint of each VT, and how initialization and memory transfers are handled. In the current design, all variables and structures are initialized, transferred to the GPU before kernel launch, transferred back to the host after kernel completion, and then freed in a single batch. Theoretically, more VTs could be launched within a program and additional efficiency squeezed out if the transfers were pipelined with some VT execution, but the current arrangement also has benefits.

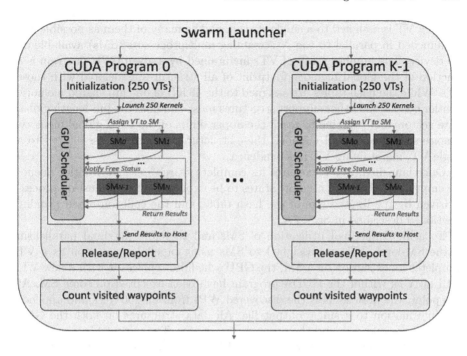

Fig. 3. Control flow for Grapple with 250 * K VTs.

Since the primary diversification techniques in Grapple are alterations in hash polynomial, search structure, and nondeterminism order, most of the host-level set-up is common across VTs. Overall, these common elements reduce the cost of this process to be nearly negligible when compared to time spent on the device. In this case, pipelining would increase overall complexity of the core code with minimal benefit. On the theme of common initialization, structures are placed in constant memory whenever possible so all VTs gain fast read-only access.

Figure 3 illustrates the control flow of Grapple. Upon start-up, a swarm script launches a CUDA program on all available hardware devices (GPUs). When there is only a single device, these K programs must sequentialize with each other, with one program launching after the execution of the previous program and its sort instance (the Linux sort utility is used to count WPs) has terminated. Internally, each CUDA program initializes a number of VTs, in this case 250, sharing common data wherever possible to minimize overhead. Examples of this includes setting up the initial state and sending WP identifiers to GPU constant memory. This initialization/pre-launch procedure runs on the CPU (host).

Each VT is assigned to a single stream, and as many of them as possible will be launched in parallel to the N streaming multiprocessors (SMs) available on the device. The number (250) of VTs maintained by a given GPU program is a function of the global memory footprint of all structures associated with those VTs. While the hash tables are assigned to the 48 KB of on-chip shared memory, frontier queues and other support structures must still hold the full-length global state vectors and combine to reach the upper limits of the GPU global memory. Despite sitting on global memory, these structures are still access-limited to a single VT, maintaining VT independence.

Once launched, a VT executes its complete search until its frontier queues are empty, and there are no more states to be explored. This exhaustion process is driven by the limited size of the hash table, and the collision-based pruning mentioned described in Sect. 2.4.

To achieve maximal utilization of SMs and therefore maximal parallelism at the SM-level, VTs are assigned to SMs using pipelining: as soon as a VT completes its execution on a SM, the GPU scheduler replaces it with a new VT, until all VTs within the CUDA program have been executed on some SM. At this point, the host collects the discovered WPs from all 250 VTs and appends this information to a single output file. All data structures on both the GPU and CPU are released, and the program terminates. The output file is read by a sort utility, and current progress reported by the swarm script. The next GPU program is launched, and the process continues until all GPU programs in the swarm are exhausted.

Note that for a single GPU system, a swarm of size 50,000 VTs requires 200 sequentially launched CUDA programs. One of the benefits of Grapple, and SV in general, is that if additional GPUs are available, even on different machines in different locations, these 200 CUDA programs can run in parallel with each other without additional modification. These other GPUs may have more memory or more SMs, allowing more VTs per program or more concurrent execution of VTs, respectively.

Due to the abridged nature of VT searches, minute changes in control flow can have a major impact on the set of visited states for each VT. As hash collisions are resolved by dropping the new entry, even differences in the order of constituent operations change the results. To better understand a VT's behavior, we offer in Algorithm 1 a comprehensive breakdown of a VT's main control loop. Furthermore, in Sect. 4, we conduct a series of tests that illuminate the effects of making even minor changes to the code.

Algorithm 1. State-Space Exploration Loop executed by each VT thread

Each of a given VT's N parallel threads does the following:

while none of thread i's output queues are empty **do**
  for all N of thread i's input queues **do**
    while input queue j is not empty **do**
      for all processes in the model **do**
        for all nondeterministic choices NDC within a process **do**
          successor = successor_generation(process, NDC, state);
          selection = (mix(a, b, state));
          hashed_value = (selection/8) % table_size;
          sel = selection%8;
          visited_state = table[hashed_value];
          table[hashed_value] |= (1<<sel);
          if (visited_state &(1 <<sel)) == 0 **then**
            Report state back to CPU for check against 100 WPs
            Pick random thread $i' \in$ N to output to
            if i' has slots **then**
              Insert the new state into queue i'
            end if//implicit else drop the state
          end if
        end for//close for (NDC)
      end for//close for (process)
    end while
  end for
  __syncthreads();
  Check output queues for emptiness
end while

The nondeterministic choice (NDC) has a variety of different implementation options. Traditionally, all nondeterministic options would be accessed in order as in standard *BFS* (parallel BFS in this case) behavior. With minor modification, all nondeterministic options can be visited in random order. To minimize the amount of branching logic, all NDC order possibilities are enumerated in constant memory, and the selection of order is completely random for each step in the loop.

As described in Sect. 2.3, Grapple VTs use a set of $N \times N$ queue structures to allow lock-free communication between threads. Each thread has a set of N input queues and N output queues, with I slots in each queue. We call an $N \times N \times I$ set of queues a *queue structure*. In Sect. 4, we consider a queue structure in Grapple to be the same as a queue in SPIN and FPGA VTs. For this to hold, I will often be as small as four or five slots.

In Grapple, the input and output queue structures are sets of pointers to a single array in GPU global memory. To avoid illegal memory access, a VT must first check that there are slots available when attempting to insert a new state. In Algorithm 1, this check happens after a state is marked visited. If there are no queue slots available, the state is dropped and its successors potentially lost. If instead the queue check happens before the state is marked visited, the same state (or a state with the same hash value) can be visited later. This second location is used in FPGA and Grapple VTs.

The logic employed with this check also plays a factor in Grapple's performance. If the check prevents writing outside the bounds of the underlying array structure, hence referred to as the *old guard*, it will still allow threads to write to unintended targets. A stricter boundary check, the *new guard*, enforces the local limitation of I. In practice, illustrated in Sect. 4, VTs with the old guard have better performance.

The reason for the better behavior of the old guard is as follows. When a thread n attempts to write to another thread q, the new guard would make sure n is not writing to $q + 1$ instead. If n is attempting to write to the (non-existent) $I + 1$ slot of q, it instead overwrites slot 0 of $q + 1$. In practice, this is a random state-drop that replaces a *shallow* state in the queue structure with a *deeper* one. Both guards lead to a state-drop, but the old guard favors keeping deep states while the new guard favors shallow states. In general, the Grapple implementation uses the old, deep-state-favoring, guard logic.

All discussion of dropped states to this point has been of random drops or partial-match drops (hash collisions). It is also possible to do complete explicit-state drops for specific state-vector matches. The default behavior of the FPGA swarm is to consider WPs to be violations. When one of these states is encountered, it is reported and dropped without generating successors. While for other models this behavior may lead to unreachable portions of the state space, it is not the case for the WP model. Our Grapple tests include variants with and without this WP dropping behavior.

4 Experimental Results

In this section, we present experimental results for Grapple. The first set of experiments use the WP benchmark to test variants of the Grapple VT design, and allow us to compare performance with the SPIN [27] and FPGA [16] swarms, as well as with our non-swarm GPU implementation [12]. All of these tests use the same 100 WPs, selected from a random distribution over the 32-bit integer space. The GPU used in these experiments is an Nvidia Geforce 660Ti GPU with 2 GB GPU global memory, and 7 SMs. This is an older, inexpensive GPU model but still allows for Grapple to show sufficient performance. SPIN experiments run Swarm 3.2 with SPIN 6.4.7, using an Intel dual-socket server that has two Xeon E5-2670v3 CPUs (24 cores total) running at 2.3 GHz and Hyper-Threading enabled (48 hardware threads total), with 128 GB of RAM. FPGA experiments are done with cycle-accurate SystemC simulations using Xilinx Vivado HLS 2017.4, targeting a Xilinx Virtex-7 XC7V690T FFG1761-3 FPGA. The test environments for the SPIN and FPGA experiments are the same as in [16]. Additionally, we include experiments using the Dining Philosopher's problem in order to demonstrate Grapple's ability to discover a known deadlock violation. Finally, we show Grapple's potential in a high-performance environment by running WP benchmark tests on Amazon's EC2 GPU cloud platform [2].

4.1 WP Benchmark

FPGA experiments use internally sequential VTs with 48 KB of storage each. The FPGA runs in batches of 44 concurrent VTs, starting a new batch when the previous one finishes. Unlike the general-purpose VT designs of the GPU and CPU swarms, which can be applied to any Promela model, the FPGA swarm is currently limited (hardwired) to the 32-bit random number generator. Fortunately, there are still some variants of this WP benchmark to test against.

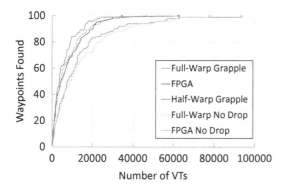

Figure 4 shows combined results of two FPGA swarm variants and three Grapple variants running the WP benchmark. In the standard configuration, WPs are recorded upon discovery, considered a violation, and the state is dropped. Non-WP states first check the queue, and are marked visited and propagate if there are slots available or drop and remain unvisited if the queue is full. This allows the state (or a colliding state) to potentially be visited later by the same VT. In later Grapple tests, we refer to this control flow as "FPGA-style", as it matches the behavior of VTs in [16].

Fig. 4. Grapple VT vs FPGA VT.

Half-warp (16 threads per VT) Grapple leads the FPGA in number of WPs from the very beginning and reaches the 100th WP in 34,500 VTs, over 28,000 fewer VTs than its counterpart. The full-warp (32 threads per VT) Grapple implementation, however, is outpaced by the FPGA. The FPGA completes the WP benchmark in 30,947 fewer VTs. While these three versions share the same control flow and queue structure size (4,096 entries), the half-warp Grapple implementation has much better performance when using the WP/VT metric. In terms of raw speed, however, the half-warp version is slower, with VTs lasting 650 ms compared to the full-warp's average of 451 ms. Both Grapple versions cannot match the hardware-level speed of the FPGA implementation, but Grapple offers fast VTs with a much easier deployment process than the FPGA swarm.

There is also an alternate control flow, wherein the 100 WPs are reported but otherwise treated like any other state. In this case, all 100 are discovered by the FPGA in 46,515 VTs or roughly 74.4% the number of VTs as the previous iteration. Full-warp Grapple also sees improvement, completing in 77,750 VTs. This is not significant enough to catch up with the FPGA or half-warp Grapple. A no-drop version of half-warp Grapple was not included in these tests.

On FPGA hardware, the swarms from Fig. 4 complete in an extremely fast 12.5 s for the original and 9.3 s for no-drop, with individual VTs lasting only ~0.2 ms. These swarms, however, were run on a cycle-accurate FPGA simulator, where one second of simulated time takes approximately one hour of wall-clock time. The simulation allows for more useful data collection without harming FPGA performance, and is cheaper and faster than deploying to a physical FPGA.

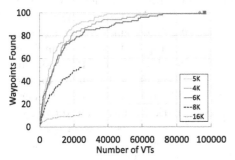

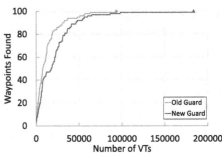

Fig. 5. Impact of frontier size on Grapple search.

Fig. 6. Impact of guard logic change on Grapple search.

Figure 5 shows the impact of the queue structure size on Grapple's performance. This test was inspired by the WP/VT difference between earlier half-warp vs full-warp tests. For the same size queue structure ($N \times N \times I$), a Grapple half-warp VT has more slots per thread (a smaller N value means a larger I value). Since the number of slots can impact state-drops (see Sect. 3), we ran a series of tests expanding the queue structure size (and thus the I value) for full-warp Grapple. When $I = 16$ or $I = 8$ (16,384 or 8,192 total queue structure size), by 25,000 VTs we determined that these versions would not outperform the $I = 4$ control and terminated the swarms. $I = 6$ performs just slightly worse than the control. Grapple achieved peak performance with $I = 5$ (5,120 queue structure size), reaching 100 WPs in 62,000 VTs. This is better than the 93,500 VTs of the control, but still worse than the 34,500 of half-warp Grapple. Since half-warp Grapple uses a queue structure of 4,096 elements ($I = 16$ with $N = 16$), but outperforms all full-warp versions in WP/VT, the difference in performance requires further study. It is likely due to a low-level bottleneck, such as register access patterns or to differences in exploration order arising from the fewer random thread options.

We also tested the impact of altering the guard logic for full-warp Grapple's queue structure, as explained in Sect. 3. Both versions use a queue structure with 4,096 entries, and otherwise identical control flow. Figure 6 shows the old guard logic maintaining a WP lead throughout the lifetime of the swarm, reaching the 100th WP in 93,500 VTs. The new guard logic takes an additional **90,000 VTs** to find all 100 WPs, with ~47% of the search spent looking for the final WP.

Unlike in Grapple and FPGA tests, where the hash table size is always 48 KB per VT, SPIN swarm experiments run on a variety of different hash table sizes. While a 48 KB hash table would be ideal for comparison purposes, a SPIN swarm requires hash tables to be multiples of 32. With the table size set to 32 KB, SPIN ran for over a week without discovering all 100 WPs, after which we terminated the search. The next step up, with 64 KB-hash-table VTs, managed to find 90 WPs in 263,220 s (just over three days). As in [16], the optimal configuration for the SPIN swarm seems to be a 256 MB table per VT. This version uncovers all 100 WPs in 10,890 s, ~3.4x as long as half-warp Grapple or ~1.8x as long as full-warp Grapple.

The optimal setting for SPIN VTs requires over 5000x the amount of memory per VT as Grapple and the FPGA. A larger memory footprint for each VT lets a VT cover a greater portion of the state-space, but at the cost of longer execution time per VT. The SPIN results suggest that either the overhead for creating many small SPIN VTs hinders their effectiveness, or that SPIN's implementation of diversification techniques favor larger VTs. While SPIN could run more concurrent VTs if more machines were available, improving performance, the same could be said for the Grapple and FPGA versions.

Non-swarm GPU tests were difficult for this model. Our original implementation in [12] called for four full explicit-state cuckoo hash tables to contain every possible state vector. Although the WP benchmark uses randomly generated 32-bit states, the states are still wrapped in a 64-bit unsigned long long integer. Following the original MC design, the total hash storage alone would be 128 GB, much larger than the 2 GB of global memory on this GPU. Converting this checker to bitstate hashing allows us to cut the hash storage to a more-reasonable 500 MB. However, this does not account for the other support structures that still use full 64-bit state vectors. The simplest solution is to run a version that is 250x the size of a single Grapple VT, since we know 250 Grapple VTs can be allocated in one CUDA program without exhausting memory. A table this size can hold just over 98 million states, a fraction of the statespace generated by the WP benchmark. Our non-swarm checker explores this space in 352 s, reaching 10 WPs. As a standalone program, the GPU MC clearly cannot compete with the full state-space exploration of Grapple.

4.2   Dining Philosophers Model

Table 1 contains results for Dining Philosophers, where each philosopher picks up the left stick, then the right, releases the left and then the right. There is a violating state (deadlock) when all philosophers pick up their respective left stick concurrently. The minimum number of VTs tested is 7, since less than 7 would take the same amount of time to run on this GPU. For versions with more processes, we use sets of 451 VTs (an arbitrary large number that fits within the GPU memory footprint), but for DP10 and DP11, we determined that more precision would be better than just saying x ≤ 451. The number of VTs needed to fully explore the state space increases dramatically when increasing the number of processes to 12. This is as expected, as DP11 has 177,146 states to fit into 392,800 slots per VT (~45% occupancy), while DP12 has 531,440 states to fit into the same number of slots (~135% occupancy). Beyond 12, we prematurely terminate the search due to the low rate of new state discovery.

Table 1. Dining Philosophers model in Grapple.

Number of processes	% of VTs finding violation	Average VT execution time	State space size	# of VTs to explore	% of state space covered by first 451VTs
10	67.72	195 ms	59048	100% in 7	100
11	46.65	366 ms	177146	100% in 14	100
12	25.55	677 ms	531440	100% in 3157	99.99
13	13.75	832 ms	1594322	99.21% in 24,805	98.65
14	11.18	882 ms	4782968	97.76% in 13,530	92.72
15	11.35	902 ms	14348906	93.19% in 50,061	76.56

The final column of Table 1 shows the percentage of the state space covered in the first 451 VTs. Due to search overlap, the number of unique states visited grows logarithmically with the number of VTs. The effect is more pronounced in a deterministic model like Dining Philosophers, since the only source of diversification in Grapple for such models is the VT's hash polynomial.

4.3 Large-Scale Results

For our large-scale experiments, we used two Amazon EC2 nodes [2], one with 4 and one with 8 Tesla V100 devices. Each device features 16 GB global memory and 80 SMs. All devices for each configuration run concurrently and their reported WPs are collected by a script on the host. As in the previous tests, each VT is independent and features data structures private to said VT. There is no inter-GPU communication other than WP counting by the script. Each CUDA program runs 2,000 VTs between reports to the host.

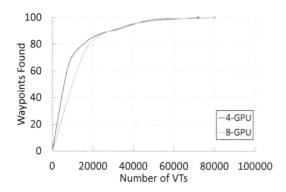

Fig. 7. Grapple with 16 threads/VT on Amazon EC2

As in Fig. 7, the 4-GPU node reaches all 100 WPs in 72,000 VTs (18,000 per GPU). The 8-GPU node reaches all 100 in 80,000 VTs (10,000 per GPU). Even with state-recording overhead they complete in 42 min and 21 min, respectively. This is faster than our previous results with such recording disabled. Turning off state-recording results in a reduction of average VT time from 1.02250 s to 203.51 ms. This is a significant reduction of 80.1%.

5   Related Work

In [23], SPIN was extended to support dual-core processors, using nested DFS to check safety and liveness properties. This work was extended to multicore systems for safety properties in [24] and liveness properties in [20]. Despite the earlier debut of a distributed model checker [11], the dual-core version of SPIN was the first parallel MC to reach wide adoption. Other work sought to avoid the naturally sequential depth-first post-order found in dual-core SPIN's nested DFS algorithm by leveraging the parallelism in breadth-first reachability analysis on both distributed [35] and multicore systems [10]. This was mainly accomplished using two algorithms: One Way Catch Them Young (OWCTY) and Maximal Accepting Predecessors (MAP). Both algorithms perform parallel reachability analysis, but differ in the way they detect cycles in the state-space graph.

Early GPU-based MC efforts focused on *a priori* graph exploration, as opposed to generating new states *on-the-fly* [9,17,22,28,32]. The first on-the-fly GPU approach used the GPU to generate new states with enabled transitions, and the CPU for duplicate detection [18]. This is not unlike waypoint counting in Grapple, but their system makes less efficient use of the GPU hardware and is not based on SV. GPUexplore [38] was introduced in 2014 along with our own GPU-based model checker [12]. While we tried to redesign SPIN to take advantage of the GPU architecture, GPUexplore worked on Labeled Transition Systems (LTSs) and followed a symbolic approach. Grapple uses VTs based on our 2014 design, so it is still very different than GPUexplore. A GPU-based on-the-fly reachability checking system for LTSs that achieved 50–100x performance over sequential search was presented in [40].

In [36], GPUs were used for strong and branching bisimilarity checking. A GPU-based method for liveness checking for finite-state concurrent system appeared in [37]. Three partial-order reduction algorithms were implemented on the GPU in [33], bringing GPUexplore closer to parity with existing CPU-based checkers. A second version of GPUexplore was released that same year, with improvements made to lock-less hashing and thread synchronization [39]. Unlike [37], this version does not include support for liveness properties. Scalability tests for GPUexplore were carried out in [13], achieving 5.5 million states/second on a 61.9 million state model. Additionally, they used GPUexplore to pit the 2015 Maxwell Architecture Nvidia Titan X GPU against the 2016 Pascal Titan X GPU, averaging a 1.73x improvement on the new device. A more in-depth comparison between cuckoo hashing and the GPUexplore table was carried out in [14], concluding that cuckoo hashing is 3x faster for random data and up to 9x faster for non-random data.

A GPU-based parameter-synthesis tool for stochastic systems was presented in [15]. Utilizing a single GPU, it achieves up to 31x the performance of sequential approaches. A multi-core version of the LTSMIN model checker [31] outperformed the 2005 multi-core SPIN and the 2008 multi-core DiVinE model checkers. In [19], a new multi-core DFS algorithm called CNDFS with better performance than the OWCTY algorithm was presented. This technique uses a swarm approach with state coloring to perform cycle detection concurrently with state-space exploration. LTSMIN saw further improvements in 2015 including support for new modeling languages [30].

In [21,34], an FPGA was used to accelerate the exploration of a relatively small 10,000-state model, achieving a 50x speed-up compared to its software equivalent. The FPGA swarm of [16], to which this work is compared, achieved a 900x improvement over a SPIN swarm for a model of a much more substantial size (4B+ states). While this scale of improvement is unlikely for a single GPU device, the process of deployment to the FPGA is much more complex compared to the GPU. Additionally, their FPGA swarm was designed specifically for the 32-bit WP model, while Grapple can handle arbitrary Promela models.

6   Conclusions

We have presented Grapple, a new framework for highly efficient explicit-state model checking on the GPU. Grapple is based on swarm verification (SV), and its features include: a parallel swarm of internally parallel verification tasks (VTs); GPU-optimized implementations of hash functions and bitstate representation of visited states; and optimal use of GPU shared memory, thereby eliminating inter-block communication/synchronization overhead. Our experimental results show that Grapple outperforms multicore SV [25] and GPU non-SV [12] approaches, and that it uses a number of VTs similar to that required by an FPGA swarm [16].

Future work includes adding support for larger state vectors, allowing us to test Grapple with larger-scale model instances from the BEEM database [3]. We will also investigate new diversification techniques, including randomized process order and alternative NDC search strategies.

References

1. About CUDA: NVIDIA developer zone. https://developer.nvidia.com/about-cuda
2. Amazon EC2 P3 instances. https://aws.amazon.com/ec2/instance-types/p3/
3. BEEM: BEnchmarks for Explicit Model checkers-ParaDiSe. http://paradise.fi.muni.cz/beem/
4. CUDA C programming guide. https://docs.nvidia.com/cuda/cuda-c-programming-guide/index.html
5. Green 500: TOP500 supercomputer sites. https://www.top500.org/green500/
6. OpenCL technology^{TM} - intel.com. http://software.intel.com/OpenCL
7. Spin-formal verification. http://spinroot.com/
8. Alcantara, D.A.F.: Efficient hash tables on the GPU. Copyright: Copyright ProQuest, UMI Dissertations Publishing 2011. Last updated 23-01-2014; First page: n/a; M3: Ph.D. (2011)
9. Barnat, J., Bauch, P., Brim, L., Česka, M.: Designing fast LTL model checking algorithms for many-core GPUs. J. Parallel Distrib. Comput. **72**(9), 1083–1097 (2012)
10. Barnat, J., Brim, L., Ročkai, P.: Scalable multi-core LTL model-checking. In: Bošnački, D., Edelkamp, S. (eds.) SPIN 2007. LNCS, vol. 4595, pp. 187–203. Springer, Heidelberg (2007). https://doi.org/10.1007/978-3-540-73370-6_13
11. Barnat, J., Brim, L., Stříbrná, J.: Distributed LTL model-checking in SPIN. In: Dwyer, M. (ed.) SPIN 2001. LNCS, vol. 2057, pp. 200–216. Springer, Heidelberg (2001). https://doi.org/10.1007/3-540-45139-0_13
12. Bartocci, E., DeFrancisco, R., Smolka, S.A.: Towards a GPGPU-parallel SPIN model checker. In: Proceedings of the 2014 International SPIN Symposium on Model Checking of Software, pp. 87–96. ACM (2014)
13. Cassee, N., Neele, T., Wijs, A.: On the scalability of the GPUexplore explicit-state model checker. In: Proceedings of the Third Workshop on Graphs as Models (GaM 2017), Uppsala, Sweden (2017)
14. Cassee, N., Wijs, A.: Analysing the performance of GPU hash tables for state space exploration. Electron. Proc. Theor. Comput. Sci. (EPTCS) **263**, 1–15 (2017)
15. Česka, M., Pilař, P., Paoletti, N., Brim, L., Kwiatkowska, M.: PRISM-PSY: precise GPU-accelerated parameter synthesis for stochastic systems. In: Chechik, M., Raskin, J.-F. (eds.) TACAS 2016. LNCS, vol. 9636, pp. 367–384. Springer, Heidelberg (2016). https://doi.org/10.1007/978-3-662-49674-9_21
16. Cho, S., Ferdman, M., Milder, P.: FPGASwarm: high throughput model checking using FPGAs. In: 28th International Conference on Field Programmable Logic and Applications (FPL). IEEE (2018)
17. Deng, Y., Wang, B.D., Mu, S.: Taming irregular EDA applications on GPUs. In: Proceedings of the ICCAD 2009 International Conference on Computer-Aided Design, ICCAD 2009, pp. 539–546. ACM, New York (2009)
18. Edelkamp, S., Sulewski, D.: Efficient explicit-state model checking on general purpose graphics processors. In: van de Pol, J., Weber, M. (eds.) SPIN 2010. LNCS, vol. 6349, pp. 106–123. Springer, Heidelberg (2010). https://doi.org/10.1007/978-3-642-16164-3_8
19. Evangelista, S., Laarman, A., Petrucci, L., van de Pol, J.: Improved multi-core nested depth-first search. In: Chakraborty, S., Mukund, M. (eds.) ATVA 2012. LNCS, pp. 269–283. Springer, Heidelberg (2012). https://doi.org/10.1007/978-3-642-33386-6_22

20. Filippidis, I., Holzmann, G.J.: An improvement of the piggyback algorithm for parallel model checking. In: Proceedings of the 2014 International SPIN Symposium on Model Checking of Software, pp. 48–57. ACM (2014)

21. Fuess, M.E., Leeser, M., Leonard, T.: An FPGA implementation of explicit-state model checking. In: Proceedings of the 2008 16th International Symposium on Field-Programmable Custom Computing Machines, FCCM 2008, Washington, DC, USA, pp. 119–126. IEEE Computer Society (2008)

22. Harish, P., Narayanan, P.J.: Accelerating large graph algorithms on the GPU using CUDA. In: Aluru, S., Parashar, M., Badrinath, R., Prasanna, V.K. (eds.) HiPC 2007. LNCS, vol. 4873, pp. 197–208. Springer, Heidelberg (2007). https://doi.org/10.1007/978-3-540-77220-0_21

23. Holzmann, G., Bošnački, D.: The design of a multicore extension of the SPIN model checker. IEEE Trans. Softw. Eng. 33(10), 659–674 (2007)

24. Holzmann, G.J.: Parallelizing the SPIN model checker. In: Donaldson, A., Parker, D. (eds.) SPIN 2012. LNCS, vol. 7385, pp. 155–171. Springer, Heidelberg (2012). https://doi.org/10.1007/978-3-642-31759-0_12

25. Holzmann, G.J.: Cloud-based verification of concurrent software. In: Jobstmann, B., Leino, K.R.M. (eds.) VMCAI 2016. LNCS, vol. 9583, pp. 311–327. Springer, Heidelberg (2016). https://doi.org/10.1007/978-3-662-49122-5_15

26. Holzmann, G.J., Joshi, R., Groce, A.: Swarm verification. In: Proceedings of the 2008 23rd IEEE/ACM International Conference on Automated Software Engineering, ASE 2008, Washington, DC, USA, pp. 1–6. IEEE Computer Society (2008)

27. Holzmann, G.J., Joshi, R., Groce, A.: Swarm verification techniques. IEEE Trans. Softw. Eng. 37(6), 845–857 (2011)

28. Hong, S., Kim, S.K., Oguntebi, T., Olukotun, K.: Accelerating CUDA graph algorithms at maximum warp. In: Proceedings of PPoPP 2011 16th ACM Symposium on Principles and Practice of Parallel Programming, pp. 267–276 (2011)

29. Jenkins, B.: A hash function for hash table lookup. https://burtleburtle.net/bob/hash/doobs.html

30. Kant, G., Laarman, A., Meijer, J., van de Pol, J., Blom, S., van Dijk, T.: LTSmin: high-performance language-independent model checking. In: Baier, C., Tinelli, C. (eds.) TACAS 2015. LNCS, vol. 9035, pp. 692–707. Springer, Heidelberg (2015). https://doi.org/10.1007/978-3-662-46681-0_61

31. Laarman, A., van de Pol, J., Weber, M.: Multi-core LTSMIN: marrying modularity and scalability. In: Bobaru, M., Havelund, K., Holzmann, G.J., Joshi, R. (eds.) NFM 2011. LNCS, vol. 6617, pp. 506–511. Springer, Heidelberg (2011). https://doi.org/10.1007/978-3-642-20398-5_40

32. Luo, L., Wong, M., Hwu, W.: An effective GPU implementation of breadth-first search. In: Proceedings of DAC 2010 47th Design Automation Conference, DAC 2010, pp. 52–55 (2010)

33. Neele, T., Wijs, A., Bošnački, D., van de Pol, J.: Partial-order reduction for GPU model checking. In: Artho, C., Legay, A., Peled, D. (eds.) ATVA 2016. LNCS, vol. 9938, pp. 357–374. Springer, Cham (2016). https://doi.org/10.1007/978-3-319-46520-3_23

34. Tie, M.E.: Accelerating explicit state model checking on an FPGA: PHAST. Master's thesis, Northeastern University (2012)

35. Verstoep, K., Bal, H., Barnat, J., Brim, L.: Efficient large-scale model checking. In: 2009 IEEE International Symposium on Parallel Distributed Processing, IPDPS 2009, pp. 1–12, May 2009

36. Wijs, A.: GPU accelerated strong and branching bisimilarity checking. In: Baier, C., Tinelli, C. (eds.) TACAS 2015. LNCS, vol. 9035, pp. 368–383. Springer, Heidelberg (2015). https://doi.org/10.1007/978-3-662-46681-0_29

37. Wijs, A.: BFS-based model checking of linear-time properties with an application on GPUs. In: Chaudhuri, S., Farzan, A. (eds.) CAV 2016. LNCS, vol. 9780, pp. 472–493. Springer, Cham (2016). https://doi.org/10.1007/978-3-319-41540-6_26

38. Wijs, A., Bošnački, D.: GPUexplore: many-core on-the-fly state space exploration using GPUs. In: Ábrahám, E., Havelund, K. (eds.) TACAS 2014. LNCS, vol. 8413, pp. 233–247. Springer, Heidelberg (2014). https://doi.org/10.1007/978-3-642-54862-8_16

39. Wijs, A., Neele, T., Bošnački, D.: GPUexplore 2.0: unleashing GPU explicit-state model checking. In: Fitzgerald, J., Heitmeyer, C., Gnesi, S., Philippou, A. (eds.) FM 2016. LNCS, vol. 9995, pp. 694–701. Springer, Cham (2016). https://doi.org/10.1007/978-3-319-48989-6_42

40. Wu, Z., Liu, Y., Sun, J., Shi, J., Qin, S.: GPU accelerated on-the-fly reachability checking. In: 2015 20th International Conference on Engineering of Complex Computer Systems (ICECCS), pp. 100–109 (2015)

41. Xiao, S., Feng, W.C.: Inter-block GPU communication via fast barrier synchronization. In: Proceedings of the IPDPS 2010 IEEE International Symposium on Parallel Distributed Processing, pp. 1–12, April 2010

Statistical Model Checking of Complex Robotic Systems

Mohammed Foughali[1(✉)], Félix Ingrand[1], and Cristina Seceleanu[2]

[1] LAAS-CNRS, Université de Toulouse, CNRS, Toulouse, France
mfoughal@laas.fr, felix@laas.fr
[2] Mälardalen University, Västerås, Sweden
cristina.seceleanu@mdh.se

Abstract. Failure of robotic software may cause catastrophic damages. In order to establish a higher level of trust in robotic systems, formal methods are often proposed. However, their applicability to the *functional layer* of robots remains limited because of the informal nature of specifications, their complexity and size. In this paper, we formalize the robotic framework G$^{en}_o$M3 and automatically translate its components to UPPAAL-SMC, a real-time statistical model checker. We apply our approach to verify properties of interest on a real-world autonomous drone navigation that does not scale with regular UPPAAL.

1   Introduction

Although robotic software is tested, both in the field and using simulators, its lack of safety hinders the deployment of robots in costly and human-interaction missions (*e.g.* home assistants, deep space). As an example, the NASA Remote Agent Experiment had to be stopped due to a deadlock, never detected during the one-year testing phase [25]. Other examples include the autonomous vehicle *Alice* [19] and the museum guide RoboX9 [32]. Such failures are mainly due to the nature of classical, scenario-based testing, unable to provide guarantees on important properties. *Formal methods* are a promising alternative, but their use in robotics is still marginal, and varies according to the software *layers* [33]. Indeed, at the *decisional layer*, in charge of high-level decision making functions (*e.g.* planning [17]), models are often formal with complete semantics, which facilitates their formal modeling and verification [7,12]. In contrast, *functional layer* components, in charge of low-level actions involving sensors and actuators (*e.g.* localization and navigation), are developed within non formal frameworks (*e.g.* ROS [26]), which makes their *formalization* particularly challenging and costly. Furthermore, the formal modeling is non reusable (it needs to be redone whenever a component evolves) and models are not guaranteed to scale. Consequently, many previous works either focus on simple case studies (usually not deployed on real robots), resort to non realistic abstractions (*e.g.* ignoring timing constraints), or propose no alternatives to deal with scalability issues (Sect. 7).

We propose in this paper the use of formal methods to verify the functional layer of robotic systems. We focus on verification by means of model checking,

F. Biondi et al. (Eds.): SPIN 2019, LNCS 11636, pp. 114–134, 2019.
https://doi.org/10.1007/978-3-030-30923-7_7

and use statistical model checking [22] to tackle scalability issues. A particular interest is given to real-time properties, *e.g.* *schedulability* and *bounded response*, crucial in robotics (examples in Sect. 6). To tackle the abovementioned problems, we (1) formalize (Sect. 3) the robotic framework G^{en}₀M3 (Sect. 2), (2) develop automatic, sound transformation from any G^{en}₀M3 specification into UPPAAL and UPPAAL-SMC models (Sects. 4, 5) and (3) verify crucial real-time properties, while avoiding non-realistic abstractions (*e.g.* all timing constraints are considered), on a real drone application (Sect. 6). We conclude with related work (Sect. 7) and lessons learned (Sect. 8).

2   Preliminaries

2.1   G^{en}₀M3

G^{en}₀M3 [23] is a tool to specify and implement robotic functional components. Each component, in charge of a functionality, ranging from sensor control (*e.g.* laser) to more integrated computations (*e.g.* navigation), is organized as shown in Fig. 1a. For space and readability, we omit in this paper *control services* and *interruption of activities*, but the interested reader may refer to [11] for details.

A component implements the core algorithms of its functionality within *activities*, which it executes following *requests* from external *clients*. Thus, the component has a (i) *control Task* to *process* the clients requests and *report* to them accordingly and (ii) one or more *execution task(s)* to execute activities. These tasks share parameters and computed values of the component through the *Internal Data Structure* (IDS). Finally, a component provides *ports* to share data with other components.

```
1   activity MoveDistance(in double distRef :"Distance in m") {
2     doc  "Move of the given distance";
3     codel <start> mdStartEngine(in distRef, in state.position, out posRef)
          yield exec, ether;
4     codel <exec> mdGotoPosition(in speedRef, in posRef, out state, port out
          Mobile) yield pause::exec, end;
5     codel <end> mdStopEngine() yield ether wcet 1 ms;
6     task motion;};
```

Listing 1: Activity *MoveDistance*

2.1.1   Behavior

We briefly explain how a component behaves. We use the support example of activity *MoveDistance* that belongs to the component DEMO, developed for illustration purposes (listing. 1).

Activities: activities are *finite-state machines* FSM, each state called a *codel*. An activity is executed by the execution task it specifies (line 6 specifies that activity *MoveDistance* is executed by the motion task).

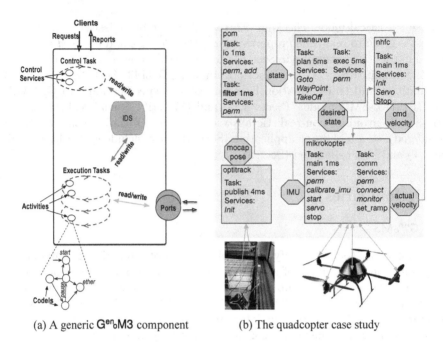

(a) A generic G^{en}$_o$M3 component   (b) The quadcopter case study

Fig. 1. Generic G^{en}$_o$M3 component & case study.

FSM: define the activity behavior through *codels* and *transitions*. A codel is a state at which a chunk of C or C++ code is executed. It specifies its arguments (*e.g.* **exec** uses the IDS fields *speedRef*, *posRef* and *state* and the port **Mobile**, line 4) and the possible *transitions* subsequent to its execution (*e.g.* **start** returns **exec** or **ether**, line 3). Taking a *pause* transition *pauses* the execution of the activity until the next *cycle* (see below) of its execution task (*e.g.* taking transition **pause::exec**, line 4, pauses the activity at codel **exec** from which it will be resumed at the next cycle of task **motion**). A codel may (optionally) specify a WCET (worst case execution time) on a given platform (*e.g.* **end** has a WCET of 1 ms, line 5). An FSM has always the codels **start** (entry point) and **ether** (end point with no code attached). When the latter is reached, the activity is *terminated* and reported to the client.

Control Task: manages requests and reports (from/to clients). When a request for an activity is received, the control task validates it and *activates* such activity (which informs the execution task in charge to execute it). Upon completion of any activity, the control task sends a report to the corresponding client.

Execution Tasks: periodic or aperiodic. With each *cycle* (triggered by period or event), an execution task runs, sequentially, all the activities it is in charge of, previously activated by the control task. The execution of an activity ends when it is paused or terminated. In the former case, the activity is resumed at the next cycle.

IDS & Concurrency: Tasks are run as parallel threads, with fine-grain concurrent access to the IDS: only the required field(s) by a codel (in its activity, run in a task) are locked when it executes and simultaneous readings are allowed.

2.1.2   Templates

G^{en}₀M3 features an automatic generation mechanism based on *templates.* A template may access all the component information (*e.g.* tasks periods, activities and their codels) and generate text files with no restrictions (examples in Sect. 5.2). There are templates that, for instance, generate component implementations for PocoLibs [1] and ROS-Comm [26] middleware. These implementation templates also collect codels execution time, which are reported (average and WCET) upon completion, and the number of occurrences of transitions in all activities (Sect. 5.2).

2.1.3   Case Study

In this paper, we consider the quadcopter in Fig. 1b. In Sect. 6, we explain how we use the components for a navigation mission. For technical details on each component (out of the scope of this paper), we refer the interested reader to [8].

```
1    process example () {
2    clock c;
3    state l0 {;10}, l1{x<=2}, l2{x<=1}; branchpoint l1_b; init l0;
4    trans  l0 -> l1 {assign x:=0; },
5           l1 -> l1_b {guard x>0; }
6           l1_b -> l0 { probability 1; },
7           l1_b -> l2 {assign x:=0; probability 2; },
8           l2 -> l0 { guard x>0; };
9    }
```

Listing 2: STA example in .xta format

2.2   UPPAAL

UPPAAL [2] is a real-time model checker. Models are based on *timed automata* (*TA*) and supported properties are mainly safety, liveness and bounded response.

Timed Automata: A TA [16] is a tuple $\langle L, l_0, X, \Sigma, E, I \rangle$ where L is a finite set of locations, $l_0 \in L$ is the initial location, X is a finite set of clocks, Σ is a finite set of actions including synchronization and internal actions, E is a finite set of edges of the form (l, g, a, φ, l'), with $l, l' \in L$, g a predicate on $\mathbb{R}^X$, $a \in \Sigma$, and φ a binary relation on $\mathbb{R}^X$, and I assigns an invariant predicate $I(l)$ to any location l.

Extending TA: In a TA, urgencies are expressed locally through invariants. For global urgencies, *e.g.* involving different TA, UTA [4] are introduced. In a UTA, when an *eager* edge (denoted ⋨) is enabled, time cannot progress and the edge must be taken (or disabled by taking another edge) immediately. TA can also be extended with data variables. We refer to UTA extended with data as DUTA. Figure 2 shows a DUTA example with two locations, *l0* (initial, denoted with an inner circle), and *l1*, and one ⚡ edge. Guards are in green, invariants in purple and operations in blue. *ex* (resp. *O*) is a Boolean expression (resp. some operations) over some variables. In this example, if the guard remains false for more than 3 time units, the DUTA *timelocks*.

UPPAAL supports a subclass of DUTA that allows (i) *urgent channels* (over which only time-constraint-free edges may synchronize), but not eager edges (example in Sect. 5) and (ii) Boolean and integer data types and functions without pointers.

2.3 UPPAAL-SMC

UPPAAL-SMC is an extension of UPPAAL based on *stochastic timed automata STA*.

Stochastic Timed Automata: An STA is a tuple $\langle TA, \mu, \gamma \rangle$ where $TA = \langle L, l_0, X, \Sigma, E, I \rangle$ is a timed automaton (Sect. 2.2), μ is the set of density delay functions $\mu_s \in L \times \mathbb{R}^X$, which can be either uniform or exponential distribution, and γ is the set of probability functions γ_s over Σ in TA.

In brief, STA extend TA with (i) density functions (on locations) and (ii) probabilities (on edges). Since we target STA as supported by UPPAAL-SMC, we show an STA example in the *.xta* format (listing 2). If the location has an associated invariant (*e.g. l1*, line 3), the density function is a uniform distribution (exponential distribution with a user-supplied rate otherwise, *e.g. 10* on *l0*, line 3). Probabilities, uniform by default, can be added using (i) a *branchpoint* (lines 5 to 7) and (ii) the keyword "probability" followed by the number of occurrences, used to compute probabilities (the probability to take the edge from *l1* to *l0* (resp. to *l2*) is 1/3 (resp. 2/3)).

Verification in UPPAAL-SMC: In this paper, we are interested in *probability evaluation*, that is estimating the probability $Pr[<= b](Op_{x \leq d}\phi)$ where b is a time bound on runs, Op is either $\Diamond$ or $\Box$ and ϕ lies within the *Weighted Metric Temporal Logic WMTL$_\leq$* [5] grammar (atomic propositions endowed with U, the *until* operator and O, the *next* operator).

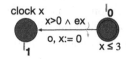

Fig. 2. A generic DUTA example

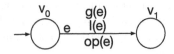

Fig. 3. A generic TTD example

3 Formalizing G^{en}₀M3

We semanticize G^{en}₀M3 components using *timed transition systems TTS* (Sect. 3.1). For readability and space, control task and aperiodic behaviors are excluded. This version preserves important mechanisms, *e.g.* concurrency, and the more complex version can be found in [11]. Since the control task is excluded, we will often refer to an execution task as simply *task*.

3.1 Timed Transition Systems

We propose a variation of TTS in [15] where (i) a dense-time model (time intervals have durations in $\mathbb{R}_{\geq 0}$ with bounds in $\mathbb{Q}_{\geq 0} \cup \infty$) is considered instead of a discrete one and (ii) more general time intervals (left- and right-open) are accepted. TTS are suitable to semanticize G^{en}₀M3. For instance, they are convenient to formalize the *global urgency constraints* (*e.g.* a codel executes *as soon as* it has the required (shared) resources, Sect. 2.1.1), as opposed to clock-based transition systems such as TA where urgencies are expressed only locally (see examples in [8]). Semantics in TTS also allowed automatic mapping to *Fiacre* in [10].

Let $\mathbb{I}$ be the set of well-formed (time) intervals. An element i of $\mathbb{I}$ can have the form: (f1) $[a, b]$ (f2) $]a, b]$ (f3) $[a, b[$ or (f4) $]a, b[$, where $a \in \mathbb{Q}_{\geq 0}$, $b \in \mathbb{Q}_{\geq 0} \cup \infty$, and with $a \leqslant b$ for f1 ($a < b$ otherwise). Interval i is thus the set of reals $x \in \mathbb{R}_{\geq 0}$ such that $a \leq x \leq b$ (f1), $a < x \leq b$ (f2), $a \leq x < b$ (f3), $a < x < b$ (f4). In any form, we say that $\downarrow i = a$ (resp. $\uparrow i = b$) is the lower (resp. upper) bound of i.

A TTS is a tuple $\langle U, S, s_0, \tau, I \rangle$ where:

- U is a finite set variables,
- S is a set of states. Each state of S is an interpretation of variables in U,
- s_0 is the initial state ($s_0 \in S$) that maps each variable in U to its initial value,
- τ is a set of transitions. Each transition $t \in \tau$ defines for every state $s \in S$ a (possibly empty) set of successors $t(s) \subseteq S$,
- $I : \tau \mapsto \mathbb{I}$ maps each transition $t \in \tau$ to a *static (time) interval* $I(t) \in \mathbb{I}$.

The semantic "meaning" of time intervals depends on the *enabledness* of transitions: if transition t is enabled at s (s is the current state of the TTS and $t(s) \neq \varnothing$) since date Δ then we can *take* t starting at date d s.t. $\Delta + \downarrow I(t) < d$ if $I(t)$ is of form (f2) or (f4) ($\Delta + \downarrow I(t) \leq d$ otherwise) and *must* take it no later than date $d' < \Delta + \uparrow I(t)$ if $I(t)$ is of form (f3) or (f4) ($d' \leq \Delta + \uparrow I(t)$ otherwise), unless it is disabled in between by taking another transition. If t is disabled, then $I(t)$ has no semantic effect (detailed semantics in [11]).

3.1.1 TTDs

A timed transition diagram TTD (inspired from [15]) is a finite directed graph with a set of vertices V and a set of edges E. The unique initial vertex is $v_0 \in V$. Each *edge* $e \in E$ is labeled with: an interval $I(e)$ (omitted if equal to $[0, \infty[$); a guard g_e (omitted if tautology); and an atomic sequence of operations op_e (omitted if has no side effects). An edge e connecting vertex v to vertex v' is denoted, interchangeably, $e \in E$ or $v \xrightarrow{e} v' \in E$. Figure 3 shows a simple generic TTD with two vertices, v_0 (initial, denoted with an incoming edge without source) and v_1, and one edge e.

3.1.2 Composition of TTDs

The parallel composition of n TTDs, $P_1, \ldots, P_n$, over a set of shared variables, U_s, results in a TTS $\{\Theta\}[\, \|_{i \in 1..n} \, P_i \,]$, where Θ gives the initial valuations of each variable in U_s and each component P_i accesses U_s and a set of local variables U_i. For detailed semantics of such TTS, we refer the interested reader to [11].

For simplicity, we stop referring to the names of edges in TTDs: $v \xrightarrow{e} v'$ (Sect. 3.1.1) will be referred to, from now on, as simply $v \rightarrow v'$, or $v \rightarrow$ (resp. $\rightarrow v'$) when the identity of v' (resp. v) is irrelevant. This is because in our G^{en}₀M3 semantics (Sect. 3.3), edges are uniquely defined through their source and target vertices.

3.2 Syntax and Syntactical Restrictions of a G^{en}₀M3 Component

3.2.1 Activity

An activity A is a tuple $\langle C_A, W_A, T_A, T_A^P \rangle$ where:
- C_A is a set of codels with at least two codels (for starting and termination, Sect. 2.1.1): $\{start_A, ether_A\} \subseteq C_A$,
- $W_A : C_A \backslash \{ether_A\} \mapsto \mathbb{Q}_{>0}$ associates to every codel its WCET (Sect. 2). The codel $ether_A$ (reserved for termination) is excluded (no code attached to it, Sect. 2.1.1),
- T_A is a set of transitions of the form $c \rightarrow c'$ (each transition is uniquely defined through its source codel c and target codel c'). We denote this relation by simply $c \rightarrow$ (or $\rightarrow c'$) when the identity of codel c (or c') is unimportant,
- $T_A^P \subseteq T_A$ is the set of *pause* transitions.

3.2.2 Task

A task T is a triple $\langle Per, \mathcal{A}, V \rangle$ where:
- $Per \in \mathbb{Q}_{>0}$ is the period,
- $\mathcal{A}$ is the non-empty set of activities T is in charge of,
- V is a set of variables.

3.2.3 Component

A component $Comp$ is a triple $\langle E, V, \mu \rangle$ where:
- E is a set of tasks,
- V is a set of variables,
- $\mu : C \mapsto \mathcal{P}(C)$ is the *conflict* function, where C is the union of all codels in all activities of all tasks in E and $\mathcal{P}(C)$ its powerset. $\mu(c)$ is the set of codels that are *in conflict* (cannot execute simultaneously) with c. If $\mu(c) = \varnothing$ then c is *thread safe* (*thread unsafe* otherwise).

3.2.4 Well-Formed Components

Well-formed components are defined by the following syntactic restrictions. For any activity A, we require that (i) each codel in $C_A \setminus \{ether_A\}$ has at least one successor in the relation defined by T_A, (ii) T_A must not include any transition whose source codel is $ether_A$ (reserved for termination), and (iii) $ether_A$ cannot be the target of a *pause* transition because the latter is for pausing while the former is for termination. These requirements can be expressed succinctly as follows:

$$\forall c \in C_A \setminus \{ether_A\} \; \exists c' \in C_A : (c \to c' \in T_A)$$
$$\forall c, c' \in C_A : (c \to c' \in T_A) \Rightarrow (c \neq ether_A)$$
$$\forall c, c' \in C_A : (c \to c' \in T_A^P) \Rightarrow (c' \neq ether_A)$$

Finally, *ether* codels are thread safe. Also, there is no conflict within the same task: any two activities A and B in the same task are executed sequentially "by construction" (one task = one thread). Therefore, we require that $\mu(c) \cap C_B = \mu(c') \cap C_A = \varnothing$ for all c in C_A and c' in C_B.

3.3 Operational Semantics of a $G^{en}_{\circ}M3$ Component

Before we go further, we need to distinguish between what the programmer specifies (reflected at the syntactical level, *e.g.* in transitions T_A, Sect. 3.2.1), and what is enforced to produce the expected behavior (*e.g. starting* and *mutual exclusion* edges, Definition 3). We present operational semantics "top-down", from component to activities.

3.3.1 Component Semantics

A component *Comp* semantics is given by the TTS $Comp = \{\Theta\}[\|_{i \in 1..n} T_i]$ where $n = | E |$ is the number of tasks in E (Sect. 3.2.3) and T_i are tasks. For each codel $c \in C$ s.t. $\mu(c) \neq \varnothing$ (Sect. 3.2.3), there is a Boolean r_c in the set of shared variables U_s (V in Sect. 3.2.3), initially false ($\Theta(r\_c) = False$ for all $r\_c \in U_s$). These variables help semanticize concurrency (Definition 3).

3.3.2 Task Semantics

The semantics of a task is given by the TTS
$T = \{\Theta\}[Tim \| M \|(\|_{A \in \mathcal{A}} A)]$ where Tim is the *timer* (Definition 1), M is the task *manager* (Definition 2), and $\|_{A \in \mathcal{A}} A$ is the composition of all activities A (Definition 3) in $\mathcal{A}$ (Sect. 3.2.2). The set of shared variables U_s (V in Sect. 3.2.2) contains: N, the set of "names" of activities to execute, sig, the period signal, and Π, the *control passing* variable. Π ranges over TTDs "names" (by abuse of notation, M is the name of the manager TTD and the name of activity A is A), N has the same type as Π excluding M, and sig is a Boolean. The initial values are $\Theta(N) = \varnothing$, $\Theta(sig) = False$, and $\Theta(\Pi) = M$ (the manager has the control when the system starts).

Definition 1 *Timer semantics. The timer semantics is given in Fig. 4.*

Changing the value of *sig* to *true* corresponds to transmitting a signal asynchronously to the *manager* (Definition 2). The time interval $[Per, Per]$ ensures that this signal is transmitted at exactly each period (each *Per* time units).

Definition 2 *Manager semantics*. *The manager semantics is given in Fig. 5.*

Vertex *wait* denotes waiting for the next period and *manage* is to execute activities, if any. The operation $\Pi := rand(N)$ gives the control to one of the activities in N (by assigning randomly an element from N to Π). The manager transits back to *wait* as soon as it has the control and N is empty.

Since $\Theta(N) = \varnothing$, no activity would ever be executed. This is because fulfilling activities requests is the role of the control task that we do not represent here. Therefore, the manager performs the operation $rrand(N)$ to initialize N randomly, over the set of activities T is in charge of; while respecting the condition $(A \in N \wedge B \in N) \Rightarrow (A \neq B)$. The operation $rrand(N)$ covers all the possible evolutions of tasks, as the resulting set of configurations of N is a superset of that obtained when a control task is present (details in [11]). Note how the guard on the edge from *wait* to *manage* does not contain the clause $\Pi = M$ because this is always true at vertex *wait* ($\Theta(\Pi) = M$ and the manager cannot lose the control at vertex *wait*).

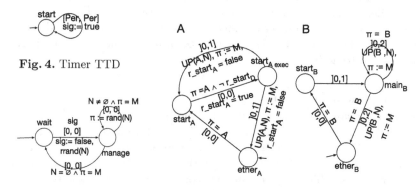

Fig. 4. Timer TTD

Fig. 5. Manager TTD   **Fig. 6.** Activities A and B in task T

Definition 3 *Activities semantics*. *The operational semantics of an activity* $\langle C_A, W_A, T_A, T_A^P \rangle$ *(Sect. 3.2.1) is given by a TTD such that:*
- *Vertices* V: *each* $c \in C_A$ *is mapped to a vertex* $c \in V$. *A vertex* $c_{exec} \in V$ *is added for each thread-unsafe codel* c ($\mu(c) \neq \varnothing$, *Sect. 3.2.3). The initial vertex* v_0 *is* $ether_A$,
- *Edges* $E = E^N \cup E^A$ *are nominal (in* E^N) *or additional (in* E^A):

  - E^N: *each transition* $c \to c'$ *in* T_A *is mapped to an edge* $c \to c'$ *(resp.* $c_{exec} \to c'$) *in* E^N *if* $\mu(c) = \varnothing$ *(resp. otherwise). We distinguish three disjoint sets of nominal edges:* $E^N = E^P \cup E^T \cup E^X$. E^P *is the set of pause*

edges that maps the set of pause transitions T^P; E^T is the set of termination edges of the form $\to$ ether and E^X the set of the remaining (execution) edges.
- *$E^A = E^S \cup E^M$ where E^S contains the starting edge ether $\to$ start and E^M the mutual exclusion edges of the form $c \to c_{exec}$ (for each thread-unsafe codel c).*

- *Time intervals I: $I(e) =]0, W_A(c)]$ iff $e \in E^N$ ($I(e) = [0, 0]$ otherwise).*
Now we define the guards and operations:
- *Each edge in $E^T \cup E^P$ is augmented with the operation $\Pi := M$ and the operation $UP(A, N)$ that removes A (the activity "name") from N,*
- *The edge in E^S, and each edge $c \to$ in $E^N \cup E^M$ such that exists an edge $\to c$ in E^P, are guarded with $\Pi = A$,*
- *Each edge $c \to$ in E^M is augmented with the operation $r\_c := true$ (see shared variables in Sect. 3.3.1).*
Finally, (i) the guard of each edge $c \to$ in E^M is conjuncted with the expression $\forall c' \in \mu(c) : \neg r\_c'$ and (ii) $r\_c := false$ is added to the operations of each edge $c_{exec} \to$ in E^N.

Nominal edges map transitions that the programmer specifies, while additional edges reflect actions enforced by G^{en}oM3 to handle starting and concurrency. Edges are uniquely defined through their source and target vertices. For activities, this can be concluded from syntax, restrictions and semantics (Sects. 3.2.1, 3.2.4 and Definition 3). For the *manager* and the *timer*, it is shown in Figs. 4 and 5.

Let us illustrate through an example how activities evolve following these semantics, and how this coincides with the behavior in Sect. 2.1.1. We consider a component with two tasks T and T'. T is in charge of two activities A and B (on which we focus) while T' is in charge of one activity D. We give the syntactical definitions of A and B:

Activity A	Activity B
- $C_A = \{start_A, ether_A\}$,	- $C_B = \{start_B, main_B, ether_B\}$,
- $W_A(start_A) = 1$,	- $W_B(start_B) = 1$, $W_B(main_B) = 2$,
- $T_A = \{start_A \to start_A,$	- $T_B = \{start_B \to main_B,$
$start_A \to ether_A\}$,	$main_B \to main_B, main_B \to ether_B\}$,
- $T_A^P = \{start_A \to start_A\}$.	- $T_B^P = \{main_B \to main_B\}$.

Now, because of the mutual exclusion between T and T', the *start* codels of A (in T) and D (in T') are in conflict: $\mu(start_A) = \{start_D\}$ (and symmetrically $\mu(start_D) = \{start_A\}$). The remaining codels are thread safe.

We apply Definition 3 to get the TTDs of A and B in Fig. 6 evolving within T (the *manager* and *timer* (generic) TTDs are given in Figs. 5 and 4, respectively). Starting an activity, from *ether* or wherever it was paused last, is subject to having the control through Π (e.g. edge $ether_B \to start_B$). At the end of execution, either by pausing (e.g. edge $main_B \to main_B$) or terminating (e.g. edge $start_A \, _{exec} \to ether_A$), the control is given back to the manager ($\Pi := M$), and the activity removes its "name" from N ($UP()$, no further execution for this activity in this cycle). Π ensures thus a *sequential* behavior within the same task, that is between the manager and each A in $\mathcal{A}$ (no two edges in two different TTDs can be enabled simultaneously).

At the codels level, outgoing edges of vertices c (the underlying codel is thread safe, *e.g.* $start_B$) and c_{exec} (otherwise, *e.g.* $start_A$) are associated with the interval $]0, W(c)]$ to reflect that the execution of a codel takes between a non-null time and its WCET. Boolean expressions involving r_c' variables, which take part in the guards on edges $c \rightarrow c_{exec}$, prevent the thread-unsafe codel c to execute if there is at least a codel in $\mu(c)$ that is already running, and the time interval $[0,0]$ allows it to execute *as soon as* this is no longer the case. For instance, the guard on $start_A \rightarrow start_A{}_{exec}$ disables this very edge (even when A has the control) as long as the activity D (in the concurrent task T', not shown here) is at vertex $start_D{}_{exec}$ (denoting the execution of $start_D$), captured through the truth of the Boolean r_start_D. Similarly, operations $r\_c := true$ on edges $c \rightarrow c_{exec}$ prevent thread-unsafe codels in $\mu(c)$ to run in parallel with c (*e.g.* $r\_start_A := true$ on $start_A \rightarrow start_A{}_{exec}$). Finally, operation $r\_c := false$ on edges of the form $c_{exec} \rightarrow$ (*e.g.* $r\_start_A := false$) allow activities with codels in conflict with c to capture the end of execution of c through the falseness of r_c.

4   Translation

TTS semantics are translated to DUTA in order to automatically map $G^{en}{}_oM3$ to UPPAAL and UPPAAL-SMC. We show the translation for activities, since it is rather straightforward for the manager and the timer (Fig. 7).

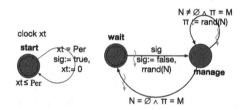

Fig. 7. DUTA translation of manager and timer

Mapping intervals into clock constraints and $\wr$ edges may lead to incorrect translations, as shown in Fig. 8 (activity B). Indeed, if B_{ta} is paused (taking $main_B \rightarrow main_B$), it will timelock after 2 time units unless it resumes the control before then (all outgoing edges from location $main_B$ are disabled). This is encountered when there is a vertex in the TTD that (i) maps a thread-safe codel and (ii) is the target of a pause edge. This problem is due to clocks evolving independently from edges enabledness in DUTA (in contrast to intervals in TTDs). We propose a generic translation for all activities.

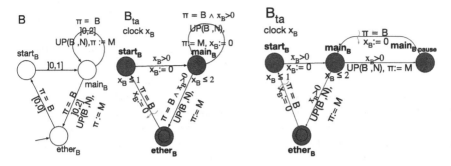

Fig. 8. Incorrect translation (activity B)   **Fig. 9.** Correct translation (activity B)

Definition 4 *Activities* A_{ta} (*DUTA*). *The DUTA translation A_{ta} of the TTD A (Definition 3), is given by the following rules:*

   - Clocks: A_{ta} has a clock x_A, whose initial valuation is zero,

   - Locations: Each vertex c in A of a thread-safe codel c s.t. there exists $\to c$ in T^P is mapped to two locations c and c_{pause}. Each remaining vertex in A is mapped to a location with the same name. Each location c that maps a vertex $c \neq ether$ of a thread-safe codel is associated with an invariant $x_A \leq \uparrow I(c \to)$ with $c \to$ any outgoing edge of c. The same invariant rule is applied to each location c_{exec},

   - Edges: - Each pause edge $c \xrightarrow{g,op} c'$ in A s.t. c' is thread safe is mapped to an edge $c \xrightarrow{x_A>0,op} c'_{pause}$, and an eager edge $c'_{pause} \xrightarrow{g,x:=0} c'$ is added.

   - Each remaining edge in A is mapped to an edge in A_{ta} with the same source and target, where: (1) intervals $[0,0]$ are mapped into $\natural$ edges, (2) each outgoing (resp. incoming) edge of a location associated with an invariant is guarded (resp. augmented) with $x_A > 0$ (resp. with $x_A := 0$), then (3) guards (resp. operations) associated with each edge result from the conjunction (resp. sequencing) of guards (resp. operations) of its TTD counterpart and the guards (resp. resets) over clocks.

These rules allow clocks to evolve unboundedly at locations c_{pause} (when the activity is paused). Resuming the activity is then equivalent to taking the edge $c_{pause} \to c$ with a clock reset to count the WCET of c starting from 0, which we may see when applying Definition 4 to activity B (Fig. 9).

Translation Soundness: DUTA models must be faithful to the $G^{en}{}_o M3$ semantics. We use weak timed bisimulation to prove that the translation is sound. Details on the proof may be found in [11].

5   Automatic Mapping

We see how the DUTA models are automatically mapped into UPPAAL and UPPAAL-SMC. In order to do so, we first present the current implementation.

Implementation: In the actual implementation (either in ROS-Comm or PocoL-ibs middleware), the set of activities to execute (N) is substituted with an array *run* of size $n = |\mathcal{A}|$ (the number of activities in the task) of *records*, starting at index 0. Each record is composed of two fields: an activity "name" m and its "status" s, that may be *requested* (r) or *idle* (d), equivalent, respectively, to $A \in N$ and $A \notin N$ in the semantics. The operation *arand*(t) initializes the status s fields of array t randomly. The variable i, initially equal to 0, ranges from 0 to n. The function *next*(t, b) browses the array t, starting from index b, and returns the index of the first element with $s = r$ ($|t|$ if such an element is not found or $b = |t|$).

The implementation of a task is then derived from its semantics as follows. For any activity A, each operation $UP(A, N)$ is replaced by $i := i + 1, i := next(run, i)$. In the manager, the guard $N \neq \varnothing$ (resp. $N = \varnothing$) is replaced by $i \neq n$ (resp. $i = n$), the operation $\Pi := rand(N)$ by $\Pi := run[i].m$, and the operation $rrand(N)$ by $arand(run), i := next(run, i)$ (in reality, the *run* array is updated by the control task, not considered in our presentation). Finally, the edge *manage* $\rightarrow$ *wait* in the manager is augmented with the operation $i := 0$. Accordingly, the implementation model of task T (Figs. 4, 5 and 6) is given in Fig. 10. Trivially, the semantics (allowing random "scheduling" of activities) is a superset of the implementation (where the order of execution of activities is predefined when initializing names fields (m) in *run*). The random scheduling at the semantics level allows to derive different implementations if needed. For DUTA, it is sufficient to apply the TTD-DUTA translation rules. Figure 11 gives the DUTA implementation of activity A (Fig. 10).

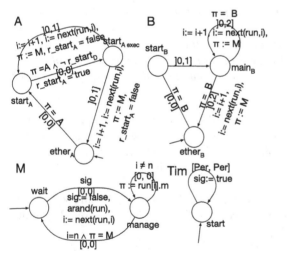
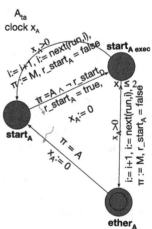

Fig. 10. TTDs in task T (implementation).

Fig. 11. DUTA (implementation) of activity A.

```
1    process A (urgent chan &exe, int[M, size_run] &pi, int[0, size_run] &i,
         CELL &run[size_run], bool &mut[size_mut]) {
2    clock x;
3    state ether, start, start_exec {x<=1}; init ether;
4    trans // behavior
5    // additional edges
6    ether -> start { guard pi = A ; sync exe!; };
7    start -> start_exec { guard pi = A && !mut[r_start_D]; sync exe!;
         assign x:= 0, mut[r_start_A]:= true; };
8    // nominal edges
9    ...
```

Listing 3: Process A (UPPAAL)

5.1 Mapping to UPPAAL

We see how to model an activity. First, we deal with urgent edges (UPPAAL only allows urgent *channels*, Sect. 2.2). We add a process *urgency* and synchronize its unique edge, over an urgent channel *exe*, with each *eager* edge in the activity (and with all eager edges in the system):

```
process Urgency(urgent chan &exe) {
state idle; init idle;
trans
         idle -> idle { sync exe?; };
}
```

Now we can model *e.g.* activity A. Listing. 3 is a partial UPPAAL model of A (only additional edges are shown). Constant $M = 0$ denotes the manager, so Π ranges over $[M, size\_run]$ (line 1) where activity names are encoded in turn as constant integers in this range. *CELL* is the record type for *run* (line 1) and *mut* is an array that facilitates implementing mutual exclusion variables (r_c becomes $mut[r\_c]$, line 1, 7).

5.2 Automatic Synthesis

We generalize the approach for automatic synthesis using the template mechanism (Sect. 2.1.2). We develop a template that generates automatically the UPPAAL model for any $G^{en}_{o}M3$ specification (made of any number of components). We show an example on how additional edges are generated for a given activity a (listing 4). The interpreter outputs everything as is, except what is enclosed in $<'$ $'>$ that it evaluates in Tcl, and in $<"$ $">$ that it evaluates and outputs the result.

In lines 3 to 7, we check each outgoing transitions of each codel (keyword yields), and append the successor to the list p if such transition is a pause. We also append the codel c to the list tu if its field *mutex*, which contains the codels c is in conflict with, is not empty. Therefore, p contains all the codels targeted by a pause and tu all thread-unsafe codels in a. At line 11, we generate the starting edge, then the mutual exclusion edges from line 12 to 20, where, for each thread-unsafe codel c, we add the guard on having the control through Π

if c is also in p (applying Definition 4 and inductively Definition 3). The task name is added to distinguish variables in different tasks.

Extending to UPPAAL-SMC: Implementation templates (Sect. 2.1.2) generate, for each transition in each activity, a line with the number of its occurrences:

```
1   <'set p [list]'>
2   <'set tu [list]'>
3   <'foreach c [$a codels] {'>
4   <'   foreach y [$c yields] {'>
5   <'      if {[$y kind] == "pause" && !($y in $p)} {lappend p $y}}'>
6   <'   if {[llength [$c mutex]]} {lappend tu $c}'>
7   <'} '>
8   ...
9   trans //behavior
10  // additional edges
11  ether-> start {guard pi_<"[$t name]"> = <"[$a name]">; sync exe!; };
12  <'foreach c in $tu {'>
13  <"[$c name]"> -> <"[$c name]">_exec {guard
14  <'   if {$c in $p} {'>
15    pi_<"[$t name]"> = <"[$a name]"> &&
16  <'   }'>!(
17  <'      foreach m [$c mutex] {'>mut[r_<"[$m name]">]
18  <'         if {$m != [lindex [$c mutex] last]} {'> || <' }'>
19  <'         }'>); sync exe!; assign x:=0, mut[r_<"[$c name]">]:= true;};
20  <'}'>
21  // nominal edges
22  ...
```

Listing 4: Generating additional edges (for an activity *a* in task *t*)

A *.proba* file is thus constructed, then passed as an argument to the UPPAAL-SMC template, together with the G$^{en}_o$M3 specification. Listing 5 shows an excerpt of the UPPAAL-SMC template. For simplicity, we only show the case where the source codel is thread safe and none of its outgoing transitions is pause or termination. Line 3 conditions adding probabilities by the existence of more than one successor. Line 5 connects the edge to a branchpoint (as shown in Sect. 5.1). Lines 6–8 generate the outgoing edges of the branchpoint and extract occurrences from the *.proba* file.

```
1   <' foreach c [$a codels] {'>
2          ...
3   <' if {[llength [$c yields]] > 1} {'>
4   <' set pr [join [list [$t name] [$a name] [$c cname] [$y cname]] /]'>
5   <"[$c name]"> -> <"[$c name]">_b {guard x>0; },
6   <' foreach y [$c yields] {'>
7   <"[$c name]">_b -> <"[$y name]"> {;probability <"[dict get $argv $pr]">;},
8   <' }}'>
9          ...
```

Listing 5: Generating probabilistic transitions (for an activity *a* in task *t*)

6   Verification Results

We use the automatically generated models (Sect. 5) to specify and verify important real-time properties on the quadcopter case study (Sect. 2.1.3). Experiments are carried out on a laptop (Intel Core i7; 16 GB of RAM). Tasks are assigned to independent cores on the hardware. Experiments, with instructions on how to reproduce them, are freely clonable from https://github.com/Mo-F/uppaal-smc-exp.

6.1   Model Checking

With UPPAAL, we get the same results as with the Fiacre template in [8]: the *stationary flight* application (excluding the component MANEUVER) scales, while the navigation application (involving all components) does not. We use UPPAAL-SMC for the latter.

6.2   Statistical Model Checking

As seen in Sect. 2, components need to receive requests from clients to run. For that, we add a client to ensure a navigation application (see below). The automatically generated UPPAAL-SMC model of the quadcopter plus the added client make 36 complex processes overall, on which we carry out the statistical verification.

6.2.1   Client

The client (Fig. 12) uses urgent channels rc_X (X is a component) to send activities requests to components, through rq_X variables. Since UPPAAL-SMC supports only broadcast channels, we guard each channel rc_X with the Boolean s_X, true only when X is ready to receive a request (which forces a rendezvous behavior). Location *hold* is for waiting an amount t between sending servoing requests (NHFC and MIKROKOPTER) and taking off (MANEUVER), as servoing must have already started before taking off (which is an important property to verify). Exponential rates are required on invariant-free locations (high rates imply a high probability to leave the location at smaller time values, but values are unimportant here because of the urgencies enforced by rc_X channels). The self-loop at location *navigate* enables, using the Boolean f, issuing a new *goto* request each time the last *goto* activity (to navigate) has ended (goal invalid, reached, or unreachable). From the same location, a request *wait* then *take_off* can be sent (to land). The client covers thus all the possible scenarios of navigation.

6.2.2   Properties of Interest

The following properties are crucial such that accidents may occur if they are not satisfied.

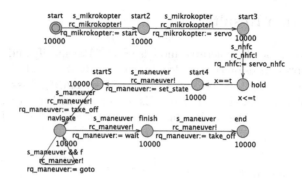

Fig. 12. UPPAAL-SMC client (quadcopter navigation).

Readiness: When requests are sent to MANEUVER, the previously requested activities from MIKROKOPTER and NHFC must have already started executing. Find the minimum value of t to satisfy this property with the highest possible probability.

Schedulability: Estimate the probability of schedulability of periodic tasks in the critical components POM, MIKROKOPTER and NHFC.

6.2.3   Verification with UPPAAL-SMC

Statistical parameters are set to a high confidence (0.98) and precision (0.005), and the runs are bounded to $b = 10s$.

Readiness: Readiness is typically a bounded response property, not supported by UPPAAL-SMC. We propose an alternative using the *Until* operator. An activity starts once its codel start begins executing, which is equivalent to reaching the location *start_exec* (since none of the codels start in this context is thread safe). Therefore, the *client* "cl" must not reach location *start4* (from which it sends requests to MANEUVER) before locations *start_exec* of each previously requested activity (*start* and *servo* (MIKROKOPTER) and *servo* in NHFC) is reached. Readiness boils down then to the conjunction of the three *Until* properties in listing 6.

```
1  ap: cl.start or cl.start2 or client.start3 or cl.hold
2  p1: ap U start_mikrokopter.start_exec
3  p2: ap U servo_mikrokopter.start_exec
4  p3: ap U servo_nhfc.start_exec
5  rp: p1 and p2 and p3
```

Listing 6: Readiness property *rp*

Note that attempting to reduce these properties to only one using the conjunction of their right terms would result in a stricter property (*e.g. start_exec* of *servo* may be left before *start_exec* of *servo_nhfc* is reached). We tune t starting from 1 ms. The highest possible probability is returned by the verifier ($\geq 99\%$ considering the precision, 0.005 ± 0.005) for all of the three properties as soon as t is equal to 8 ms. Results for *p3* for different values of t are given in Table 1.

Table 1. Analysis results for p3 (listing 6) with the query $Pr[<= b]p3$.

t (ms)	Results	Runs	Time
7	$Pr \in [0.98, 0.99]$	3279	12
8	$Pr \in [0.99, 1]$	1595	6
100	$Pr \in [0.99, 1]$	390	3

Table 2. Analysis results for schedulability (POM)

Task	Query	Results	Runs	Time
io	$Pr[<= b]vs_{io}$	$Pr \in [0, 0.01]$	390	966
filter	$Pr[<= b]vs_{filter}$	$Pr \in [0, 0.01]$	390	962

Therefore, in order to ensure a high probability of satisfying *Readiness*, t may have any value larger than 8 ms. We fix it to 1 s.

Schedulability: It is reduced to a reachability property. Indeed, it is sufficient to verify that whenever the *manager* is executing activities (at location *manage*), no new period signal is received (*sig* is false), see Fig. 7. The probability of violating this property is the lowest possible for all tasks of the critical components POM, MIKROKOPTER and NHFC ($\leq 1\%$). Examples of results on POM tasks are given in Table 2 with vs_T being the violation of schedulability of task T: $<> manager\_T.manage$ and sig_T.

6.2.4   Discussion

While we cannot verify some properties in a precise way (due to scalability issues with model checking), the results we get with UPPAAL-SMC are encouraging. We verify important properties up to a high probability, which is better than classical scenario-based testing. The verification is cost effective: around 15 min in the worst case, and a remarkably low memory consumption (less than 15 mb). Nevertheless, two main issues are encountered, besides non exhaustivity. First, though 99% is fair for this application, we generally lack precise requirements expressed probabilistically in the robotics domain. Second, the expressiveness of UPPAAL-SMC query language is limited (*e.g.* bounded response properties are not supported). While we often manage, with some artefacts, to verify closer alternatives, such artefacts need a proficiency with formal languages that robotic practitioners do not possess.

7   Related Work

Model Checking: The synchronous language ESTEREL [3] is used in some model-checking-based verification works such as [18,30,31], where the robotic specifications are either translated by hand to, or hard-coded in ESTEREL. Efforts such as [24] rely on automatic translation of *RoboChart* models into CSP [27] in order to verify real-time properties. However, RoboChart is not a robotic framework (its models are not executable on robotic platforms). That is, robotic applications, initially specified in a robotic framework, need to be modeled first in RoboChart, then translated into CSP. An attempt to formalize ROS components is developed in [13] where UPPAAL is used to verify buffer-related properties (no overflow). Only the message passing part (publisher/subscriber) is modeled, manually, and crucial bounded response properties (*e.g.* messages are delivered within a bounded amount of time), are not verified. Our work distinguishes itself across three main aspects: (i) this is the first work that fully formalizes a robotic framework for functional-layer specifications, (ii) modeling is fully automatized and (iii) only real-world applications are analyzed.

Statistical & Probabilistic Model Checking: Real-time statistical/probabilistic model checking has been used to verify systems in various domains such as communication protocols [21], railway systems [6] and decisional robotics [29]. At the functional layer of robotic systems, statistical and probabilistic model checkers are seldom used. The work presented in [14] is a notable exception. ROS graphs are formalized in an ad-hoc fashion (no operational semantics given), then, on an autonomous vehicle case study, PRISM [20] estimates the probability of finding an object in a bounded amount of time. To the best of our knowledge, our work presented here is the first that applies real-time statistical model checking to complex, concurrent functional layer, where formal models are sound and automatic. The choice of UPPAAL-SMC is motivated by the fact that the automatic translation gives us the opportunity to use regular UPPAAL and resort to UPPAAL-SMC when models do not scale.

Comparison to Our Previous Work: In our previous efforts to verify the quadcopter, model checking scaled only for the stationary flight, excluding the MANEUVER component [8,9]. This is the first work that verifies the navigation application, involving all the components, through sound and automatic bridging with UPPAAL-SMC.

8   Conclusion

We propose in this paper automatic and sound generation of formal models from robotic specifications, and obtain encouraging results on a real application. Our contributions advance the state of the art toward a correct and practical verification of robotic systems.

However, it is difficult to set the probabilities for properties because we lack this kind of requirements in robotics. We need to investigate further this problem. Moreover, the restricted query language of UPPAAL-SMC forced us to reason on alternatives using the supported operators only. For a robotic programmer, this could be discouraging since it requires a good knowledge of the tool, the query language and the underlying logic. A possible future work consists therefore in developing query-to-query transformations that are transparent to the practitioner. Finally, we are interested in verifying some hardware-related properties using SMC such as energy consumption (as in [28]).

References

1. The PocoLibs middleware. https://git.openrobots.org/projects/pocolibs
2. Behrmann, G., David, A., Larsen, K.G.: A tutorial on UPPAAL. In: Bernardo, M., Corradini, F. (eds.) SFM-RT 2004. LNCS, vol. 3185, pp. 200–236. Springer, Heidelberg (2004). https://doi.org/10.1007/978-3-540-30080-9_7
3. Berry, G.: The Esterel v5 language primer: version v5_91. Centre de mathématiques appliquées, Ecole des mines and INRIA (2000)
4. Bornot, S., Sifakis, J., Tripakis, S.: Modeling urgency in timed systems. In: de Roever, W.-P., Langmaack, H., Pnueli, A. (eds.) COMPOS 1997. LNCS, vol. 1536, pp. 103–129. Springer, Heidelberg (1998). https://doi.org/10.1007/3-540-49213-5_5
5. Bulychev, P., et al.: Monitor-based statistical model checking for weighted metric temporal logic. In: Bjørner, N., Voronkov, A. (eds.) LPAR 2012. LNCS, vol. 7180, pp. 168–182. Springer, Heidelberg (2012). https://doi.org/10.1007/978-3-642-28717-6_15
6. Cappart, Q., Limbrée, C., Schaus, P., Quilbeuf, J., Traonouez, L.M., Legay, A.,Q.: Verification of interlocking systems using statistical model checking. In: 2017 IEEE 18th International Symposium on High Assurance Systems Engineering (HASE), pp. 61–68. IEEE (2017)
7. Cimatti, A., Roveri, M., Bertoli, P.: Conformant planning via symbolic model checking and heuristic search. Artif. Intell. 159(1–2), 127–206 (2004)
8. Foughali, M.: Toward a correct-and-scalable verification of concurrent robotic systems: insights on formalisms and tools. In: International Conference on Application of Concurrency to System Design (ACSD), pp. 29–38 (2017)
9. Foughali, M., Berthomieu, B., Dal Zilio, S., Hladik, P.E., Ingrand, F., Mallet, A.: Formal verification of complex robotic systems on resource-constrained platforms. In: International Conference on Formal Methods in Software Engineering (FormaliSE), pp. 2–9 (2018)
10. Foughali, M., Berthomieu, B., Dal Zilio, S., Ingrand, F., Mallet, A.: Model checking real-time properties on the functional layer of autonomous robots. In: Ogata, K., Lawford, M., Liu, S. (eds.) ICFEM 2016. LNCS, vol. 10009, pp. 383–399. Springer, Cham (2016). https://doi.org/10.1007/978-3-319-47846-3_24
11. Foughali, M., Dal Zilio, S., Ingrand, F.: On the semantics of the GenoM3 framework. Technical report, LAAS-CNRS (2019)
12. Hähnel, D., Burgard, W., Lakemeyer, G.: GOLEX—Bridging the gap between logic (GOLOG) and a real robot. In: Herzog, O., Günter, A. (eds.) KI 1998. LNCS, vol. 1504, pp. 165–176. Springer, Heidelberg (1998). https://doi.org/10.1007/BFb0095437
13. Halder, R., Proença, J., Macedo, N., Santos, A.: Formal verification of ROS-based robotic applications using timed-automata. In: International Conference on Formal Methods in Software Engineering (FormaliSE), pp. 44–50. IEEE/ACM (2017)
14. Hazim, M.Y., Qu, H., Veres, S.M.: Testing, verification and improvements of timeliness in ROS processes. In: Alboul, L., Damian, D., Aitken, J.M.M. (eds.) TAROS 2016. LNCS (LNAI), vol. 9716, pp. 146–157. Springer, Cham (2016). https://doi.org/10.1007/978-3-319-40379-3_15
15. Henzinger, T.A., Manna, Z., Pnueli, A.: Timed transition systems. In: de Bakker, J.W., Huizing, C., de Roever, W.P., Rozenberg, G. (eds.) REX 1991. LNCS, vol. 600, pp. 226–251. Springer, Heidelberg (1992). https://doi.org/10.1007/BFb0031995

16. Henzinger, T., Nicollin, X., Sifakis, J., Yovine, S.: Symbolic model checking for real-time systems. Inf. Comput. **111**(2), 193–244 (1994)
17. Ingrand, F., Ghallab, M.: Deliberation for autonomous robots: a survey. Artif. Intell. **247**, 10–44 (2017)
18. Kim, M., Kang, K.C.: Formal construction and verification of home service robots: a case study. In: Peled, D.A., Tsay, Y.-K. (eds.) ATVA 2005. LNCS, vol. 3707, pp. 429–443. Springer, Heidelberg (2005). https://doi.org/10.1007/11562948_32
19. Kress-Gazit, H., Wongpiromsarn, T., Topcu, U.: Correct, reactive, high-level robot control. IEEE Robot. Autom. Mag. **18**(3), 65–74 (2011)
20. Kwiatkowska, M., Norman, G., Parker, D.: PRISM 4.0: verification of probabilistic real-time systems. In: Gopalakrishnan, G., Qadeer, S. (eds.) CAV 2011. LNCS, vol. 6806, pp. 585–591. Springer, Heidelberg (2011). https://doi.org/10.1007/978-3-642-22110-1_47
21. Kwiatkowska, M., Norman, G., Sproston, J.: Probabilistic model checking of deadline properties in the IEEE 1394 FireWire root contention protocol. Formal Aspects Comput. **14**, 295–318 (2003)
22. Legay, A., Delahaye, B., Bensalem, S.: Statistical model checking: an overview. In: Barringer, H., Falcone, Y., Finkbeiner, B., Havelund, K., Lee, I., Pace, G., Roşu, G., Sokolsky, O., Tillmann, N. (eds.) RV 2010. LNCS, vol. 6418, pp. 122–135. Springer, Heidelberg (2010). https://doi.org/10.1007/978-3-642-16612-9_11
23. Mallet, A., Pasteur, C., Herrb, M., Lemaignan, S., Ingrand, F.: GenoM3: building middleware-independent robotic components. In: International Conference on Robotics and Automation (ICRA), pp. 4627–4632. IEEE (2010)
24. Miyazawa, A., Ribeiro, P., Li, W., Cavalcanti, A., Timmis, J.: Automatic property checking of robotic applications. In: International Conference on Intelligent Robots and Systems (IROS), pp. 3869–3876. IEEE (2017)
25. Pecheur, C.: Verification and validation of autonomy software at NASA. Technical report, NASA Ames Research Center (2000)
26. Quigley, M., et al.: ROS: an open-source Robot Operating System. In: ICRA Workshop on Open Source Software, p. 5 (2009)
27. Roscoe, A.: Understanding Concurrent Systems. Springer, London (2010). https://doi.org/10.1007/978-1-84882-258-0
28. Seceleanu, C., Vulgarakis, A., Pettersson, P.: REMES: a resource model for embedded systems. In: International Conference on Engineering of Complex Computer Systems (ICECCS), pp. 84–94 (2009)
29. Sekizawa, T., Otsuki, F., Ito, K., Okano, K.: Behavior verification of autonomous robot vehicle in consideration of errors and sisturbances. In: International Computer Software and Applications Conference (COMPSAC), pp. 550–555 (2015)
30. Simon, D., Pissard-Gibollet, R., Arias, S.: Orccad, a framework for safe robot control design and implementation. In: National Workshop on Control Architectures of Robots: Software Approaches and Issues (CAR) (2006)
31. Sowmya, A., So, D.T.-W., Tang, W.H.: Design of a mobile robot controller using Esterel tools. Electron. Notes Theor. Comput. Sci. **65**(5), 3–10 (2002)
32. Tomatis, G., et al.: Designing a secure and robust mobile interacting robot for the long term. In: International Conference on Robotics and Automation (ICRA), pp. 4246–4251. IEEE (2003)
33. Volpe, R., Nesnas, I., Estlin, T., Mutz, D., Petras, R., Das, H.: The CLARAty architecture for robotic autonomy. In: Aerospace Conference, pp. 1–121 (2001)

STAD: Stack Trace Based Automatic Software Misconfiguration Diagnosis via Value Dependency Graph

Yuan Liu, Xi Wang$^{(\boxtimes)}$, Lintao Xian, and Zhongwen Guo

Ocean University of China, Qingdao, China
liuyuan6787@stu.ouc.edu.cn, {wangxi6696,guozhw}@ouc.edu.cn,
xianlintao@qq.com

Abstract. Configurable software allows users to customize software behaviors through configurations. However, software misconfigurations that lead to the hard-to-diagnose system crash failures could inflict enormous harm to users and should be diagnosed with a high priority. To address this problem, we present a systematic approach (and its tool implementation, called STAD) to diagnosing misconfigurations based on static code analysis. Our approach analyzes the value dependency between variables obtained by exploring the stack trace, generates the *value dependency graph* (VDG), recommends the root cause of a misconfiguration via the VDG, and utilizes the correlation between configuration options to improve our recommendation results. There are two advantages compared with existing approaches: STAD does not require software crash reproduction, and users do not need to provide configuration options and their *option read points* (i.e. the statements that access the values of configuration options). We evaluated STAD on 8 misconfigurations from JChord built on Java. STAD can successfully diagnose all misconfigurations with less average number of false positives compared with existing approaches. In addition, STAD runs in less than one minute for each misconfiguration, making debugging more efficient.

Keywords: Misconfiguration diagnosis · Value dependency graph · Configuration options · Static analysis

1 Introduction

To meet specific user demands, configurable software allows users to customize software behaviors with sufficient configuration options. However, due to the configuration complexity caused by the increase of configuration options and configuration constraints, and the lack of user domain knowledge, software misconfigurations occur frequently. In recent years, misconfigurations have become

This work is supported by the National Science Foundation of China (NSFC) under Grant No. 61827810.

© Springer Nature Switzerland AG 2019
F. Biondi et al. (Eds.): SPIN 2019, LNCS 11636, pp. 135–152, 2019.
https://doi.org/10.1007/978-3-030-30923-7_8

one of the main causes of system failures [18]. For example, in September 2018, a MongoDB server belonging to Veeam exposed hundreds of millions of records because of a misconfiguration [12]. In November 2018, a DNS server misconfiguration caused an outage of AWS in Seoul for about two hours [20]. Rabkin and Katz [13] pointed out that misconfigurations are the primary cause of Hadoop cluster failures, in terms of the number of technical support cases and support time. Similar problems have also been confirmed in other types of systems, such as storage systems [10,19], data-intensive systems [21] and cloud systems [9].

Yin et al. [19] reported that mistaken parameter values account for 70%–85% of all misconfigurations and that a significant portion of misconfigurations can cause crashes. A crash not only leads to a poor user experience, but also damages the interests of users. In addition, the magnitude of the hazard is usually positively correlated with the duration of the crash. So, misconfigurations that lead to the system crash failures should be diagnosed with a high priority.

Diagnosing such misconfigurations is very time-consuming and tedious. To deal with this predicament, many researchers are committed to developing tools to achieve automatic misconfiguration diagnosis [2,7,13,23]. However, many tools such as ConfAid [2] and ConfDiagnoser [23] assume that users can rerun the software with previously misconfigured configuration settings to reproduce crash errors. Unfortunately, manual crash reproduction is labor-intensive and tiresome [5]. And automatic crash reproduction is difficult, either introduces non-trivial performance overhead, or fails to reproduce many crashes in practice because of scalability issues, such as the *path explosion* problem [4] and the *object creation challenge* [16]. Moreover, crash reproduction can infringe on user privacy as it is likely to collect user personal configuration settings. ConfDoctor [7] can diagnose misconfigurations without program re-execution and crash reproduction, but it requires users to manually search for configuration options in a document and find *option read points* for each configuration option from the source code. Here an *option read point* (*orp*) is a statement that accesses a configuration option value. For most configurable software, their source code has at least thousands of lines and their documents have dozens of pages. Manual labor is huge and error-prone. Moreover, because of the limitations of development resources, the documents of some software cannot be updated in time, and even some software does not provide supporting documents, so that users cannot obtain accurate and complete configuration options. Locating *orps* from the source code requires professional code analysis capabilities, which is an obstacle for ordinary users.

Our approach (and its tool implementation STAD) aims to address the above-mentioned challenges. The key idea of STAD is to track the value flow of variables through the methods related to the crash stack trace, then label the variables that are directly associated with configuration options, and finally output a ranked list of suspicious configuration options that may cause the misconfiguration. STAD determines the entry statement and relevant methods for the diagnosis analysis by exploring the stack trace, and identifies the configuration options and corresponding *orps* based on the classes managing configuration APIs. Besides, STAD computes the correlation between configuration options by considering the line spacing between *orps* to improve the recommendation results. As a lightweight approach, STAD does not need crash reproduction, code instrumentation or personal configuration settings. It needs only the crash stack trace of the current misconfiguration. The contributions of this work are the following ones.

- Aimed at a new configuration convention we found, a novel approach to extracting configuration options and locating *orps* for programs is presented.
- A systematic approach to diagnosing software misconfigurations is presented. It uses only static analysis.
- An empirical evaluation on 8 misconfigurations from JChord[1] and a comparison with three existing approaches demonstrate the usefulness of our approach.

The rest of this paper is organized as follows. We first present the overview of our approach. In Sect. 3, we detail our approach. Section 4 describes the implementation. In Sect. 5, we evaluate the accuracy and efficiency of our approach, and compare our approach with three existing approaches. Section 6 discusses related work. We summarize our conclusions in Sect. 7.

2 Technique Overview

The key-value configuration structure has been adopted by many configuration mechanisms, such as the Unix system environment, the Windows Registry and the Java Properties API [14]. In this paper, we focus on this type of configuration structure. Configurable software commonly contains a base class for managing the configuration options and configuration APIs intensively [6]. We adopt this coding convention and call this class the *main configuration class* (*mcc*). Each module of software may have its own configuration class, and these classes usually inherit from the *mcc*.

Figure 1 illustrates the workflow of our technique. STAD only takes as input the crash stack trace, the source code and the name of the *mcc*. STAD first preprocesses the stack trace to obtain a sorted set of statements related to stack frames (Sect. 3.1), and identifies all configuration options and *orps* corresponding to each option (Sect. 3.2). Then, STAD analyzes the value dependency between variables to generate the value dependency graph (VDG) based on the sorted statements set, configuration options and *orps* (Sect. 3.3). Different from [15], here the VDG is a directed graph where each vertex represents a variable and a directed edge (a, b) stands for variable a depending on variable b in terms of value. Finally, STAD recommends the suspicious options by analyzing the VDG and report the ranked results to users (Sect. 3.4).

We use Java as an example to explain the technical details, but the technology can be extended to other object oriented languages that support stack trace. Besides, the configuration options are set and manipulated at the source code

---

[1] JChord: https://bitbucket.org/psl-lab/jchord/.

level [3]. The misconfiguration options reside in the source code of the application instead of the libraries. So we exclude the standard JDK library and the third-party libraries when analyzing the source code. This practice was used in several past papers [7,13].

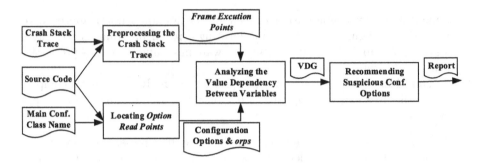

Fig. 1. Workflow of our misconfiguration diagnosis technique.

3   Systematic Diagnosis Analysis

This section describes our analysis in more detail, presenting four subanalyses in turn according to the diagnostic process.

3.1   Preprocessing the Crash Stack Trace

A crash stack trace comprises the exception type and an ordered list of crash stack frames of size of k as shown in Fig. 2. Each crash stack frame contains the fully qualified class name, the name of the method called up, as well as the file name and line number where the call happened. And each frame points to one specified execution point (usually called one *frame execution point*) which is denoted by fep_i, for $i = 1, \ldots, k$ (see Fig. 2). The fep_1 is the point where an unhandled error was detected, and the method containing fep_{j+1} called the method containing fep_j $(j = 1, \ldots, k-1)$ at the statement fep_{j+1}. We preprocess the crash stack trace according to the following two steps.

Filtering the Crash Stack Trace. We adopt two rules to filter the crash stack trace to get frames. First, we omit the first line that indicates the exception type and only extract frames that range from the second line to the end line. Second, the top several frames occasionally point to the libraries, and we exclude them by matching the full qualified class names with regular expressions. We define T as a sorted set of the frames obtained after filtering:

$$T = \{t_i, i = 1, \ldots, n\}$$

where t_i represents a crash stack frame obtained after filtering, and n is the number of these frames.

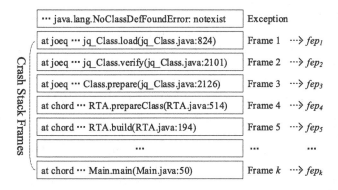

Fig. 2. A crash stack trace.

| 1. public class Config {
| 2.   public final static String **maxHeap** =
| System.getProperty("**chord.max.heap**");
| 3.   public final static String **maxStack** =
| System.getProperty("**chord.max.stack**");
| 4.   public final static String **jvmargs** =
| System.getProperty("**chord.jvmargs**");
| ...
| n. }

```
< option variable access> ::=
   < option variable name> |
   < reference>. < option variable name>

< option variable name> ::= < identifier>

< reference> ::= < expression>
...
```

Fig. 3. An example of *option variable* declarations.

Fig. 4. A segment of BNF grammar specification for accessing an *option variable*.

Locating Frame Execution Points. Each frame t_i in T can be only mapped to one *frame execution point* fep_i according to the file name and the line number in t_i. We define F as a sorted set of the $feps$ located based on T:

$$F = \{fep_i, i = 1, \ldots, n\}$$

where n is equal to the size of T.

3.2   Locating Option Read Points

ORPLocator [6] can locate the majority of *orps* in some software. However, it only considers the convention that configuration classes provide developers with methods whose names start with the prefix *get* for obtaining configuration option values. We observe that some software, for example, JChord, does not provide such *get*-methods. Developers need obtain configuration option values by accessing the variables declared in configuration classes. These variables are used to store configuration option values, and we call them the *option variables*, such as *maxHeap*, *maxStack* and *jvmargs* in Fig. 3. For the latter case, we propose a new approach to extracting configuration options and locating *orps*.

Identifying Configuration Classes. To obtain all configuration options and *orps*, we identify all configuration classes including the *mcc* and *mcc*'s subclasses. A configuration class is denoted by *conf* and all configuration classes are stored into a set called C. If a class inherits from *conf*, we also add it to C.

Searching for Option Variable Names. There is a consistent one-to-one match between each *option variable* and each configuration option. For a configuration option, STAD determines its *option variable* in accordance with two assumptions. First, each *option variable* can only be assigned once and is initialized with library functions to ensure the consistency of the option value. Second, each configuration option name is a string composed of words and separators. The separators are usually "." or "_".

We define P as the set of key-value pairs to store the *option variable* names, and in each pair the value (i.e. $M_{option}(c_i)$) is also a set of key-value pairs:

$$P = \{\langle c_i, M_{option}(c_i)\rangle, i = 1, \ldots, t\}$$

where c_i represents the name of $conf_i$ in C, in each pair of $M_{option}(c_i)$ the key represents the *option variable* name and the value represents the configuration option name, and t is the size of C.

Algorithm 1. Getting *option variable* names and option names.

Auxiliary functions:
searchAllDeclofClassFields(c): get the declaration statements of static fields in class c
getClassFieldName(stmt): get the *option variable* name from the statement *stmt*
getOptionName(stmt): get the option name from the statement *stmt*
orderPbyInheritance(): order P by key, and the base class precedes all its child classes
getSuperClass(c): get the name of the base class of class c
Global: P, C
getClassVarOptionMap()

```
 1: for each c in C do
 2:     statements ⇐ searchDeclStaticFields(c)
 3:     if statements is not null then
 4:         M_option(c) ⇐ null
 5:         for each stmt in statements do
 6:             key ⇐ getClassFieldName(stmt)
 7:             value ⇐ getOptionName(stmt)
 8:             M_option(c).put(key, value)
 9:         end for
10:         P.put(c.name, M_option(c))
11:     end if
12: end for
13: orderPbyInheritance()
14: for each p in P do
15:     superClassName ⇐ getSuperClass(p.key)
16:     if superClassName is not null then
17:         p.value ⇐ p.value ∪ P.get(superClassName)
18:     end if
19: end for
```

The algorithm for computing P is shown in Algorithm 1. We compute $M_{option}(c_i)$ based on $conf_i$ and $conf_i$'s base class because a subclass can inherit the static fields from its base class.

Locating Access Sites of Option Variables. An access site of an *option variable* is the statement where the *option variable* is accessed. Obviously, an access site of an *option variable* is an *orp*. An *option variable* can have multiple access sites. The grammar of accessing an *option variable* is depicted in Fig. 4.

As the grammar shows, an *option variable* can be accessed in two ways: by its name or with a reference. For the latter usage, we consider three cases. So we locate the access sites of an *option variable* according to the following four cases. For an access site, we use the file name and the line number to indicate an *orp*.

- As a static field, an *option variable* can be directly accessed using its name inside the *conf* where it is declared.
- The *<reference>* refers to a class name.
- The *<reference>* refers to an instance of *conf* or a method call expression that returns an instance of *conf*.
- The *<reference>* refers to an instance creation expression.

We do not consider accessing an *option variable* by the *this* or *super* keyword, because the *this* and *super* cannot access a static field in Java.

We define the collection of located results L as a set of key-value pairs, and the value (i.e. $M_{orps}(c_i)$) of each pair is also a set of key-value pairs:

$$L = \{\langle c_i, M_{orps}(c_i)\rangle, i = 1, \ldots, t\}$$

where c_i represents the name of $conf_i$ in C, in each pair of $M_{orps}(c_i)$ the key represents the *option variable* name and the value represents the corresponding *orps*, and t is the size of C.

Linking Option Read Points to Options. P has the same keys (i.e. configuration class names) with L. And for a fixed c_i, $M_{orps}(c_i)$ has the same keys (i.e. *option variable* names) with $M_{option}(c_i)$. So we can build a table mapping each *orp* to the configuration option name most directly related to it.

3.3 Analyzing the Value Dependency Between Variables

Our investigation shows that the root cause of a statement throwing a runtime error is the abnormal value of a variable in the statement. And the mistaken value of a configuration option causes the abnormal value to appear via the value dependency between variables. We determine the value dependency between variables based on the statements with assignment operations, and use the VDG to describe it.

Unlike traditional data dependency analysis, we do not try to find all possible dependencies, but make full use of stack trace to find the most relevant dependencies between variables instead of statements, which can greatly reduce the computational space. The workflow of analyzing the value dependency between variables is shown in Fig. 5.

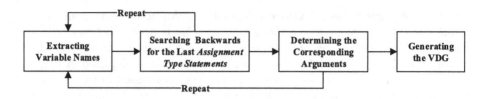

Fig. 5. Workflow of analyzing the value dependency between variables.

Extracting Variable Names from a Statement. We classify statements into *assignment type statements* and *non-assignment type statements*. The *assignment type statements* consist of assignment statements, *for-each* statements and *setter* methods call statements. We consider the *assignment type statements* as the basis of analyzing the value dependency between variables. We consider the following four cases to extract the variable names, and use the set V to store them.

First, for an assignment statement, we determine whether a basic assignment operator (i.e. "=") is included. If it contains a "=", we extract variable names from the right of "=". If it contains a compound assignment operator, such as "+=" and "/=", the left operand also impacts itself, so we extract variable names from both right and left of the compound assignment operator. Specially, for an object initialization statement, we extract the parameter from the parameter list of the constructor. Because of one or more parameters of the constructor, we need to build the correspondence between the instance variables and the parameters of the constructor in advance.

Second, for a *for-each* statement, for instance, *for (type var : array), var* is assigned by per element of *array*, so we extract the name of *array*.

Third, for a *setter* method call statement, we extract the parameter name from the parameter list of the *setter* method.

Last, for a *non-assignment type statement*, we take all variables into consideration because we can't determine which variable's value is abnormal.

After extracting a list of variable names from a statement, we remove duplicates from the list, and mark the location for each variable using a class name and a method name.

Searching Backwards for the Last Assignment Type Statement. For a variable in V, we propose Algorithm 2 to search backwards for the last *assignment type statement* of it. The statement in which the variable is extracted is denoted by *analStmt*. We search inside the method where *analStmt* is located, and use the line number to compute the distance between an *assignment type statement* and *analStmt*.

We specifically consider the situation whether *analStmt* is inside a conditional block. If *analStmt* is not inside a conditional block, we search all conditional blocks backwards because we are not sure which conditional block the program has executed; otherwise, we only search the conditional block inside which *analStmt* is and ignore the others.

Algorithm 2. Searching backwards for the last assignment type statement(s) of the variable.

Auxiliary functions:
getAllAsgmtTypeStmts(varName): get all *assignment type statements* that assign values to the variable named *varName*
getLineNum(analStmt): get the line number of the statement *analStmt*
isInDiffBlock(stmt1, stmt2): determine whether *stmt1* and *stmt2* are inside different blocks of the same conditional statement
Input: the variable name *varName* and the statement *analStmt* where the variable is located
Output: the last *assignment type statement(s)* of the variable
getAsignStmts(*varName, analStmt*)

1: *preAsgmtTypeStmts* ⇐ null
2: *allStmts* ⇐ *getAllAsgmtTypeStmts(varName)*
3: *ln* ⇐ *getLineNum(analStmt)*
4: **if** *allStmts* is not null **then**
5:    remove the elements whose line numbers are greater than *ln* from *allStmts*
6:    sort *allStmts* in descending order of line number
7:    **for** each *stmt* in *allStmts* **do**
8:       **if** *isInDiffBlock(analStmt, stmt)* **then**
9:          *allStmts.remove(stmt)*
10:      **end if**
11:   **end for**
12:   *asgmtTypeStmt* ⇐ *allStmts*[0]
13:   *preAsgmtTypeStmts.add(asgmtTypeStmt)*
14:   **for** each *stmt* in *allStmts* **do**
15:      **if** *isInDiffBlock(asgmtTypeStmt, stmt)* **then**
16:         *preAsgmtTypeStmts.add(stmt)*
17:         *asgmtTypeStmt* ⇐ *stmt*
18:      **end if**
19:   **end for**
20: **end if**
21: **return** *preAsgmtTypeStmts*

Determining the Corresponding Arguments. Since Java passes arguments by value, there is the value dependency between parameters and arguments. Given a parameter, we determine the corresponding argument by taking the following steps. First, we compute the index of the parameter in the parameter list and store the index into a set S. Second, we find the method call statement based on F. Last, we use the index to search for the argument in the argument list.

Generating the Value Dependency Graph. By integrating the previous steps, Algorithm 3 is proposed to analyze the value dependency between variables inside a method. If an *orp* is found, we add the configuration option name related to it to V and stop looking for a new *assignment type statement* for this option. For each element in V, we use E to store their value dependencies. After performing the analysis, we generate the VDG using V and E.

Algorithm 3. Intraprocedural value dependency analysis.

Auxiliary functions:
isOptionReadStmt(analStmt): get configuration option names if the statement *analStmt* is an *orp*
getVarNames(analStmt): extract variable names from the statement *analStmt*
maintainEdges(): maintain E when a new vertex is added to V
getParmIndex(varName, analStmt): get the position of the variable named *varName* in the parameter list of the statement *analStmt*
getParmIndex(varName, analStmt): is the function from Algorithm 2
Global: V, E, S, *varNameLst* (a list of variable names extracted from statements)
getValueDependencyInfo(analStmt)

```
 1: optionNames ⇐ isOptionReadStmt(analStmt)
 2: varNames ⇐ getVarNames(analStmt)
 3: if varNames is empty then
 4:    if optionNames is not empty then
 5:       V.add(optionNames)
 6:       maintainEdges(optionNames)
 7:    end if
 8:    return
 9: else
10:    V.add(varNames)
11:    varNameLst.add(varNames)
12:    if F does not contain analStmt then
13:       if optionNames is not empty then
14:          V.add(optionNames)
15:          maintainEdges(optionNames)
16:       end if
17:       maintainEdges(varNames)
18:    end if
19: end if
20: while varNameLst is not empty do
21:    stmts ⇐ getAsignStmts(varNameLst[0], analStmt)
22:    if stmts is not empty then
23:       for each stmt in stmts do
24:          maintainEdges(varNameLst[0])
25:          varNameLst.remove(varNameLst[0])
26:          getValueDependencyInfo(stmt)
27:       end for
28:    else
29:       maintainEdges(varNameLst[0])
30:       varNameLst.remove(varNameLst[0])
31:       S.put(varNameLst[0], getParmIndex(varNameLst[0], analStmt))
32:    end if
33: end while
```

Moreover, the crash stack trace usually involves multiple methods. Therefore, based on Algorithm 3, we designed Algorithm 4 which is suitable for multiple associated methods. Taking fep_1 of F as the entry statement, when S is empty or all *feps* are analyzed, Algorithm 4 ends.

A callee can be called by multiple callers, but Algorithm 4 can precisely determines the caller of a callee based on F (details in Sect. 3.1). So we consider that STAD is context-insensitive.

Algorithm 4. Interprocedural value dependency analysis.

Auxiliary functions:
$getArgumentNames(index, stmt)$: get the argument name via the parameter index
Global: F, V, E, S
mainValueDependencyAnalysis()

```
 1: for each stmt in F do
 2:     if S is not empty then
 3:         for each s in S do
 4:             edges ⇐ edges + s.key+ "," + getArgumentNames(s.value, stmt) + "@"
 5:         end for
 6:     end if
 7:     S.clear()
 8:     getValueDependencyInfo(stmt)
 9:     if S is empty then
10:         break
11:     end if
12: end for
```

3.4 Recommending Suspicious Configuration Options

The collection of variable names that are extracted from the statement fep_1 is denoted by V_1. For a vertex v_i in the VDG, the shortest path distance between v_i and V_1 is defined as:

$$d(v_i) = min(\{Distance(v_j, v_i) \mid v_i \in V, v_j \in V_1\})$$

where the $Distance(v_j, v_i)$ is used to compute the path distance from v_j to v_i. If v_j cannot reach v_i, $d(v_i)$ is infinite.

The suspicious configuration options are stored into a sorted set Ω. We use the following strategy to compute Ω.

VDG with Option Names. If there is only one configuration option name, we directly add it to Ω. If not, we first compute the shortest path distances between option names and V_1, then add these option names to Ω in ascending order of the distance.

Moreover, Zhang et al. [22] reported that there are rich correlations between configuration options. If there is a configuration correlation between option A and option B, the misconfiguration of option A may affect the access of option B. In this situation, we find that the crash stack trace is usually related to option B instead of option A. And there is a method in which both option A and option B are read. We exploit such correlations to improve our recommendation results. For each option X in Ω, we first search for the options whose $orps$ and the $orps$ of X are located inside the same methods. Then we compute the line spacing between $orps$. These two steps are easy to accomplish via the table obtained in

Sect. 3.2. Last, we append these option names to Ω in ascending order of the line spacing.

VDG Without Option Names. This situation is caused by the incomplete location of *orps*. Because during the software maintenance, developers may not centralize the new configuration options into the configuration classes for management, but instead declare the *option variables* where needed and access them. However, we find that these *option variables* are among the extracted variables that do not depend on other variables.

For the VDG, we define the sorted set V_2 as the collection of vertexes that are not starting points of directed edges. First, we compute $d(v_k)$ for each vertex v_k in V_2, remove the vertexes from V_2 whose distances are infinite, and sort V_2 in ascending order of $d(v_k)$. Then, for each vertex in V_2, we search for the declaration statement of the variable represented by the vertex, extract the option name based on the second rule described in Sect. 3.2, and add the option name into Ω. Last, similar to the first situation (i.e. VDG with Option Names), for each option in Ω, we search for the options that may have a correlation with it and add them into Ω.

4 Implementation

We implemented a tool called STAD as our technique prototype. STAD is built on Java and relies on the srcML² toolkit. The srcML toolkit supports converting the source code into an XML document. Different types of statements are identified by different XML elements. Therefore, STAD analyzes the source code by searching for and analyzing XML elements. STAD uses the XPath (version 2.0) to analyze the XML document directly and uses Graphviz³ to visualize the value dependency between variables.

5 Evaluation

To evaluate how effective and efficient is STAD in systematically diagnosing misconfigurations, we investigated the following aspects. (1) The effectiveness and time cost of STAD in extracting configuration option names and locating *option read points*. (2) The effectiveness and time cost of STAD in misconfiguration diagnosis. (3) Comparison with existing techniques on misconfiguration diagnosis.

5.1 Experimental Setup

We evaluated STAD on JChord (version 2.1) which is a program analysis platform for Java. We reproduced 8 misconfigurations listed in Table 1. The configuration option names for each error are shown in column "Erroneous Configuration Option" in Table 5. These misconfigurations are from [8] and have been used to evaluate ConfAnalyzer [13], ConfDiagnoser [23] and ConfDoctor [7].

---

² srcML: https://www.srcml.org/.
³ Graphviz: https://www.graphviz.org/.

Table 1. Misconfigurations of JChord used in the evaluation.

Error ID	Description of misconfiguration
1	No main class is specified
2	No main method in the specified class
3	Running a nonexistent analysis
4	Invalid context-sensitive analysis name
5	Printing nonexistent relations
6	Disassembling nonexistent classes
7	Invalid reflection kind
8	Wrong classpath

We ran our experiment on a laptop with Intel Core i7 6700HQ (2.6 GHz) and 8 GB physical memory, running Windows 10.

5.2 Results and Analyses

Locating Option Read Points. The configuration options provided by JChord can be got from the online document[4]. For the corresponding *orps*, two people located them from the source code and resolved the discrepancies. The number of *orps* found by two people was 209 and 214, respectively. After inspected, 209 identical *orps* were identified and we adopted these 209 *orps*. We treat a line of code as an object to be evaluated when analyzing inter-rater agreement. The Cohen Kappa score is near 0.987.

Table 2. The overall results of STAD.

Item	STAD	Documented	Documented and Found	
			#Found	%Found
Configuration options	59	60	56	93.3%
orps	211	209	203	97.1%

Accuracy. The overall results are shown in Table 2. STAD identifies 59 configuration options and 211 *orps*. For documented configuration options and *orps*, it finds 56 out of the 60 options (93.3%) and 203 out of the 209 *orps* (97.1%). The reasons why the 4 options are not identified by STAD are shown in Table 3.

Time Cost. As shown in Table 4, column "*orps*" represents the time cost of STAD in extracting configuration options and locating *orps*. The time cost is only related to the source code, so it takes 30 s for each error. This far exceeds manual identification. Note that this is a one-time effort, and it is suitable for the diagnosis of different misconfigurations of the same software.

---

[4] https://www.seas.upenn.edu/~mhnaik/chord/user_guide/properties.html.

Table 3. The reasons why options are not found by STAD.

ID	Option name	Description
1	chord.props.file	Option values are directly accessed by the Java Properties API
2	chord.args.<id>	
3	chord.ssa	Option name is changed
4	chord.print.methods	Option is removed

Table 4. Time cost of STAD (seconds).

Error ID	Stack trace	*orps*	Value dependency	Suspects	Total
1	12	30	3	10	55
2	12	30	2	10	54
3	5	30	3	3	41
4	6	30	8	1	45
5	4	30	2	3	39
6	4	30	4	3	41
7	4	30	3	4	41
8	11	30	2	6	49

Misconfiguration Diagnosis. As shown in Table 5 (Column "STAD"), STAD can diagnose all misconfigurations.

Accuracy. STAD successfully identifies the root cause of all misconfigurations. For all errors except error #8, STAD gets the root cause configuration options without false positives; for error #8, the root cause configuration option ranks second. The average number of false positives in STAD output is 0.1. For error #4[5], there are not configuration option names in the VDG and its V_2 contains four variable names, namely *format*, *key*, *ctxtKindStr* and *legalVals*. All variables except *ctxtKindStr* are parameters, and there are no declaration statements with initialization for them. The *ctxtKindStr* represents the *option variable* corresponding to the configuration option *chord.ctxt.kind*. For error #8, the option *chord.class.path* has a configuration correlation with the option *chord.main.class*, causing a crash stack trace about *chord.main.class*. So STAD firstly recommends *chord.main.class* instead of *chord.class.path*.

Time Cost. As shown in Table 4, column "Stack trace", "Value dependency" and "Suspects" represents preprocessing the crash stack trace, analyzing the value dependency between variables and recommending suspicious configuration

---

[5] all VDGs of 8 errors can be obtained from: https://www.jianguoyun.com/p/DZ3TiAwQlOmKBhiYrsMB.

Table 5. Experimental results of misconfiguration diagnosis with different techniques. Data in the column "ConfAnalyzer", "ConfDiagnoser" and "ConfDoctor" is taken from [13,23] and [7] respectively. Column "#FPs" represents the number of times a correct option was mistaken for a suspicious one.

Error ID	Erroneous Configuration Option	STAD		ConfAnalyzer		ConfDiagnoser		ConfDoctor	
		#FPs	Success	#FPs	Success	#FPs	Success	#FPs	Success
1	chord.main.class	0	Y	0	Y	0	Y	1	Y
2	chord.main.class	0	Y	0	Y	0	Y	0	Y
3	chord.run.analyses	0	Y	0	Y	16	Y	0	Y
4	chord.ctxt.kind	0	Y	2	Y	0	Y	0	Y
5	chord.print.rels	0	Y	0	Y	14	Y	0	Y
6	chord.print.classes	0	Y	0	Y	15	Y	0	Y
7	chord.reflect.kind	0	Y	2	Y	0	Y	0	Y
8	chord.class.path	1	Y	1	N	7	Y	21	Y
Ave. of FPs—Success ratio (%)		0.1	100	0.6	87.5	5.7	100	2.7	100

options respectively. Obviously, the total time cost for each misconfiguration diagnosis is less than 1 min. This is fast enough to satisfy most scenarios. If we store the results of locating *orps*, STAD can save at least half of the time for diagnosing a misconfiguration.

Comparison with Existing Techniques. We compared STAD with three existing approaches, ConfAnalyzer [13], ConfDiagnoser [23], and ConfDoctor [7]. The experimental results are shown in Table 5. ConfAnalyzer cannot pinpoint the root cause of error #8, because the option value flows into the system calls. ConfDiagnoser gives too many false positives for error #3, #5 and #6. The worst ranking for ConfDoctor is error #8 because ConfDoctor cannot capture the dependency between command line arguments and configuration options [7]. The average number of false positives in STAD is less than other approaches.

5.3   Discussion

Limitations. First, STAD is suitable for diagnosing configuration errors that can produce a stack trace. Second, as we describe in Sect. 2, STAD focuses on the key-value configuration structure. There are also some software that adopts the Spring XML configuration model. This model uses the XML elements, such as <bean> and <property>, to manage the configuration settings. Third, our implementation and experiments are restricted to Java. Fourth, we evaluated STAD on misconfigurations involving just one configuration error. Last, STAD does not consider the method calls when extracting variable names.

Threats to Validity. First, JChord may not be representative, though it has been selected as a subject program in many evaluations of papers. Second, all 8 errors are created by ConfErr [11] and they do not cover all real error types, such as compatibility errors. Thus we cannot claim the results can be generalized to an arbitrary program.

6 Related Work

The most closely related work is misconfiguration diagnosis based on program analysis. Such methods diagnose misconfigurations by identifying the statements and execution paths that are affected by configuration options via data flow analysis and control flow analysis [1,2,7,13,17,23]. ConfAnalyzer [13] builds a map between configuration options and program points by data flow and locates related options by the map and line numbers in the exception. ConfDiagnoser [23] first gets all judge statements affected by configuration options by thin slicing, then obtains an execution profile of these judge statements under a misconfiguration by program instrumentation, finally infers the root cause by comparing the execution profile with the correct profile. ConfDoctor [7] gets the set of statements affected by each configuration option via forward slicing, and obtains the set of statements affected by stack trace via backward slicing, then compares the two sets for each option, finally ranks the suspicious configuration options by computing the correlation degrees. ConfAid [2] instruments program binaries to get the causal dependencies introduced through control and data flow as the program executes, and uses these dependencies to link the erroneous behavior to specific option. SPEX [17] gets all configuration variables related to configuration options by data flow analysis, then infers configuration constraints via the data flow of these variables, finally infers the root cause based on the constraints. X-ray [1] diagnoses the misconfiguration by summarizing the performance cost of each configuration option and can diagnose misconfigurations with the abnormal performances.

There are several differences to the above techniques. First, many previous techniques employ dynamic analysis [1,2,23]. STAD adopts only static analysis, does not need users to reproduce misconfigurations, and does not depend on code instrumentation, avoiding the performance overhead. Second, manual labeling is required to determine the range and the start position of the static analysis for ConfAnalyzer [13] and SPEX [17]. STAD can automatically analyze the stack trace and define the start or end statement. Third, ConfDoctor is similar to STAD. However, ConfDoctor assumes that the configuration options are published and *orps* can be located completely by searching for option names in source code [7]. STAD can automatically extract options and locate *orps* for each option.

7 Conclusion

This paper describes STAD, a technique to diagnose misconfigurations without the crash reproduction and the manual extraction of configuration options and *orps*. STAD focuses on the misconfigurations that caused by mistaken parameter values and lead to system crashes. STAD recommends the suspicious configuration options based on the VDG and the configuration correlation between options. Unlike previous work, STAD analyzes the variables directly rather than the statements. The empirical evaluation shows that our technique is highly effective and efficient in misconfiguration diagnosis.

In future work, we plan to handle some limitations in our technique. For instance, we will analyze the method calls when we extract variables from statements. Besides, configuration constraints have a great effect on misconfiguration diagnosis, we will focus on the mining and representation of configuration constraints. We also plan to develop techniques to guide users to configure software safely to avoid some misconfigurations.

References

1. Attariyan, M., Chow, M., Flinn, J.: X-ray: automating root-cause diagnosis of performance anomalies in production software. In: Proceedings of the 10th USENIX Conference on Operating Systems Design and Implementation, OSDI 2012, pp. 307–320. USENIX Association, Berkeley (2012)
2. Attariyan, M., Flinn, J.: Automating configuration troubleshooting with dynamic information flow analysis. In: Proceedings of the 9th USENIX Conference on Operating Systems Design and Implementation, OSDI 2010, pp. 237–250. USENIX Association, Berkeley (2010)
3. Behrang, F., Cohen, M.B., Orso, A.: Users beware: preference inconsistencies ahead. In: Proceedings of the 2015 10th Joint Meeting on Foundations of Software Engineering, pp. 295–306. ACM (2015)
4. Boonstoppel, P., Cadar, C., Engler, D.: RWset: attacking path explosion in constraint-based test generation. In: Ramakrishnan, C.R., Rehof, J. (eds.) TACAS 2008. LNCS, vol. 4963, pp. 351–366. Springer, Heidelberg (2008). https://doi.org/10.1007/978-3-540-78800-3_27
5. Chen, N., Kim, S.: STAR: stack trace based automatic crash reproduction via symbolic execution. IEEE Trans. Softw. Eng. **41**(2), 198–220 (2015). https://doi.org/10.1109/TSE.2014.2363469
6. Dong, Z., Andrzejak, A., Lo, D., Costa, D.: ORPLocator: identifying read points of configuration options via static analysis. In: 2016 IEEE 27th International Symposium on Software Reliability Engineering (ISSRE), pp. 185–195, October 2016. https://doi.org/10.1109/ISSRE.2016.37
7. Dong, Z., Andrzejak, A., Shao, K.: Practical and accurate pinpointing of configuration errors using static analysis. In: 2015 IEEE International Conference on Software Maintenance and Evolution (ICSME), pp. 171–180, September 2015. https://doi.org/10.1109/ICSM.2015.7332463
8. Dong, Z., Ghanavati, M., Andrzejak, A.: Automated diagnosis of software misconfigurations based on static analysis. In: 2013 IEEE International Symposium on Software Reliability Engineering Workshops (ISSREW), pp. 162–168, November 2013. https://doi.org/10.1109/ISSREW.2013.6688897
9. Gunawi, H.S., et al.: What bugs live in the cloud? A study of 3000+ issues in cloud systems. In: Proceedings of the ACM Symposium on Cloud Computing, SOCC 2014, pp. 7:1–7:14. ACM, New York (2014). https://doi.org/10.1145/2670979.2670986
10. Jiang, W., Hu, C., Pasupathy, S., Kanevsky, A., Li, Z., Zhou, Y.: Understanding customer problem troubleshooting from storage system logs. In: Proceedings of the 7th Conference on File and Storage Technologies, FAST 2009, pp. 43–56. USENIX Association, Berkeley (2009)

11. Keller, L., Upadhyaya, P., Candea, G.: ConfErr: a tool for assessing resilience to human configuration errors. In: 2008 IEEE International Conference on Dependable Systems and Networks With FTCS and DCC (DSN), pp. 157–166, June 2008. https://doi.org/10.1109/DSN.2008.4630084
12. O'Donnell, L.: Millions of records exposed in Veeam misconfigured server (2018). https://threatpost.com/millions-of-records-exposed-in-veeam-misconfigured-server/137361/. Accessed 11 Sept 2018
13. Rabkin, A., Katz, R.: Precomputing possible configuration error diagnoses. In: Proceedings of the 2011 26th IEEE/ACM International Conference on Automated Software Engineering, ASE 2011, pp. 193–202. IEEE Computer Society, Washington (2011). https://doi.org/10.1109/ASE.2011.6100053
14. Rabkin, A., Katz, R.: Static extraction of program configuration options. In: Proceedings of the 33rd International Conference on Software Engineering, ICSE 2011, pp. 131–140. ACM, New York (2011). https://doi.org/10.1145/1985793.1985812
15. Weise, D., Crew, R.F., Ernst, M., Steensgaard, B.: Value dependence graphs: representation without taxation. In: Proceedings of the 21st ACM SIGPLAN-SIGACT Symposium on Principles of Programming Languages, pp. 297–310. ACM (1994)
16. Xiao, X., Xie, T., Tillmann, N., de Halleux, J.: Precise identification of problems for structural test generation. In: Proceedings of the 33rd International Conference on Software Engineering, ICSE 2011, pp. 611–620. ACM, New York (2011). https://doi.org/10.1145/1985793.1985876
17. Xu, T., et al.: Do not blame users for misconfigurations. In: Proceedings of the Twenty-Fourth ACM Symposium on Operating Systems Principles, SOSP 2013, pp. 244–259. ACM, New York (2013). https://doi.org/10.1145/2517349.2522727
18. Xu, T., Zhou, Y.: Systems approaches to tackling configuration errors: a survey. ACM Comput. Surv. **47**(4), 70:1–70:41 (2015). https://doi.org/10.1145/2791577
19. Yin, Z., Ma, X., Zheng, J., Zhou, Y., Bairavasundaram, L.N., Pasupathy, S.: An empirical study on configuration errors in commercial and open source systems. In: Proceedings of the Twenty-Third ACM Symposium on Operating Systems Principles, SOSP 2011, pp. 159–172. ACM, New York (2011). https://doi.org/10.1145/2043556.2043572
20. Yong-ik, L., Kim, M.: Server error in Amazon cloud network disrupts web-based services in Korea (2018). https://pulsenews.co.kr/view.php?year=2018&no=732347. Accessed 23 Nov 2018
21. Yuan, D., et al.: Simple testing can prevent most critical failures: an analysis of production failures in distributed data-intensive systems. In: Proceedings of the 11th USENIX Conference on Operating Systems Design and Implementation, OSDI 2014, pp. 249–265. USENIX Association, Berkeley (2014)
22. Zhang, J., et al.: EnCore: exploiting system environment and correlation information for misconfiguration detection. In: Proceedings of the 19th International Conference on Architectural Support for Programming Languages and Operating Systems, ASPLOS 2014, pp. 687–700. ACM, New York (2014). https://doi.org/10.1145/2541940.2541983
23. Zhang, S.: ConfDiagnoser: an automated configuration error diagnosis tool for Java software. In: 2013 35th International Conference on Software Engineering (ICSE), pp. 1438–1440, May 2013. https://doi.org/10.1109/ICSE.2013.6606737

Extracting Safe Thread Schedules from Incomplete Model Checking Results

Patrick Metzler[1]([⊠]), Neeraj Suri[1], and Georg Weissenbacher[2]

[1] Technische Universität Darmstadt, Darmstadt, Germany
patrick.metzler@posteo.net, suri@cs.tu-darmstadt.de
[2] TU Wien, Vienna, Austria
georg.weissenbacher@tuwien.ac.at

Abstract. Model checkers frequently fail to completely verify a concurrent program, even if partial-order reduction is applied. The verification engineer is left in doubt whether the program is safe and the effort towards verifying the program is wasted.

We present a technique that uses the results of such incomplete verification attempts to construct a (fair) scheduler that allows the safe execution of the partially verified concurrent program. This scheduler restricts the execution to schedules that have been proven safe (and prevents executions that were found to be erroneous). We evaluate the performance of our technique and show how it can be improved using partial-order reduction. While constraining the scheduler results in a considerable performance penalty in general, we show that in some cases our approach—somewhat surprisingly—even leads to faster executions.

1 Introduction

Automated verification of concurrent programs is inherently difficult because of exponentially large state spaces [38]. State space reductions such as partial-order reduction (POR) [10,16,17] allow a model checker to focus on a subset of all reachable states while the verification result is valid for all reachable states. However, even reduced state spaces may be intractably large [17] and corresponding programs infeasible to (automatically) verify, requiring manual intervention.

We propose a novel model checking approach for safety verification of potentially non-terminating programs with a bounded number of threads, non-deterministic scheduling, and shared memory. Our approach iteratively generates *incomplete verification results* (IVRs) to prove the safety of a program under a (semi-)deterministic scheduler. The scheduling constraints induced by an IVR

P. Metzler—Supported by the German Academic Exchange Service (DAAD).
N. Suri—Research supported in part by H2020-SU-ICT-2018-2 CONCORDIA GA 830927 and BMBF-Hessen TUD CRISP.
G. Weissenbacher—Supported by the Vienna Science and Technology Fund (WWTF) through grant VRG11-005 and the Austrian Science Fund (FWF) via the Austrian National Research Network S11403-N23 (RiSE).

© Springer Nature Switzerland AG 2019
F. Biondi et al. (Eds.): SPIN 2019, LNCS 11636, pp. 153–171, 2019.
https://doi.org/10.1007/978-3-030-30923-7_9

can be enforced by *iteratively relaxed scheduling* [29], a technique to enforce fine-grained orderings of concurrent memory events. When the scheduling constraints of an IVR are enforced, all executions (under all non-deterministic inputs) are safe, even if the underlying (operating system) scheduler is non-deterministic. Thereby, the program can be executed safely before a (potentially infeasible) complete verification result is available. Executions can still exploit concurrency and the number of memory accesses that are executed concurrently may even be increased. As the model checking problem is eased, additional programs become tractable. Furthermore, IVRs can be used to safely execute unsafe programs which are safe under at least one scheduler. E.g., instead of programming synchronization explicitly, our model checking algorithm can be used to synthesize synchronization so that all executions are safe.

We use the producer-consumer example from Fig. 1 to explain our approach. The verifier analyses an initial schedule, e.g., where thread T_1 and T_2 produce and consume in turns, and emits an IVR $\mathcal{R}_1$, guaranteeing safe executions under this schedule. With its second IVR, the verifier might verify the correctness of producing two items in a row and the scheduling constraints can be relaxed accordingly. When the verifier hits an unsafe execution (the

```
1  initially:
2    empty buffer of
       size N
3    count = 0
4    mutex = 0
5  thread T₁:
6    while true:
7      produce()
8  thread T₂:
9    while true:
10     consume()

11 produce:
12   lock(mutex)
13   if count < N:
14     put item
15     count += 1
16   unlock(mutex)
17 consume:
18   lock(mutex)
19   remove item
20   count -= 1
21   unlock(mutex)
```

Fig. 1. Producer-consumer problem with bug

consumer produces an underflow), it emits an unsafe IVR for debugging. If the verifier accomplishes to analyze all possible executions of the program, it will report the final result *partially safe*, as the program can be used safely under all inputs but unsafe executions exist. Had there been no unsafe or safe IVR, the final result would be *safe* or *unsafe*, respectively.

This paper shows how to instantiate our approach by answering these questions: 1. Which state space abstractions are suitable for iterative model checking? The abstraction should be able to represent non-terminating executions and facilitate the extraction of schedules. 2. How to formalize and represent suitable IVRs? IVRs should be as small as possible in order to allow short iterations, while they must be large enough to guarantee fully functional executions under all possible program inputs. More precisely, for every possible program input, an IVR must cover a program execution. 3. What are suitable model checking algorithms that can be adapted to produce IVRs? A suitable algorithm should easily allow to select schedules for exploration.

2   Incomplete Verification Results

2.1   Basic Definitions

A *program* P comprises a set S of states (including a distinct initial state) and a finite set $\mathcal{T}$ of threads. Each state $s \in S$ maps program counters and variables to values. We use $\mathsf{l}(s)$ to denote the program location of a state s, which comprises a local location $\mathfrak{l}_T(s)$ for each thread $T \in \mathcal{T}$. W.l.o.g. we assume the existence of a single error location that is only reachable if the program P is not safe.

A state formula ϕ is a predicate over the program variables encoding all states s in which $\phi(s)$ evaluates to true. A transition relation R relates states s and their successor states s'. Each tread T is partitioned into local transitions $R_{\mathfrak{l},\mathfrak{l}'}$ such that $\mathfrak{l} = \mathfrak{l}_T(s)$ and $\mathfrak{l}' = \mathfrak{l}_T(s')$ for all s, s' satisfying $R_{\mathfrak{l},\mathfrak{l}'}(s, s')$ and $R_{\mathfrak{l},\mathfrak{l}'}$ leaves the program locations and variables of other threads unchanged. We use $Guard(R)$ to denote a predicate encoding $\exists s' . R(s, s')$, e.g., $Guard(R_{13,14})$ is (count $<$ N) for the transition from location 13 to 14 in Fig. 1. We say that $R_{\mathfrak{l},\mathfrak{l}'}$ (or T, respectively) is *active* at location $\mathfrak{l}$ and *enabled* in a state s iff $\mathfrak{l}(s) = \mathfrak{l}$ and s satisfies $Guard(R)$. Multiple transitions of a thread T at a location can be active, but we allow only one transition R to be enabled at a given state and define $enabled_T(s) := \{R\}$ if R exists and $enabled_T(s) := \emptyset$ otherwise.

If there exist states s for which no transition of a thread T is enabled (e.g., in line 12 in Fig. 1), T may block. We assume that such locations $\mathfrak{l}_T(s)$ are (conservatively) marked by $may\text{-}block(\mathfrak{l}_T(s))$.

An *execution* is a sequence $s_0, T_1, s_1, \ldots$, where s_0 is the initial state and the states s_i and s_{i+1} in every adjacent triple (s_i, T_i, s_{i+1}) are related by the transition relation of T_i. An execution that does not reach the error location is *safe*. A *deadlock* is a state s in which no transitions are enabled. W.l.o.g. we assume that all finite executions correspond to deadlocks and are undesirable; intentionally terminating executions can be modelled using terminal locations with self-loops.

An execution τ is (strongly) *fair* if every thread T_i enabled infinitely often in τ is also scheduled infinitely often [5]. We assume that fairness is desirable and enforce it by our algorithm presented in Sect. 3. Other notions of fairness such as weak fairness can be enforced analogously.

Non-determinism can arise both through scheduling and non-deterministic transitions. A *scheduler* can resolve the former kind of non-determinism.

Definition 1 (scheduler). *A scheduler* $\zeta : (S \times \mathcal{T})^* \times S \to \mathcal{T}$ *of a program P is a function that takes an execution prefix $s_0, T_1, \ldots, T_n, s_n$ and selects a thread that is enabled at s_n, if such a thread exists. A scheduler ζ is* deadlock-free *(fair, respectively) if all executions possible under ζ are deadlock-free (fair).*

A scheduler for the program of Fig. 1, for instance, must select T_1 rather than T_2 for the prefix $s_{init}, T_1, s_1, T_1, s_2, T_1, s_3, T_2, s_4, T_2, s_5$, since at that point the lock is held by T_1 and $enabled_{T_2}(s_5) = \emptyset$.

Non-deterministic transitions are the second source of non-determinism. If $R_{\mathfrak{l},\mathfrak{l}'}$ of thread T allows multiple successor states for a state s, we presume the existence of input symbols X such that each $\iota \in X$ determines a unique successor state s' by selecting an $R^{\iota}_{\mathfrak{l},\mathfrak{l}'} \subseteq R_{\mathfrak{l},\mathfrak{l}'}$ with $R^{\iota}_{\mathfrak{l},\mathfrak{l}'}(s, s')$.

Definition 2 (input). *An input is a function $\chi : (S \times \mathcal{T})^* \to X$, which chooses an input symbol depending on the current execution prefix.*

In conjunction, an input and a scheduler render a program completely deterministic: the input χ and scheduler ζ select a transition in each step such that each adjacent triple (s_i, T_{i+1}, s_{i+1}) is uniquely determined.

For Partial Order Reduction (POR), we assume that a symmetric independence relation $\parallel$ on transitions of different threads is given, which induces an equivalence relation on executions. Two transitions R_1 and R_2 are only independent if they are from distinct threads, they are commutative at states where both R_1 and R_2 are enabled, and executing R_1 does neither enable nor disable R_2. We write $R_1 \nparallel R_2$ if R_1 and R_2 are not independent.

2.2 Requirements on Incomplete Verification Results

Our goal is to ease the verification task by producing incomplete verification results (IVRs) which prove the program safety under reduced non-determinism, i.e., only for a certain scheduler. We only allow "legitimate" restrictions of the scheduler that do not introduce deadlocks or exclude threads. Inputs must not be restricted, since this might reduce functionality and result in unhandled inputs.

Hence, we define an IVR to be a function $\mathcal{R}$ that maps execution prefixes to sets of threads, representing scheduling constraints. An IVR for the program from Fig. 1, for instance, may output $\{T_1\}$ in states with an empty buffer, meaning that only thread T_1 may be scheduled here, and $\{T_2\}$ otherwise, so that an item is produced if and only if the buffer is empty. A scheduler $\zeta_{\mathcal{R}}$ *enforces* (the scheduling constraints of) an IVR $\mathcal{R}$ if $\zeta_{\mathcal{R}}(\tau) \in \mathcal{R}(\tau)$ for all execution prefixes τ. IVR $\mathcal{R}$ *permits* all executions possible under a scheduler that enforces $\mathcal{R}$.

The remainder of this subsection discusses the requirements on useful IVRs. We define *safe, realizable, deadlock-free, fairness-admitting*, and *fair* IVRs. In the following subsection, we instantiate IVRs with abstract reachability trees (ARTs).

Safety. An IVR $\mathcal{R}$ can either expose a bug in a program or guarantee that all permitted executions are safe. Here, we are only concerned with the latter case. An IVR $\mathcal{R}$ is *safe* if all executions permitted by $\mathcal{R}$ are safe. An unsafe IVR permits an unsafe execution and is called a *counterexample*.

Completeness. To reduce the work for the model checker, a safe IVR $\mathcal{R}$ should ideally have to prove the correctness of as few executions as possible. At the same time, it should cover sufficiently many executions so that the program can be used without functional restrictions. For instance, the IVR $\mathcal{R}(\tau) := \emptyset$, for all τ, is safe but not useful, as it does not permit any execution. Consequently, $\mathcal{R}$ should permit at least one enabled transition, in all non-deadlock states, which is done by *realizable* IVRs: an IVR $\mathcal{R}$ is *realizable* if at least one scheduler that enforces $\mathcal{R}$ exists. Furthermore, an IVR should never introduce a deadlock: an IVR $\mathcal{R}$ is *deadlock-free* if all schedulers that enforce $\mathcal{R}$ are deadlock-free.

Fairness. In general, we deem only fair executions desirable. The IVR $\mathcal{R}(\tau) := \{T_1\}$, for instance, is deadlock-free for the program of Fig. 1 but useless, as no item is consumed. A deadlock-free IVR *admits fairness* if there exists a fair scheduler enforcing $\mathcal{R}$ (i.e., a fair execution of the program is possible).

If a scheduler permits both fair and unfair executions, it might be difficult to guarantee fairness at runtime. In such cases, a *fair* IVR can be used: A deadlock-free IVR $\mathcal{R}$ is *fair* if all schedulers enforcing $\mathcal{R}$ are fair.

2.3   Abstract Reachability Trees as Incomplete Verification Results

In this subsection, we instantiate the notion of IVRs using abstract reachability trees (ARTs), which underly a range of software model checking tools [9,21,23,28] and have recently been used for concurrent programs [39]. Due to the explicit representation of scheduling choices from the beginning of an execution up to an (abstract) state, ARTs are well-suited to represent IVRs. Model checking algorithms based on ARTs perform a path-wise exploration of program executions and represent the current state of the exploration using a tree in which each node v corresponds to a set of states at a program location $\mathsf{l}(v)$. These states, represented by a predicate $\phi(v)$, (safely) over-approximate the states reachable via the program path from the root of the ART (ϵ) to v. Edges expanded at v correspond to transitions starting at $\mathsf{l}(v)$. A node w may *cover* v (written $v \triangleright w$) if the states at w include all states at v ($\phi(v) \Rightarrow \phi(w)$); in this cases, v is covered (*covered*(v)) and its successors need not be further explored. (Intuitively, executions reaching v are continued from w.) Formally, an ART is defined as follows:

Definition 3 (abstract reachability tree [28,39]). *An* abstract reachability tree *(ART) is a tuple $\mathscr{A} = (V, \epsilon, \rightarrow, \triangleright)$, where $(V, \rightarrow)$ is a finite tree with root $\epsilon \in V$ and $\triangleright \subseteq V \times V$ is a covering relation. Nodes v are labeled with global control locations and state formulas, written $\mathsf{l}(v)$ and $\phi(v)$, respectively. Edges $(v, w) \in \rightarrow$ are labeled with a thread and a transition, written $v \xrightarrow{T,R} w$.*

Intuitively, an ART $\mathscr{A}$ is *well-labeled* [28] if $\mathscr{A}$'s $\rightarrow$-edges represent the transitions of the program and edges $v \triangleright w$ indicate that all states modeled by node v are also modeled by node w. Formally, $\mathscr{A}$ is well-labeled if for every edge $v \xrightarrow{T,R_{\mathsf{l},\mathsf{l}'}} w$ in $\mathscr{A}$ we have that (i) $\phi(\epsilon)$ represents the initial state, (ii) $\phi(v)(s) \wedge R_{\mathsf{l},\mathsf{l}'}(s,s') \Rightarrow \phi(w)(s')$ and $\mathsf{l}_T(v) = \mathsf{l}$ and $\mathsf{l}_T(w) = \mathsf{l}'$, and (iii) for every v, w with $v \triangleright w$, $\phi(v) \Rightarrow \phi(w)$ and $\neg covered(w)$.

An incomplete ART $\mathscr{A}_{p-c}$ for the producer-consumer problem of Fig. 1 is shown on the right. Nodes show the state formulas and edges are labeled with the thread and statement corresponding to the transition.

ART-Induced Schedulers. A well-labeled ART $\mathscr{A}$ directly corresponds to an IVR $\mathcal{R}_\mathscr{A}$ that simulates an execution by traversing $\mathscr{A}$. We define $\mathcal{R}_\mathscr{A}$ as follows: Let $\tau = s_0, T_1, s_1, \ldots, s_n$ be an execution prefix. If $\mathscr{A}$ contains no path that corresponds to τ, $\mathcal{R}_\mathscr{A}$ leaves the schedules for this execution unconstrained. Otherwise, let v_n be the last node of the path in $\mathscr{A}$ that corresponds to τ. $\mathcal{R}_\mathscr{A}$ permits exactly those threads that are expanded at v_n (or at w if v_n is covered by some node w). E.g., the execution prefix $\tau = s_0, T_1, s_1$ corresponds to the path from ϵ to v_1 in $\mathscr{A}_{p-c}$. As only T_1 is expanded at v_1, $\mathcal{R}_{\mathscr{A}\,p-c}$ allows only $\{T_1\}$ after τ.

Safety. An ART is *safe* if whenever $\mathfrak{l}_T(v)$ is the error location then $\phi(v) = \textit{false}$. As only safe executions may correspond to a path in a safe ART (cf. Theorem 3.3 of [39]), $\mathcal{R}_\mathscr{A}$ is a safe IVR.

Completeness. In order to derive a deadlock-free IVR from a well-labeled ART $\mathscr{A}$, we have to fully expand at least one thread T at each node v that represents reachable states (where T is fully expanded at v if v has an outgoing edge for every active transition of T at $\mathfrak{l}_T(v)$). However, there may exist reachable states s represented by $\phi(v)$ for which no action of T is enabled (i.e., $\mathit{enabled}_T(s) = \emptyset$). If T is the only thread expanded at v, $\mathcal{R}_\mathscr{A}$ is not realizable. This situation can arise for locations $\mathfrak{l}$ at which T may block (marked with $\mathit{may\text{-}block}(\mathfrak{l}_T)$).

Consequently, whenever $\mathit{may\text{-}block}(\mathfrak{l}_T(v))$ in a *deadlock-free* ART $\mathscr{A}$, we require that $\phi(v)$ is strong enough to entail that the transitions R of T expanded at v (or at the node covering v, respectively) are enabled (i.e., $\phi(v) \Rightarrow \mathit{Guard}(R)$). For instance, $\phi(v_1)$ in the ART shown above proves the enabledness of T_1 at v_1, as $\phi(v_1) \Rightarrow \mathsf{mutex} = 0$ and $\mathsf{lock(mutex)}$ is enabled if $\mathsf{mutex} = 0$.

Lemma 1. *If an ART $\mathscr{A}$ is deadlock-free, $\mathcal{R}_\mathscr{A}$ is a deadlock-free IVR.*

Fairness. IVRs derived from deadlock-free ARTs do not necessarily admit fairness if the underlying ART contains cycles (across $\triangleright$ and $\rightarrow$ edges) that represent unfair executions. In order to make sure a deadlock-free ART *admits fairness* we implement a scheduler that allows $\mathscr{A}$ to schedule each thread infinitely often (whenever it is enabled infinitely often) by requiring that every $(\triangleright \cup \rightarrow)$-cycle is "fair", defined as follows.

Definition 4 (ART admitting fairness). *A deadlock-free ART $\mathscr{A} = (V, \epsilon, \rightarrow, \triangleright)$ admits fairness if every $(\triangleright \cup \rightarrow)$-cycle contains, for every thread T that is enabled at a node of the cycle, a node v such that T is expanded at v.*

Lemma 2. *If an ART $\mathscr{A}$ admits fairness, $\mathcal{R}_\mathscr{A}$ is an IVR that admits fairness.*

Note that the expansion of a thread T at a node in a cycle does not guarantee that the transition is part of the cycle. A slight modification of the fairness condition for ARTs leads to a sufficient condition for ARTs as fair IVRs, as the following definition and lemma show. The difference in the fairness condition is that all enabled threads are expanded *within* each $(\triangleright \cup \rightarrow)$-cycle c, which we denote by $\mathit{fair}(c)$. The $(\triangleright \cup \rightarrow)$-cycle shown on the right, for instance, is fair.

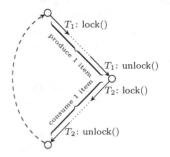

Algorithm 1 Part 1: Iterative IMPACT for concurrent programs: main procedure (based on [39])

input	: Program with threads $\mathcal{T}$
intermediate outputs:	fair ARTs $\mathscr{A}_1 \subseteq \mathscr{A}_2 \subseteq \ldots \subseteq \mathscr{A}_n$ and unsafe ARTs
output	: safe, partially safe, or unsafe

```
    Data: 𝒜 = (V, ε, →, ▷) := ({ε}, ε, ∅, ∅),        17  Function Iteration()
          W := {ε}, I := {}                             18      W := New_Schedule_Start()
1   Function Main()                                     19      if W = ∅ then
2       while true do                                   20          return no progress
3           status := Iteration()                       21      while W ≠ ∅ do
4           if status = no progress then                22          select and remove v from W
5               break                                   23          Close(v)
6           else if status = counterexample             24          if v not covered then
                then                                     25              status := Refine (v)
7               yield 𝒜 as an unsafe IVR                26              if status = counterexample then
8           else                                        27                  return counterexample
9               𝒜' := Remove_Error_Paths(𝒜)             28              status := Check_Enabledness(v)
10              yield 𝒜' as a safe IVR                  29              if status = no progress then
11      if 𝒜 is safe then                               30                  return no progress
12          return safe                                 31              Expand (v)
13      else if Remove_Error_Paths(𝒜)                   32      return progress
            admits fairness then
14          return partially-safe
15      else
16          return unsafe
```

Definition 5 (fair ART). A deadlock-free ART $\mathscr{A} = (V, \epsilon, \rightarrow, \triangleright)$ is fair if $fair(c)$ holds for every $(\triangleright \cup \rightarrow)$-cycle c.

Lemma 3 (fairness). For all fair ARTs $\mathscr{A}$, $\mathcal{R}_{\mathscr{A}}$ is a fair IVR.

Given an ART $\mathscr{A}$ that admits fairness, one can generate a fair ART $\mathscr{A}'$ such that $\mathcal{R}_{\mathscr{A}}$ permits all executions permitted by $\mathcal{R}_{\mathscr{A}'}$.

3 Iterative Model Checking

A suitable algorithm for our framework must generate fair IVRs. We use model checking based on ARTs (cf. Sect. 2.3), which allows us to check infinite executions and explicitly represent scheduling. Nevertheless, other program analysis techniques such as symbolic execution are also suitable to generate IVRs. In particular, our algorithm (Algorithm 1 parts 1 and 2) constitutes an iterative extension of the IMPACT algorithm [28] for concurrent programs [39]. We chose IMPACT as a base for our algorithm because it has an available implementation for multi-threaded programs, which we use to evaluate our approach in Sect. 5.

IMPACT generates an ART by path-wise unwinding the transitions of a program. Once an error location is reached at a node v, IMPACT checks whether the path π from the ART's root to v corresponds to a feasible execution. If this is the case, a property violation is reported; otherwise, the node labeling is strengthened via interpolation. Thereby, a well-labeled ART is maintained. Once the ART is complete, its node labeling provides a safety proof for the program.

Algorithm 1 Part 2: Iterative IMPACT for concurrent programs

---

continued:
1 **Function** Check_Enabledness(v)
2      $\pi := v_0 \xrightarrow{T_1, R_1} v_1 \ldots \xrightarrow{T_n, R_n} v_n$ §
         § path from ϵ to v
3   **if** *not may-block*$(\mathsf{l}v_{n-1})T\_n$ **then**
4   **return** *progress*
5   **if** $R_1 \wedge \ldots \wedge R_{n-1} \wedge \neg Guard(R_n)$ *is unsat* **then**
6          $\phi(v) := \phi(v) \wedge Guard(R_n)$
7   **else**
8   **return** Backtrack(v)
9 **Function** Close(v)
10   **for** *all uncovered nodes w that have been created before v* **do**
11   **if** $\mathsf{l}(w) = \mathsf{l}(v) \wedge (\phi(v) \Rightarrow \phi(w))$ §
             § $\wedge \forall c \in C_{\mathscr{A}}(v, w). fair(c)$
             then
12             $\triangleright := \triangleright \cup \{(v, w)\}$
13             $\triangleright := \triangleright \setminus \{(x, y) : v \rightsquigarrow y\}$
14   **for** T *with* $v \xrightarrow{T} v'$ §
                 § *and not* $w \xrightarrow{T} w'$ **do**
15   add (v, T) to I

16 **Function** Backtrack(v)
17     $\pi := v_0 \xrightarrow{T_1, R_1} v_1 \ldots \xrightarrow{T_n, R_n} v_n$ §
         § path from ϵ to v
18     $i := n - 1$
19   **while** $i \geq 0$ **do**
20   **if** $\exists T, v'_i. v_i \xrightarrow{T} v'_i \notin \mathscr{A}$ §
             § $\wedge (\texttt{Skip}(v_i, T) = false)$
             then
21   add $v_i \xrightarrow{T} v'_i$ to $\mathscr{A}$
22             $W := W \cup \{v'_i\}$
23   prune $\xrightarrow{T_{i+2}, R_{i+2}} v_{i+3} \ldots$ §
                 § $\ldots \xrightarrow{T_n, R_n} v_n$ from $\mathscr{A}$
24             $\phi(v_{i+1}) := false$
25   **return** *progress*
26         $i := i - 1$
27   **return** *no progress*
28
29 **Function** Expand(v)
30     $T := \texttt{Schedule\_Thread}(v)$
31   Expand_Thread (T, v)

In each iteration, our extended algorithm yields an IVR which is either unsafe (a counterexample) or fair (can be used as scheduling constraints). If the algorithm terminates, it outputs "safe", "partially safe", or "unsafe", depending on whether the program is safe under all, some, or no schedulers. Procedure *Main()* repeatedly calls *Iteration()* (line 3), which, intuitively, corresponds to an execution of the original algorithm of [39] under a deterministic scheduler. *Iteration()* (potentially) extends the ART $\mathscr{A}$. If no progress is made ($\mathscr{A}$ is unchanged), the algorithm terminates (lines 12, 14, and 16). Otherwise, an intermediate output is yielded: either $\mathscr{A}$ as an intermediate output (line 7) or $\mathscr{A}$ with all previously found counterexamples removed, i.e., the largest fair ART that is a subgraph of $\mathscr{A}$, denoted by *Remove_Error_Paths()*.

Iteration() maintains a work list W of nodes v to be explored via *Close(v)* (Algorithm 1 part 2), which tries to find (as in [39]) a node that covers v. In addition to the covering check of [39], we check fairness, where $C_{\mathscr{A}}(v, w)$ denotes all cycles that would be closed by adding the edge $v \triangleright w$ (line 11 of Algorithm 1 part 2). If such a node w is found, any thread T that is expanded at v but not at w (line 14 of Algorithm 1 part 2) must not be skipped at w by POR. Instead of expanding T instantaneously at w (as in [39]), which would explore another schedule, T is added to the set I so that it can be explored in a subsequent iteration. If no covering node for v is found, v is refined, which returns *counterexample* if v has a feasible error path (line 25). Otherwise (line 28), *Check_Enabledness()* (Algorithm 1 part 2) performs a deadlock check by testing whether the last action that leads to v is enabled in all states represented by the predecessor node. If not, deadlock-freedom is not guaranteed and *Backtrack()* tries to find a substitute node where exploration can continue.

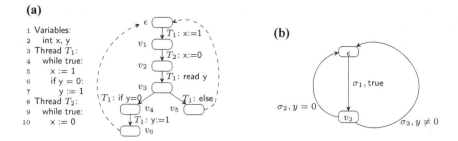

Fig. 2. (a) Section paths. (b) A program schedule

The deterministic scheduler of *Iteration()* is controlled by *New_Schedule_-Start()* and *Schedule_Thread()*. The former selects a set of initial nodes for the exploration (line 18 of Algorithm 1 part 1); the latter decides which thread to expand at a given node (line 30 of Algorithm 1 part 2). We use a simple heuristic that selects the first (in breadth-first order) node which is not yet fully expanded and use a round-robin scheduler for *Schedule_Thread* that switches to the next thread once a back jump occurs (e.g., the end of a loop body is reached). Additionally, *Schedule_Thread* returns only threads that are necessary to expand at the given node after POR (cf. *Skip()* [39]). More elaborate heuristics are conceivable but out of the scope of this paper.

The correctness of Algorithm 1 w.r.t. safety follows from the correctness of [28] and [39]. Additionally, Algorithm 1 is also fair:

Lemma 4 (fairness of Algorithm 1). *Any safe ART $\mathscr{A}$ generated by Algorithm 1 is fair.*

4   Partial-Order Reduction

A naive enforcement of the context switches at the relevant nodes of a safe IVR $\mathcal{R}_{\mathscr{A}}$ would result in a strictly sequential execution of the transitions, foiling any benefits of concurrency. To enable parallel executions, we introduce *program schedules* that relax the scheduling constraints by means of partial-order reduction (POR). Note that this application of POR concerns the enforcement of scheduling constraints and occurs in addition to POR applied by our model checking algorithm when constructing an ART (cf. Sect. 3). Nevertheless, dependency information that is used for POR during model checking can be reused so that redundant computations are avoided.

The goal is to permit the parallel execution of independent transitions (in different threads) whose order does not affect the outcome of the execution represented by $\mathscr{A}$ (i.e., the resulting traces are Mazurkiewicz-equivalent). Using traditional POR to construct such scheduling constraints poses two challenges: 1. Executions may be infinite, but we need a finite representation of scheduling constraints. 2. The control flow of an execution may be unpredictable, i.e., it is a priori unclear which scheduling constraints will apply. We solve issue 1 by partitioning ARTs into *sections* and associate a finite schedule with every section. To address issue 2, we require that sections do not contain branchings (control flow and non-deterministic transitions).

Consider the program and corresponding ART in Fig. 2a. The if-statement of T_1 is modeled as a separate read transition followed by a branching at node v_3. We define three section paths $\pi_1 := \epsilon \to v_1 \to v_2 \to v_3$, $\pi_2 := v_3 \to v_4 \to v_6 \to \epsilon$, and $\pi_3 := v_3 \to v_5 \to \epsilon$. After π_1 has been executed, a scheduler can distinguish the cases $y = 0$ and $y \neq 0$ and schedule π_2 or π_3 accordingly.

Formally, a *section path* $v_1 \xrightarrow{R_1} \dots \xrightarrow{R_n} v_{n+1}$ corresponds to a branching-free path in an ART whose first transition may be guarded. A section path follows $\to_{\mathscr{A}}$ edges, skipping covering edges $\rhd$. The *section schedule* of a section path describes the Mazurkiewicz equivalence class of the contained transitions and is defined as the smallest partial order $\sigma = (V_\sigma, \to_\sigma)$ such that $V_\sigma = \{e_1, \dots, e_n\}$ and $\to_\sigma \supseteq \{(e_i, e_j) : i < j \land R_i \nparallel R_j\}$, where $e_i, 1 \leq i \leq n$ is the occurrence of transition R_i at position i. The section schedule of π_1 is $(\{e_1, e_2, e_3\}, \{(e_1, e_2), (e_1, e_3)\})$ with $e_1 \triangleq T_1 : \texttt{x:=1}$, $e_2 \triangleq T_2 : \texttt{x:=0}$, and $e_3 \triangleq T_1 : \texttt{read y}$.

A *program schedule* Σ comprises several section schedules. Σ is a labeled graph $(V_\Sigma, \to_\Sigma)$. Each node $v \in V_\Sigma$ is the start of a section path π in $\mathscr{A}$. Each edge is labeled with the section schedule of π and the guard $Guard(R)$ of the first transition R in π. As $\mathscr{A}$ is deadlock-free, there exists a thread T which is fully expanded at v in $\mathscr{A}$ and we require that Σ likewise has outgoing edges at v labeled with T for each transition of T at v. Figure 2b shows a program schedule for our example program.

A scheduler can enforce the scheduling constraints of a program schedule by picking a section schedule that matches the current execution prefix and scheduling an event whose predecessors (according to the section schedule) have already been executed. Hence, all independent events in a section can be executed concurrently without synchronization. All events of a section schedule have to appear before the first event of the next section schedule, so that the states reached between sections correspond to nodes of the program schedule.

A program schedule of an ART $\mathscr{A}$ that admits fairness permits exactly those executions that correspond to a path in $\mathscr{A}$ (modulo Mazurkiewicz equivalence). In particular, as Mazurkiewicz equivalence preserves safety properties [17], only safe executions are permitted.

Lemma 5 (correctness). *Let $\mathscr{A}$ be an ART that admits fairness and Σ a program schedule for $\mathscr{A}$. All program executions induced by Σ are equivalent to an execution that corresponds to a path in $\mathscr{A}$.*

5   Evaluation

In five case studies, we evaluate our iterative model checking algorithm and scheduling based on IVRs. We use the IMPARA model checker [39], as it is the only available implementation of model checking for non-terminating, multi-threaded programs based on a forward analysis on ARTs we have found. IMPARA uses lazy abstraction with interpolants based on weakest preconditions. We extend the tool by implementing our algorithm presented in Sect. 3. IMPARA accepts C programs as inputs, however, some language features are not supported and we have rewritten programs accordingly.[1] We refer to the (non-iterative) IMPARA tool as IMPARA-C (for complete verification) and to our extension of Impara with iterative model checking as IMPARA-IMC.

Based on the ARTs constructed by IMPARA, program schedules are generated automatically and encoded as vector clocks. We instrument the benchmark programs with a call-back to a specially designed user space scheduler directly before and after each access to a global variable. The result is a multi-threaded program that executes concurrent memory accesses according to a given program schedule. All experiments have been executed on a 4-core Intel Core i5-6500 CPU at 3.2 GHz. We report median values averaged over five runs.

5.1 Infeasible Complete Verification

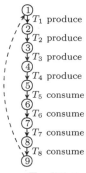

Even for a moderate number of threads, complete verification, i.e., verification of a program under all possible schedules and inputs, may be infeasible. In particular, IMPARA-C times out (after 72 h) on a corrected variant of the producer consumer problem (Fig. 1) with four producers and four consumers. IMPARA-IMC produces the first IVR $\mathcal{R}_1$ after 4:29:53 h. A simplification of $\mathcal{R}_1$ is depicted on the right; it covers all executions in which the threads appear to execute their loop bodies atomically in the order $T_1, T_2, \ldots, T_8$. While the main bottleneck for IMPARA-C is state explosion and finding many coverings for different schedules, we observe that the main issue to produce $\mathcal{R}_1$ is to find a single covering that comprises all threads, i.e., to find a fair cycle.

The subsequent IVRs $\mathcal{R}_2, \ldots, \mathcal{R}_8$ are found much faster than the first IVR, after 19:31, 12:3, 6:13, 28:0, 9:25, 8:27, and 8:40 min. We stop the model checker after eight IVRs. According to our implementation of New_Schedule_Start() in Algorithm 1, IVR $\mathcal{R}_i$ permits, in addition to all executions permitted by $\mathcal{R}_{i-1}$, those executions in which the threads appear in the order $T_i, T_1, \ldots, T_{i-1}, T_{i+1}, \ldots, T_8$. Hence, $\mathcal{R}_8$ gives the scheduler more freedom than $\mathcal{R}_1$, which may result in a better execution performance, e.g., because a producer which has its item available earlier does not have to wait for all previous producers.

---

[1] E.g., Pthread mutexes, some uses of the address-of operator, and reuse of the same function by several threads are not supported. We solve these issues by rewriting our benchmark programs so that IMPARA handles them correctly and their intuitive semantics is not changed. We will publish our modifications to IMPARA, including two bug fixes.

5.2 Deadlocks

A common issue with multi-threaded programs are deadlocks, which may occur when multiple mutexes are acquired in a wrong order, as in the program on

```
1 Thread T₁:
2   while true:
3     lock(mutex1)
4     lock(mutex2)
5     execute_critical_section()
6     unlock(mutex2)
7     unlock(mutex1)
```

```
8  Thread T₂:
9    while true:
10     lock(mutex2)
11     lock(mutex1)
12     execute_critical_section()
13     unlock(mutex2)
14     unlock(mutex1)
```

the right, in which two threads use two mutexes to protect their critical sections. A deadlock is reached, e.g., when T_2 acquires mutex2 directly after T_1 has acquired mutex1. A monolithic verification approach would try to verify one or more executions and, as soon as a deadlock is found, report the execution that leads to the deadlock as a counterexample. With manual intervention, this counterexample can be inspected in order to identify and fix the bug.

In contrast, IMPARA-IMC logs both safe and unsafe IVRs. The first IVR found in this example covers all executions in which Threads 1 and 2 execute their loop bodies in turns, with Thread 1 beginning. As expected, executing the program with enforcing the first program schedule never leads to a deadlock. Executing the uninstrumented program (without scheduling constraints) leads to a deadlock after only a few hundred loop iterations. Hence, IMC enables to safely use the program deadlock-free and without manual intervention.

5.3 Race Conditions Through Erroneous Synchronization

```
1 Threads
2   T₁: while true: produce()
3   T₂: while true: produce()
4   T₃: while true: consume()
5   T₄: while true: consume()
```

```
6  produce:
7    if buffer_is_not_full():
8      lock()
9      assert buffer_is_not_full()
10     add_item()
11     unlock()
```

```
12 consume:
13   if buffer_is_not_empty():
14     lock()
15     assert buffer_is_not_empty()
16     remove_item()
17     unlock()
```

The above program shows a variant of the producer-consumer problem with two producers and two consumers which uses erroneous synchronization: both the produce and consume check the amount of free space without acquiring the mutex first. For example, a buffer underflow occurs if the buffer contains only one item and the two consumers concurrently find that the buffer is not empty; although the buffer becomes empty after the first consumer has removed the last item, the second consumer tries to remove another item.

The first IVR found by IMPARA-IMC is depicted simplified on the right. The simplification merges all individual edges of a procedure into a single edge, which is possible as IMPARA-IMC does not apply context switches inside of procedures during the first iteration. Since both procedures appear to be executed atomically, no assertion violation is found during the first iteration. We ran the

program with a program schedule corresponding to the first IVR. As expected, we have not observed any assertion violations.

5.4 Declarative Synchronization

Figure 3 shows an extension of a benchmark used in [15], which is a simplified extract of the multi-threaded Frangipani file system. The program uses a time-varying mutex: depending on the current value of the busy bit, a disk block is protected by m_busy or m_inode. We want to evaluate whether we can use IMPARA-IMC to generate safe program schedules even if all mutexes are (intentionally) removed from the program.

```
 1 Variables:              8 Thread T1:            18 Thread T2:           24 Thread T3:
 2   int block             9   while true:         19   while true:        25   while true:
 3   boolean busy         10     lock(m_inode)     20     lock(m_busy)      26     lock(m_inode)
 4   boolean inode        11     if not inode:     21     if not busy:      27     lock(m_busy)
 5   mutex m_inode        12       lock(m_busy)    22       block := 0      28     inode := false
 6   mutex m_busy         13       busy := true    23     unlock (m_busy)   29     busy := false
 7 Initially: inode = busy 14       unlock(m_busy)                         30     unlock(m_inode)
                          15       inode := true                          31     unlock(m_busy)
                          16     block := 1
                          17     unlock(m_inode)
```

Fig. 3. The file system benchmark

```
 1 Thread T1:                10 Thread T2:            17 Thread T3:
 2   while true:             11   while true:         18   while true:
 3     if not inode:         12     if not busy:      19     atomic−begin
 4       busy := true        13       atomic−begin    20     assume inode = busy
 5       inode := true       14       assume not busy 21     inode := false
 6     atomic−begin          15       block := 0      22     busy := false
 7     assume inode and busy 16       atomic−end      23     atomic−end
 8     block := 1
 9     atomic−end
```

Fig. 4. The file system benchmark with synchronization constraints in assume statements

For this purpose, we use a variant of the file system benchmark where all mutexes are removed and synchronization constraints are declared as assume statements, shown in Fig. 4. It is sufficient to assure for T_1 that the block is written only if it is allocated, i.e., both inode and busy are true. For T_2, it is sufficient to assure that the block is only reset if it is not busy, i.e., busy = false. Finally, for T_3, it is necessary to assure that the block is deallocated only if it is already deallocated or fully allocated, i.e., inode = busy.

Running IMPARA-IMC on the file system benchmark without mutexes yields a first program schedule that schedules T_1, T_2, T_3 repeatedly in this order, according to our simple heuristic for an initial IVR. However, although all executions permitted by this schedule are fair, the if-condition of T_2 always evaluates to false and T_2 never performs useful work. To obtain a more useful schedule, we inform the model checker

```
 1 Thread T2':
 2   while true:
 3     atomic−begin
 4     assume not busy
 5     block := 0
 6     atomic−end
```

that the (omitted) else-branch of Thread T_2 is not useful. We encode this information by inserting else: assume false. After simplifying the code, we obtain T_2' as depicted on the right. For the updated code, IMPARA-IMC yields a first scheduler that schedules T_3 before T_2 before T_1, so that all threads perform useful work.

5.5 Performance

Table 1 shows the performance impact of enforcing IVRs on several correct programs. Each program is model-checked once until the first IVR (IMPARA-IMC) and once completely (IMPARA-C). As a baseline, the program is run without schedule enforcement (unconstrained). The first IVR is enforced without (Opt0), and with optimizations (Opt1, Opt2). Opt1 applies POR and omits operations on synchronization objects (mutexes, barriers).[2] Opt2 uses, in addition to Opt1, longer section schedules (by replicating a section eight times) and stronger partial-order reduction that identifies independent accesses to distinct indices of an array. Additionally, for the producer-consumer benchmark, we apply a compiler-like optimization, removing and reordering events to reduce the number of constraints.[3] Both Opt1 and Opt2 enable the concurrent execution of more memory accesses, e.g., because the beginning of a critical section can already be executed before a thread arrives at a constrained access that has to wait. The schedules for each benchmark (Opt0–Opt2) are obtained from the first IVR. As all benchmarks use unbounded loops, we measure the execution time performance by counting useful (i.e., with a successful concurrent access such as a produced item) loop iterations and terminating the execution after 2 s.

Table 1. Experimental results (to: timeout, rounded to full seconds). Performance is measured in number of useful (e.g., with a successful concurrent access such as a produced item) loop iterations within a time limit of 2 s.

Benchmark	Model checking		Performance (higher is better)			
	Time 1st IVR	IMPARA-C	Opt0	Opt1	Opt2	Unconstr
prod.-cons. 1p 1c	**2 m 0 s**	to (72 h)	4 864 489	7 466 093	**11 370 258**	8 199 202
prod.-cons. 2p 2c	**23 m 47 s**	to (72 h)	3 400 187	5 959 041	8 428 598	**11 643 208**
prod.-cons. 4p 4c	**4 h 29 m 53 s**	to (72 h)	1 327 063	2 576 695	3 676 876	**7 210 796**
double lock 1 ms	0 s	0 s	1 845	1 834	**3 217**	1 797
file system	0 s	0 s	3 667	4 877 035	6 705 672	**23 822 129**
barrier	1 s	4 m 14 s	1 238 720	8 285 228	**14 586 849**	1 077 907

We use the producer-consumer implementation (with correct synchronization and buffer size 1000) from SV-COMP [1] (stack_safe), modified with an

---

[2] As enforcing an IVR is redundant to synchronization over existing mutexes and barriers, omitting them is safe.

[3] Opt2 follows a general algorithm, however we do not automate our implementation of Opt2, as it would be a large effort to implement compiler optimizations. Our implementation of Opt1 is automated.

unbounded loop and with 1, 2, and 4 producers and consumers. The double lock benchmark is a corrected version (lock operations in T_2 reversed) of the dead-lock benchmark (Sect. 5.2), where the critical section is simulated by sleeping for 1 ms; the uncorrected version reached a deadlock after only 172 loop iterations. The file system benchmark from SV-COMP (time_var_mutex_safe) is extended with a third thread and again with unbounded loops as in Sect. 5.4. The barrier benchmark uses two barriers to implement ring communication between threads.

As the model checking columns of Table 1 show, IMPARA-IMC finds the first IVR often much faster than or at least as fast as it takes IMPARA-C for complete model checking; it can produce an IVR even for our largest benchmarks, where IMPARA-C times out. For a buffer size of 5, IMPARA-C can verify the producer-consumer benchmark even with eight threads but again, IMPARA-IMC is considerably faster in finding the first IVR. Subsequent IVRs were generated considerably faster than the first IVR, which might be caused by caching of facts in the model checker.

Somewhat surprisingly, some benchmarks are slower when executed unconstrained. We conjecture that this is caused by more memory accesses being executed in parallel under Opt2. In all but one cases, Opt2 is considerably faster than Opt1, which is considerably faster than Opt0. The highest overhead is observed for the file system benchmark, where Opt2 is about 3.5 times slower than the unconstrained execution. We conjecture that the high overhead here stems from an unequal distribution of loop iterations among threads, when executed unconstrained: the loop body of T_2 was executed nearly 100 times more frequently than T_1, while it is shorter and probably faster. Opt0–Opt2 execute all threads nearly balanced. In addition to the Pthread barriers used in the barrier benchmark, we tried a variant with busy waiting barriers, where the unconstrained execution showed a performance of 13 567 135, which is still slower than Opt2. When the buffer size of the producer-consumer benchmark with eight threads is reduced to 5, the performance of unconstrained executions decreases to 3 240 136 compared to 3 392 111 with Opt2.

Even in repeated executions of the experiment, the unconstrained variant of double lock showed only "starving" executions in the sense that the second thread was never able to acquire the mutexes before the timeout of 2 s. Hence, the constrained executions improve on the operating system scheduler in terms of a balanced execution of all threads.

In order to compare to the enforcement of *input-covering schedules* [7] (explained in Sect. 6), we measure the overhead of our scheduler implementation on the pfscan benchmark used there. Pfscan is a parallel implementation of grep and uses 1 producer and 2 consumer threads to distribute tasks, consisting of reading and searching a file for a given query. As input, we use 8 files with 100 MB of random content each. We evaluate 4 different schedules[4], which show an overhead between 3% and 10% (with Opt2). Hence, IVRs can perform much better than input-covering schedules (60% overhead reported in [7]).

---

[4] As IMPARA cannot handle several features used by pfscan (such as condition variables, structs, and standard output), we manually generate initial IVRs.

6 Related Work

Unbounded model checking [18,20,32,39] is a technique to verify the correctness of potentially non-terminating programs. In our setting, we deploy algorithms that use abstract reachability trees (ARTs) [21,28,39] to represent the already explored state space and schedules, and perform this exploration in a forward manner. Instead of discarding an ART after an unsuccessful attempt to verify a program, we use the ART to extract safe schedules.

Conditional model checking [8] reuses arbitrary intermediate verification results. In contrast to our approach, they are not guaranteed to prove the safety of a program that is functional under all inputs and does not enforce the preconditions (e.g., scheduling constraints) of the intermediate result.

Context bounding [31,35,36] eases the model checking problem by bounding the number of context switches. It is limited to finite executions and unlike our approach, does not enforce schedules at runtime.

Automated fence insertion [2,3,13,24,26] transforms a program that is safe under sequential consistency to a program that is also safe under weaker memory models. While the amount of non-determinism in the ordering of events is reduced, non-determinism due to scheduling can not be influenced. Synchronization synthesis [19] inserts synchronization primitives in order to prevent incorrect executions, but may introduce deadlocks.

Deterministic multi-threading (DMT) [4,6,7,11,12,27,30,34] reduces non-determinism due to scheduling in multi-threaded programs. Schedules are chosen dynamically, depending on the explicit input, and can not be enforced by a model checker. Nevertheless, there are combinations with model checking [11] and instances which schedule based on previously recorded executions [12].

We are aware of only one DMT approach that supports symbolic inputs [7]. Similar to our *sections*, *bounded epochs* describe infinite schedules as permutations of finite schedules. Via symbolic execution, an *input-covering* set of schedules is generated, which contains a schedule for each permutation of bounded epochs. As all permutations need to be analyzed (even if they are infeasible), state space explosion through concurrency is only partially avoided; indeed, the experimental evaluation shows that the analysis is infeasible even for five threads when the program has many such permutations. In contrast, we do not require race-freedom, use model checking, sections may contain multiple threads, omit infeasible schedules, and allow a safe execution from the first schedule on, i.e., an IVR can be considerably smaller than an input-covering set of schedules.

Deterministic concurrency requires a program to be deterministic regardless of scheduling. In [37], a deterministic variant of a concurrent program is synthesized based on constraints on conflicts learned by abstract interpretation. In contrast to DMT, symbolic inputs are supported, however no verification of general safety properties is done and the degree of non-determinism is not adjustable, in contrast to IVRs.

Sequentialized programs [14, 22, 25, 32, 33, 36] emulate the semantics of a multi-threaded program, allowing tools for sequential programs to be used. The amount of possible schedules is either not reduced at all or similar to context bounding.

7 Conclusion

We present a formal framework for using IVRs to extract safe schedules. We state why it is legitimate to constrain scheduling (in contrast to inputs) and formulate general requirements on model checkers in our framework. We instantiate our framework with the IMPACT model checking algorithm and find in our evaluation that it can be used to 1. model check programs that are intractable for monolithic model checkers, 2. safely execute a program, given an IVR, even if there exist unsafe executions, 3. synthesize synchronization via assume statements, and 4. guarantee fair executions. A drawback of enforcing IVRs is a potential execution time overhead, however, in several cases, constrained executions turned out to be even faster than unconstrained executions.

References

1. Benchmark suite of the competition on software verification (SV-COMP). https://github.com/sosy-lab/sv-benchmarks
2. Abdulla, P.A., Atig, M.F., Chen, Y.-F., Leonardsson, C., Rezine, A.: Counter-example guided fence insertion under TSO. In: Flanagan, C., König, B. (eds.) TACAS 2012. LNCS, vol. 7214, pp. 204–219. Springer, Heidelberg (2012). https://doi.org/10.1007/978-3-642-28756-5_15
3. Abdulla, P.A., Atig, M.F., Chen, Y.-F., Leonardsson, C., Rezine, A.: MEMORAX, a precise and sound tool for automatic fence insertion under TSO. In: Piterman, N., Smolka, S.A. (eds.) TACAS 2013. LNCS, vol. 7795, pp. 530–536. Springer, Heidelberg (2013). https://doi.org/10.1007/978-3-642-36742-7_37
4. Aviram, A., Weng, S., Hu, S., Ford, B.: Efficient system-enforced deterministic parallelism. In: OSDI. USENIX Association (2010)
5. Baier, C., Katoen, J.P.: Principles of Model Checking. MIT Press, Cambridge (2008)
6. Bergan, T., Anderson, O., Devietti, J., Ceze, L., Grossman, D.: CoreDet: a compiler and runtime system for deterministic multithreaded execution. In: ASPLOS. ACM (2010)
7. Bergan, T., Ceze, L., Grossman, D.: Input-covering schedules for multithreaded programs. In: OOPSLA (2013)
8. Beyer, D., Henzinger, T.A., Keremoglu, M.E., Wendler, P.: Conditional model checking: a technique to pass information between verifiers. In: FSE. ACM (2012)
9. Beyer, D., Keremoglu, M.E.: CPACHECKER: a tool for configurable software verification. In: Gopalakrishnan, G., Qadeer, S. (eds.) CAV 2011. LNCS, vol. 6806, pp. 184–190. Springer, Heidelberg (2011). https://doi.org/10.1007/978-3-642-22110-1_16
10. Clarke, E.M., Grumberg, O., Minea, M., Peled, D.: State space reduction using partial order techniques. STTT 2(3), 279–287 (1999)

11. Cui, H., et al.: Parrot: a practical runtime for deterministic, stable, and reliable threads. In: SOSP. ACM (2013)

12. Cui, H., Wu, J., Gallagher, J., Guo, H., Yang, J.: Efficient deterministic multi-threading through schedule relaxation. In: SOSP. ACM (2011)

13. Fang, X., Lee, J., Midkiff, S.P.: Automatic fence insertion for shared memory multiprocessing. In: ICS. ACM (2003)

14. Fischer, B., Inverso, O., Parlato, G.: CSeq: a concurrency pre-processor for sequential C verification tools. In: ASE. IEEE (2013)

15. Flanagan, C., Freund, S.N., Qadeer, S.: Thread-modular verification for shared-memory programs. In: Le Métayer, D. (ed.) ESOP 2002. LNCS, vol. 2305, pp. 262–277. Springer, Heidelberg (2002). https://doi.org/10.1007/3-540-45927-8_19

16. Flanagan, C., Godefroid, P.: Dynamic partial-order reduction for model checking software. In: POPL. ACM (2005)

17. Godefroid, P. (ed.): Partial-Order Methods for the Verification of Concurrent Systems - An Approach to the State-Explosion Problem. LNCS, vol. 1032. Springer, Heidelberg (1996). https://doi.org/10.1007/3-540-60761-7

18. Günther, H., Laarman, A., Sokolova, A., Weissenbacher, G.: Dynamic reductions for model checking concurrent software. In: Bouajjani, A., Monniaux, D. (eds.) VMCAI 2017. LNCS, vol. 10145, pp. 246–265. Springer, Cham (2017). https://doi.org/10.1007/978-3-319-52234-0_14

19. Gupta, A., Henzinger, T.A., Radhakrishna, A., Samanta, R., Tarrach, T.: Succinct representation of concurrent trace sets. In: POPL. ACM (2015)

20. Henzinger, T.A., Jhala, R., Majumdar, R.: Race checking by context inference. In: PLDI. ACM (2004)

21. Henzinger, T.A., Jhala, R., Majumdar, R., Sutre, G.: Lazy abstraction. In: POPL, pp. 58–70. ACM (2002)

22. Inverso, O., Tomasco, E., Fischer, B., La Torre, S., Parlato, G.: Bounded model checking of multi-threaded C programs via lazy sequentialization. In: Biere, A., Bloem, R. (eds.) CAV 2014. LNCS, vol. 8559, pp. 585–602. Springer, Cham (2014). https://doi.org/10.1007/978-3-319-08867-9_39

23. Kroening, D., Weissenbacher, G.: Interpolation-based software verification with WOLVERINE. In: Gopalakrishnan, G., Qadeer, S. (eds.) CAV 2011. LNCS, vol. 6806, pp. 573–578. Springer, Heidelberg (2011). https://doi.org/10.1007/978-3-642-22110-1_45

24. Kuperstein, M., Vechev, M.T., Yahav, E.: Automatic inference of memory fences. In: FMCAD. IEEE (2010)

25. Lal, A., Reps, T.W.: Reducing concurrent analysis under a context bound to sequential analysis. Formal Methods Syst. Des. **35**(1), 73–97 (2009)

26. Linden, A., Wolper, P.: A verification-based approach to memory fence insertion in PSO memory systems. In: Piterman, N., Smolka, S.A. (eds.) TACAS 2013. LNCS, vol. 7795, pp. 339–353. Springer, Heidelberg (2013). https://doi.org/10.1007/978-3-642-36742-7_24

27. Liu, T., Curtsinger, C., Berger, E.D.: DTHREADS: efficient deterministic multithreading. In: SOSP. ACM (2011)

28. McMillan, K.L.: Lazy abstraction with interpolants. In: Ball, T., Jones, R.B. (eds.) CAV 2006. LNCS, vol. 4144, pp. 123–136. Springer, Heidelberg (2006). https://doi.org/10.1007/11817963_14

29. Metzler, P., Saissi, H., Bokor, P., Suri, N.: Quick verification of concurrent programs by iteratively relaxed scheduling. In: ASE. IEEE Computer Society (2017)

30. Mushtaq, H., Al-Ars, Z., Bertels, K.: DetLock: portable and efficient deterministic execution for shared memory multicore systems. In: High Performance Computing, Networking Storage and Analysis. IEEE (2012)
31. Musuvathi, M., Qadeer, S.: Iterative context bounding for systematic testing of multithreaded programs. In: PLDI. ACM (2007)
32. Nguyen, T.L., Fischer, B., La Torre, S., Parlato, G.: Lazy sequentialization for the safety verification of unbounded concurrent programs. In: Artho, C., Legay, A., Peled, D. (eds.) ATVA 2016. LNCS, vol. 9938, pp. 174–191. Springer, Cham (2016). https://doi.org/10.1007/978-3-319-46520-3_12
33. Nguyen, T.L., Schrammel, P., Fischer, B., La Torre, S., Parlato, G.: Parallel bug-finding in concurrent programs via reduced interleaving instances. In: ASE. IEEE Computer Society (2017)
34. Olszewski, M., Ansel, J., Amarasinghe, S.P.: Kendo: efficient deterministic multi-threading in software. In: ASPLOS (2009)
35. Qadeer, S., Rehof, J.: Context-bounded model checking of concurrent software. In: Halbwachs, N., Zuck, L.D. (eds.) TACAS 2005. LNCS, vol. 3440, pp. 93–107. Springer, Heidelberg (2005). https://doi.org/10.1007/978-3-540-31980-1_7
36. Qadeer, S., Wu, D.: KISS: keep it simple and sequential. In: PLDI. ACM (2004)
37. Raychev, V., Vechev, M., Yahav, E.: Automatic synthesis of deterministic concurrency. In: Logozzo, F., Fähndrich, M. (eds.) SAS 2013. LNCS, vol. 7935, pp. 283–303. Springer, Heidelberg (2013). https://doi.org/10.1007/978-3-642-38856-9_16
38. Valmari, A.: The state explosion problem. In: Reisig, W., Rozenberg, G. (eds.) ACPN 1996. LNCS, vol. 1491, pp. 429–528. Springer, Heidelberg (1998). https://doi.org/10.1007/3-540-65306-6_21
39. Wachter, B., Kroening, D., Ouaknine, J.: Verifying multi-threaded software with impact. In: FMCAD. IEEE (2013)

Learning Guided Enumerative Synthesis
for Superoptimization

Shikhar Singh$^{(\boxtimes)}$, Mengshi Zhang, and Sarfraz Khurshid

University of Texas, Austin, USA
{shikhar_singh,mengshi.zhang,khurshid}@utexas.edu

Abstract. The field of program synthesis has seen substantial recent progress in new ideas, e.g., program sketching and synthesis modulo pruning, and applications, e.g., in program repair and superoptimization, which is our focus in this paper. The goal of superoptimization is to generate a program which is functionally equivalent to the given program but is optimal with respect to some desired criteria. We develop a learning-based approach to guide the exploration of the space of candidate programs to parts of the space where an optimal solution likely exists. We introduce the techniques of bulk and sequence orderings which enable this directed search. We integrate these machine learning techniques with an enumerative superoptimizer and experimentally evaluate our framework using a suite of subjects. Our findings demonstrate that machine learning techniques can play a useful role in reducing the amount of candidate program space that the enumerative search must to explore in order to find an optimal solution; for the subject programs, the reduction is up to 80% on average.

Keywords: Superoptimization · Program synthesis ·
Enumerative search · Machine learning

1 Introduction

Program synthesis addresses the problem of automatic generation of code typically with respect to a given specification that captures the intention of the user [25]. Program synthesis techniques have been applied to solve problems in a variety of domains, including program repair [12], robotics [29], tutoring systems [22], and superoptimization [27,31,34,38]. Various approaches to synthesize programs have been proposed and studied, e.g., program sketching [2], where the user provides a partial program with "holes" in it for the synthesizer to fill out in such a way that the completed program satisfies the given correctness criteria. The user intent can also be captured using natural language inputs [13] or input-output demonstrative examples [16,21] to facilitate synthesis. We focus on a class of well-known synthesis approaches that have two main components: a search capability to explore the program space to seek valid programs, and

© Springer Nature Switzerland AG 2019
F. Biondi et al. (Eds.): SPIN 2019, LNCS 11636, pp. 172–192, 2019.
https://doi.org/10.1007/978-3-030-30923-7_10

some equivalence or correctness checker to determine the feasibility of the solution [7,35]. The specific steps of the search over the program space have a direct impact on the efficiency of the synthesizer.

In superoptimization, which is our focus, the specification takes the form of a program for which a functionally equivalent optimal candidate is desired using a synthesis-based method [34]. The optimality criterion can be the code size, memory accesses, energy efficiency etc. In contrast with optimizing compilers, superoptimizers search for all programs in very large program spaces rather than relying on a set of rewrite rules. Conceptually, superoptimization considers the optimization avenues which a compiler will apply and can discover optimizations which a compiler may miss. For example, superoptimizers are shown to discover peephole optimization rules for compilers [5,18]. In one instance, a superoptimizer optimized a complex multiplication kernel to achieve a speed-up of 60% over an optimizing compiler [33,38].

Several synthesis approaches have been developed and studied in the context of superoptimization. Symbolic or constraint-solving based techniques formulate the synthesis task as a boolean satisfiability problem [2,41]. The input specifications and the programming language constructs are encoded into a single formula and any solution to the formula is a desired program. While this technique can be slow, it is useful in synthesizing constant values in a program. Stochastic search based techniques [38,39] sample the search space by randomly mutating the input program and using a cost function to determine the acceptance of the candidate. Stochastic superoptimization is fast and capable of synthesizing long programs. However, there is a possibility of getting caught in a local minima, which leads to sub-optimal solutions. Enumerative program synthesis involves generating expressions according to the language grammar and encoding the semantic specifications of the language into a satisfiability modulo theory (SMT) [6] formula. Enumerative search coupled with an equivalence checker has proven to be effective [23,40,43]. However, these systems find it hard to scale beyond a few lines of code when using expressive representations, especially ones allowing for a large range of constants and hence require intelligent pruning techniques [3,5]. Recent superoptimization frameworks use multiple types of search techniques that collaborate and complement each other to optimize a variety of programs [34].

Enumeration-based synthesis is the specific synthesis approach we focus on in this paper. Our insight is that there exist opportunities in the enumeration process to employ machine learning-based search techniques to help optimize the search. Specifically, we utilize feed-forward networks [36] and sequence translation models [42], which, to the best of our knowledge, have not been used in prior work on enumerative superoptimization.

This paper introduces effective methods from machine learning to direct state space exploration and likely find superoptimization solutions faster. We develop our techniques in the context of the ARMv7 Instruction Set Architecture (ISA). As our training data, we use over 26000 programs and optimize them using a recent superoptimizer called Greenthumb [33]. This enables learning of the optimization rules applied by the superoptimizer. We devise learning strategies to recognize patterns which the superoptimizer uses to optimize programs. The learned model is used to guide the search towards regions in program space that are likely to contain an optimal solution. For example, if the model determines that a program containing instructions A, B, C can be optimized to a program containing instructions C and E, this information can be used to prioritize exploration of programs comprising C and E when the superoptimizer is presented with a program which has instructions A, B and C.

We devise two learning strategies to direct the search towards regions in the space of candidate programs which likely contain an optimal solution. *Bulk ordering* looks at the input code and recommends a ranked ordering of instructions. A higher ranking indicates a higher likelihood of the instruction being present in the optimized code. *Sequence ordering* analyzes the input code and generates a collection of ranked orderings of instructions, one for each location in the optimized sequence. This results in a fine-grained ordering which relies on the input program as well as the location of the instruction being searched. We develop a feed-forward neural network (FNN) [36] model to accomplish bulk ordering. The network takes as input an encoded representation of the input program and outputs instructions that need to be searched first when exploring optimal candidates. We accomplish sequence ordering using a sequence-to-sequence [42] network comprised of gated recurrent unit networks [9], which are commonly used in machine language translation tools. The objective is to learn an optimized sequence for a given unoptimized sequence of instructions. We study the enumerative superoptimization process and identify overheads that are incurred at different phases of the search. During a *search phase*, the search algorithm looks for the next instruction in the candidate being synthesized. The instructions enumerated during this phase comprise the *search overhead*. If the search determines that no program of current size can satisfy correctness, it restarts and looks for longer candidates. The instructions enumerated during this *expansion phase* cause the *expansion overhead*. We develop two strategies to address these overheads. *Prioritization* aims to reduce the search overhead while *pruning* reduces the number of instructions enumerated during the expansion phase. Prioritization and pruning techniques are realized using the rankings suggested by the ordering schemes. Finally, we equip the enumerative search with prioritization and pruning capabilities made possible by bulk and sequence orderings and perform an experimental evaluation, which demonstrates a significant reduction of overheads.

This paper makes the following contributions:

- **Learning to optimize enumerative search.** We study the performance of enumerative search to identify sources of inefficiencies and propose *pruning* and *prioritization* techniques to address the bottlenecks. These techniques are made feasible by *ordering schemes* that direct the search algorithm towards regions in the program space that are likely to contain the optimal solution. We devise two learning strategies to realize the proposed ordering schemes. Bulk ordering generates one ranked ordering for the whole input and is implemented using a feed-forward neural network. Sequence ordering generates a series of rankings, one for each instruction in the optimal sequence, and is formulated as a sequence learning task and implemented using a sequence to sequence translation network.

- **Integration.** The learned models for bulk and sequence orderings are integrated with an enumerative superoptimizer. This provides the search core, the capability to incorporate pruning and prioritization techniques which are used to guide the search making it more efficient.
- **Dataset.** To train the machine learning models, we generate a corpus of over 26000 unoptimized and optimized code sequence pairs that follow the ARMv7 ISA specifications. These sequences vary in length, instruction mix, number of variables etc. Our dataset is publicly available at:
  https://github.com/Shikhar8990/TrainingPrograms_Superoptimization
  Datasets like these can play an important role in superoptimizer development and analysis.
- **Evaluation.** We perform an experimental evaluation of our approach. The results show that learning has a useful role in synthesis-based superoptimization. The test suite comprises 15 synthetic programs which are designed to test the efficacy of our scheme in identifying different optimization avenues. Our approach achieves an average of 80% reduction in the instructions enumerated for the subject programs.

2   Background

2.1   Enumerative Superoptimization

This section describes the basic enumerative superoptimization search procedure. Given a test suite as a desired correctness criteria, the search enumerates candidate expressions of increasing size. A candidate that passes all the test cases is given to the equivalence checker. If the candidate is functionally equivalent to the specification and has a lower cost (according to the optimality criterion) than all previously found candidates (including the specification), it becomes the current solution. In case the candidate is not equivalent, the search is provided a counterexample in the form of a test case which gets added to the test suite. This process continues until all equivalent programs of lesser cost than the specification are enumerated, the search times out, or it is determined that no such candidate exists.

2.2   Illustration

Modern superoptimizers formulate enumerative synthesis as a graph search problem [34]. The nodes in the graph denote the current state of the program execution (represented by the values of active variables/registers, overflow, sign flags etc). A directed edge between two nodes is an instruction that changes the program state by modifying one or more values. We illustrate the enumerative search based synthesis procedure for a sample program in ARMv7 assembly language. The objective is to synthesize a program of minimum possible length which takes two integers as inputs and returns 1 if the numbers are equal and returns 0 otherwise. The system is also provided a program that computes the desired result as a reference implementation that has to be optimized.

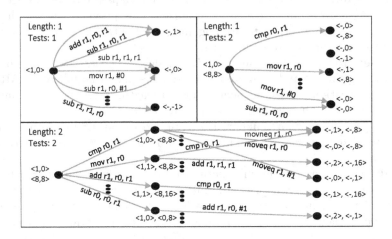

Fig. 1. Enumerative search procedure

Figure 1 illustrates the various steps in the search procedure. The program state is represented using two registers R0 and R1 which contain the program inputs (we do not show the program status flags for simplicity). The output of the program is stored in R1. The enumerator is provided an initial test input (1, 0) and the expected output (0). Using this test input, the search starts generating programs of size one to determine if a single instruction brings about a change in the program state such that R1 contains the desired result. At the end of the first search step, the feasible candidates that pass the test are provided to an SMT solver, which checks for program equivalence with the reference implementation. In this case, the equivalence checker provides another test case and none of the single instruction programs generate the desired output for both tests. At this point, the search graph is expanded by enumerating all legal instructions, which results in multiple intermediate states. This is followed by a second search phase which enumerates programs comprising two instructions. At each stage, the set of instructions that are considered for either search or expansion comprise the *opcode pool*. We define one search and expansion phase as an *epoch*.

3   Our Approach

3.1   Optimizing Enumerative Search

The illustrative example in the previous section highlights two distinct enumeration overheads. The search overhead comprises of instructions which are enumerated in the search phase while the expansion overhead includes the instructions enumerated to expand the search graph i.e. increase the size of the program to be searched. These overheads can become prohibitively large when expressive ISAs and language representations are used, resulting in increased search times and resource requirements. We introduce two concepts to reduce the search and expansion overheads of enumerative search.

Prioritization. Prioritization aims to reduce the search overhead by reordering the opcode pool such that instructions that are more likely to be present in the optimal candidate are searched first.

Algorithm 1. Enumerative Search Loop - Bulk Ordering

       ▷ p_{SPEC} is the unoptimized program, $numInsts$ is the number of instructions to consider when expanding the graph

input: $numInsts$, p_{SPEC}

output: p_{OPT} ▷ p_{OPT} is the optimized program

1: $orderedPool \leftarrow$ BULKPRIORITIZATION(p_{SPEC}) ▷ Prioritized list of instructions
2: $prunedPool \leftarrow$ BULKPRUNING$(orderedPool, numInsts)$ ▷ List containing $numInsts$ instructions
3: $p_{SIZE} \leftarrow 1$ ▷ start with single instruction programs
4: $p_{COST} \leftarrow$ COST(p_{SPEC}) ▷ Initial cost
5: $Graph \leftarrow$ INITIALIZEGRAPH$()$
6: **while** true **do**   ▷ Main search loop
    ▷ Search phase
7:     **for all** $inst \in orderedPool$ **do**
8:         $(p_{CAND}, found) \leftarrow$ FINDCANDIDATE$(Graph, inst, p_{SPEC})$
9:         **if** $found$ **then**
10:            **if** COST$(p_{CAND}) < p_{COST}$ **then**
11:              $p_{COST} \leftarrow$ COST(p_{CAND}) ▷ Update the current cost
12:              $p_{OPT} \leftarrow p_{CAND}$ ▷ Found a cheaper candidate
    ▷ Expansion phase
13:     $p_{SIZE} \leftarrow p_{SIZE} + 1$
    ▷ Restrict the graph expansion using $prunedPool$
14:     $Graph \leftarrow$ EXPANDGRAPH$(Graph, prunedPool)$

Pruning. Pruning reduces the size of the search graph that is built during the expansion phase. In the illustrative example, if the opcode pool is limited to the instructions that are likely to be present in the optimal candidate, this can lead to significant reduction in expansion overheads.

3.2 Ordering Schemes

Both prioritization and pruning require the opcode pool used by the enumerative search to be modified in a particular fashion. Prioritization uses a ranked ordering of instructions while pruning removes lower-ranked instructions from the

---

Algorithm 2. Enumerative Search Loop - Sequence Ordering

   ▷ p_{SPEC} is the unoptimized program, $numInsts$ is the number of instructions to consider when expanding the graph

input: $numInsts$, p_{SPEC} **output:** p_{OPT} ▷ p_{OPT} is the optimized program

1: $p_{SIZE} \leftarrow 1$ ▷ Start with single instruction programs
2: $p_{COST} \leftarrow \text{COST}(p_{SPEC})$ ▷ Initial cost
3: $Graph \leftarrow \text{INITIALIZEGRAPH}()$
4: $orderedPool \leftarrow \text{SEQPRIORITIZATION}(p_{SPEC}, p_{SIZE})$ ▷ Initialize ordered pool
5: **while** true **do**   ▷ Main search loop
    ▷ Search phase
6:    **for all** $inst \in orderedPool$ **do**
7:       $(p_{CAND}, found) \leftarrow \text{FINDCANDIDATE}(Graph, inst, p_{SPEC})$
8:       **if** $found$ **then**
9:          **if** $\text{COST}(p_{CAND}) < p_{COST}$ **then**
10:            $p_{COST} \leftarrow \text{COST}(p_{CAND})$ ▷ Update the current cost
11:            $p_{OPT} \leftarrow p_{CAND}$ ▷ Found a cheaper candidate
    ▷ Expansion phase
12:    $p_{SIZE} \leftarrow p_{SIZE} + 1$
    ▷ Generate an $orderedPool$ for the current p_{SIZE}
13:    $orderedPool \leftarrow \text{SEQPRIORITIZATION}(p_{SPEC}, p_{SIZE})$
    ▷ Generate a $prunedPool$ for the current p_{SIZE}
14:    $prunedPool \leftarrow \text{SEQPRUNING}(orderedPool, numInsts)$
15:    $Graph \leftarrow \text{EXPANDGRAPH}(Graph, prunedPool)$

---

opcode pool when expanding the graph. We describe two approaches to achieve this ordering.

Bulk Ordering. This type of ordering generates one ordered opcode pool for the entire search. It reads the input program and emits a ranked ordering of instructions that are likely to exist in the program. This ranking is used to prioritize and prune the opcode pool. Algorithm 1 describes the bulk ordering procedure. It begins with an input program p_{SPEC} and an empty graph. The function BULKPRIORITIZATION reads the input program and generates a ranked list, which is used in the search phase. BULKPRUNING is called to generate the pruned opcode pool, which is used by the synthesizer to grow the graph. This function takes as input parameters, the ordered pool generated in the previous line, and $numInsts$ - the number of instructions to consider when expanding the graph. For example, if $numInsts$ is 10, the graph will be expanded using only the top 10 instructions from the ordered pool. The FINDCANDIDATE procedure takes as input the current graph, the instruction being considered, and the reference specification (p_{SPEC}) and determines if an equivalent candidate can be synthesized using sub-programs in $Graph$ and the current instruction. It returns a tuple containing a $found$ flag which is $true$ if an equivalent candidate (p_{CAND}) is found. In case an equivalent candidate is found, the current cost and p_{OPT}

are updated if this candidate is cheaper than all the previous candidates. After all the instructions in the ordered pool are searched, *Graph* is expanded using the pruned pool generated by BULKPRUNING and the search resumes to look for a candidate with one instruction more than the previous iteration.

Sequence Ordering. In sequence ordering, a ranking is generated for each epoch; every search and expansion phase is provided a distinct ranking of instructions. Sequence ordering aims to generate a more descriptive ordering which depends not only on the input program but also on the position of that instruction in the candidate program. The intuition is that the preference ordering can change depending on the location of the instruction. For example, when searching for optimal candidates of size 2, bulk ordering will generate the same rankings for both instructions 1 and 2 while sequence ordering (Algorithm 2) will generate distinct rankings for the two instructions. To accomplish this, after every expansion phase, a distinct ordering is generated for the new instruction that needs to be searched. The pruning (SEQPRUNING) and prioritization (SEQPRIORITIZATION) functions are called at every epoch (one iteration of the while loop). Distinguishing it from the bulk ordering counterpart, the sequence prioritization method requires additional information about instruction location, which is equal to the current size of the program (p_{SIZE}).

4   Learning Framework

This section describes the machine learning infrastructure used to accomplish bulk and sequence ordering. As previously discussed, our approach is to use a large collection of unoptimized code sequences and their optimized counterparts to learn optimization avenues and scenarios for a specific language representation. We formulate a scheme to encode these code-sequence pairs into a format that can be used by machine learning models. We represent programs as vectors, which are provided to the networks for training and inference. We use a feed-forward network to generate bulk orderings while sequence ordering is achieved using a sequence-to-sequence translation network.

4.1   Corpus Generation

To generate a large database of code sequences, we developed a random program generator which can emit programs adhering to the ARMv7 standard. In machine language terminology, the part of the instruction which specifies the operation to be performed is called an *opcode*. The values on which the operation is to be performed are called operands. These values can be directly specified as a part of the instruction (called immediate operands), or the opcodes can also use the values in special locations called registers. The program generator has knobs for regulating instruction mix, length, opcode flavors (different formats in which an opcode can be used) and range of immediate values. The current version of the program generator can synthesize 20 different opcodes. It uses 4 registers and 5-bit constants to generate the operands. The maximum length of the program is capped at 8. We generated around 125000 sequences and all of them were provided to Greenthumb to find an optimal equivalent program, should one exist. The objective was to make the corpus diverse enough so that Greenthumb discovers various kinds of optimization techniques applicable under different scenarios. Out of around 125000 programs, Greenthumb was able to discover optimal solutions for around 26000, which were used for training.

4.2   Learning Bulk Ordering

Feed-Forward Networks. Feed-forward neural networks (FNNs) are one of the oldest and most widely studied networks. They find application in non-linear regression and classification tasks [36, 44]. These networks comprise neural populations structured in layers. In these networks, a connection is allowed only between a particular layer and its successors. There are no backward or intra-layer connections. Along with the input and output layers, a network can have one or more hidden layers. If every neuron in one layer is connected to every neuron in the successive layer, the layers are said to be fully connected. FNNs with one or more hidden layers are commonly called multi-layer perceptrons. The network learns through a process called back-propagation [37] where the weight of each unit is modified according to a loss function which quantifies the error between the predicted and actual outputs. FNNs are well suited for learning bulk orderings as they can be trained to classify an instruction being present or absent in the optimized program for a given input program.

Implementation. Figure 2 depicts the feature extraction and encoding process. Each instruction in the code sequence is converted to a token. A token retains information about the opcode and the type of operands that are used. It strips the instruction of the register numbers and values of operands. This makes the learning problem tractable by reducing the feature space. We list all possible ways in which the opcode can be used and assign it a position in a 1-D array. For example, the opcode ADD can exist with 3 register operands, 2 registers, and 1 immediate operand, with an optional conditional suffix and with a secondary shift operation on the second register operand. This is done for all opcodes, which results in 92 unique tokens. Each token is assigned a unique index in a vector and the presence of an instruction is recorded by incrementing the value at the corresponding token location by 1. These values are then normalized with respect to the total number of instructions in the program.

After a design space exploration, we configured the FNN to have 2 hidden layers with 16 and 8 hidden units respectively. The network has 92 units in the input and output layers, one for each token in the feature vector. The activations of the output layer are sorted, and this provides a ranked ordering of tokens/instructions. The training was carried out for 100 epochs with a batch size of 32. The neural network was implemented and trained using Keras [10] with the Tensorflow [1] back-end.

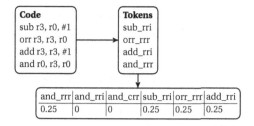

Fig. 2. Feature generation and encoding for bulk ordering

4.3 Learning Sequence Orderings

Seq2seq Networks. Recurrent Neural Networks (RNNs) are special types of artificial neural networks that have been the subject of recent interest by the machine learning community [19,47]. This architecture was conceived by Elman in 1990 [15]. Conventional FNNs are oblivious to sequential information or ordering in time; they generate a prediction by considering only the current input. RNNs are capable of considering not only the current input but also its past decisions. An RNN unit has "memory" and a notion of a state, and this allows it to learn and interpret sequences. Information about the sequence is embedded into its state and it looks at its present state as well as the current input when making predictions. There is a feedback loop from the output of the unit back into it and this keeps updating its internal state and letting information persist. Gated Recurrent Units [9] (GRUs) are a special type of RNNs which have found application in various sequence learning and sequence-to-sequence translation (seq2seq) tasks [11,42]. Seq2seq network architecture consists of two GRU networks - an encoder and a decoder. The encoder processes the input sequence to generate an output and update its internal state. The output of the encoder is discarded and the final internal state acts as a "context" for the decoder. A decoder is another GRU network which predicts the next token in the target sequence when provided with all previous tokens. During training, the input to the decoder is the desired target sequence and the output is the same target sequence but shifted by one time-step. The target sequences are provided explicit "START" and "STOP" tokens to signal the beginning and end of the sequence. The initial internal state of the decoder is determined by the "context" provided by the encoder. This process of learning is called *Teacher Forcing* [30]. During inference, the input sequence is provided to encoder while the decoder is given only a "START" token which signals is to start decoding using the final encoder context. Seq2seq networks are well suited for learning sequence orderings as they can be trained to learn the position of an instruction in the optimized code for a given input program.

Implementation. The feature generation process for sequence ordering is shown in Fig. 3. The input and output sequences are converted to their token representations and each token is assigned a distinct index in a one dimensional

vector. Each instruction in the code sequence is assigned one such vector with
the value at the corresponding token index set to 1. The vectors are consolidated
to create a 2-dimensional structure of one-hot vectors. Our implementation of
the seq2seq network comprises 256 GRU units in both the encoder and decoder.
The 2-D structure corresponding to the input code sequence is fed to the encoder
and for each token predicted in the output sequence by the decoder, we record
and sort the output activations to derive one ranked ordering per token. The network was trained for 1000 epochs with a batch size of 32. We used the pytorch-
seq2seq [17,32] library to configure the network. This network configuration was
determined after evaluating several different configurations.

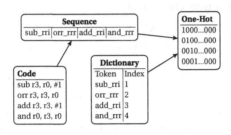

Fig. 3. Feature generation and encoding for sequence ordering

5   Evaluation

5.1   Subjects

To test the ordering schemes, we create a handwritten suite comprising 15 programs ranging in length from to 2 to 5 instructions. The destination register of
the last instruction contains the result of the program. These program lengths
are typical of the state-of-art work on applying learning to program synthesis [4]
and was chosen to be a reasonable design parameter to evaluate our scheme.
Programs of the length we consider are also appropriate in determining if the
learned models can recognize fundamental optimizations, and each subject in the
suite can be optimized using one or more of these optimization techniques. The
programs are classified into three non-exclusive categories. Category A programs
can be optimized by combining two or more instructions into one. Category B
programs can be optimized by avoiding redundant data movement while Category C programs contain instructions that have no effect and can be eliminated.
Table 1 lists these programs and their optimized counterparts.

5.2   Integration with Enumerative Search

This section describes the integration of the learned models with an enumerative searcher to enable pruning and prioritization. We take the enumerative

Table 1. Benchmark programs

progID	Original	Optimized	Category
1	add r0, r0, r1 add r0, r0, r1	add r0, r0, r1, lsl #1	A
2	mov r0, r1 mov r2, r0	mov r2, r1	B

3	mov r0, r1
	mov r2, r0
	mov r3, r2
		mov r3, r1	B

4	mov r0, r1 add r2, r2, r0	add r2, r1, r2	B

5	orr r0, r1, r3
	sub r2, r0, #2
	mov r1, r2
		orr r2, r1, r3
		sub r1, r2, #2
			B

6	add r0, r1, r2
	sub r0, r0, r3
	mov r1, r0
	eor r3, r1, r2
		sub r3, r3, r2
		sub r0, r1, r3
		eor r3, r0, r2
			B

7	mvn r0, r1 add r2, r1, r0	mvn r2, #0	A
8	mvn r0, r0 mvn r1, r1 rsb r2, r1, r0	sub r2, r1, r0	A
9	add r1, r1, #0 add r2, r1, r0	add r2, r0, r1	C
10	sub r1, r1, #0 add r2, r1, r0	add r2, r0, r1	C
11	orr r1, r1, #0 add r2, r1, r0	add r2, r0, r1	C
12	mvn r0, r1 orr r2, r1, r0	mvn r2, #0	A

13	cmp r0, r1
	movlt r2, r1
	movge r2, r1
	add r3, r2, r3
		add r3, r1, r3	C

14	mvn r0, r1 and r2, r0, r2 mvn r3, r2 rsb r3, r3, r0	bic r3, r2, r1 rsb r3, r1, r3	AB

15	add r0, r0, r1
	add r0, r0, r1
	mov r2, r0
	sub r3, r2, #0
	and r3, r3, r1
		add r3, r0, r1, lsl #1
		and r3, r1, r3
			ABC

search provided in the Greenthumb framework [33] and extend it to incorporate the ordering schemes. As described in the previous sections, sequence and bulk models suggest an ordering of instructions. The instruction encodings used for learning contain information about the opcode and the type of operands. This encoding provides a template for the enumerative search to generate instructions. For example, using a token *sub_rri*, the enumerator will generate instructions using sub as an opcode, a register and an immediate (constant) on which the operation is performed and a destination register to store the result. The search strategy determines the exact register names and constant values. Three configurations are used for experimentation - Vanilla configuration is enumerative search without any modifications, Bulk and Sequence configurations implement bulk and sequence pruning/prioritization respectively. For the optimality criteria, we use a model that assigns a certain cost to each instruction in the language. Instructions which are more complex and take longer to complete incur higher penalties.

5.3 Enumeration Overheads

To make a case for the necessity of an ordering scheme like ours, we run the test programs on the vanilla configuration. Each program is run five times and the number of instructions searched to reach the optimal solution is recorded. Figure 4 plots the average (left y-axis) and standard deviation (right y-axis) of the number of instructions searched during the superoptimization process. One way to quantify the unnecessary program space that is explored is to count the number of instructions that are enumerated before an optimal candidate is found. For subject programs containing 2 instructions, this value ranges from 3 instructions for program 12 to as high as 154 for program 1. For programs of length 3, the search explores 40 instructions for program 8 while program 5 requires enumerating around 1500 instructions. These overheads become more pronounced as the size of the program increases. In order to optimize program 6, which has a length of 4, almost 8000 instructions are enumerated. Most programs exhibit a high variation in search overhead across identical runs. The reason for this is that during every search and expansion phase, the superoptimizer shuffles the opcode pool. This non-determinism hinders reproducibility and makes performance analysis rather difficult. These observations call for a need to develop a more structured approach to explore the program space.

5.4 Performance of Ordering Schemes

This section discusses the efficacy of bulk and sequence orderings when used to prioritize and prune the program space.

Prioritization. Figure 5 depicts the impact of prioritization on the search overhead. The test programs are run with pruning turned off. The number of instructions enumerated during the search phase is recorded for both bulk and sequence

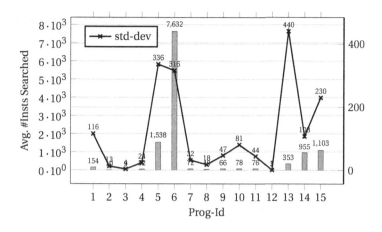

Fig. 4. Average and std-dev of instructions searched - vanilla configuration

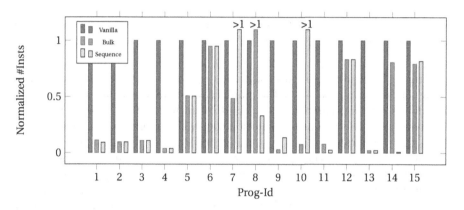

Fig. 5. Impact of prioritization on search overhead

ordering and are normalized with respect to the number of instructions enumerated in the vanilla configuration. Ordering schemes can reduce the search overhead anywhere between 10% and 90%. Bulk ordering proves more efficient for some programs while sequence ordering proves efficient for others. For example, the solution to program 14 consists of 2 instructions - *bic* (bit clear) with 3 registers followed by *rsb* (reverse subtract) with 3 registers. Sequence ordering assigns top rank to *bic* with three registers and third rank to *rsb* with three registers. As a result, the search is directed towards these instructions, which enables it to find the optimal solution without having to search invalid instructions. Without sequence ordering, the synthesizer had to search over 900 extra instructions before reaching the same solution. For three cases – sequence ordering in programs 7 and 10 and bulk ordering in program 8 – the ordering schemes degrade the performance. This is because of the inefficient ordering suggested by our models. The solution to program 8 is a single instruction *sub* (subtract) or *rsb* (reverse subtract) which uses three registers. Bulk ordering assigns a rank of 18 and 19 to these instructions, which is not a good prediction. Vanilla configuration, on the other hand, picks *sub* with three registers as the third choice, which results in fewer instructions being searched.

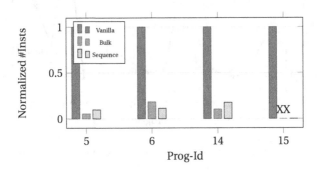

Fig. 6. Impact of pruning on expansion overhead

Pruning. The objective of this study was to evaluate the impact of ordering schemes in restricting the size of the graph that is built when the size of the optimal candidate being searched is increased by an instruction. Since 4 programs in the test suite yield an optimal solution comprising more than one instruction, we use these programs to study pruning performance. Figure 6 compares the expansion overheads of the ordering techniques with the vanilla configuration. We allow the search to expand the graph using only the top 10 instructions recommended by bulk and sequence orderings. The four test programs are run with prioritization turned off and only instructions enumerated in the expansion phase are counted. The number of instructions is normalized with respect to the vanilla configuration. Three out of four test programs show more than 80% reduction in expansion overhead. For program 15, the optimal solution comprises an *add* instruction with 3 registers and a secondary shift operation. This instruction does not find a place in the top 10 rankings of either bulk (rank 12) or sequence (rank 32) orderings. As a result, the graph does not contain this instruction and the search is unable to find an optimal solution. The choice of considering only the top 10 instructions was to underline the importance of careful determination of how much a graph should be pruned. While aggressive pruning leads to greater overhead reduction, there is also an increased risk of not enumerating instructions essential to the search process. For example, had we chosen to consider the top 12 instructions instead of top 10, bulk pruning would have found the solution to program 15 but also increased the expansion overhead for the rest of the programs.

Prioritization and Pruning. In this section, pruning and prioritization are combined and their impact on the overall enumeration overhead is studied. Enumerative search is extended to incorporate bulk and sequence orderings according to the scheme described in Sect. 3. Figure 7 shows the total reduction in enumeration overhead across both search and expansion phases. The orderings are unable to find a solution for program 15 because an instruction required for the optimal solution is pruned out by both the schemes (discussed in the previous section). Bulk ordering proves beneficial in all of the remaining 14 programs while sequence ordering is able to reduce the number of enumerated instructions in 12 programs. Both these techniques result in an average overhead reduction of 80%. Bulk ordering performs better in some cases while sequence ordering performs better in others. It was anticipated that the sequence ordered pruning and prioritization would exhibit superior performance as it was expected to generate a more fine-grained ordering. However, bulk ordering proved to be more efficient. Since sequence translation models are very difficult to train, we suspect that further training is required along with a larger dataset. We continue to experiment with the model to improve its performance.

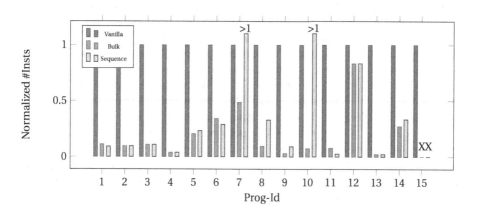

Fig. 7. Impact of prioritization and pruning on total overhead

6   Limitations and Future Work

Our approach shares the limitations of other machine learning based approaches, specifically the quality of training data is crucial for the approach's effectiveness. While we created a diverse corpus of subjects, our evaluation results may not generalize to programs that have characteristics different from the ones we used. Moreover, similar to other heuristics that prune search space, our learning-based pruning technique may lead the search to completion without finding a solution that could have been found by an exhaustive search that did not use pruning. Scalability remains a major challenge for learning based program synthesis and making our technique efficient and practical for larger programs remains an active area of research.

The focus of our work is enumerative search. Modern superoptimizers, such as Greenthumb, use a combination of search strategies. We plan to apply learning to different search algorithms to create a more comprehensive solution for superoptimization in future work.

7 Related Work

Massalin [31] first introduced the concept of superoptimization in 1987 for code written in the assembly of the Motorola 68020 ISA. Massalin's superoptimizer was able to synthesize code comprising a few instructions. Since then, several approaches and techniques to superoptimize have been developed. These techniques vary in terms of the target code environment, search algorithms, the speed of search, computational overheads, size of the synthesized code etc. STOKE is a stochastic superoptimizer for the x86_64 ISA [38] that uses a random search to rapidly explore the incredibly vast program space to come up with an optimized version of the given program. Stochastic search starts with an input program and generates modifications on that program. A *proposal distribution* determines the probability of a particular modification. The new candidate is accepted or rejected based on correctness and optimality criteria. Reinforcement learning [46] is demonstrated to have improved the performance of the STOKE superoptimizer by learning the *proposal distribution* using the semantics of the input program [8]. To the best of our knowledge, our proposed technique is the first to apply machine learning to enumerative superoptimization. Enumerative synthesis is crucial to a comprehensive superoptimization framework as it ensures optimality of the solution.

In the more general context of program synthesis, machine learning techniques, such as probabilistic inference [20, 24, 26] and Genetic Programming [28, 45] have shown to be useful in previous work. Machine learning has also been applied to inductive program synthesis where input-output examples are used to generate code in a domain-specific language. One approach uses recurrent neural networks to synthesize code in a language comprising regular expression-based string transformations [14]. *DeepCoder* [4] combines enumerative search and learning to synthesize programs. For a given language representation comprising several high level functions, a neural network is trained to learn the likelihood of a function being present for a given set of inputs and outputs to the program, and this information is used to guide the search. The technique implemented in [48] extends [4] to incorporate information about intermediate program states to predict the next instruction. A key difference between Deepcoder and our work is that Deepcoder considers inductive program synthesis using examples of input/output values, whereas we consider superoptimization where the input is an unoptimized program and the output is its optimized version.

8   Conclusion

This paper presented an approach based on machine learning for more effective superoptimization using program synthesis based on enumerative search. We introduced ordering schemes that give priority to instructions that are likely to exist in an optimal program. Bulk ordering scheme analyzes the input code and recommends a ranked ordering of instructions. Sequence ordering scheme generates a collection of ranked orderings of instructions, one for each location in the optimized sequence. Using these ordering schemes, we developed pruning and prioritization techniques which guide the enumerative search towards regions in the program space that likely contain an optimal solution. We developed learning-based techniques to implement bulk and sequence orderings and integrated them with an enumerative superoptimizer to implement prioritization and pruning. An experimental evaluation of our approach using a suite of superoptimization subjects demonstrates that machine learning techniques can play a useful role in reducing the amount of program space that the enumerative search has to explore in order to find an optimal solution.

Acknowledgments. This work started as a class project for *Program Synthesis* taught by Dr. Keshav Pingali at UT Austin. The authors are grateful for his valuable input.

This research was partially supported by the US National Science Foundation under Grant Nos. CCF-1704790 and CCF-1718903.

References

1. Abadi, M., et al.: TensorFlow: a system for large-scale machine learning. In: Proceedings of the 12th USENIX Conference on Operating Systems Design and Implementation, OSDI 2016, pp. 265–283. USENIX Association, Berkeley (2016). http://dl.acm.org/citation.cfm?id=3026877.3026899
2. Alur, R., et al.: Syntax-guided synthesis. In: 2013 Formal Methods in Computer-Aided Design, pp. 1–8, October 2013. https://doi.org/10.1109/FMCAD.2013.6679385
3. Alur, R., Radhakrishna, A., Udupa, A.: Scaling enumerative program synthesis via divide and conquer. In: Legay, A., Margaria, T. (eds.) TACAS 2017. LNCS, vol. 10205, pp. 319–336. Springer, Heidelberg (2017). https://doi.org/10.1007/978-3-662-54577-5_18
4. Balog, M., Gaunt, A.L., Brockschmidt, M., Nowozin, S., Tarlow, D.: DeepCoder: learning to write programs. arXiv preprint arXiv:1611.01989 (2016)
5. Bansal, S., Aiken, A.: Automatic generation of peephole superoptimizers. In: Proceedings of the 12th International Conference on Architectural Support for Programming Languages and Operating Systems, ASPLOS XII, pp. 394–403. ACM, New York (2006). https://doi.org/10.1145/1168857.1168906
6. Barrett, C., Sebastiani, R., Seshia, S., Tinelli, C.: Satisfiability modulo theories. In: Frontiers in Artificial Intelligence and Applications, vol. 185, pp. 825–885, 1st edn (2009). https://doi.org/10.3233/978-1-58603-929-5-825

7. Bornholt, J., Torlak, E., Grossman, D., Ceze, L.: Optimizing synthesis with metasketches. In: Proceedings of the 43rd Annual ACM SIGPLAN-SIGACT Symposium on Principles of Programming Languages, POPL 2016, pp. 775–788. ACM, New York (2016). https://doi.org/10.1145/2837614.2837666
8. Bunel, R., Desmaison, A., Kumar, M.P., Torr, P.H.S., Kohli, P.: Learning to superoptimize programs. CoRR abs/1611.01787 (2016)
9. Cho, K., van Merrienboer, B., Bahdanau, D., Bengio, Y.: On the properties of neural machine translation: encoder-decoder approaches. CoRR abs/1409.1259 (2014). http://arxiv.org/abs/1409.1259
10. Chollet, F.: Keras (2015). https://github.com/fchollet/keras
11. Chung, J., Gülçehre, Ç., Cho, K., Bengio, Y.: Empirical evaluation of gated recurrent neural networks on sequence modeling. CoRR abs/1412.3555 (2014). http://arxiv.org/abs/1412.3555
12. D'Antoni, L., Samanta, R., Singh, R.: QLOSE: program repair with quantitative objectives. In: Chaudhuri, S., Farzan, A. (eds.) CAV 2016. LNCS, vol. 9780, pp. 383–401. Springer, Cham (2016). https://doi.org/10.1007/978-3-319-41540-6_21
13. Desai, A., et al.: Program synthesis using natural language. CoRR abs/1509.00413 (2015). http://arxiv.org/abs/1509.00413
14. Devlin, J., Uesato, J., Bhupatiraju, S., Singh, R., Mohamed, A.R., Kohli, P.: RobustFill: neural program learning under noisy I/O. arXiv preprint arXiv:1703.07469 (2017)
15. Elman, J.L.: Finding structure in time. Cogn. Sc. **14**(2), 179–211 (1990). https://doi.org/10.1016/0364-0213(90)90002-E. http://www.sciencedirect.com/science/article/pii/036402139090002E
16. Feser, J.K., Chaudhuri, S., Dillig, I.: Synthesizing data structure transformations from input-output examples. In: Proceedings of the 36th ACM SIGPLAN Conference on Programming Language Design and Implementation, PLDI 2015, pp. 229–239. ACM, New York (2015). https://doi.org/10.1145/2737924.2737977
17. Gao, K.: IBM pytorch-seq2seq (2017). https://github.com/IBM/pytorch-seq2seq/
18. Granlund, T., Kenner, R.: Eliminating branches using a superoptimizer and the GNU C compiler. In: Proceedings of the ACM SIGPLAN 1992 Conference on Programming Language Design and Implementation, PLDI 1992, pp. 341–352. ACM, New York (1992). https://doi.org/10.1145/143095.143146
19. Graves, A.: Generating sequences with recurrent neural networks. CoRR abs/1308.0850 (2013). http://arxiv.org/abs/1308.0850
20. Gulwani, S.: Dimensions in program synthesis. In: Proceedings of the 12th International ACM SIGPLAN Symposium on Principles and Practice of Declarative Programming, PPDP 2010, pp. 13–24. ACM, New York (2010). https://doi.org/10.1145/1836089.1836091
21. Gulwani, S.: Automating string processing in spreadsheets using input-output examples. In: Proceedings of the 38th Annual ACM SIGPLAN-SIGACT Symposium on Principles of Programming Languages, POPL 2011, pp. 317–330. ACM, New York (2011). https://doi.org/10.1145/1926385.1926423
22. Gulwani, S.: Applications of program synthesis to end-user programming and intelligent tutoring systems. In: Proceedings of the Companion Publication of the 2014 Annual Conference on Genetic and Evolutionary Computation, GECCO Comp 2014, pp. 5–6. ACM, New York (2014). https://doi.org/10.1145/2598394.2598397
23. Gulwani, S., Jha, S., Tiwari, A., Venkatesan, R.: Synthesis of loop-free programs. In: Proceedings of the 32nd ACM SIGPLAN Conference on Programming Language Design and Implementation, PLDI 2011, pp. 62–73. ACM, New York (2011). https://doi.org/10.1145/1993498.1993506

24. Gulwani, S., Jojic, N.: Program verification as probabilistic inference. In: Proceedings of the 34th Annual ACM SIGPLAN-SIGACT Symposium on Principles of Programming Languages, POPL 2007, pp. 277–289. ACM, New York (2007). https://doi.org/10.1145/1190216.1190258
25. Gulwani, S., Polozov, O., Singh, R.: Program synthesis. Found. Trends® Program. Lang. **4**(1–2), 1–119 (2017). https://doi.org/10.1561/2500000010
26. Jojic, V., Gulwani, S., Jojic, N.: Probabilistic inference of programs from input/output examples, April 2018
27. Joshi, R., Nelson, G., Randall, K.: Denali: A goal-directed superoptimizer. In: Proceedings of the ACM SIGPLAN 2002 Conference on Programming Language Design and Implementation, PLDI 2002, pp. 304–314. ACM, New York (2002). https://doi.org/10.1145/512529.512566
28. Katz, G., Peled, D.: Genetic programming and model checking: synthesizing new mutual exclusion algorithms. In: Cha, S.S., Choi, J.-Y., Kim, M., Lee, I., Viswanathan, M. (eds.) ATVA 2008. LNCS, vol. 5311, pp. 33–47. Springer, Heidelberg (2008). https://doi.org/10.1007/978-3-540-88387-6_5
29. Kuniyoshi, Y., Inaba, M., Inoue, H.: Learning by watching: extracting reusable task knowledge from visual observation of human performance. IEEE Trans. Robot. Autom. **10**(6), 799–822 (1994). https://doi.org/10.1109/70.338535
30. Lamb, A., Goyal, A., Zhang, Y., Zhang, S., Courville, A., Bengio, Y.: Professor forcing: a new algorithm for training recurrent networks. ArXiv e-prints, October 2016
31. Massalin, H.: Superoptimizer: a look at the smallest program. In: Proceedings of the Second International Conference on Architectural Support for Programming Languages and Operating Systems, ASPLOS II, pp. 122–126. IEEE Computer Society Press, Los Alamitos (1987). https://doi.org/10.1145/36206.36194
32. Paszke, A., et al.: Automatic differentiation in PyTorch. In: NIPS-W (2017)
33. Phothilimthana, P.M., Thakur, A., Bodik, R., Dhurjati, D.: Greenthumb: superoptimizer construction framework. In: Proceedings of the 25th International Conference on Compiler Construction, CC 2016, pp. 261–262. ACM, New York (2016). https://doi.org/10.1145/2892208.2892233
34. Phothilimthana, P.M., Thakur, A., Bodik, R., Dhurjati, D.: Scaling up superoptimization. SIGPLAN Not. **51**(4), 297–310 (2016). https://doi.org/10.1145/2954679.2872387
35. Polozov, O., Gulwani, S.: FlashMeta: a framework for inductive program synthesis. In: Proceedings of the 2015 ACM SIGPLAN International Conference on Object-Oriented Programming, Systems, Languages, and Applications, OOPSLA 2015, pp. 107–126. ACM, New York (2015). https://doi.org/10.1145/2814270.2814310
36. Ruck, D.W., Rogers, S.K., Kabrisky, M., Oxley, M.E., Suter, B.W.: The multilayer perceptron as an approximation to a Bayes optimal discriminant function. IEEE Trans. Neural Netw. **1**(4), 296–298 (1990). https://doi.org/10.1109/72.80266
37. Rumelhart, D.E., Hinton, G.E., Williams, R.J.: Learning representations by backpropagating errors. In: Neurocomputing: Foundations of Research, pp. 696–699. MIT Press, Cambridge (1988). http://dl.acm.org/citation.cfm?id=65669.104451
38. Schkufza, E., Sharma, R., Aiken, A.: Stochastic superoptimization. In: Proceedings of the Eighteenth International Conference on Architectural Support for Programming Languages and Operating Systems, ASPLOS 2013, pp. 305–316. ACM, New York (2013). https://doi.org/10.1145/2451116.2451150

39. Schkufza, E., Sharma, R., Aiken, A.: Stochastic optimization of floating-point programs with tunable precision. In: Proceedings of the 35th ACM SIGPLAN Conference on Programming Language Design and Implementation, PLDI 2014, pp. 53–64. ACM, New York (2014). https://doi.org/10.1145/2594291.2594302

40. Solar-Lezama, A., Rabbah, R., Bodík, R., Ebcioğlu, K.: Programming by sketching for bit-streaming programs. In: Proceedings of the 2005 ACM SIGPLAN Conference on Programming Language Design and Implementation, PLDI 2005, pp. 281–294. ACM, New York (2005). https://doi.org/10.1145/1065010.1065045

41. Solar-Lezama, A., Tancau, L., Bodik, R., Seshia, S., Saraswat, V.: Combinatorial sketching for finite programs. In: Proceedings of the 12th International Conference on Architectural Support for Programming Languages and Operating Systems, ASPLOS XII, pp. 404–415. ACM, New York (2006). https://doi.org/10.1145/1168857.1168907

42. Sutskever, I., Vinyals, O., Le, Q.V.: Sequence to sequence learning with neural networks. CoRR abs/1409.3215 (2014). http://arxiv.org/abs/1409.3215

43. Udupa, A., Raghavan, A., Deshmukh, J.V., Mador-Haim, S., Martin, M.M., Alur, R.: TRANSIT: specifying protocols with concolic snippets. In: Proceedings of the 34th ACM SIGPLAN Conference on Programming Language Design and Implementation, PLDI 2013, pp. 287–296. ACM, New York (2013). https://doi.org/10.1145/2491956.2462174

44. Ruck, D.W., Rogers, S., Kabrisky, M.: Feature selection using a multilayer perceptron 2, July 1993

45. Weimer, W., Nguyen, T., Le Goues, C., Forrest, S.: Automatically finding patches using genetic programming. In: Proceedings of the 31st International Conference on Software Engineering, ICSE 2009, pp. 364–374. IEEE Computer Society, Washington, DC (2009). https://doi.org/10.1109/ICSE.2009.5070536

46. Williams, R.J.: Simple statistical gradient-following algorithms for connectionist reinforcement learning. Mach. Learn. 8(3), 229–256 (1992). https://doi.org/10.1007/BF00992696

47. Zheng, S., et al.: Conditional random fields as recurrent neural networks. CoRR abs/1502.03240 (2015). http://arxiv.org/abs/1502.03240

48. Zohar, A., Wolf, L.: Automatic program synthesis of long programs with a learned garbage collector. CoRR abs/1809.04682 (2018). http://arxiv.org/abs/1809.04682

Applying Model Checking Approach with Floating Point Arithmetic for Verification of Air Collision Avoidance Maneuver Hybrid Model

Sergey Staroletov[1(✉)] and Nikolay Shilov[2]

[1] Polzunov Altai State Technical University, Barnaul, Russia
serg_soft@mail.ru
[2] Innopolis University, Innopolis, Russia
shiloviis@mail.ru

Abstract. A term *Cyber-Physical System* (CPS) refers to a mathematically described (specified) real-world process, that combines discrete changes of pre-defined control states (a cyber part) and changes of controllable continuous-time states (a physical part). In this paper, we present a model-checking approach to verification of Cyber-Physical Systems. The primary goal of the paper is to try using SPIN verifier and Promela language to specify and verify a safety property of a CPS for Air Collision Avoidance. The main "obstacle" preventing model checking the CPSs is the absence of a floating-point arithmetic in input languages of model checkers. In this paper, we describe an implementation of a standard floating-point arithmetic in Promela language as well as results of verifying an Air Collusion Avoidance model using this implementation and comparison of our approach with other approaches. Also, we stress an importance of verified standard mathematical functions used in CPSs solutions.

Keywords: Cyber-Physical Systems · Model checking · SPIN · Promela · Floating-point arithmetic · Standard IEEE-754

1 Introduction

A term *Cyber-Physical System* (CPS) refers to a mathematically described (specified) real-world process, that combines discrete changes of pre-defined control states (a cyber part) and evaluation of controllable continuous-time states (a physical part)—the time is passing and these controllable variables of a model are changing according to some mathematical specification (e.g., they are solutions of a system of ODE—Ordinary Differential Equations).

© Springer Nature Switzerland AG 2019
F. Biondi et al. (Eds.): SPIN 2019, LNCS 11636, pp. 193–207, 2019.
https://doi.org/10.1007/978-3-030-30923-7_11

These systems can be modeled as Hybrid automata [11] which represent discrete-time and continuous-time transitions; such models are known as Hybrid models and specified using the Hybrid Dynamic Logic [13]. According to A. Platzer [15], the syntax of hybrid programs is defined as follows:

$$\alpha ::= x := e \mid ?Q \mid x' = f(x)\&Q \mid \alpha \cup \alpha \mid \alpha; \alpha \mid \alpha^* \qquad (1)$$

where α is a meta-variable for the hybrid programs, x is a meta-variable for program variables, e is a meta-variable for the first-order real-valued terms, f is a meta-variable for the continuous real functions, and Q is a meta-variable for the first-order formulas over real numbers. The construct ';' means here the sequential composition, '$\cup$'—is the non-deterministic choice, '?'—is the condition operator, and '*'—is the non-deterministic iteration (like Kleene-star).

In this work, we are mostly interested in verification of safety properties of Cyber-Physical Systems [12], express that *a specified (bad) situation will never happen* during a system execution.

Of course, such systems can be implemented as C++ or Java programs by solving the differential equations of the CPS analytically (i.e. explicitly) prior to coding or by solving the ODEs numerically in runtime (for example, using the Runge-Kutta method). The Model-Driven Developing (MDD) approach is becoming more and more popular nowadays to describe the behavior of a CPS in various forms of flowcharts, it could be expressed in Modelica declarative language [8], using Berkeley's Ptolemy [5] or Matlab Simulink [1]. Then the CPS can be numerically simulated many times and each simulation can be tested against a particular safety property (i.e. that a particular bad situation never happens in every particular simulation exercise).

However, numerical simulation and test-based validation cannot guarantee a safety property of a CPS: simulation just shows some plots with key parameters and/or listings of their current values, but unexpected unsafe behavior may be missed in simulation (while the corresponding real-world process may influence people or harm hardware and can cost a lot).

It this paper we deal with a demo CPS to model the Air Collision Prevention Maneuver [6,14], which is a simplification of aircraft control system, and *the absence of collision of two planers* as a safety property (more precisely—that *two aircraft should not be in a circle of a given radius*).

Formal verification is a way to prove mathematically that a model program meets formal requirements (that specify a correct model behavior). In the Model Checking approach [4], these requirements are usually expressed in a temporal logic, such as LTL or CTL. The models for verification are usually written in a special modeling language, which simplifies conventional imperative or functional programming languages (by using enumerable types, fix-size finite memory, etc.) but adds non-deterministic transitions and some features for inter-process communication and synchronization.

The main advantage of a formal verification is a chance to prove the correctness of a model for all the possible behaviors (but not only for simulated ones). Of course, the formal model of a system or formal specification of the system' requirements could be incorrect or be incomplete, so we cannot claim that the formal verification makes the system totally correct, but still any formal verification is a good way to validate the formal model against the formal specification beforehand implementing real system code.

In this paper, we address the problem of verifying CPSs. Currently, the model checking approach is not applied here because of the absence of floating-point types. We present a way to implement floating-point arithmetic in Promela language for the SPIN verifier. A CPS for Air Collision Avoidance is used as a running verification example. Also, we count of resulting internal states and discuss the feasibility and scalability of the approach to CPS modeling and verification with a comparison to other formal techniques.

For sake of paper completeness, let us conclude the introductory section with a very brief characteristic of used tools SPIN and Promela (more detailed sketch is unnecessary for SPIN workshop audience) and the problem with floating-point within these tools.

SPIN is a verifier for models written in a special Promela input language [22] with respect to given LTL requirements constructed using key variables of the model. To deal with CPSs models, we may relay upon the following language features:

- it is an actor-based (process-oriented) language,
- it is primarily designed to describe protocols interoperations,
- it has C-styled syntax and fix-size finite data types,
- it uses function inlining quite similar to the macros in C,
- it allows non-deterministic transitions.

We can state that Promela language is ideal for modeling cyber parts of CPSs, but it is not so convenient to model physical parts. As the paper deals with modeling of CPSs, we should found a way to use continuous time in model programs, and hence, the fixed-point or the floating-point arithmetic should be applied for it. Of course, using floating-point arithmetic is more interesting because of higher accuracy: since CPSs are modeled with differential equations, there are many "opportunities" to increase the total error with an imprecise data type.

Unfortunately, the Promela language comes neither with fixed-point nor floating-point types. The official site says [23]:

There are no floating-point numbers in basic Promela because the purpose the language is to encourage abstraction from the computational aspects of a distributed application while focusing on the verification of process interaction, synchronization, and coordination.

So, the model checking approach implemented in SPIN is designed not to check the calculations; the purpose is to check interoperations. But later in the paper, the approach will be used to verify also a system that represents the Air Collision Prevention model with a lot of floating-point calculations.

The rest of the paper has the following structure. In the next very short Sect. 2 we present the collision avoidance model. The floating-point arithmetic and its implementation are presented in the Sect. 3. In the last Sect. 4 we present our verification process and outcome of our verification experiment (Subsect. 4.1), compare our approach with some other approaches (Subsect. 4.2) and conclude discussing topics for further research (Subsect. 4.3).

2   The Roundabout Maneuver

The Roundabout Maneuver is a behavior of aircraft to make Collision Avoidance, and it is a subject to cooperation in air traffic control. The avoidance of collision is achieved by an agreement on some common angular velocity ω_{xy} and common centre c_{xy} around which both can fly by the circle safely without coming closer to each other not more than R_{safe} [14]. In this section, it is stating how we can model two planers which are going to enter the Maneuver and what safety property should be specified verified to prove the correctness of the Collision Avoidance.

2.1   Flight Dynamic

According to [14], the flight dynamic can be modeled as a system:

$$\begin{cases} x_1 = v \cdot cos\theta \\ x_2 = v \cdot sin\theta \\ \theta' = \omega \end{cases} \qquad (2)$$

where $x = (x_1, x_2)$ is a planar position, v—a linear velocity, ω—an angular velocity, θ—an angular orientation. After introducing the linear speed vector $d = (d_1, d_2) = (vcos\theta, vsin\theta)$ from (2) the following differential equation for two aircraft is derived:

$$\begin{cases} x_1' = d_1, \ x_2' = d_2 \\ d_1' = -\omega \cdot d_2, \ d_2' = \omega \cdot d_1 \\ y_1' = e_1, \ y_2' = e_2 \\ e_1' = -\omega_y \cdot e_2, \ e_2' = \omega_y \cdot e_1 \end{cases} \qquad (3)$$

where also $y = (y_1, y_2)$ is a second planar position, $e = (e_1, e_2)$ – a second linear speed vector, ω_y – an angular velocity of the second planer.

The system (3) can be solved analytically (manually with pen-and-paper or symbolically with using tools like Mathematica or Maxima [21]):

$$
\begin{cases}
x_1(t) = x_1(0) + \dfrac{d_1(0) \cdot sin(\omega \cdot t) + d_2(0) \cdot (cos(\omega \cdot t) - 1)}{\omega} \\[2mm]
x_2(t) = x_2(0) + \dfrac{d_2(0) \cdot sin(\omega \cdot t) + d_1(0) \cdot (1 - cos(\omega \cdot t))}{\omega} \\[2mm]
d_1(t) = d_1(0) \cdot cos(\omega \cdot t) - d_2(0) \cdot sin(\omega \cdot t) \\[1mm]
d_2(t) = d1(0) \cdot sin(\omega \cdot t) + d_2(0) \cdot cos(\omega \cdot t) \\[1mm]
y_1(t) = y_1(0) + \dfrac{e_1(0) \cdot sin(\omega_y \cdot t) + e_2(0) \cdot (cos(\omega_y \cdot t) - 1)}{\omega_y} \\[2mm]
y_2(t) = y_2(0) + \dfrac{e_2(0) \cdot sin(\omega_y \cdot t) + e_1(0) \cdot (1 - cos(\omega_y \cdot t))}{\omega_y} \\[2mm]
e_1(t) = e_1(0) \cdot cos(\omega_y \cdot t) - e_2(0) \cdot sin(\omega_y \cdot t) \\[1mm]
e_2(t) = e_1(0) \cdot sin(\omega_y \cdot t) + e_2(0) \cdot cos(\omega_y \cdot t)
\end{cases}
\tag{4}
$$

Numeric simulation of the system has been implemented in C++. The program (available on GitHub [18]) in a loop increases the time variable t to some Δt, calculates positions according to (4) and plots them. An example result is shown in Fig. 1.

Fig. 1. Roundabout Maneuver simulation

2.2 The Maneuver

When two aircraft move according to (4), they can proceed to the Roundabout Maneuver, but the safety property (specified below in the next Subsect. 2.3) should be held as a precondition.

The procedure of the Maneuver:

$$
\begin{cases}
d_1 = -\omega_{xy} \cdot x_2 - cc_2 \\
d_2 = \omega_{xy} \cdot x_1 - cc_1 \\
e_1 = -\omega_{xy} \cdot y_2 - cc_2 \\
e_2 = \omega_{xy} \cdot y_1 - cc_1
\end{cases}
\tag{5}
$$

where ω_{xy} is a common angular velocity, cc_1 and cc_2—new centers of aircraft curves.

2.3 The Safety Property

Before and during the Maneuver the aircraft should be outside the circle with radius R_{safe}. So, we have the following precondition to the entry procedure of the Maneuver and the safe property to verify:

$$(x_1 - y_1)^2 + (x_2 - y_2)^2 \geqslant R_{safe}^2 \qquad (6)$$

3   Floating-Point Arithmetic

In this section we recall IEEE-754 representation of floating-point numbers and operations. Nowadays the floating-point arithmetic is (usually) implemented in hardware (co-processors and processors). Because of the absence of floating-point arithmetic in a particular language (e.g. Promela), floating-point numbers and operations should be coded in a "software mode", that means they should be written according to algorithms based on the representation of the numbers in the memory to calculate the operations results and maintain the representation format.

3.1   Integer Based Representation of Floating-Point Numbers

As there is a 32-bit type in Promela (the *int* datatype), it is possible to represent floating-point numbers as integers, then implement the floating-point operations, and there will be a type that is a "very similar" to *float* (i.e. real number single precision) data type in C. The internal representation of float in 32 bits is depicted below:

$$\overbrace{Sign(0,1)}^{1 \text{ bit}} \overbrace{Exponent}^{8 \text{ bit}} \overbrace{Mantissa}^{23 \text{ bit}} \qquad (7)$$

In this representation *Sign* is the bit equals to 0 for positives and 1—for negatives; *Exponent* and *Mantissa* are the power of the binary exponent of the number and its multiplier respectively; the number represented by (7) is equal to

$$Float(32bit) = (-1)^{Sign} \cdot 2^{128+Exponent} \cdot \frac{Mantissa}{2^{23}}, \qquad (8)$$

where 23 is the size of the mantissa in bits and 128 is the bias value for 8-bit exponent representation.

3.2 Algorithms of Software Floating-Point Arithmetic

– *Adding* two positive floating-point numbers: before we add numbers, they need to have a common exponent, so the adding firstly getting a more prominent exponent of two numbers, than modifying the other number by shifting to the right to the diff of two exponents and then actually adding the two mantises. If the resulting mantissa is bigger than the maximum allowed value, the resulting exponent is decreased, and the result is shifted to the right.
– *Subtracting* two floating-point numbers, a bigger and a lower: we should first find a maximum exponent of the two, then shift the other mantissa to the right according to the exponent diff, do the actual subtracting of the mantises and then check the sign of the result, if the result is negative, change the sign and put the absolute value as the result.
– Subtracting and adding numbers with *different signs* and comparisons: these cases can be resolved by checking the signs and apply operations to add or to subtract with a possible change of the sign of the result.
– *Multiplying* two floating-point numbers: the resulting exponent is the sum of the two exponents, the resulting mantissa is the product of the two mantises shifted by 8 each other (otherwise the overflow occurs) and then the result should be shifted to achieve the number not to exceed the maximum allowed mantissa and the resulting sign is the modulo-2 sum of the two signs.
– *Dividing* two floating-point numbers is the hardest operation to implement. The resulting exponent is the subtraction of the two exponents, and the resulting sign is the modulo 2-sum of the two signs, the resulting mantissa is calculated by the iterative process of adding next division product and getting the remainder and repeat to div the remainder by the second number while remainder is more than a given bound. To div two numbers in integers and reduce an error and number of loops, we execute a process of shifting the first number to the left to the highest possible value and shifting the second number to the right while it has 0 as a low bit in the base of 2 representation.
– Some *common procedures* are executed before any operation, these are: getting the sign, exponent and mantissa from a number by shifting and putting a mask; and after any operation—shifting the resulting mantissa to achieve the highest possible number not more than $2^{mantissa\ bits}$ (see (8)), and every shifting should be done with updating the exponent. The resulting number is formatted according to the (7).

3.3 Implementation of the Floating-Point Arithmetic

Implementation of the 32-bit floating-point arithmetic uses some Promela language features such as function inlining (macros) and bitwise operations (provided because the language has been constructed for protocols verification). The implementation is freely available on GitHub [19].

The developing process was as follows:

– firstly, these algorithms were implementing as functions in C [19],

– then these functions were tested on random numbers (using Unit-testing),
– and finally C-functions were rewritten in Promela.

We have started with C-implementation because this language offers more convenient debugging and testing support. An example of the implementation of floating-point multiplication (the most straightforward operation) is given in Listing 1.1.

Listing 1.1. Implementation of multiplication of floating-point numbers in Promela

```
inline mul_float(result, a_pass, b_pass){
    int a_mul = a_pass; //create copies
    int b_mul = b_pass;
    if ::(a_mul == 0 || b_mul == 0) ->
    result = 0;
        ::else -> {
            int ea = a_mul >> MANTISSA_BITS,
            eb = b_mul >> MANTISSA_BITS;
            byte sign_a = a_mul >>
            (MANTISSA_BITS + EXP_SIZE);
            byte sign_b = b_mul >>
            (MANTISSA_BITS + EXP_SIZE);
            ea = ea & EXP_MASK;
            eb = eb & EXP_MASK;
            //resulting exponent
            int e = ea + eb - EXP_BIAS;
            a_mul = a_mul & MASK;
            b_mul = b_mul & MASK;
            //resulting mantissa
            int p_mul = ((a_mul >> 8) *
            (b_mul >> 8))
            >> (MANTISSA_BITS - 16);
            //resulting sign
            bit sign = (sign_a + sign_b) % 2;
            e = (sign << EXP_SIZE) + e;
            result = p_mul |
            (e << MANTISSA_BITS);
        }
    fi
}
```

In the listing we note the shifting operator that truncates the resulting value to satisfy the size of the mantissa, and here is a point to loosing precision for floating-point values especially that presented inaccurately due to the impossibility to represent them as a decomposition of a number in powers of two. (But it is an "official" truncation according to the standard.)

Some additional operations were implemented to allow to create floating-point numbers in code and to show their values in the simulation mode.

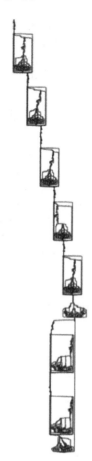

Fig. 2. The sine function implementation internal automaton

- *float_from_int(result, x, rate_of_minus10)* creates a floating-point value *result* by dividing the value of *x* by the value of $10^{rate\_of\_minus10}$; for example, the following code snippet defines the approximation π with 5 digits in the decimal part:

```
int pi;
float_from_int(pi, 3141592, 6);
//3141592*10^{-6}
```

- *print_float_representation(float_num)* prints the number *float_num* in human-readable format (8); for example, the value of the constant `pi` defined above will be printed as `pi = [0 2 3294144]` that is $51471 * 2^{-14}$. (If we put this value to a calculator or, for example, into the Google's search string, we will get 3.14154052734).

Trigonometric functions (our hybrid model has the differential equation solution with sin / cos) can be implemented as Taylor series. Currently, the sine is implemented as the sum (9) bounded to a given precision or count of terms and the cosine is implemented based on the identity (10).

$$sin(x) = x - \frac{x^3}{3!} + \frac{x^5}{5!} - ... \tag{9}$$

$$cos(x) = sin(\frac{\pi}{2} - x) \tag{10}$$

(Please refer to [17] for criticism and verification of this approach).

In Fig. 2 the sine internal automaton generated by iSpin and graphviz tools is shown to illustrate a complexity of implementation of floating-point standard functions in Promela. A comprehensive verification of standard functions (like sine verification in [10,17]), is out of scope of our paper, but it is possible to apply the model checking approach to verify the standard functions in floating-point arithmetic.

4   Main Results and Conclusion

4.1   Verification of the Example

The overall process is presented in Fig. 3. First we had solved the CPS system and got a solution (4) for X, D, Y, T. Then we had created a model simulator of the CPS with a visualization of two aircraft position for "playing" with the model and adjusting its initial values. (Simultaneously it was used for dynamic checks of the safety condition (6).) Next we had implemented 32-bit floating-point arithmetic (as described in the Sect. 3), sine and cosine functions. After all these it has become possible to implement the CPS model behavior according to formulas (4–6).

In the code [19] we show how to implement this CPS. The implementation sets the initial values for x_1, x_2, y_1, y_2, etc., then loops (adding Δt to t) and calculates values for the solution of the differential equation according to (4) (which are coded as inline functions in Promela). The LTL formula representing the safety property (6) is $[](safe == 1)$ where $safe$ variable is setting as a result of evaluating (6) after calculating values of all variables of (4).

The verification result output for $t \in [0..1]$ is shown in Fig. 4. The model checker has utilized more than 2 GB of memory, about 8000 bytes for the state vector (SPIN's VECTORZ parameter [9]) and generated more than 250.000 states. It looks like that verifying such systems is near the limit of Model Checking approach applicability, so we did not test the method on potentially all t intervals using the non-deterministic addition.

4.2   Comparison with Other Related Methods

Actually, the ODE system that model the Roundabout Maneuver is included as an example in the KeYmaera [15], an interactive proof assistant designed to

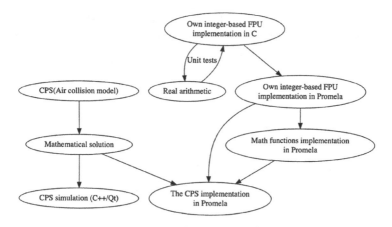

Fig. 3. CPS verification software engineering process

```
./spin -a fpu.pml
ltl check_me: [] ((safe==1))
gcc -DMEMLIM=1024 -O2 -DVECTORSZ=15000 -DMEMLIM=3072 -DXUSAFE -w -o pan pan.c
./pan -m1000000 -a -n -c1
Pid: 18166

(Spin Version 6.4.8 -- 2 March 2018)
        + Partial Order Reduction

Full statespace search for:
        never claim         + (check_me)
        assertion violations + (if within scope of claim)
        acceptance   cycles  + (fairness disabled)
        invalid end states - (disabled by never claim)

State-vector 7856 byte, depth reached 533151, errors: 0
    266576 states, stored
        1 states, matched
    266577 transitions (= stored+matched)
        0 atomic steps
hash conflicts:        7 (resolved)

Stats on memory usage (in Megabytes):
 2004.323 equivalent memory usage for states (stored*(State-vector + overhead))
 2016.680 actual memory usage for states
  128.000 memory used for hash table (-w24)
   53.406 memory used for DFS stack (-m1000000)
    3.958 memory lost to fragmentation
 2194.136 total actual memory usage



pan: elapsed time 4.99 seconds
No errors found -- did you verify all claims?
```

Fig. 4. The CPS verification results with SPIN

specify and verify Hybrid systems. The tool implements the dynamic differential logic (DDL) that extends Pratt's dynamic logic by adding the following axioms [16]: Hoare's assignment rule; solution of the symbolic initial value problem; iteration axiom; modal modus ponens from modal logic; induction schema for loops; variation of Harel's convergence rule, suitably adapted to hybrid systems over $\mathbb{R}$; Barcan formula; vacuous modalities, Gödel's necessitation rule for modal logic and an axiom for reducing differential equations with evolution domain constraints to equations without it, so it is now possible to write and check invariants for modalities after runs of (1).

Fig. 5. The CPS verification results with KeYmaera tool

The main advantages of KeYmaera are initial system description in the original equations (not in code), ability to verify over potentially all the possible values for some parameters, opportunity to extend the class of verifying systems by providing lemmas for particular types of equations. But verification using this tool additionally requires linkage of external tools like Reduce, Orbital and SMT to simplify the system at every step of the proving process by providing the real arithmetic, ODE solution or counterexample generation ability. In Fig. 5 the result of verification of the system with KeYmaera is shown. We note that the proof tree consists of 138 nodes of DDL simplification rules and for our type of ODE system it can be done fully automatically (otherwise it requires to simplify the system step-by-step since KeYmaera is an interactive theorem prover).

A part of the reasons preventing introduction of KeYmaera to industrial practice is the absence of a convenient DSL language and/or a GUI to describe the model systems, but some steps to solve the problem have been attempted [2]. Another disadvantage of KeYmaera is inherited from dynamics logic that doesn't support parallel processes and their interaction.

Listing 1.2. Axioms for proving the Sine function in ACSL using bounded Taylor series recursive implementation

```
logic real SinN {l} (
real x, real sum,
real current, integer i, integer i_max);

axiom SinNEmpty: \forall
real x, real sum, real current,
integer i, integer i_max;
(\abs(current) <= EPS) || (i == i_max) ==>
SinN(x, sum, current, i, i_max) == sum + current;

axiom SinNNext: \forall
real x, real sum, real current,
integer i, integer i_max;
\abs(current) > EPS ==>
SinN(x, sum, current, i, i_max) ==
SinN(x, sum + current,
current * (−1.0 * x * x /
((2 * i) * (2 * i + 1))), i + 1, i_max);
```

It is also possible to try to verify C code [18] of a model using a deductive approach [7] by providing code contracts (requires, ensures and loop invariants), for example, as annotations in ACSL language [3], and then verifying them with Frama-C WP (the Weakest Precondition) tool. But due to the lack of proper support of real arithmetic and the lemmas for trigonometric functions a verifying engineer now will definitely have troubles to verify such systems (while some successful attempts have been reported [20]). For example, now we have ended up with verifying the part of the CPS in C code, it required to write bounded (to a given accuracy or iteration count) sine axioms (see Listing 1.2) as a recursive solution for (9) and check it in a loop invariant. As it is shown in this listing, deductive verification here corresponds to logical predicates that use the *real* type (a general type with clear real arithmetic), and to prove the computations we need to make type-conversion to the float type and use Frama-C real model which does not care about possible rounding errors, NaNs, etc.

4.3   Concluding Remarks

In this paper, the Air Collision Avoidance system has been modeled and verified with the model checking approach. The approach is based on implementation of floating-point arithmetic and some standard functions. The created code can be potentially used as a library to verify (with some degree of accuracy) other CPS models. Moreover, the code for a CPS system with using this library can be generated from a system description. Using our approach by implementing the IEEE-754 standard and verify the model, we can say that our proof will be correspond to the behaviour of real code that use the same arithmetic standard.

The implementation of floating-point arithmetic very close to the standard can be applied further for obtaining lemmas to do deductive verification. We are also planning to use the Promela model to check some properties of real computations instead of tests.

We hope in the conclusion that the approach may be used for modeling and verifying hybrid models with communicating actors. In the paper, we modeled just a simple single-actor (or one-process) system, but what if two aircraft communicating together as actors and at the same time a physical process is performing according to some differential equations? We believe that such systems can be modeled in Promela, however, these systems are extremely hard for verification, and perhaps some different verification techniques or their combinations should be used.

Acknowledgement. The research is partially supported by Russian Basic Research Foundation grant no. 17-01-00789 *Platform-independent approach to formal specification and verification of standard mathematical functions.*

References

1. Ali, R.B., Schulte, H., Mami, A.: Modeling and simulation of a small wind turbine system based on PMSG generator. In: Evolving and Adaptive Intelligent Systems 2017, pp. 1–6 (2017)
2. Baar, T., Staroletov, S.: A control flow graph based approach to make the verification of cyber-physical systems using KeYmaera easier. Model. Anal. Inf. Syst. **25**(5), 465–480 (2018)
3. Baudin, P., et al.: ACSL: ANSI/ISO C Specification Language Version 1.13. http://frama-c.com/download/acsl-implementation-Chlorine-20180501.pdf
4. Clarke Jr., E.M., et al.: Model Checking (Cyber-Physical Systems). MIT Press, Cambridge (2018)
5. Cremona, F., et al.: Hybrid co-simulation: it's about time. Softw. Syst. Model. **18**, 1–25 (2017)
6. Damm, W., Pinto, G., Ratschan, S.: Guaranteed termination in the verification of LTL properties of non-linear robust discrete time hybrid systems. Int. J. Found. Comput. Sci. **18**(1), 63–86 (2007)
7. Filliâtre, J.-C.: Deductive software verification. Int. J. Softw. Tools Technol. Transfer **13**, 397 (2011)
8. Fritzson, P.: Principles of Object-oriented Modeling and Simulation with Modelica 2.1. Wiley, Hoboken (2010)
9. Geldenhuys, J., de Villiers, P.J.A., Rushby, J.: Runtime efficient state compaction in spin. In: Dams, D., Gerth, R., Leue, S., Massink, M. (eds.) SPIN 1999. LNCS, vol. 1680, pp. 12–21. Springer, Heidelberg (1999). https://doi.org/10.1007/3-540-48234-2_2
10. Harrison, J.: Formal verification of floating point trigonometric functions. Lect. Notes Comput. Sci. **1954**, 217–233 (2000)
11. Henzinger, T.A.: The theory of hybrid automata. In: Inan, M.K., Kurshan, R.P. (eds.) Verification of Digital and Hybrid Systems, pp. 265–292. Springer, Heidelberg (2000). https://doi.org/10.1007/978-3-642-59615-5_13

12. Kindler, E.: Safety and liveness properties: a survey. Bull. Eur. Assoc. Theor. Comput. Sci. **53**, 268–272 (1994)
13. Platzer, A.: Differential dynamic logic for hybrid systems. J. Autom. Reasoning **41**(2), 143–189 (2008)
14. Platzer, A.: Differential-algebraic dynamic logic for differential-algebraic programs. J. Log. Comput. **20**, 309–352 (2008)
15. Platzer, A.: Logical Foundations of Cyber-Physical Systems. Springer, Heidelberg (2018)
16. Platzer, A.: The complete proof theory of hybrid systems. In: Proceedings of the 2012 27th Annual IEEE/ACM Symposium on Logic in Computer Science. IEEE Computer Society (2012)
17. Shilov, N., Faifel, B., Shilova, S., Promsky, A.: Towards platform-independent specification and verification of the standard trigonometry functions. arXiv:1901.03414 [cs.LO]. (2019). https://arxiv.org/abs/1901.03414
18. Staroletov, S.: Roundabout Maneuver Simulator. https://github.com/SergeyStaroletov/RoundAboutManeuver
19. Staroletov, S.: FPU Arithmetics In Integers. https://github.com/SergeyStaroletov/FloatArithInIntegers
20. Titolo, L., Moscato, M.M., Muñoz, C.A., Dutle, A., Bobot, F.: A formally verified floating-point implementation of the compact position reporting algorithm. In: Havelund, K., Peleska, J., Roscoe, B., de Vink, E. (eds.) FM 2018. LNCS, vol. 10951, pp. 364–381. Springer, Cham (2018). https://doi.org/10.1007/978-3-319-95582-7_22
21. Maxima, A Computer Algebra System. http://maxima.sourceforge.net/
22. Spin Version 6 – Promela Grammar. http://spinroot.com/spin/Man/grammar.html
23. Spin: Promela reference. float – floating point numbers. http://spinroot.com/spin/Man/float.html

Conformance Testing of Schedulers for DSL-based Model Checking

Nhat-Hoa Tran[1](✉)[iD] and Toshiaki Aoki[2][iD]

[1] National University of Civil Engineering, Hanoi 11657, Vietnam
hoatn@nuce.edu.vn
[2] Japan Advanced Institute of Science and Technology,
Nomi, Ishikawa 923-1211, Japan
toshiaki@jaist.ac.jp

Abstract. When we verify concurrent systems executed under a real operating system (OS), we should take the scheduling policy of the OS into account. However, with a specific implementation of an OS, the description of the scheduling policy does not exist or not clear to describe the behaviors of the real scheduler. In this case, we need to make assumptions in the specification by ourselves. Therefore, checking the correctness of the specification of the scheduling policy is important because it affects the verification result. In this paper, we propose a method to validate the correspondence between the specification of the scheduling policy and the implementation of the scheduler using testing techniques. The overall approach can be regarded as conformance testing. As a result, we can find the inconsistency between the implementation and the specification. That indicates the incorrectness of the specification. To deal with testing, we propose a domain-specific language (DSL) to specify the test generation with the scheduling policy. A search algorithm is introduced to determine the executions of the processes. The tests are generated automatically and exhaustively by applying model-based testing (MBT) techniques. Based on this method, we develop a tool for generating the tests. We demonstrate our method with Linux FIFO scheduling policy. The experiments show that we can facilitate the test generation and check the specification of the scheduling policy easily.

Keywords: Conformance testing · Domain-specific language ·
Model checking · Test generation · Scheduling policy ·
Model-based testing

1 Introduction

The executions of the processes of a real software system are determined by a scheduler. Therefore, verifying systems with considering all possible interleavings of the behaviors of the processes in the presence of the scheduler can produce spurious bugs because some of the executions may not exist. Thus, the scheduling policy needs to be taken into account during the verification to increase the

© Springer Nature Switzerland AG 2019
F. Biondi et al. (Eds.): SPIN 2019, LNCS 11636, pp. 208–225, 2019.
https://doi.org/10.1007/978-3-030-30923-7_12

accuracy. In fact, many kinds of schedulers, which adopt different strategies, are used in a real OS. For example, the Linux scheduler supports different policies for non-real-time and real-time tasks based on their priorities, such as *round-robin* and *first-in-first-out*. That means dealing with facilitating the variation of schedulers is also needed.

To overcome these problems, in previous work [20], we proposed a method to verify systems using model checking techniques. Our method is based on specifying the way to explore the state space using a DSL [7] to handle the executions of the processes. This method is named *DSL-based Model Checking*. In our approach, we introduced a DSL named SchDSL[1] to describe the scheduling policies. The main purpose of the DSL is to provide a high-level support for the succinct specification of various scheduling policies. Based on the specification of the behaviors of the scheduler, a search algorithm is realized to explore the state space following the scheduling policy to verify the system. With this approach, the problem now is that the quality of the specification of the policy in the DSL affects the verification result. Therefore, ensuring the correctness of the specification is necessary and important.

In our research, we aim at verifying software systems run on real OSs. However, it is difficult to find the corresponding specification of the implementation of the scheduler. We mean that there is no specification for a specific implementation or the corresponding specification is not clear to describe the behaviors of the real scheduler. For example, the specification of real-time FIFO policy of Linux OS indicates that if a call to the functions `sched_setscheduler/sched_setparam` to increase the priority of the running or runnable `SCHED_FIFO` thread, it *may preempt* the current thread with the same priority [13]. Thus, there are two options for the implementation: (1) the corresponding process preempts the current process and (2) this running process isn't preempted. In fact, there are multiple versions of Linux OS and which option is implemented on each version of Linux is not described in the specification. In addition, the behaviors of the scheduler in a real OS can be observed only in executing the system. Therefore, using testing techniques is an appropriate approach to check the correspondence between the specification of the policy and the implementation in a real OS. That helps us to increase the confidence of the specification of the policy.

To address these problems, we propose a method to generate the tests to check the correspondence between the specification of the scheduling policy and the implementation. The main idea is that we can apply conformance testing techniques to check whether the implementation of the scheduler follows the specification. As a result, we can find the inconsistency between the implementation and the specification. That indicates the incorrectness of the specification. To make the tests, we apply MBT techniques. Firstly, we extend our DSL for specifying the test generation. This language aims to facilitate the specification of the scheduling policy with the definition of the test generation. Secondly, we propose a search algorithm to visit every state of the system to realize the

---

[1] SchDSL stands for 'Scheduling DSL'.

executions of the processes. Each execution following the search (called an execution path or a trail) is used to generate a test. All of the necessary information for the search and for generating the tests is realized automatically from the specification of the scheduling policy and the definition of the tests in the DSL.

We have implemented our method on a tool named SSpinJa[2] and conducted the experiments for generating the tests. We have applied our approach to checking the correspondence between the specification and the implementation of the real-time FIFO scheduling policy of Linux OS. The results show that our method is practical. With this approach, we can check the correspondence between the specification of the scheduling policy and the implementation of the scheduler.

The rest of the paper is organized as follows: Sect. 2 gives the detail of our approach. The DSL is introduced in Sect. 3. The method for generating the tests is shown in Sect. 4. The implementation of our method is introduced in Sect. 5. In Sect. 6, we show a case study with the experimental results for generating test cases and test programs to check the specification of the scheduling policy with the implementation of Linux OS. Section 7 presents the related work. Finally, the conclusion and future work are given in Sect. 8.

2   Approach

Our method for the testing is to check that the behaviors specified in the specification are the same as the real ones (meaning that they are accepted by the real scheduler). Figure 1 depicts an example of a system using *priority* scheduling policy with 3 processes (P, Q and R). In this example, process P has the highest priority and process R has the lowest one. The only action of each process is terminating itself. We know that when the current process terminates, the scheduler will select the highest priority process to run. Therefore, with this example, firstly, process P is selected because it has the highest priority; this process terminates; then process Q runs; at the end, process R is selected and also terminates. To ensure the correspondence between the scheduling policy and the implementation of the real scheduler, these behaviors of the scheduler is necessary to check. With this example, we have only one execution of the system, which can be tested by checking the running order of these processes.

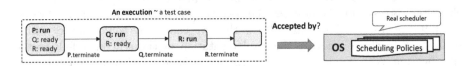

Fig. 1. An example for the testing

Here, we face these two following problems: (a) how to chose a suitable set of processes with their attributes (called an environment) for the testing, and (b)

---

[2] https://sites.google.com/site/trannhathoa/home/sspinja (accessed: 1-Jun-2019).

how to create the tests from the corresponding environment. In addition, with a concurrent system, there are multiple executions of the processes. It leads to the fact that manually making the tests is error-prone and time-consuming. That means a systematic approach is necessary. To address these problems, we apply MBT techniques to generate the tests automatically and exhaustively. Our method is as follows, first, we extend our DSL to define the tests generated. Then, we determine the necessary environments for the testing. After that, we apply model checking techniques to indicate the executions of the system to generate the tests using the specification of the test above. We then apply the tests with the real implementation of the scheduler in an OS. Our method for the testing is depicted in Fig. 2. It includes three main steps.

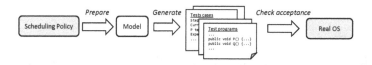

Fig. 2. Testing method

In the first step, a model is used to represent the behaviors of the system. With a scheduling policy, this model includes a set of processes and a scheduler. We call the processes and their attributes as an environment. Actually, the environment is necessary for the testing because the processes are used to perform the scheduling tasks. In the second step, we explore the model of the system (realized by the set of processes and the scheduler) to determine the executions of these processes following the scheduling policy. Each execution indicates a test case to generate the tests. The corresponding code for a test (test case or test program) is now constructed by mapping the behaviors of the system to the codes generated (this method is depicted in Fig. 3). In the last step, we perform the tests to check whether these executions are accepted by the real scheduler in an OS. That means the behaviors specified by the scheduling policy exist in the real scheduler.

Fig. 3. Method for generating the tests

Our approach for generating the tests is depicted in Fig. 4; the corresponding parts are explained in details in Sect. 3. The main points are as follows.

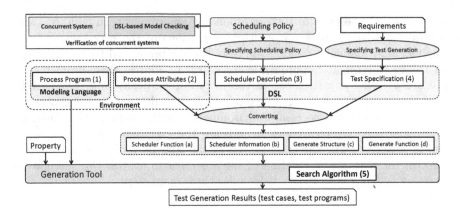

Fig. 4. Test generation approach

Firstly, the behaviors of the processes and the attributes of the processes are specified in (a) *process program* (1) and (b) *process attributes* (2). The information needed for performing scheduling tasks is generated from the description of the scheduling policy in the DSL (called *scheduler description* (3)). Here, the *scheduler function* (a) is used to perform the scheduling tasks (i.e. handling the scheduling events[3]) and the *scheduler information* (b) is for determining the state of the system. Based on the description of the scheduler, a *search algorithm* (5) is realized to explore the system state space.

Secondly, we aim to check the correspondence between the specification of the scheduling policy and the real behaviors of the scheduler. Actually, in the specification, the behaviors of the scheduler are specified in the *scheduling events*. Therefore, we need to check the correspondence between these events and the behaviors of the real scheduler. That means the code generated needs to be considered with the *scheduling events*.

Thirdly, to generate the test, we extend our DSL to specify the tests generated. The description of the test (called *test specification* (4)) is used to generate (1) a *generate structure* (c) and (2) a *generate function* (d). These two artifacts are used to generate the tests following the search on the state space, where (a) the *generate structure* determines the structure of the tests (i.e. test cases, test programs) and (b) the *generate function* is used to construct the tests.

Fourthly, the code (of the tests) is determined in the search using the *search algorithm* (5). Each test can be realized (on-the-fly) from the trail that (1) leads to the violation of a property (expressed by an assertion statement in the *process program*) at a state of the system (an error happens) or (2) contains a state that has been visited (an execution of the processes is found). We then apply the tests to check whether the implementation of the scheduler follows the specification to guarantee the correctness of the specification of the scheduling policy.

---

[3] We deal with the behaviors of the scheduler based on handling scheduling events.

As shown in Fig. 4, the quality of the policy affects the verification result. That means checking the correctness of the specification of the scheduling policy is necessary and important. The validated scheduling policy now helps to ensure the correctness of the concurrent systems in the verification.

3   DSL for Scheduling Policies and Test Generation

3.1   Language for Scheduling Policies

In the previous work [20], to facilitate the scheduling policies, we propose a DSL for specifying the scheduling tasks. Our DSL contains two types of the specification: (a) the attributes of the processes and (b) the behaviors of the scheduler. An example for specifying the *priority* scheduling policy is depicted in Fig. 5. With this example, the behaviors of the processes, the attributes of the processes, and the behaviors of the scheduler are specified in (a) *process program*, (b) *process attribute*, and (c) *scheduler description*, respectively.

```
int a, b;
proctype P() {
next:
if
    :: (a+b) < 100000 -> a++; goto next;
    :: else -> sch_api_self(terminate)
fi;
}
proctype Q() {
next:
if
    :: (a+b) < 100000 -> b++; goto next;
    :: else -> sch_api_self(terminate)
fi;
}
init { sch_exec(P()); sch_exec(Q()); }
```
a) Process program

```
def process Priority {
    attribute{ var byte priority; }
    proctype P() { this.priority = 5; }
    proctype Q() { this.priority = 3;
}
init { [{P(), Q()}] }
```
b) Process attribute

```
scheduler Priority () {
    data { collection ready using priorityOrder; }
    event handler {
        select_process (process p) {
            get process from ready to run;
        }
        new_process (process target) {
            move target to ready;
            if (!running_process.isNull()) {
                if (target.priority > running_process.priority) {
                    move running_process to ready;
                }
            }
        }
    }
    interface { function terminate(process target) { remove target; } }
}
comparator {
    variable { int x; }
    comparetype priorityOrder(process p_n, p_o) {
        x = p_n.priority - p_o.priority;
        if (x>0) return greater;
        else if (x==0) return equal; else return less;
    }
}
```
c) Scheduler description

Fig. 5. An example for the scheduling policy

The behaviors of the processes are described in a modeling language, which is based on Promela [8]. The set of processes and their initial attributes are determined in the *process attribute* (b). That can be done by defining (a) the attributes of the processes, (b) the process types (i.e. the processes with the same behaviors) with the initial values for the attributes, and (c) the initialization of these processes. In the example, we define two processes (P and Q); the priority of P is greater than that of Q; these two processes are executed at the same time.

The main task of a scheduler is selecting a process for the execution and changing the running statuses of the processes (e.g. blocking a process). There is a situation that multiple processes can be selected to run (e.g. the processes with the same priority). To deal with this fact, we order processes using their attributes for the selection. Firstly, we introduce collections, which are defined in the *data* part of the *scheduler description* (c), to represent the statuses of the processes. Each collection is an abstract data type that maintains a partially ordered set (poset) of the processes. Secondly, we define the ordering method for the processes by declaring a function in the *comparator* part. In the example (as shown in Fig. 5), a collection named `ready` is used. This collection uses function `priorityOrder` to order the processes. With this function, the process with higher priority will be placed in front of the other in the collection. If two processes have the same priority, they will have the same order.

To perform the scheduling tasks, the scheduler handles the scheduling events, which are defined in the *event handlers* and the *interface functions* of the *scheduler description* (as shown in Fig. 5c). Some of these events are pre-defined, which are `new_process`, `select_process`, and `clock`. The event `new_process` occurs when a new process arrives to the system. The event `select_process` is for selecting a process to run. The event `clock` is a timer event, which happens following the occurrence of each action of the process[4]. Besides, to allow the communication between the processes and the scheduler, such as a process can increase its priority, we provide an interface to define the scheduling tasks performed by the process (called *process scheduling events*). That is showed in the *interface functions* part. In the example (Fig. 5), the scheduler handles two events (`new_process` and `select_process`). When a new process (indicated by `target`) arrives, if its priority is greater than that of the current process (indicated by `running_process`), the current process will be preempted (by putting it to the `ready` collection). This makes the scheduler select another process to run. To do that, the scheduler obtains a process from this collection. That behavior is specified in the `select_process` event handler. In this example, an interface function named `terminate` is defined to terminate the current process.

3.2   Language for the Test Generation

In our work, the scheduling policy is specified in the DSL. To indicate the behaviors of the system, we need to prepare the set of processes with the corresponding attributes (called an environment). Actually, the number of processes with their attributes can be determined based on the purpose of the testing. For example, to check the selection of the scheduler with *priority* policy, we can use only 2 processes with different values for the priorities of these processes. In fact, the values for the attributes can be limited, e.g. we can use different priorities in the range [0..2] for the processes. Moreover, we can determine the behaviors needed for the testing, e.g. the processes perform scheduling tasks, such as terminating itself or executing a new process. We now can determine the environment(s) to realize the model of the system, which indicates the behaviors of the processes following the scheduling policy. We then use this model to generate the tests (test cases and test programs).

---

[4] We consider that an action of the process takes one time unit.

```
int cnt ;
proctype P () {
  do
    :: d_step{
      sch_api_self(terminate);
      cnt--
    };
    :: d_step{
      sch_api_self(runP);
      if
        :: cnt <= 2 -> cnt++ ;
        :: else skip ;
      fi ;
    };
    :: skip;
  od
}
init {
  sch_exec(P());
  sch_exec(P());
  cnt = 2 ;
}
```

a) Process program

```
def process linux_0 {
  proctype P () {}
}
init {
  [{P(),P()}]
}
```

b) Process attribute

```
scheduler linux() {
  generate {
    configuration {
      option = { Searching };
      directory = "TestGen";
      file name = "Testcase" ;
      file extension = "txt" ;
      test case = (header + "\n") + (behaviors) ;
    }
    component { header { genln 'Test case following the search' ; } }
    system {
      behavior =('Step '+ getStep()+'/'+getTotalStep() + '\\n' + pre_take) +
        ('Process'+<PID>+<InstanceID> + ' action: ' + action +
        ', then cnt = ' + Sys(cnt) + '\\n') + (post_take + '\\n') ;
    }
  }
  data { collection ready with fifo ; }
  event handler{
    select_process (process target_process) {
      get process from ready to run;
    }
    new_process (process target_process) {
      move target_process to ready ;
    }
    pre_take (){ genln 'Current process count = ' + Sys(cnt); }
    post_take (){ genln 'Expected process count = ' + Sys(cnt); }
  }
  interface {
    function terminate () { remove running_process; }
    function runP() { new P(), 3; }
  }
}
```

c) Scheduler description with test specification

Fig. 6. An example for the test generation

To generate the tests, we extend the DSL to specify the codes generated following the behaviors of the scheduler. We use FIFO scheduling policy to demonstrate the specification of the test generation (as shown in Fig. 6). This example contains three files for describing the behaviors of the processes, the attributes of the processes and the behaviors of the scheduler with the description of test generation, which are specified in *process program* (a), *process attribute* (b), and *scheduler description with test specification* (c), respectively.

We support two types of the test, i.e. *test case* and *test program*. In general, each *test case* contains multiple steps, which indicate the current values of the variables, the behavior of the system, and the expected values for these variables. A *test program* is a program for testing a part of the system (e.g. the scheduler). The program usually has a structure (e.g. the header for the declaration, the main function for performing the program and the functions that express the behaviors of the processes). The structure of a test can be defined using the component(s) defined in the *component* part. Some special components including init, processes, behaviors and error are pre-defined, where: (1) the init component is used for initializing the test generation (e.g., we can use this component to prepare the declaration of the test programs); (2) the processes component corresponds to the set of processes; (3) the behaviors component indicates the set of actions of a process; (4) the error component points out the corresponding error (violation of a property indicating by an assertion in the *test program*), which happens during the execution of the processes.

To support the test generation, we introduce two more events: pre_take and post_take. These events are for dealing with the pre-processing and post-processing of each behavior (action) of a process. For instance, we can display the current value of a variable before taking an action (pre_take) and the expected value of this variable after taking this action (post_take) in a test case. To generate the tests, we introduce statements gen and genln for generating the code following the scheduling events (the difference between gen and genln is that the code generated using genln is with the line break, but gen is not).

In the example (as shown in Fig. 6), we specify the *test cases* generation. Each test case contains two components (header and behaviors). The structure of the tests and the template of each component are defined. We use the string operator to produce each component. The code generated is specified in the events pre_take and post_take using the genln statements. The value of the variable cnt defined in the *process program* can be get using the function Sys(). The codes generated indicate the current value of the cnt variable before taking an action of the current process and the expected value of the variable after taking this action. We use the string operations to concatenate the codes and the components (in text string) with functions getStep() and getTotalStep() (the index of the step and the number of steps in a test case).

4   Test Generation with Scheduling Policies

We propose an algorithm to generate the tests following the search using the scheduling policy and the test specification. To deal with the scheduling policy, the behaviors of the scheduler are considered. The algorithm is shown in Algorithm 1, which is an extension of the algorithm introduced in [20]. Our idea for the generation is that the codes generated (by mapping the behaviors of the system with the text strings) are recorded during the search and are used to generate the tests after an execution being found.

The algorithm performs a search starting from function START (line 3) to visit every state that is reachable from the initial state Σ_0 of the system. The behaviors of the system following the scheduling policy are determined by these following functions. Function SCH_SELECT (line 14) is used to obtain the processes for the execution (it happens when the system has no running process). This function can return an empty set (line 15) indicating that no process can be executed. In this case, the system only performs the timer action (*clock*) determined by function SCH_CLOCK (line 16). Otherwise, all actions of the processes selected (line 26, 27) are considered. Function SCH_TAKE (line 28) performs an action a of the process to change the system state: $\Sigma_a = \text{SCH\_TAKE}(a, \Sigma)$.

To generate the tests, the data structures corresponding to a *test sequence* ($\mathcal{TS}$) and the result of the *test generation* ($\mathcal{TG}$) are used, where $\mathcal{TS}$ is an ordered set of *generation steps* (a *generation step* corresponds to the code generated following a behavior of the system) and $\mathcal{TG}$ is an unordered set of strings representing the result of the test generation. We also introduce the following functions: (1) Function *getIO* (line 17, 30) is used to get the values of the variables at a state of the system; (2) Function *genCode* (line 17, 30) is used to generate the corresponding code following a behavior of the system; (3) Function *Add_step* (line 17, 30) is used to add a *generation step* to the *test sequence*; (4) Function *Remove_last_step* (line 42) is for removing the last *generation step* from the

Algorithm 1. *Test generation algorithm following the search*

```
 1:  Input: Σ₀                                                    ▷ initial state
 2:  Output: 𝒯𝒢                                                   ▷ test generation
 3:  procedure START
 4:      Stack: 𝒮𝒯 = ∅
 5:      State space: 𝒮𝒫 = ∅
 6:      Test sequence: 𝒯𝒮 = ∅
 7:      Test generation: 𝒯𝒢 = ∅
 8:      Push(𝒮𝒯, Σ₀)
 9:      Add_state(𝒮𝒫, Σ₀)
10:      SEARCH
11:  end procedure
12:  procedure SEARCH
13:      Σ = Top(𝒮𝒯)
14:      P = SCH_SELECT(Σ)
15:      if P == ∅ then
16:          Σᵗ = SCH_CLOCK(Σ)
17:          Add_step(𝒯𝒮, ⟨⟨getIO(Σ), getIO(Σᵗ)⟩, genCode(⟨Σ, clock, Σᵗ⟩)⟩)
18:          if Contains(𝒮𝒫, Σᵗ) == false then
19:              Push(𝒮𝒯, Σᵗ)
20:              Add_state(𝒮𝒫, Σᵗ)
21:              SEARCH
22:          else
23:              Add_test(𝒯𝒢, genTest(𝒯𝒮))
24:          end if
25:      else
26:          for p ∈ P do
27:              for a ∈ p.L_p do
28:                  Σₐ = SCH_TAKE(a, Σ)
29:                  Σₐᵗ = SCH_CLOCK(Σₐ)
30:                  Add_step(𝒯𝒮, ⟨⟨getIO(Σ), getIO(Σₐᵗ)⟩, genCode(⟨Σ, a, Σₐᵗ⟩)⟩)
31:                  if Contains(𝒮𝒫, Σₐᵗ) == false then
32:                      Push(𝒮𝒯, Σₐᵗ)
33:                      Add_state(𝒮𝒫, Σₐᵗ)
34:                      SEARCH
35:                  else
36:                      Add_test(𝒯𝒢, genTest(𝒯𝒮))
37:                  end if
38:              end for
39:          end for
40:      end if
41:      Pop(𝒮𝒯)
42:      Remove_last_step(𝒯𝒮)
43:  end procedure
```

test sequence; (5) Function *genTest* (line 23, 36) is used to generate the test from the *test sequence*; (6) Function *Add_test* (line 23, 36) is used to add a test derived from the *test sequence* ($\mathcal{TS}$) to the set of tests ($\mathcal{TG}$). This function is called when the search reaches to a visited state.

We note that, if the error is determined at the current state, e.g. taking an action that leads to the violation of a property, we can generate a test from the current *test sequence*. This fact is not shown in this algorithm.

5   Implementation

We extend our tool named SSpinJa, which is first introduced in [20], to deal with the test generation with the scheduling policy. The architecture of our tool is shown in Fig. 7. The back-end of the tool was extended from SpinJa [12], which is a re-implementation of Spin model checker [10]. SpinJa is developed in Java using the object-oriented design principle with the aim to extend easily while being competitive in memory usage and runtime. We used XText framework [3] for the implementing of the DSL. XText is a framework for the development of programming languages and DSL. It supports a full infrastructure including parser, linker, type checker, compiler as well as the editing environment for the development.

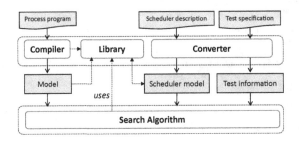

Fig. 7. The architecture of the tool.

We follow the compilation approach to prepare the necessary information beforehand. The *process program* in the modeling language is compiled into a model (in Java) which uses the libraries of SSpinJa. A converter under the XText framework was built to generate all necessary information from the description of the scheduling policy and from the test specification. This information is for performing the scheduling tasks and generating the tests following the behaviors of the system. The information generated includes (1) the implementation of the process, (2) the implementation of the collections with ordering methods, (3) the implementation of the scheduler, (4) the structure of the tests and (5) the generation functions. We implemented the search algorithm in the tool for exploring the system state space to generate the tests.

6   Case Studies

In this section, we introduce case studies to check the correspondence between the policy specified in the DSL with the implementation of the real scheduler. Real-time FIFO policy on Linux OS was used in the experiments. The experiments were conducted on Intel Core i7, 3.4 GHz CPU with 32G RAM.

Test Cases Generation. In this experiment, we generated test cases corresponding to the behaviors of the processes defined in the *process program* with FIFO scheduling policy. The description of the policy with the test generation in the DSL is depicted in Fig. 6. Because the specification of Linux scheduling policy indicates that the process with higher priority always preempts the current process, we only used the processes with the same priority to check the selection of the scheduler. With the real-time policies, we used only one configuration for the testing (the processes had the same priority). The test generation was indicated following the search to cover all the states of the system. With this experiment, 14 test cases were generated. The results for the generation are listed in Table 1.

Test Programs Generation. In the next experiment, we generated test programs following the scheduling specified in the DSL to check the correspondence between the description of the policy with the implementation of the scheduler. The real-time FIFO policy and Linux Ubuntu version 12.04.5 are used. Base on the specification of Linux scheduling policy [13], there is a case that when a process arrives, it may preempt the current process if they have the same priority. That means we can not determine which process will be executed next. In this experiment, only the case that the processes had the same priority was considered. Therefore, we created the processes with the same priority and checked which process was selected to run. To generate the test programs, we indicated the scheduling tasks in the *process program* (e.g. terminates itself or executes another process). In comparison with the previous experiment (the test cases generation), the attributes of the processes, and the behaviors of the scheduler are kept. The specification for the test generation was changed to specify the code generated for the test programs. In this experiment, 29 programs were generated. A summary of the results is represented in Table 1.

Table 1. Test generation result

	No. tests	States	Memory (MB.)	Time (s)
Test cases generation	14	16	21.119	0.03
Test programs generation	29	16	21.2529	0.05

For executing the test programs, there is no specification of the implementation of this Linux version indicating which process will be selected to run if a process with the same priority as the current one arrives at the system (i.e. the current process *may be* preempted). In this situation, we can make the assumption that for an implementation of Linux OS, the scheduler can select any process among these processes to run. In fact, with our approach, a test is generated following only an execution of the system. Thus, it cannot handle all the possible executions of these processes. To check the specification of the scheduling policy with the implementation of the scheduler, our method is based on executing the test program multiple times with checking the execution orders of the processes. Here, we count the actions of the processes (called *steps*). A test program is passed (in testing) if all the actions are performed in the right order. We wrote a test script to execute the tests generated and handle the results of the execution. The bound of times to try for each program was set to 1000000. In this experiment, all the tests were passed after 1388702 times to try in total 2371.407 s. The detail results are shown in Table 2.

Table 2. Test program execution results

Test program	Passed	No. steps	Times to try	Time (s)
Program_0.c	Yes	4	674	1.147
Program_1.c	Yes	2	1	0.004
Program_2.c	Yes	4	81	0.214
Program_3.c	Yes	2	1	0.004
Program_4.c	Yes	4	89	0.215
Program_5.c	Yes	7	813	2.429
Program_6.c	Yes	7	264453	451.564
Program_7.c	Yes	4	52284	89.027
Program_8.c	Yes	8	159024	272.397
Program_9.c	Yes	2	12140	20.730
Program_10.c	Yes	4	595	1.138
Program_11.c	Yes	3	15904	27.686
Program_12.c	Yes	6	52659	92.072
Program_13.c	Yes	6	6023	10.440
Program_14.c	Yes	8	52506	88.996
Program_15.c	Yes	8	400181	681.109
Program_16.c	Yes	4	676	1.149
Program_17.c	Yes	8	107358	182.041
Program_18.c	Yes	5	18433	31.164
Program_19.c	Yes	8	635	1.118
Program_20.c	Yes	3	629	1.084
Program_21.c	Yes	3	14044	23.764
Program_22.c	Yes	4	25	0.074
Program_23.c	Yes	8	209274	355.802
Program_24.c	Yes	4	11002	18.633
Program_25.c	Yes	7	923	1.695
Program_26.c	Yes	7	8135	15.364
Program_27.c	Yes	6	1	0.008
Program_28.c	Yes	6	139	0.339

Discussion. As shown in Table 2, all the tests are passed. That means all the behaviors specified in the specification exist in the real scheduler. In other words, the specification can specify the behaviors of the scheduler. The experiments also showed that our approach is practical. In fact, we can generate the test programs for checking the correspondence between the specification of the FIFO policy and the implementation of the Linux scheduler. This is done easily with the support of the DSL. In addition, with the test specification in the DSL, all the test cases and the test programs were generated automatically. The behaviors of the processes are modeled in the *process program*. Here, we use the search to explore the corresponding system state space, therefore, all the states of the system are covered and represented in the tests.

The execution orders of the processes affect the code generated. For example, which process selected among the processes with the same priority will lead to the different code generated in comparison with the others. In our implementation, all of the duplicate results in the test generation will be removed. Therefore, although using the same *process program* and the same scheduling policy, the number of test cases (in the first experiment) and the number of test programs (in the second experiment) are different. Besides, in our approach, the specification of the scheduling policy and the test specification in the DSL is reusable and flexible to deal with the variation of the behaviors of the scheduler with the test generation. The number of lines of description code for each scheduling policy and for the test generation used in the experiments is really small in comparison with the results of the tests generated (as shown in Table 3). In other words, using the DSL is an effective way for the specification.

Table 3. Number of lines of the code generated

Experiment	No. lines of the specification	Test generation results
Test cases generation (a)	**72**	**14** test cases, **317** lines
Test programs generation (b)	**124**	**29** test programs, **3058** lines

Actually, with our method, we can check the correspondence between the specification of the scheduling policy and the real strategy implemented in the OS. That helps us to increase the confidence of the specification of the scheduling policy to ensure the correctness of software systems. Here, with the automatic test generation, we can easily deal with the quality assurance of the software product (i.e. the system with the scheduling policies). In another hand, with the conformance testing approach, by assuming the correctness of the specification of the scheduling policy, we can generate the tests to check the correctness of the implementation of the scheduler in an OS.

However, there is a case that the specification of the scheduling policy is not clear to describe the behaviors of the scheduler (as shown in the specification of Linux FIFO scheduling policy). That means there are multiple options for the implementation of the scheduler. We call them as non-deterministic behaviors of the scheduler. For testing these behaviors, executing a test program many times to check the satisfaction is an ineffective approach because it only shows the satisfaction indicated by the program and can not prove the dissatisfaction. Besides, we can see that the average times to try and the average time for executing the programs corresponding to the number of the steps in these experiments are varied (as shown in Fig. 8). The problem is now how to design a suitable test program which can cover the non-deterministic behaviors of the system mentioned above.

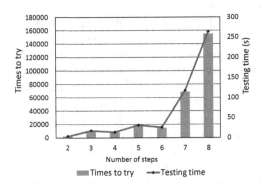

Fig. 8. Experimental results.

7   Related Work

Our work uses testing techniques to deal with checking the correspondence between the specification and the implementation. Recent researches use designed models taken from UML diagrams, such as state diagram, activity diagram, use cases diagram and sequence diagram for test cases generation [15,18,19]. There are works to deal with this problem using technologies from verification (model-checking, SAT solving and constraint satisfaction) [1,6,16,17]. With the behaviors of each process representing in the model of the system, we can find the executions that lead to the violation of a property (counter-examples) or satisfy the property (witness) using model checking approach. In addition, there are tools, such as SAL [9] and STG [5], for the test generation. SAL uses a specification with Boolean *trap variables* representing test goals to generate the tests. STG use symbolic generation techniques to deal with the state space explosion problem. In our approach, we apply MBT techniques for the test generation. Our research uses the search to explore the state space and generate the tests following the behaviors of the system as these approaches do. However, these works and tools do not deal with the scheduling policies as our work does.

The research proposed by Chen and Aoki [4] introduces the scheduler in the system model to generate test cases with the help of Spin model checker for conformance testing of OSEK/VDX OS. In fact, Spin can print out the information of the system during the checking phase using embedded C function of Promela. Their work uses this functionality to produce the log corresponding to the invoked system services and the current state of the system. Using that log, another tool will generate test cases for checking the implementation of the system. This is a practical work. However, because this work is based on the support of the model checker, we can see that the approach has several limitations. Firstly, the scheduler is modeled and embedded in the model of the system. Thus, the checking phase needs to consider many behaviors of the system and store unnecessary information of the scheduler. Secondly, we need to build another tool to complete the generation with the results produced by the model checker. Thirdly, it is difficult to deal with other scheduling policies for generating the tests. In comparison with this work, our method can be regarded as conformance testing as this work does. However, our purpose for this research is different and we have already overcome these problems above.

In our approach, we propose a DSL to facilitate the specification of the scheduling policies and the test generation. There are some works introducing the DSL for the test generation. For specifying system operations, the work [11] introduced a DSL to extract the test cases from use case definitions. However, it only focuses on automating the system test process and does not deal with the scheduler. Paiva et al. [14] proposed a DSL for automatic generation of test cases from the specification of a system. This work focus on interactive components of the system and lack of behaviors of the system. To deal with verifying the event-based systems, Cyrille Artho et al. presented a tool named Modbat [2], which provides a DSL for constructing the state machine based on the explicit representation of system states. That means the behaviors of the system are modeled as finite state machine explicitly in the DSL proposed. Our research is different from these works because our DSL is for specifying the scheduling policies with the test generation and the system state space is built on-the-fly during the verification.

Our DSL is based on the language introduced in the previous work [20]. This language aims to deal with the variation of the scheduling policies used in model checking techniques. For generating the tests, in this work, we extend our language for specifying the tests generated. In fact, several elements were added to the DSL for defining the tests with the structure and the template of the tests. For exploring the state space, we also introduce a new search algorithm to construct the tests. The test generation is produced using the searching trails resulted by the verification.

8   Conclusion

This paper presents an approach to check the correspondence between the specification of the scheduling policy and the implementation in an OS using testing techniques. The overall method can be regarded as conformance testing. As a result of testing, we can find the inconsistency between the specification and the implementation of the real scheduler. If no inconsistency is found, we can increase the confidence of the quality of the scheduling policy before making any verification of the system run on the real OS.

The advantages of our approach are: (1) the specification of the tests in the DSL is flexible to generate the tests, (2) the descriptions of the system can be reused completely, and (3) the approach is practical.

We have the following contributions for this paper. First, we propose a DSL to provide a high-level support for the succinct specification of the test generation with the scheduling policies. Second, we propose a search algorithm to explore the state space to generate the tests following the behaviors of the scheduler. Third, we implement our method in a tool to generate the tests exhaustively and automatically.

In the future, we plan to study some heuristic methods for selecting suitable execution paths for the test generation. In addition, we are going to overcome the problem of checking the non-deterministic behaviors of the systems.

References

1. Ammann, P.E., Black, P.E., Majurski, W.: Using model checking to generate tests from specifications. In: Proceedings Second International Conference on Formal Engineering Methods, 1998, pp. 46–54. IEEE (1998)
2. Artho, C.V., et al.: Modbat: a model-based API tester for event-driven systems. In: Bertacco, V., Legay, A. (eds.) HVC 2013. LNCS, vol. 8244, pp. 112–128. Springer, Cham (2013). https://doi.org/10.1007/978-3-319-03077-7_8
3. Bettini, L.: Implementing Domain-Specific Languages with Xtext and Xtend. Packt Publishing Ltd., Birmingham (2013)
4. Chen, J., Aoki, T.: Conformance testing for OSEK/VDX operating system using model checking. In: 2011 18th Asia Pacific Software Engineering Conference (APSEC), pp. 274–281. IEEE (2011)
5. Clarke, D., Jéron, T., Rusu, V., Zinovieva, E.: STG: a symbolic test generation tool. In: Katoen, J.-P., Stevens, P. (eds.) TACAS 2002. LNCS, vol. 2280, pp. 470–475. Springer, Heidelberg (2002). https://doi.org/10.1007/3-540-46002-0_34
6. DeMilli, R., Offutt, A.J.: Constraint-based automatic test data generation. IEEE Transact. Softw. Eng. **17**(9), 900–910 (1991)
7. Fowler, M.: Domain-Specific Languages. Pearson Education, London (2010)
8. Gerth, R.: Concise PROMELA reference (1997). http://spinroot.com/spin/Man/Quick.html
9. Hamon, G., De Moura, L., Rushby, J.: Automated test generation with SAL. CSL Technical Note p. 15 (2005)
10. Holzmann, G.J.: The SPIN Model Checker: Primer and Reference Manual, vol. 1003. Addison-Wesley Reading, Boston (2004)
11. Im, K., Im, T., McGregor, J.D.: Automating test case definition using a domain specific language. In: Proceedings of the 46th Annual Southeast Regional Conference on XX, pp. 180–185. ACM (2008)
12. de Jonge, M., Ruys, T.C.: The SPINJA model checker. In: van de Pol, J., Weber, M. (eds.) SPIN 2010. LNCS, vol. 6349, pp. 124–128. Springer, Heidelberg (2010). https://doi.org/10.1007/978-3-642-16164-3_9
13. Kerrisk, M.: SCHED(7) Linux Programmer's Manual. http://man7.org/linux/man-pages/man7/sched.7.html, accessed 10 Jan 2017
14. Paiva, A.C., Faria, J.P., Vidal, R.M.: Automated specification-based testing of interactive components with AsmL. In: QUATIC, pp. 119–126 (2004)
15. Patel, P.E., Patil, N.N.: Testcases formation using UML activity diagram. In: 2013 International Conference on Communication Systems and Network Technologies (CSNT), pp. 884–889. IEEE (2013)

16. Peleska, J., Vorobev, E., Lapschies, F.: Automated test case generation with SMT-solving and abstract interpretation. In: Bobaru, M., Havelund, K., Holzmann, G.J., Joshi, R. (eds.) NFM 2011. LNCS, vol. 6617, pp. 298–312. Springer, Heidelberg (2011). https://doi.org/10.1007/978-3-642-20398-5_22

17. Seater, R., Dennis, G.: Automated test data generation with SAT (2005). http://groups.csail.mit.edu/pag/6.883/projects/mutant-test-generation.pdf

18. Shirole, M., Kumar, R.: UML behavioral model based test case generation: a survey. ACM SIGSOFT Softw. Eng. Notes **38**(4), 1–13 (2013)

19. Swain, S.K., Mohapatra, D.P., Mall, R.: Test case generation based on use case and sequence diagram. Int. J. Softw. Eng. **3**(2), 21–52 (2010)

20. Tran, N.H., Chiba, Y., Aoki, T.: Domain-specific language facilitates scheduling in model checking. In: 2017 24th Asia-Pacific Software Engineering Conference (APSEC), pp. 417–426. IEEE (2017)

A Study of Learning Data Structure Invariants Using Off-the-shelf Tools

Muhammad Usman[(✉)], Wenxi Wang[(✉)], Kaiyuan Wang[(✉)], Cagdas Yelen[(✉)],
Nima Dini[(✉)], and Sarfraz Khurshid[(✉)]

University of Texas at Austin, Austin, TX 78712, USA
{muhammadusman,wenxiw,kaiyuanw,cagdas,nima.dini,khurshid}@utexas.edu

Abstract. Data structure invariants play a key role in checking correctness of code, e.g., a model checker can use an invariant, e.g., acyclicity of a binary tree, that is written in the form of an assertion to search for program executions that violate it, e.g., erroneously introduce a cycle in the structure. Traditionally, the properties are written manually by the users. However, writing them manually can itself be error-prone, which can lead to false alarms or missed bugs. This paper presents a controlled experiment on applying a suite of off-the-shelf machine learning (ML) tools to learn properties of dynamically allocated data structures that reside on the program heap. Specifically, we use 10 data structure subjects, and systematically create training and test data for 6 ML methods, which include decision trees, support vector machines, and neural networks, for binary classification, e.g., to classify input structures as valid binary search trees. The study reveals two key findings. One, most of the ML methods studied – with off-the-shelf parameter settings and without fine tuning – achieve at least 90% accuracy on all of the subjects. Two, high accuracy is achieved even when the size of the training data is significantly smaller than the size of the test data. We believe future work can utilize the learnt invariants to automate dynamic and static analyses, thereby enabling advances in machine learning to further enhance software testing and verification techniques.

Keywords: Data structure invariants · Machine learning · Korat

1 Introduction

Data structure invariants are properties that the data structures in a program must satisfy in valid states, e.g., a binary search tree implementation must create structures that are trees, i.e., contain no cycles, and consist of keys that appear in the tree in the correct search order. In object-oriented programs such invariants are termed class invariants and are expected to hold in all publicly-visible states [28,34].

Data structure invariants play a key role in testing and verification. For example, when written as assertions they enable a number of assertion-based checking

© Springer Nature Switzerland AG 2019
F. Biondi et al. (Eds.): SPIN 2019, LNCS 11636, pp. 226–243, 2019.
https://doi.org/10.1007/978-3-030-30923-7_13

techniques. To illustrate, in software testing, they serve as test assertions as well as a basis of automated test generation [4,27]; in model checking, they serve as target assertions that a model checker can try to violate, i.e., find a program execution that leads to an assertion violation [20,23,33,47]; in runtime verification, they provide a basis for error recovery using data structure repair [11,13]; and in static analysis, they enable deep semantic checking [8,24,35,40,42,48].

Data structure invariants are often written manually by users who want to utilize them for automated testing or verification. However, writing complex invariants manually itself can be error-prone and errors in invariants can lead to false alarms or undetected faults. To reduce the burden on the user to write invariants, researchers have developed several techniques for automatically creating invariants using various forms of analyses. While a vast majority of the techniques utilize static or dynamic analysis [10,12,14,26,29,32,35,40,42,43,48], a few techniques have leveraged machine learning methods to characterize invariants [16,30] and serve as a basis for our work.

This paper presents a controlled experiment on applying a suite of off-the-shelf machine learning (ML) tools to learn invariants of dynamically allocated data structures. Specifically, we use 6 ML methods that include four methods based on decision trees [39], as well as support vector machines [9] and multi-layer perceptrons [36]. As data structure subjects we use structural invariants of 10 data structures that have been studied before in several contexts [4,13,16], including most recently for training binary classifiers using feed-forward artificial neural networks [16].

The subjects were introduced in the public distribution of the automated test input generator Korat [1,4] and were originally developed for the purpose of evaluating Korat's input generation. Each data structure contains a Java method called *repOk* that implements an executable check for the properties that represent the corresponding structural invariants (and a variety of other methods). Given a *repOk* method and a bound on the input size, e.g., 5 nodes for a binary search tree, Korat performs a backtracking search over the space of all candidate inputs (up to the size bound) for *repOk* to systematically enumerate all inputs for which *repOk* returns true. For increased efficiency, Korat only considers non-isomorphic candidates. During its search, Korat typically inspects each candidate by running *repOk* on it to get feedback for pruning the search, and as a result outputs only the *valid* inputs, i.e., inputs for which *repOk* returns true.

Our study methodology is as follows. For each data structure subject invariant and ML model, we first create training and test data, then we train the ML model using the training data, and finally we evaluate it using the test data. To create the training/test data, we use Korat to exhaustively explore the bounded input space and create every valid input. The set of all valid inputs forms the positive samples and a subset of invalid inputs inspected by Korat forms the negative samples. In general, for complex structural properties, the number of valid structures is much smaller than the number of invalid structures. Therefore, to avoid training an incorrect model that simply learns to predict false with high probability, we use *balanced* sets of samples such that there are the same number of positive and negative samples. To study how *learnable* the invariants are we vary the ratio of training and test data from 75 to 25 respectively, which is common in the field of machine learning, to 10 to 90 respectively, which allow us to study the setting where the training data is relatively scarce.

The study reveals two key findings. One, most of ML methods studied – with off-the-shelf parameter settings and without fine tuning – achieve at least 90% accuracy on all of the subjects. Two, the accuracy is achieved even when the size of the training data is significantly smaller than the size of the test data. We find the results quite encouraging and believe machine learning methods hold much promise in developing new techniques for more effective software analysis.

The training and test/evaluation datasets used in our study are publicly available at: https://github.com/muhammadusman93/Spin2019KoratML.

2   Background: Korat and Learning

This section provides the necessary background on the Korat test input generator [4] and basic machine learning models that we use in our study.

2.1   Korat

Korat is a framework for automatic test input generation for Java programs. It takes as input a Java predicate, termed *repOk* method, and a finitization on the input domain, and generates all possible inputs for which the predicate returns true. Korat repeatedly executes *repOk* on candidate inputs, monitors the object fields accessed by *repOk* for each input, and uses this information to create next candidates to consider. Korat implements a backtracking search that prunes large parts of the input space while preserving the completeness of the search and correctness of the generated valid test input. Moreover, Korat generates only non-isomorphic inputs and does not consider any isomorphic candidates during search, which significantly reduces the number of generated inputs and time overhead.

To illustrate, Fig. 1 shows the `BinaryTree` class, including the `repOk` predicate and finitization `finBinaryTree`. The binary tree has a root field of type `Node` and a `size` field that is a primitive integer. The `Node` class declares a `left` field and a `right` field, representing the left child and the right child of the node. The method `repOk` checks if its input does not have any cycle and has the correct value for size. `repOk` returns `true` if the checked property holds and `false` otherwise. The finitization method `finBinaryTree` specifies a bound on the total number of nodes, and the min and max values for size.

The Korat search internally represents each candidate input structure using a candidate vector of integer indices whose length depends on the finitization and elements that represent object fields. Each element of the candidate vector indexes into an appropriate domain of values for the corresponding field. To illustrate, for a finitization of up to 3 nodes (Node 1, Node 2, and Node 3) and

```
class BinaryTree {
  static class Node {
    Node left, right; }

  Node root;
  int size;

  boolean repOk() {
    if (root == null) return size == 0;
    // checks that tree has no cycle
    Set visited = new HashSet();
    visited.add(root);
    LinkedList workList = new LinkedList();
    workList.add(root);
    while (!workList.isEmpty()) {
      Node current = (Node) workList.removeFirst();
      if (current.left != null) {
        if (!visited.add(current.left)) return false;
        workList.add(current.left);
      }
      if (current.right != null) {
        if (!visited.add(current.right)) return false;
        workList.add(current.right);
      }
    }
    // checks that size is consistent
    return (visited.size() == size); }

  static IFinitization finBinaryTree(int size) {
    return finBinaryTree(size, size, size); }

  static IFinitization finBinaryTree(int nodesNum, int minSize,
                                     int maxSize) {
    IFinitization f = FinitizationFactory.create(BinaryTree.class);
    IObjSet nodes = f.createObjSet(Node.class, nodesNum, true);
    f.set("root", nodes);
    f.set("size", f.createIntSet(minSize, maxSize));
    f.set("Node.left", nodes);
    f.set("Node.right", nodes);
    return f; }}
```

Fig. 1. BinaryTree repOk and finitization

size equal to 3, Korat creates a candidate vector of length 8: index 0 represents the value of the root field; index 1 represents the size (and its value is fixed as 0 since size is allowed to take only one value, i.e., 3); indexes 2 and 3 represent the left and right children of Node 1 respectively; likewise indexes 4, 5 and 6, 7 represent the left/right children of Node 2 and Node 3 respectively. The value of each index that represents a node ranges from 0 to 3, representing 4 possibilities: [null, Node 1, Node 2 and Node 3]. This finitization defines a bounded exploration space of size $4 \times 1 \times (4 \times 4)^3 = 16,384$ since the tree root and each of left and right fields of each of the 3 nodes have 4 possible values, and the tree size is fixed to 1 value.

The Korat search generates the following candidate vectors for a binary tree using this finitization:

0 0 0 0 0 0 0 0 :: 0 1
1 0 0 0 0 0 0 0 :: 0 2 3 1
1 0 0 1 0 0 0 0 :: 0 2 3
1 0 0 2 0 0 0 0 :: 0 2 3 4 5 1
1 0 0 2 0 1 0 0 :: 0 2 3 4 5
1 0 0 2 0 2 0 0 :: 0 2 3 4 5
1 0 0 2 0 3 0 0 :: 0 2 3 4 5 6 7 1 ***
1 0 0 2 0 3 0 1 :: 0 2 3 4 5 6 7

....

1 0 2 3 1 0 0 0 :: 0 2 3 4
1 0 2 3 2 0 0 0 :: 0 2 3 4
1 0 2 3 3 0 0 0 :: 0 2 3 4

Each row shows two entities separated by :: . The first entity is the candidate vector and is shown before :: . The second entity is field access ordering and is shown after :: . Valid structures are marked by ***.

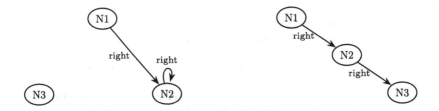

Fig. 2. Invalid binary tree   **Fig. 3.** Valid binary tree

To illustrate, the candidate vector [1 0 0 2 0 2 0 0] represents an invalid binary tree as shown in Fig. 2. The first index states that Node 1 is the root node. The left child of Node 1 is null and the right child of Node 1 is Node 2. Similarly, the left child of Node 2 is null and the right child of Node 2 is Node 2 itself. Both children of Node 3 are null. Thus, the candidate vector represents an invalid binary tree because Node 2 has a self-loop (cycle).

Another example candidate vector [1 0 0 2 0 3 0 0] represents a valid binary tree as shown in Fig. 3. This candidate vector shows that Node 1 is the root node. The left child of Node 1 is null and the right child of Node 1 is Node 2. Similarly, the left child of Node 2 is null and the right child of Node 2 is Node

3. Both children of node 3 are `null`. Since the binary tree has no cycle, and it has size 3 with 3 nodes reachable from the root, the binary tree is valid.

For this finitization, Korat creates and inspects 63 candidate structures (out of 16384 total candidates while pruning the rest), and outputs 5 of them as valid binary trees with 3 nodes. Korat search breaks isomorphisms, which helps to reduce the number of structures to be explored and generated, thus speeding up the search – note, none of the structures explored by Korat are isomorphic. To illustrate Korat's backtracking search, when Korat finds that the candidate vector [1 0 0 2 0 2 0 0] makes the `repOk` returns false and the last accessed field is the right child of Node 2, it simply increases the value of index 5 (from 2 to 3) and point the right child of Node 2 to Node 3. Korat knows that the left and right children of Node 3 do not affect the result of `repOk` since those fields are not read by `repOk` for the given candidate and thus can be ignored for this combination of values for fields accessed. This pruning helps Korat remove a lot of invalid structures in practice.

2.2 Machine Learning Models

The machine learning models used in the study are Decision Tree (DT) Classifier [39], ensemble Decision Tree Classifiers (including Random Forest Tree Classifier (RFT) [22], Gradient Boosting Tree Classifier (GBDT) [18] and Adaboost Decision Tree Classifier (ADT) [17]), Support Vector Machine (SVM) [9], and Multi-Layer Perceptron (MLP) [36]. We used Python programming language and Scikit-Learn library [2] to implement these machine learning models.

2.2.1 Decision Tree Classifiers

DT classifier takes a tree as a classifier where each leaf node represents the label of the class, and each intermediate node represents a test on a feature. DT is easy to train and can handle qualitative features without using dummy encoding. However, DT is not good in understanding complex relationships between features and is sensitive to the changes in training data.

2.2.2 Ensemble Decision Tree Classifiers

RFT classifier is based on the bootstrap aggregating (Bagging) technique. The underlying idea is to create multiple decision trees and then combine their results to predict the final classification labels. This technique reduces variance of the model and also does not increase bias, and usually overcomes the problem of over-fitting if sufficient number of decision trees are used. GBDT classifier uses a differentiable loss function and creates a strong model using many weak models. ADT classifier makes use of the results of previous trees to select the next trees so that the focus can be shifted on samples which are much harder to classify. Here, multiple weak learners work together to make a strong classifier. After every iteration, weights are assigned to the training samples and higher weight samples get more priority in later trees.

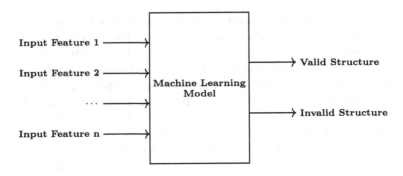

Fig. 4. Architecture of the experimental setup

2.2.3 Support Vector Machine

SVM is a non-probabilistic binary linear classifier and assigns each training sample to one of the two categories. They use a technique called kernel trick in which the data is mapped to a higher dimension making it linearly separable. This makes SVM useful in high dimensional spaces, and flexible with different kernel functions. However, when the number of features is more than the training samples, it is critical to choose the right kernel function and regularization parameters.

2.2.4 Multi-layer Perceptron

MLP is a type of artificial neural network consisting of multiple layers. The first layer is called the input layer and the last layer is called the output layer, with at least one hidden layer in between. The algorithm applies back propagation technique for training, using different non-linear activation functions like tanh and relu. MLP are fully connected and each connection has a weight which is updated during the training phase usually by Stochastic Gradient Descent [41] approach. The main advantage of MLP is its excellent performance in classification, although more training data is needed which makes the training phase time-consuming.

2.3 Encoding Data Structures as Inputs to ML Models

The Korat candidate vector representation provides an immediate encoding for input structures as inputs for binary classification using machine learning models as shown in recent work [16]. Once the finitization is defined, the length of the candidate vector and the ranges of values each element in the vector are precisely defined. Thus, if the candidate vector has length n, the machine learning model for binary classification has n input features and one output (in $\{0, 1\}$), which represents whether the input structure is valid (1) or not (0).

Figure 4 illustrates the experimental setup.

3   Study Subjects

As data structure subjects we select 10 subjects from the standard Korat distribution [1,4]. The subjects include a variety of textbook data structures implemented in Java: singly-linked lists (*SLL*), sorted lists (*SL*), binary trees (*BT*), binary search trees (*BST*), red-black trees (*RBT*), binary heaps (*BH*), heap arrays (*HA*), Fibonacci heaps (*FH*), disjoint sets (*DS*), and directed acyclic graphs (*DAG*).

4   Study Methodology

In this section, we present our study methodology including generation of training and test data using Korat, selection of finitization bounds for Korat, selection of positive and negative samples, and learning with machine learning classifiers.

4.1   Generation of Training and Test Data

For each data structure invariant, we use Korat to generate the training and test data for the machine learning models. Inputs that satisfy the invariants are termed *positive data* and inputs that violate the property are termed *negative data*. The inputs generated by Korat serve as positive data and the candidates explored by Korat but found to violate an invariant serve as a pool for selecting negative data. Given the structural complexity of all our subjects, the number of valid structures is much smaller than the number of invalid structures. For each subject, we create balanced [38] pools of positive and negative data. Section 4.2 explains how we select the finitization bounds in view of the learning quality of the ML models. Section 4.3 further describes how we select positive and negative data.

Each data sample consists of a candidate vector whose elements serve as features, and a binary label that specifies whether the candidate is valid or invalid. Since different data structures have different fields and may have different finitizations, the positive and negative data for different subjects may vary in length. However, for one subject, each data sample has the same length. To illustrate, for the binary tree subject, for a finitization that allows 10 nodes, the candidate vector has length 22 where the first two fields are root and size of the tree and each of the subsequent two fields represent left and right child of one of the 10 nodes. Thus, each data sample has 23 entries, 22 that are features defined by the Korat candidate vector and 1 that defines whether the candidate is valid or invalid.

4.2   Selection of Finitization Bounds

The finitization bound chosen for each structure determines the space of input candidates that Korat searches and the number of valid structures it creates. Note that different data structures can have very different numbers of valid structures for the same size, e.g., the number of binary search trees with n nodes is much greater than the number of red-black trees for n nodes due to the height-balance property of red-black trees.

Our main criteria for setting the finitization bound for Korat was to select the smallest bound such that there were sufficient amount of training and test data for the application of machine learning models and at the same time if manual tuning of parameters is needed, the amount of data does not create an impractical problem. Specifically, we chose the bound of at least 10,000 positive data, i.e., valid structures, for all but one of our subjects.

As we explain in Sect. 4.3, we select the same number of negative samples as positive samples, so we have at least 20,000 samples for each data structure invariant (except one). To illustrate, we have to set the finitization bound of Binary-Tree property to 10 nodes, which generates 16796 positive samples.

For one of our subjects, namely red-black trees, we chose a finitization bound of 9 nodes, which gave fewer than 10,000 valid solutions since generation for a higher bound timed out. Specifically, we used the bound of 9,0,9,9, which specifies the number of nodes, the minimum size of the tree, the maximum size of tree and the number of unique integer keys in the tree respectively. For this bound, there are 6753 positive samples and 2262280 negative samples. The positive samples consist of all non-isomorphic red-black trees that can be formed with up to 9 nodes where each node contains a key from a set of 9 unique integer values. Table 1 shows for each subject, the finitization bound (as provided to the finitization method of the subject using --args command line option), the size of the state space for the given finitization, the number of valid structures found by Korat, the number of invalid structures explored by Korat, and finally the total number of structures explored by Korat.

Table 1. Candidate structures explored by Korat for each data structure subject.

Subject	Finitization bound	State space	Valid explored	Invalid explored	Total explored
SLL	0,9,10,10	2^{75}	26443	500868	527311
BST	8,0,8,0,7	2^{81}	12235	3613742	3625977
BH	7	2^{109}	107416	154372	261788
BT	10	2^{72}	16796	798304	815100
SL	0,8,9,9	2^{96}	24310	150962	175272
HA	6	2^{23}	13139	51394	64533
DS	5	2^{39}	41546	372309	413855
RBT	9,0,9,9	2^{135}	6753	2262280	2269033
FH	5	2^{82}	52281	112084	164365
DAG	6	2^{108}	19696	185197	204893

4.3   Selection of Positive and Negative Samples

The positive samples consist of every (non-isomorphic) valid structure generated by Korat for the chosen finitization bound. To balance the dataset, we randomly select the same amount of negative samples as the positive ones from the full negative dataset that consists of each candidate Korat explored but found to be invalid. To illustrate, the Disjoint-Set invariant had 41546 positive samples and 372309 negative samples. We kept all of the 41546 positive samples and randomly selected 41546 samples from 372309 negative samples.

4.4   Learning with Machine Learning Classifiers

A key factor in applications of machine learning models is the ratio of training and test data. Traditionally, ratios of 80:20 or 75:25 for training:test are commonly used. We use 4 different ratios in our study. Specifically, we performed experiments using each of the following training:test ratios – 75:25, 50:50, 25:75, and 10:90. Thus, on one extreme, we explore the more traditional setting where 75% of data are used for training and 25% are used for evaluation, and on the other extreme, we explore the unconventional setting of using just 10% data for training and 90% for evaluation. As is common practice in evaluating ML models, our training and test data had no overlap. Moreover, due to the use of Korat, not only is there no intersection in the training and test datasets but also the two datasets don't contain isomorphic structures.

We ran experiments using base ML models taken off-the-shelf, and also using manually tuned models. The tuned models performed only slightly better than base models but the overhead in finding tuned hyper-parameters outweighed the increase in accuracy. Therefore, we report the results of base models only in Tables 2 and 3.

We report counts of True Negatives (TN), False Positives (FP), False Negatives (FN) and True Positives (TP) in Tables 2 and 3. True Negative is when the ground truth label is 0 and the classifier correctly predicted label 0. False Positive is when the ground truth label is 0 but the classifier wrongly predicted label 1. False Negative is when the ground truth label is 1 but the classifier wrongly predicted label 0. True Positive is when the ground truth label is 1 and the classifier correctly predicted label 1. In addition, we use four metrics to report the results of the classification: Precision, Recall, Accuracy and F1 score. Precision is calculated as $\frac{TP}{TP+FP}$. Recall is calculated as $\frac{TP}{TP+FN}$. Accuracy is calculated as $\frac{TP+TN}{TP+TN+FP+FN}$. F1 score is calculated as $\frac{2*Precision*Recall}{Precision+Recall}$.

5   Experimental Results

Experiments were performed with training data percentage of 10%, 25%, 50%, and 75%, and in each case the rest of the data was used for testing, i.e., evaluation of accuracy. In this section, we included detailed results obtained using 10% training data (Tables 2 and 3) and the remaining detailed results are included in

Table 2. Classification results for 10:90 training:test ratio

Property	Model	TN	FP	FN	TP	Accuracy	Precision	Recall	F1
SLL	DT	23728	37	39	23794	0.9984	0.9984	0.9984	0.9984
	RFT	23659	106	25	23808	0.9972	0.9956	**0.9990**	0.9973
	GBDT	23729	36	24	23809	**0.9987**	**0.9985**	**0.9990**	**0.9987**
	ABT	22402	1363	396	23437	0.9630	0.9450	0.9834	0.9638
	SVM	23196	569	24	23809	0.9875	0.9767	**0.9990**	0.9877
	MLP	23691	74	24	23809	0.9979	0.9969	**0.9990**	0.9979
BST	DT	10092	921	865	10145	0.9189	0.9168	0.9214	0.9191
	RFT	10258	755	580	10430	0.9394	0.9325	0.9473	0.9399
	GBDT	10149	864	192	10818	**0.9521**	0.9260	**0.9826**	**0.9535**
	ABT	10030	983	324	10686	0.9407	0.9158	0.9706	0.9424
	SVM	10325	688	1630	9380	0.8947	0.9317	0.8520	0.8900
	MLP	10337	676	380	10630	**0.9521**	**0.9402**	0.9655	0.9527
BH	DT	96447	211	155	96536	0.9981	0.9978	0.9984	0.9981
	RFT	96258	400	215	96476	0.9968	0.9959	0.9978	0.9968
	GBDT	95902	756	382	96309	0.9941	0.9922	0.9960	0.9941
	ABT	93536	3122	1958	94733	0.9737	0.9681	0.9797	0.9739
	SVM	96391	267	50	96641	0.9984	0.9972	**0.9995**	0.9984
	MLP	96523	135	123	96568	**0.9987**	**0.9986**	0.9987	**0.9987**
BT	DT	14979	180	51	15023	**0.9924**	**0.9882**	0.9966	**0.9924**
	RFT	14520	639	607	14467	0.9588	0.9577	0.9597	0.9587
	GBDT	14774	385	194	14880	0.9808	0.9748	0.9871	0.9809
	ABT	13369	1790	0	15074	0.9408	0.8939	**1.0000**	0.9440
	SVM	10467	4692	4996	10078	0.6796	0.6823	0.6686	0.6754
	MLP	14323	836	499	14575	0.9558	0.9458	0.9669	0.9562
SL	DT	21687	154	83	21834	**0.9946**	**0.9930**	0.9962	**0.9946**
	RFT	21306	535	216	21701	0.9828	0.9759	0.9901	0.9830
	GBDT	21262	579	160	21757	0.9831	0.9741	0.9927	0.9833
	ABT	18212	3629	3476	18441	0.8376	0.8356	0.8414	0.8385
	SVM	21345	496	12	21905	0.9884	0.9779	**0.9995**	0.9885
	MLP	21537	304	15	21902	0.9927	0.9863	0.9993	0.9928

the GitHub repository and summarized here due to space limitation. We choose to include 10% here because it is the most interesting case as we train on a relatively small percentage of data and still are able to classify the data structure invariants with surprisingly high accuracy. The key results are as follows.

For 10% training data ratio (i.e., 90% test data), the maximum accuracy for the subject invariants was 99.87%, which was achieved for the binomial heap invariant using multi-layer perceptrons (MLPs). The minimum accuracy was

Table 3. Classification results for 10:90 training:test ratio

Property	Model	TN	FP	FN	TP	Accuracy	Precision	Recall	F1
HA	DT	11735	99	46	11771	**0.9939**	**0.9917**	**0.9961**	**0.9939**
	RFT	11523	311	351	11466	0.9720	0.9736	0.9703	0.9719
	GBDT	11218	616	95	11722	0.9699	0.9501	0.9920	0.9706
	ABT	8852	2982	2812	9005	0.7550	0.7512	0.7620	0.7566
	SVM	9993	1841	536	11281	0.8995	0.8597	0.9546	0.9047
	MLP	10439	1395	576	11241	0.9167	0.8896	0.9513	0.9194
DS	DT	33595	3700	3053	34435	0.9097	0.9030	0.9186	0.9107
	RFT	33730	3565	2820	34668	**0.9146**	**0.9068**	0.9248	**0.9157**
	GBDT	31978	5317	2623	34865	0.8938	0.8677	0.9300	0.8978
	ABT	30079	7216	8561	28927	0.7890	0.8003	0.7716	0.7857
	SVM	30595	6700	2352	35136	0.8790	0.8399	**0.9373**	0.8859
	MLP	32849	4446	2350	35138	0.9091	0.8877	**0.9373**	0.9118
RBT	DT	5807	276	107	5966	0.9685	0.9558	0.9824	0.9689
	RFT	5865	218	65	6008	0.9767	**0.9650**	0.9893	0.9770
	GBDT	5826	257	17	6056	**0.9775**	0.9593	**0.9972**	**0.9779**
	ABT	5836	247	32	6041	0.9770	0.9607	0.9947	0.9774
	SVM	5849	234	155	5918	0.9680	0.9620	0.9745	0.9682
	MLP	5848	235	84	5989	0.9738	0.9622	0.9862	0.9741
FH	DT	45893	1063	1217	45933	0.9758	**0.9774**	0.9742	0.9758
	RFT	44078	2878	3489	43661	0.9323	0.9382	0.9260	0.9320
	GBDT	42326	4630	2913	44237	0.9198	0.9053	0.9382	0.9214
	ABT	37152	9804	9024	38126	0.7999	0.7955	0.8086	0.8020
	SVM	40973	5983	2187	44963	0.9132	0.8826	0.9536	0.9167
	MLP	45885	1071	1100	46050	**0.9769**	0.9773	**0.9767**	**0.9770**
DAG	DT	16162	1579	966	16746	**0.9282**	**0.9138**	**0.9455**	**0.9294**
	RFT	15708	2033	1852	15860	0.8904	0.8864	0.8954	0.8909
	GBDT	15000	2741	1638	16074	0.8765	0.8543	0.9075	0.8801
	ABT	14560	3181	3266	14446	0.8182	0.8195	0.8156	0.8176
	SVM	14296	3445	2013	15699	0.8460	0.8200	0.8863	0.8519
	MLP	15677	2064	2010	15702	0.8851	0.8838	0.8865	0.8852

75.50% for the heap array invariant using Adaboost trees. Overall, decision trees (DTs) performed the best on data structure invariants whereas Adaboost trees (ABTs) performed the worst for the invariants studied. DT average accuracy is 96.79%; random forest (RFT) average accuracy is 95.61%; gradient boosting tree (GBDT) average accuracy is 95.46%; ABT average accuracy is 87.95%; support vector machine (SVM) average accuracy for Korat is 90.54%; and MLP average accuracy is 95.59%.

For 25% training data ratio (i.e., 75% test data), the results observed were as follows. The maximum accuracy for the subject invariant was 99.99%, which was achieved for the Singly-linked list invariant using MLP. The minimum accuracy was 71.60% for the sorted list invariant using SVM. Overall, decision trees performed the best on data structure invariants whereas Adaboost Trees performed the worst of the models studied. DT average accuracy is 98.33%; RFT average accuracy is 97.34%; GBDT average accuracy is 95.55%; ABT average accuracy is 88.14%; SVM average accuracy is 92.30%; and MLP average accuracy is 97.87%.

For 50% training data ratio (i.e., 50% test data), the results observed were as follows. The maximum accuracy for the subject invariant was 99.98%, which was achieved for the heap array invariant using DT and binomial heap invariant using MLP. The minimum accuracy was 75.13% for the binary tree invariant using SVM. Overall, decision trees performed the best on data structure invariants whereas Adaboost trees performed the worst of the models studied. DT average accuracy is 98.96%; RFT average accuracy is 98.16%; GBDT average accuracy is 95.78%; ABT average accuracy is 88.16%; SVM average accuracy is 93.64%; and MLP average accuracy is 98.92%.

For 75% training data ratio (i.e., 25% test data), results observed as follows. The maximum accuracy for the subject invariant was 100%, which was achieved for the heap array invariant using DT and sorted list using MLP. The minimum accuracy was 78.08% for the binary tree invariant using Adaboost Tree. Overall, decision trees performed the best on data structure invariants whereas Adaboost Trees performed the worst of the models studied. DT average accuracy is 99.27%; RFT average accuracy is 98.58%; GBDT average accuracy is 95.65 %; ABT average accuracy is 88.28%; SVM average accuracy is 94.45%; and MLP average accuracy is 99.24%.

Overall, from the study we conclude that decision trees are quite good in predicting structurally complex properties whereas Adaboost trees have the least accuracy. We also observe that overall the accuracy ranges from a low of 71.60% to a high of 100.00%.

All experiments were performed on an Intel i7-4700MQ (2.40 GHz) processor with 8 GB of RAM.

6   Threats to Validity

In our experiments, we use a fixed size for each subject. The ML classifiers may perform worse for smaller sizes of subjects due to less available training data and better for larger sizes of subjects due to more available training data.

The negative examples generated by Korat makes the irrelevant fields their default values because setting those fields to any value does not change the false result of *repOk*. So those examples are canonical compared to the entire negative example space. As a consequence, our results may not hold for other negative examples.

As explained in Sect. 2.1, the training data from Korat was always correctly labeled. Thus, this data had no noise. However, in practical situations, the training data does not have this quality. Normally, training data has some samples which are labeled wrong or have missing values. This situation did not occur here and this is one of the main reason behind high accuracy values observed during the course of this study.

Another threat to validity is the undersampling technique used in this study. We can see that the negative cases had a much larger state space and we have to do undersampling to make the classes balanced. Also it is impossible to generate all the negatives in some cases. For example, the structures explored for the Red-Black Tree invariant were 2269033. We tried to randomly sample the negative samples but more work should be done in future to find a better way of dealing with imbalanced classes and dealing with large state space.

7   Related Work

A number of research projects introduced the use of machine learning methods in learning properties of software systems [5,7,16,19,30,44]. In the specific context of structural properties of data structures, to our knowledge, Malik [30] first introduced the use of a machine learning method, namely support vector machines, for characterizing the properties, specifically by utilizing graph spectra [6]. Most recently, Molina et al. [16] introduced the first use of feed-forward artificial neural networks as binary classifiers for data structure properties and showed their trained networks had high accuracy and worked better than an approach [14] for using dynamic analysis for detecting likely program invariants.

Our study is closest to Molina et al.'s work and extends it in three important directions. One, we evaluate 6 machine learning models, including decision trees and support vector machines, that were not studied in their work that only used neural networks. Two, we use 4 data structure subjects that were not in their study as well as 6 subjects that were in their study. Three, we study several different ratios of test/training data whereas their study did not consider any specific test/training ratio, rather the ratio in their study was driven by the training data generated by the test generation tool Randoop [37]. Moreover, we have no overlap between test and training data whereas in their study there was up to >50% overlap for positive cases (e.g., for binary search trees and red-black trees) and for each subject the test data contained all of the training data. Overall, the results of our study generally corroborate their findings, but in addition, enhance them along new dimensions.

There is a rich body of work on using dynamic analysis and static analysis in detecting and generating (likely) program invariants [12,14,26,32,35,40,42,43, 48]. Ernst [14,15] is a widely studied tool for generating likely program invariants. The key idea in Daikon is to use a collection of pre-defined property templates and observe program states at control points of interest to check which of the properties consistently hold at those points, and then to consider those as likely invariants. While Daikon is quite effective at properties over integers and arrays, its effectiveness is relatively low for structural properties. Deryaft [29] followed Daikon's spirit to introduce a technique for generating likely structural invariants and can handle complex data structures. However, a key issue with the Daikon family of techniques is that they require a collection of property templates and can only create invariants based on those properties (and boolean connections among them).

There is a large body of work on program synthesis [3,21,31] and sketching [46] that is applicable to invariant generation in principle. We believe machine learning methods can also be helpful in improving some of these techniques, e.g., by guiding the search in the space of candidate programs [25,45].

8   Conclusion

This paper presented a controlled experiment on applying a suite of off-the-shelf machine learning (ML) tools to learn properties of dynamically allocated data structures that reside on the program heap. Specifically, we used 10 data structure subjects, and systematically created training and test data for 6 ML methods, which include decision trees, support vector machines, and neural networks, for binary classification, e.g., to classify input structures as valid binary search trees. The study had two key findings. One, most of ML methods – with off-the-shelf parameter settings and without fine tuning – achieves at least 90% accuracy on all of the subjects. Two, the accuracy is achieved even when the size of the training data is significantly smaller than the size of the test data. We believe machine learning models offer a promising approach to characterize data structure invariants.

Acknowledgments. This research was partially supported by the US National Science Foundation under Grant Nos. CCF-1704790 and CCF-1718903.

References

1. Korat GitHub repository. https://github.com/korattest/korat
2. Scikit-Learn Library. https://scikit-learn.org/stable/. Accessed 18 Aug 2019
3. Bodik, R.: Program synthesis: opportunities for the next decade. In: 20th ACM SIGPLAN International Conference on Functional Programming, p. 1 (2015)
4. Boyapati, C., Khurshid, S., Marinov, D.: Korat: automated testing based on Java predicates. In: ACM SIGSOFT International Symposium on Software Testing and Analysis, pp. 123–133 (2002)
5. Briand, L.C., Labiche, Y., Liu, X.: Using machine learning to support debugging with tarantula. In: 18th IEEE International Symposium on Software Reliability, pp. 137–146 (2007)
6. Brouwer, A.E., Haemers, W.H.: Spectra of Graphs. Springer, New York (2012). https://doi.org/10.1007/978-1-4614-1939-6
7. Chen, Y.-F., Hong, C.-D., Lin, A.W., Rümmer, P.: Learning to prove safety over parameterised concurrent systems. In: Formal Methods in Computer Aided Design (FMCAD), pp. 76–83 (2017)
8. Clarke, E.M., Kroening, D., Yorav, K.: Behavioral consistency of C and verilog programs using bounded model checking. In: 40th Design Automation Conference, (DAC), pp. 368–371 (2003)

9. Cortes, C., Vapnik, V.: Support-vector networks. Mach. Learn. **20**(3), 273–297 (1995)
10. Csallner, C., Tillmann, N., Smaragdakis, Y.: DySy: dynamic symbolic execution for invariant inference. In: 30th International Conference on Software Engineering, pp. 281–290 (2008)
11. Demsky, B., Rinard, M.C.: Automatic detection and repair of errors in data structures. In: Proceedings of the 2003 ACM SIGPLAN Conference on Object-Oriented Programming Systems, Languages and Applications, OOPSLA, pp. 78–95 (2003)
12. Dillig, I., Dillig, T., Li, B., McMillan, K.: Inductive invariant generation via abductive inference. In: ACM SIGPLAN International Conference on Object Oriented Programming Systems Languages & Applications, pp. 443–456 (2013)
13. Elkarablieh, B., Garcia, I., Suen, Y.L., Khurshid, S.: Assertion-based repair of complex data structures. In: IEEE/ACM International Conference on Automated Software Engineering, pp. 64–73 (2007)
14. Ernst, M.D., Czeisler, A., Griswold, W.G., Notkin, D.: Quickly detecting relevant program invariants. In: International Conference on Software Engineering, pp. 449–458 (2000)
15. Ernst, M.D., et al.: The daikon system for dynamic detection of likely invariants. Sci. Comput. Program. **69**(1–3), 35–45 (2007)
16. Molina, F., Degiovanni, R., Ponzio, P., Regis, G., Aguirre, N., Frias, M.F.: Training binary classifiers as data structure invariants. In: International Conference on Software Engineering (ICSE), May 2019
17. Freund, Y., Schapire, R.E.: A decision-theoretic generalization of on-line learning and an application to boosting. J. Comput. Syst. Sci. **55**(1), 119–139 (1997)
18. Friedman, J.H.: Greedy function approximation: a gradient boosting machine. Ann. Stat. **29**(5), 1189–1232 (2001)
19. Garg, P., Neider, D., Madhusudan, P., Roth, D.: Learning invariants using decision trees and implication counterexamples. In: 43rd Annual ACM SIGPLAN-SIGACT Symposium on Principles of Programming Languages, pp. 499–512 (2016)
20. Godefroid, P.: Model checking for programming languages using VeriSoft. In: 24th ACM SIGPLAN-SIGACT Symposium on Principles of Programming Languages, pp. 174–186 (1997)
21. Gulwani, S., Dimensions in program synthesis. In: 12th International ACM SIGPLAN Symposium on Principles and Practice of Declarative Programming, pp. 13–24 (2010)
22. Ho, T.K.: Random decision forests. In: Third International Conference on Document Analysis and Recognition, vol. 1 (1995)
23. Holzmann, G.: The SPIN Model Checker: Primer and Reference Manual, 1st edn. Addison-Wesley Professional, Boston (2011)
24. Jackson, D., Vaziri, M.: Finding bugs with a constraint solver. In: International Symposium on Software Testing and Analysis (ISSTA), pp. 14–25 (2000)
25. Jha, S., Gulwani, S., Seshia, S.A., Tiwari, A.: Oracle-guided component-based program synthesis. In: 32nd ACM/IEEE International Conference on Software Engineering, vol. 1, pp. 215–224 (2010)
26. Jump, M., McKinley, K.S.: Dynamic shape analysis via degree metrics. In: 8th International Symposium on Memory Management (ISMM), pp. 119–128 (2009)
27. Korel, B.: Automated software test data generation. IEEE Trans. Softw. Eng. **16**(8), 870–879 (1990)
28. Liskov, B., Guttag, J.V.: Program Development in Java - Abstraction, Specification, and Object-Oriented Design. Addison-Wesley, Boston (2001)

29. Malik, M., Pervaiz, A., Uzuncaova, E., Khurshid, S.: Deryaft: a tool for generating representation invariants of structurally complex data. In: ACM/IEEE 30th International Conference on Software Engineering (2008)
30. Malik, M.Z.: Dynamic shape analysis of program heap using graph spectra: NIER track. In: 33rd International Conference on Software Engineering (ICSE), pp. 952–955 (2011)
31. Manna, Z., Waldinger, R.: A deductive approach to program synthesis. ACM Trans. Program. Lang. Syst. **2**(1), 90–121 (1980)
32. McMillan, K.L.: Quantified invariant generation using an interpolating saturation prover. In: Ramakrishnan, C.R., Rehof, J. (eds.) TACAS 2008. LNCS, vol. 4963, pp. 413–427. Springer, Heidelberg (2008). https://doi.org/10.1007/978-3-540-78800-3_31
33. Mera, E., Lopez-García, P., Hermenegildo, M.: Integrating software testing and run-time checking in an assertion verification framework. In: Hill, P.M., Warren, D.S. (eds.) ICLP 2009. LNCS, vol. 5649, pp. 281–295. Springer, Heidelberg (2009). https://doi.org/10.1007/978-3-642-02846-5_25
34. Meyer, B.: Class invariants: concepts, problems, solutions. CoRR, abs/1608.07637 (2016)
35. Møller, A., Schwartzbach, M.I.: The pointer assertion logic engine. In: ACM SIGPLAN Conference on Programming Language Design and Implementation (PLDI), pp. 221–231 (2001)
36. Murtagh, F.: Multilayer perceptrons for classification and regression. Neurocomputing **2**(5), 183–197 (1991)
37. Pacheco, C., Lahiri, S.K., Ernst, M.D., Ball, T.: Feedback-directed random test generation. In: 29th International Conference on Software Engineering, pp. 75–84 (2007)
38. Provost, F.: Machine learning from imbalanced data sets 101. In: Proceedings of the AAAI 2000 Workshop on Imbalanced Data Sets, vol. 68, pp. 1–3. AAAI Press (2000)
39. Quinlan, J.R.: Induction of decision trees. Mach. Learn. **1**(1), 81–106 (1986)
40. Reynolds, J.C.: Separation logic: a logic for shared mutable data structures. In: 17th Annual IEEE Symposium on Logic in Computer Science (2002)
41. Robbins, H., Monro, S.: A stochastic approximation method. Ann. Math. Stat. **22**(3), 400–407 (1951)
42. Sagiv, S., Reps, T.W., Wilhelm, R.: Parametric shape analysis via 3-valued logic. In: 26th ACM SIGPLAN-SIGACT Symposium on Principles of Programming Languages, pp. 105–118 (1999)
43. Sankaranarayanan, S., Sipma, H.B., Manna, Z.: Non-linear loop invariant generation using gröbner bases. In: 31st ACM SIGPLAN-SIGACT Symposium on Principles of Programming Languages, pp. 318–329 (2004)
44. Si, X., Dai, H., Raghothaman, M., Naik, M., Song, L.: Learning loop invariants for program verification. In: Bengio, S., Wallach, H., Larochelle, H., Grauman, K., Cesa-Bianchi, N., Garnett, R. (eds.) Advances in Neural Information Processing Systems, vol. 31, pp. 7751–7762 (2018)
45. Singh, S., Zhang, M., Khurshid, S.: Learning guided enumerative synthesis for superoptimization (2019, under submission)

46. Solar-Lezama, A.: Program synthesis by sketching. Ph.D. thesis (2008)
47. Visser, W., Havelund, K., Brat, G.P., Park, S.: Model checking programs. In: Fifteenth IEEE International Conference on Automated Software Engineering (ASE), pp. 3–12 (2000)
48. Zee, K., Kuncak, V., Rinard, M.C.: Full functional verification of linked data structures. In: ACM SIGPLAN Conference on Programming Language Design and Implementation, pp. 349–361 (2008)

VeriVANca: An Actor-Based Framework for Formal Verification of Warning Message Dissemination Schemes in VANETs

Farnaz Yousefi$^{1(\boxtimes)}$, Ehsan Khamespanah^{2,5}, Mohammed Gharib^4,
Marjan Sirjani^{3,5}, and Ali Movaghar^1

^{1} Department of Computer Engineering,
Sharif University of Technology, Tehran, Iran
`faryousefi@ce.sharif.edu`
^{2} School of Electrical and Computer Engineering,
University of Tehran, Tehran, Iran
^{3} School of IDT, Mälardalen University, Västerås, Sweden
^{4} School of Computer Science,
Institute for Research in Fundamental Science (IPM), Tehran, Iran
^{5} School of Computer Science,
Reykjavik University, Reykjavik, Iceland

Abstract. One of the applications of Vehicular Ad-hoc NETworks, known as VANETs, is warning message dissemination among vehicles in dangerous situations to prevent more damage. The only communication mechanism for message dissemination is multi-hop broadcast; in which, forwarding a received message has to be regulated using a scheme regarding the selection of forwarding nodes. When analyzing these schemes, simulation-based frameworks fail to provide guaranteed analysis results due to the high level of concurrency in this application. Therefore, there is a need to use model checking approaches for achieving reliable results. In this paper, we have developed a framework called VeriVANca, to provide model checking facilities for the analysis of warning message dissemination schemes in VANETS. To this end, an actor-based modeling language, Rebeca, is used which is equipped with a variety of model checking engines. To illustrate the applicability of VeriVANca, modeling and analysis of two warning message dissemination schemes are presented. Some scenarios for these schemes are presented to show that concurrent behaviors of the system components may cause uncertainty in both behavior and performance which may not be detected by simulation-based techniques. Furthermore, the scalability of VeriVANca is examined by analyzing a middle-sized model.

Keywords: Model checking · Warning message dissemination · Vehicular Ad-Hoc Networks (VANETs) · Rebeca · Actor model

© Springer Nature Switzerland AG 2019
F. Biondi et al. (Eds.): SPIN 2019, LNCS 11636, pp. 244–259, 2019.
https://doi.org/10.1007/978-3-030-30923-7_14

1   Introduction

VANETs have attracted much attention in both academia and industry during the last years. The emergence of autonomous vehicles and the safety concerns regarding the use of these vehicles in the near future have highlighted the possible use of VANETs in safety enhancement of future transportation system. Using VANETs in such mission critical applications, calls for reliability assurance of algorithms. One of the applications in this domain is the use of vehicle to vehicle communication for Warning Message Dissemination (WMD) in dangerous situations to prevent further damage. In this application, vehicles broadcast warning messages to inform each other of the upcoming hazard. To increase the number of vehicles receiving the warning message, the receiving nodes should forward the message. To hold the trade-off between the traffic in the network and maximum number of vehicles receiving the message, a number of schemes regarding the selection of forwarding nodes has been proposed [14]. More details about WMD in VANETs are presented in Sect. 2.

A number of simulation-based tools and techniques have been used for the analysis of these WMD schemes. However, concurrent execution of system components reduces the effectiveness of simulation-based approaches for such mission critical applications. This is because simulation-based approaches cannot provide high level of confidence for the correct behavior of the system. In such cases, there is a need to apply formal verification for achieving reliable results. Formal verification is used in applications of VANETs such as cooperative collision avoidance [7], intersection management using mutual exclusion algorithms [2], and collaborative driving [10]. However, to the best of our knowledge, there is no work on formal verification of WMD application in VANETs.

In this paper, we introduce VeriVANca as a framework for the analysis of WMD schemes in VANETs. To this end, we develop VeriVANca in Timed Rebeca [9], a real-time extension of Rebeca [15]. Rebeca is an operational interpretation of the actor model with formal semantics, supported by a variety of analysis tools [8]. In the actor model, all the elements that are running concurrently in a distributed system are modeled as actors. Communication among actors takes place by asynchronous message passing. These structures and features match the needs of VANETs as they consist of autonomous nodes which communicate by message passing. This level of faithfulness helps in having a more natural mapping between the actor model and VANETs, making models easier to develop and understand. In Sect. 3 Timed Rebeca is briefly introduced using the counting-based scheme example.

To illustrate the applicability of this approach, we have modeled a distance-based scheme [16] and a counting-based scheme [17] using VeriVANca. Results of model checking for the distance-based scheme show that concurrent execution of the system components enables multiple execution traces some of which cause starvation and may not be detected using simulation-based techniques (Sect. 4.1). We also observed that, in a given scenario, multiple values may be achieved for the performance when considering the interleaving of concurrently executing components. Our further investigations yield that having multiple performance results is not limited to one scenario but is common. More details on these cases are presented in Sect. 4.2. Furthermore, to examine the scalability of VeriVANca, a middle-sized model of a four-lane street with about 40 vehicles is analyzed. We observed that if scaling up the number of vehicles results in creation of very congested areas, the size of the state space and analysis time is increased dramatically. However, scaling up the model without creation of new congested areas, results in smooth increase in the size of the state space and analysis time as presented in Sect. 4.3.

2   Warning Message Dissemination in VANETs

WMD is an application developed for VANETs that tends to increase the safety and riding experience of passengers. In this application, a warning message is disseminated between vehicles in the case of any abnormal situations such as car accidents or undesirable road conditions. Received warning messages are used either to activate an automatic operation such as reducing speed to avoid chained accidents (increasing safety) or are shown as alerts to inform the driver of the upcoming hazard so that the driver can do operations such as changing their route (improving the riding experience).

Using WMD in safety-critical applications, requires providing high reliability for the application in developed solutions. Besides, some characteristics of VANETs such as high mobility of the nodes and fast topology changes, makes routing algorithms commonly used in MANETs (Mobile Ad-hoc NETworks) inapplicable to VANETs [20]. Therefore, the only approach for implementation of message dissemination in VANETs is multi-hop broadcast of the message. In this approach, the receiving nodes are responsible for re-broadcasting the message to the others. However, this can result in broadcast storm problem in the network. In order to tackle this problem, a number of schemes have been proposed for WMD as described in the following subsection.

2.1   Message Dissemination Schemes

Message dissemination schemes are algorithms that specify how a forwarding node is selected in a VANET. The selection of a forwarding node is performed based on some criteria such as distance between senders and receivers, number of received messages by a node, probabilities associated with nodes, topology of the network, etc. [14]. In this paper, two schemes—a distance-based and a counting-based scheme—are modeled using the proposed framework.

The distance-based scheme, called TLO (The Last One) [16], makes use of location information of the vehicles to select the forwarding node. In this scheme, upon a message broadcast, the farthest receiver in the range of the sender is selected as the forwarding TLO node. Other vehicles in the range know that they are not the farthest node and do not forward the received message. However, they wait for a while to make sure of successful broadcast of the TLO node. Receiving the warning message from the TLO node, means that the sending of the message has been successful and they do not forward the warning message. Otherwise, the algorithm is run once again to select the next TLO forwarding node.

In the counting-based scheme [17], an integer number is defined as counter threshold. Each receiving node counts the number of received messages in a time interval. At the end of that time interval, the receiver decides on being a forwarding node based on the comparison of the value of its counter and the value of counter threshold. If the value of the counter is greater than the value of counter threshold, the receiver assumes that enough warning messages are disseminated in its vicinity; therefore, it avoids forwarding the message. Otherwise, the receiver forwards the warning message.

2.2   Analysis Techniques

Different analysis techniques have been developed for the analysis of message dissemination schemes in VANETs. Simulation-based approaches are widely used for the analysis of applications of in this domain. Gama et al. developed a model and analyzed three different message dissemination schemes using Veins simulator [4]. Sanguesa et al. have used ns-2 simulator in two independent works regarding the selection of optimal message dissemination scheme. In [12], they aim to select the optimal broadcasting scheme for the model in each scenario and in [13], the selection of the optimal scheme is performed for each vehicle based on vehicular density and the topological characteristics of the environment where the vehicle is located in. In a more comprehensive work [14] authors have developed a framework in ns-3 simulator for comparing different schemes. Note that although this approach is used in many applications, it does not guarantee correctness of results as it does not consider concurrent execution of system components.

Another technique used for the analysis of WMD in VANETs is the analytical approach. In this approach, a system is modeled by mathematical equations and the analysis is performed by finding solutions to the equation system. For example, in [11], Saeed et al. have derived difference equations that their solutions yield the probability of all vehicles receiving the emergency warning message. This value is computed as a function of the number of neighbors of each vehicle, the rebroadcast probability, and the dissemination distance. In another work, a probabilistic multi-hop broadcast scheme is mathematically formulated and the packet reception probability is reported for different configurations, taking into account the topology of the network and as a result, major network characteristics such as vehicle density and the number of one-hop neighbors [6]. This approach guarantees achieving correct results but it is not modular and developing mathematical formula needs a high degree of user interaction and a high degree of expertise.

As the third technique, model checking is a general verification approach which provides ease of modeling similarly to simulation-based approaches in addition to guaranteeing the correctness of results due to its mathematical foundation. To the best of our knowledge, there is no framework which provides model checking facilities for the analysis of WMD schemes in VANETs.

3 Rebeca Language

Rebeca is a modeling language based on Hewitt and Agha's actors [1]. Actors in Rebeca are independent units of concurrently running programs that communicate with each other through message passing. The message passing is an asynchronous non-blocking call to the actor's corresponding message server. Message servers are methods of the actor that specify the reaction of the actor to its corresponding received message. In the Java-like syntax of Rebeca, actors are instantiated from reactive class definitions that are similar to the concept of classes in Java. Actors in this sense can be assumed as objects in Java. Each reactive class declares the size of its message buffer[1], a set of state variables, and the messages to which it can respond. Reactive classes have constructors with the same name as their reactive class, that are responsible for initializing the actor's state.

Basically, in Rebeca the concept of known rebecs was introduced for an actor to specify the actors to which it can send messages. However, to implement applications in ad-hoc networks, a more flexible sending mechanism is needed. Two Rebeca extensions b-Rebeca [18] and w-Rebeca [19] have been proposed to provide more complex sending mechanism. In b-Rebeca the concept of known rebecs is eliminated and it is assumed that the only communication mechanism among actors is broadcasting; hence, only a fully connected network can be modeled. Note that the type of broadcasting introduced in b-Rebeca is not the same as the location-based broadcasting in VANETs. In location-based broadcasting, only the actors in the range of each other are connected in the Rebeca model. Regarding this assumption, a counter-based reduction technique is used in b-Rebeca to reduce the state space size of the model making it impossible to send messages to a subset of actors.

The other extension w-Rebeca, which is developed for model checking of wireless ad-hoc networks, uses an adjacency matrix in the model checking engine, to consider connectivity of actors. In this approach, by random changes in the value of adjacency matrix, all the possible topologies of the network are considered in the model checking. Note that users are allowed to define a set of topological constraints and the topologies that do not fulfill the constraints are not considered in the model checking. w-Rebeca does not support timing in the model which is essential for developing models in the domain of VANET, since there are some real-time properties that need to be considered. Besides, considering all possible topologies—some of which may not be possible in the reality of the model—results in a bigger state space for the model. In addition, considering these infeasible topologies, may cause false-negative results when checking correctness properties.

---

[1] Message queue in Rebeca and message bag in Timed Rebeca.

3.1   Explaining Rebeca by the Example of Counting-Based Scheme

In this subsection, we introduce Timed Rebeca [9] using the example of the counting-based scheme presented in the previous section. A Timed Rebeca model consists of a number of reactive class definitions which provide type and behavior specification for the actors instantiated from them. There are two reactive classes BroadcastingActor and Vehicle in the implementation of counting-based WMD in VeriVANca as shown in Listing 1.

Each reactive class consists of a set of state variables and a message bag with the size specified in parentheses after the name of the reactive class in the declaration. For example, reactive class Vehicle has state variables isAv, direction, latency, counter, etc. The size of the message bag for this reactive class is set to five. The local state of each actor consists of the values of its state variables and the contents of its message bag. Being an actor-based language, Timed Rebeca benefits from asynchronous message passing among actors. Upon receiving a message, the message is added to the actor's message bag. Whenever the actor takes a message from the message bag, the routine which is associated with that message is executed. These routines are called message servers and are implemented in the body of reactive classes.

```
1   env int RANGE = 10;
2   env int THRESHOLD_WAITING = 4;
3   env int MESSAGE_SEND_TIME = 1;
4   env int C_THRESHOLD = 3;
5   abstract reactiveclass BroadcastingActor (5) {
6      statevars { int id, x, y; }
7      abstract msgsrv receive(int data);
8      void broadcast(int data) { ... }
9      double distance(BroadcastingActor bActor, BroadcastingActor cActor){...}
10  }
11  reactiveclass Vehicle extends BroadcastingActor(5){
12     statevars{
13        boolean isAV;
14        int direction, latency, destX, destY, counter;
15     }
16     Vehicle (/*List of Parameters*/){
17        /*Variables Initializations*/
18        if (isAV) {
19           self.alertAccident();
20        } else
21           self.move() after(latency);
22     }
23     msgsrv alertAccident(){ ... }
24     msgsrv move() { ... }
25     msgsrv stop () { ... }
26     msgsrv finishWait(int hop) { ... }
27     msgsrv receive(int hopNum) { ... }
28  }
29  main {
30     Vehicle v1():(0,0,10,RIGHT,1,10,10,true), v2():(1,10,0,UP,2,10,10,false),
```

```
31 |    v3():(2,-1,0,RIGHT,1,10,0,false), v4():(3,0,1,DOWN,2,0,-10,false),
32 |    v5():(4,3,0,LEFT,1,-10,0,false);
33 | }
```

Listing. 1. Counting-based scheme in Timed Rebeca

As depicted in Listing 1, the message servers of the reactive class `Vehicle` are `move`, `receive`, `alertAccident`, `stop`, and `finishWait`. In order for an actor to be able to send a message to another actor, the sender has to have a direct reference to the receiver actor. For example, in Line 19, the message `alertAccident` is sent to `self` which represents a reference to the actor itself. However, in order to model a WMD scheme in VANETs, the warning message should reach actors which are in the range of the sender actor. In other words, actors should receive messages based on some criteria, i.e., their location in this application. We used the inheritance mechanism of Timed Rebeca to implement this customized sending strategy.

3.2 Customized Message Sending in VeriVANca

In object-oriented design, inheritance mechanism enables classes to be derived from another class and form a hierarchy of classes that share a set of attributes and methods. Using this approach, we encapsulated a broadcasting mechanism in a reactive class called `BroadcastingActor` and all other behaviors of vehicles are implemented in `Vehicle` reactive class which is derived from `BroadcastingActor`. In `BroadcastingActor`, the `broadcast` method shown in Listing 2 mimics the sending mechanism of vehicles in VANET.

As mentioned before, broadcasting data results in receiving a message containing that data by the vehicles in the range of the sender actor. In the body of this method, all actors—that are derived from `BroadcastingActor`—are examined in terms of their distance to the sender (Line 5). If the distance between an actor and the sender is less than the specified threshold, called `RANGE` (Line 6), the data is sent to the actor by an asynchronous message server call of `receive` (Line 7). As `BroadcastingActor` has no idea about the behavior of vehicles, upon receiving the `receive` message, the template method design pattern [5] is used in the implementation of `receive`. So, the `receive` message server is defined as an abstract message server in `BroadcastingActor` and its body is implemented in `Vehicle`. The behavior of the WMD scheme is implemented in `Vehicle`.

```
 1 | void broadcast(int data) {
 2 |   ArrayList<ReactiveClass> allActors = getAllActors();
 3 |   for(int i = 0; i < allActors.size(); i++) {
 4 |     BroadcastingActor ba = (BroadcastingActor)allActors.get(i);
 5 |     double distance = distance (ba , self);
 6 |     if(distance < RANGE) {
 7 |       ba.receive(data) after (MESSAGE_SEND_TIME);
 8 |     }
 9 |   }
10 | }
```

```
11  double distance(BroadcastingActor bActor , BroadcastingActor
       cActor){
12    return sqrt(pow(cActor.x - bActor.x, 2) + pow(cActor.y -
         bActor.y, 2));
13  }
```

Listing. 2. Body of broadcast Method in Broadcasting Actor

3.3 Counting-Based Scheme in VeriVANca

For the case of counting-based scheme, three message servers `alertAccident`, `finishWait`, and `receive` provide the behavior of the scheme. When `Vehicle` actors are instantiated, their constructor methods are executed resulting in sending one of the following messages to themselves:

- `alertAccindent`: sent by the accident vehicle to start the WMD algorithm (Line 8)
- `move`: sent by the other actors to begin moving with their pre-defined `latency`; an actor performs this through sending `move` message periodically to itself (Line 10).

```
1   reactiveclass Vehicle extends BroadcastingActor(5){
2
3     statevars{ ... }
4     Vehicle (...){
5       ...
6       counter = 0;
7       if (isAV) {
8          self.alertAccident();
9       } else
10         self.move() after(latency);
11    }
12    msgsrv alertAccident(){
13      broadcast(0);
14    }
15    msgsrv finishWait(int hop){
16      if (counter < C_THRESHOLD)
17        broadcast(hop++);
18    }
19    msgsrv receive(int hopNum) {
20      if (counter == 0) {
21        self.finishWait(hopNum) after (THRESHOLD_WAITING);
22        counter = 1;
23      } else {
24        counter++;
25      }
26    }
27  }
```

Listing. 3. Body of message servers in Vehicle Actor

The algorithm of counting-based scheme, as implemented in Listing 3, begins by serving `alertAccident` message in the accident vehicle. Upon the execution of `receive`, if the `counter`, which is initially set to zero for all actors (Line 6), is zero—meaning that it is the first time the actor is receiving the warning message—a watchdog timer is started. This is implemented by sending the `finishWait` message to the actor itself with the arrival time of `THRESHOLD_WAITING`. In addition, the value of `counter` is set to one to indicate that this is the first call of `receive` (Lines 20–22). The next calls of `receive` result in increasing the value of `counter`, which represents the number of received warning messages. When message server `finishWait` is executed by an actor, showing that the watchdog timer is expired, the value of `counter` is compared with the threshold considered for the counter (`C_THRESHOLD`). By not exceeding the threshold, i.e., the area around the actor is not covered by enough number of warning messages, the actor broadcasts the warning message (Lines 16 and 17).

3.4 Reusability of VeriVANca

To illustrate the reusability of VeriVANca, we show how the model of the counting-based scheme can be altered to present another scheme (the TLO scheme) by making minor modifications to the code. At the first step, we implemented the algorithm in a method called `runTLO`. As shown in Listing 4, the bodies of the message servers `finishWait` and `receive` are rewritten to mimic the behavior of the scheme in the event of expiration of the watchdog timer and receiving a warning message respectively.

```
1  msgsrv finishWait(int hopNum) {      13      if (isTLO()) {
2    if (isWaiting)                     14          broadcast(hopNum++);
3      runTLO(hopNum);                  15          received = true;
4  }                                    16      } else {
5  msgsrv receive(int hopNum) {         17          isWaiting = true;
6    if(!isWaiting)                     18          self.finishWait(hopNum)
7      runTLO(hopNum);                              after(THRESHOLD_WAITING);
8    else                              19      }
9      isWaiting = false;              20  }
10  }                                  21  }
11  void runTLO(int hopNum) {
12    if (!received) {
```

Listing. 4. Needed modifications for TLO scheme

In the TLO scheme, explained in Sect. 2.1, upon receiving the warning message for the first time, the `runTLO` method is called. In the body of this method, if the value of state variable `received` is false—meaning that the actor has not received the duplicate warning message from a selected TLO node as a sign of its successful broadcast—, the `isTLO` method is called. This method is implemented in the `BroadcastingActor` and checks if the actor is the furthest node in the range of the sender and returns the result as a boolean value. If the return value is true, the actor is the last one in the range and is selected as the TLO node to forward the warning message; so, it broadcasts the message by increasing the value of `hopNum` by one (Line 15). Then the value of `received` is set to true to show that broadcasting has been successful. In case the actor is not the last one in the range (Line 17), the actor should wait for a while to make sure that the selected TLO node has successfully broadcasted the warning message. To this end, the actor sets the value of `isWaiting` to true to show that the actor is in the waiting mode, and then sets the watchdog timer by sending message `finishWait` to itself by execution time of `THRESHOLD_WAITING` (Line 19). The message server `receive`, like in the previous scheme, mimics receiving the warning message. In the body of this message server, if the value of `isWaiting` is false, meaning that the actor is not in the waiting mode, `isTLO` is executed to select the TLO forwarding node. Otherwise, `isWaiting` is set to false since this message is interpreted as a successful broadcast of the TLO node. The `finishWait` message server is executed upon expiration of the watchdog timer and it checks the value of `isWaiting`. In the case of false value for `finishWait`, the actor has not received the warning message from the selected TLO node, so, `runTLO` is called to select the next TLO forwarding node.

4   Experimental Results

To demonstrate the applicability of VeriVANca, both of the schemes presented in the former section are analyzed in different configurations. As mentioned before, concurrent behaviors of the system components may cause uncertainty which is clearly observable in the presented scenarios, but may not be detected using simulation-based techniques. For the case of the TLO scheme, we show that nondeterminism causes starvation and for the case of the counting-based scheme, it causes different results in the performance of the algorithm. Furthermore, we illustrate that the approach is scalable regarding the number of cars with traffic patterns that do not contain congested areas. Note that the following experiments have been executed on a Macbook Air with Intel Core i5 1.3 GHz CPU and 8 GB of RAM, running macOS Mojave 10.14.2 as the operating system. Development of these experiments are performed in Afra, modeling and verification IDE of Rebeca family languages [3].

4.1   Starvation Scenario in TLO Scheme

In this section, we present an observed scenario that using the TLO scheme causes starvation and affects the reliability of the scheme in some executions. The steps of the scenario is depicted in Fig. 1. In 1(a), position of the vehicles is shown in the time of the accident between vehicles A and B. In the next step, vehicle B starts broadcasting the warning message and vehicles C and D receive the message as they are in the range of B (Fig. 1(b)). Upon receiving the warning message, these vehicles execute the TLO algorithm and since they both have the same distance from B, they forward the received warning message and the vehicles E and F receive the warning message from these two vehicles. When vehicles E and F execute the TLO algorithm, racing between the following two scenarios happen.

1. **E broadcasts before F:** vehicles G and H receive the warning message from E. Upon execution of TLO algorithm by G and H, Vehicle H is selected as the TLO forwarding node and forwards the message. Meanwhile, vehicle G is waiting for receiving the warning message from H to make sure that the broadcasting has been successful. If in the waiting time of G, vehicle H forwards the warning message, the message will be interpreted as acknowledgement of the successful broadcast of H and although G is TLO node in this step, it will not forward the message. In this case, the vehicle J does not receive the warning message.

2. **F broadcasts before E:** vehicle G receive the warning message from F and after the execution of TLO algorithm, it forwards the message as the selected TLO node and vehicle J will receive the warning message in this scenario.

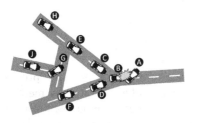

(a) Accident between A and B

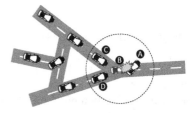

(b) B broadcasts the warning message

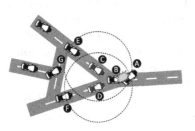

(c) C and D are both selected as TLO nodes to forward the warning message

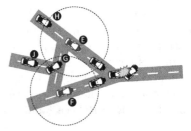

(d) Order of broadcasting between E and F results in two cases

Fig. 1. A scenario of TLO scheme which results in two execution alternatives that one of them causes starvation for vehicle J

This example shows that concurrent execution of the algorithm in nodes causes nondeterministic behavior which may violate correctness properties of the application. To avoid such cases, all the possible nondeterministic behaviors have to be considered in any analysis framework. However, simulation-based techniques, commonly used for the analysis of these systems, fail to report a result by considering all the possible execution traces. This highlights the necessity of applying formal methods in the development of applications of VANETs with critical mission.

4.2   Nondeterminism in Performance of the Counting-Based Scheme

The configuration depicted in Fig. 2(a) is used for the analysis of the counting-based scheme (explained in Sect. 3.1). In this scenario, the value of C_THRESHOLD is set to 2 and the RANGE is set to 4. The scenario begins with the vehicle A broadcasting the warning message (Fig. 2(b)). This broadcast results in increasing the counters of the vehicles A, B, C, and E by one. In the next round two following cases may happen.

1. **The watchdog timer of vehicle E expires after receiving the message from B:** In this case, as the counter has reached the threshold, E does not forward the warning message as shown in Fig. 2(c). Following this case, the algorithm continues with vehicles D, H, and F being selected as forwarding nodes and rebroadcasting the message Figs. 2(d)–(f). As a result, it takes 5 hops for all the vehicles to get informed of the warning message. Note that the same scenario happens when C forwards the message before the expiration of the watchdog timer of E.
2. **The watchdog timer of vehicle E expires before receiving warning message from B and C:** In this case, since the counter of E is less than the threshold, E must forward the warning message (Fig. 3(a)). In the next step, vehicle F broadcasts the message and all non-informed vehicles receive the warning message and algorithm finishes in 3 hops.

Achieving two different numbers for performance of this algorithm shows that beside correctness properties, providing guaranteed values for performance results requires applying formal verification techniques as well. We analyzed this scenario with different values for range and counter threshold, the result of three of them are shown in Fig. 4. The results show that this phenomenon is not rare and can be observed in many cases.

4.3   Scalability Analysis

For the purpose of scalability analysis, we have modeled a four-lane street which contains about 30 vehicles. These vehicles are distributed in a way that there is no congested area in the street as shown in Fig. 5(a). The execution time of this model is 11 s and the number of reached states and transitions are 19,588 and 110,627 respectively. To determine the scalability, we added new cars in two ways. First, we increased the length of the street and added new vehicles to the tail of the street of Fig. 5(a). To avoid creating congested areas, we kept the same distribution while adding new vehicles. This way of scaling resulted in 15 s, 23,734 states, and 133,255 transitions for 35 vehicles and 18 s, 25,872 states, and

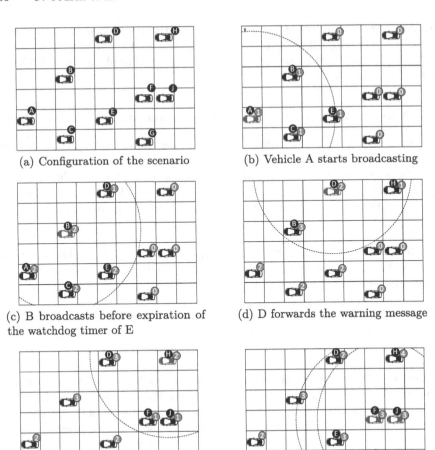

(a) Configuration of the scenario

(b) Vehicle A starts broadcasting

(c) B broadcasts before expiration of the watchdog timer of E

(d) D forwards the warning message

(e) H rebroadcasts the message

(f) F and (or) J forward(s) the message and algorithm finishes

Fig. 2. A case of the scenario for the counting-based scheme

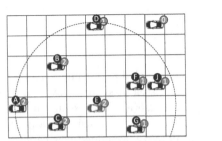
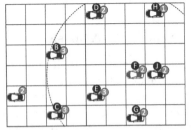

(a) E is selected as forwarder (instead of B as depicted in Figure 2(c))

(b) F broadcasts the message and algorithm finishes

Fig. 3. Another case of the scenario for the counting-based scheme

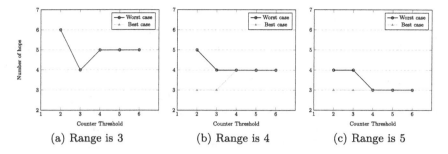

(a) Range is 3   (b) Range is 4   (c) Range is 5

Fig. 4. Analysis results of the counting-based scheme with different values for the range and counter threshold (Note that Y axis shows the number of hops required for termination of the algorithm)

143,727 transitions for 40 vehicles (i.e. about 1.3 times more than the first case). As an estimation of the supported maximum size of the model regarding the state space size limit of Afra, the number of vehicles can be increased up to 100 if having distribution which does not create congested areas. In the second way, new vehicles were added in a way to increase congestion in some areas (Fig. 5(b)). Scaling in this way increases the execution time of the model to 120 s and the number of reached states and transitions to 157,086 and 1,265,839, respectively (i.e. about 10 times more than the previous case). This is because of the fact that in a congested area, the number of delivered warning messages to each vehicle grows rapidly and all the possible orders of execution for messages with the same execution time are considered in the model checking. This results in a sharp growth in the size of the state space and model checking time consumption.

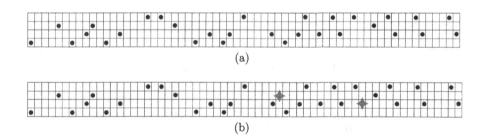

Fig. 5. Configuration of the scenario used for scalability analysis

5   Conclusion and Future Work

Lack of a framework for formal modeling and efficient verification of warning message dissemination schemes in VANETs is the main obstacle in using these schemes in real-world applications. In this paper, we presented VeriVANca, an actor-based framework, developed using Timed Rebeca for modeling warning message dissemination schemes in VANETs. Model of schemes developed in VeriVANca can be analyzed using Afra, the model checking tool of Timed Rebeca. We showed how warning message dissemination schemes can be modeled using VeriVANca by implementing two of these schemes. Scenarios in these schemes were explored to illustrate the effectiveness of the approach in checking correctness properties and performance evaluation of the schemes. We further explained how easily the model of a scheme can be transformed to present another scheme by making minor modifications. Providing this level of guarantee in correctness and performance of warning message dissemination schemes, enables engineers to benefit from these schemes in the development of smart cars.

Considering different members of Rebeca family modeling language, VeriVANca can be used for addressing other characteristics of schemes such as their probabilistic behavior. Since Afra supports different members of Rebeca family, models with these characteristics can be analyzed using Afra.

VeriVANca can be used for the analysis of scenarios with limited congested areas. However, to be able to use the framework for large-scale models containing congested areas, we are going to develop a partial order reduction technique. This reduction relies on the fact that reaction of a vehicle to received warning messages is independent of their sender; therefore, different orders of execution (interleaving) for messages received at the same time can be ignored without affecting the result of model checking.

Acknowledgments. The work on this paper has been supported in part by the project "Self-Adaptive Actors: SEADA" (163205-051) of the Icelandic Research Fund and DPAC Project (Dependable Platforms for Autonomous Systems and Control) at Mälardalen University, Sweden.

References

1. Agha, G., Hewitt, C.: Concurrent programming using actors: exploiting large-scale parallelism. In: Maheshwari, S.N. (ed.) FSTTCS 1985. LNCS, vol. 206, pp. 19–41. Springer, Heidelberg (1985). https://doi.org/10.1007/3-540-16042-6_2
2. Luo, A., Wu, W., Cao, J., Raynal, M.: A generalized mutual exclusion problem and its algorithm. In: ICPP, pp. 300–309. IEEE Computer Society (2013)
3. de Boer, F.S., et al.: A survey of active object languages. ACM Comput. Surv. **76:50**(5), 1–76:39 (2017)
4. Gama, Ó., Nicolau, M.J., Costa, A., Santos, A., Macedo, J., Dias, B.: Evaluation of message dissemination methods in VANETs using a cooperative traffic efficiency application. In: IWCMC, pp. 478–483. IEEE (2017)
5. Gamma, E., Helm, R., Johnson, R., Vlissides, J.: Design Patterns: Elements of Reusable Object-oriented Software. Addison-Wesley Longman Publishing Co. Inc., Boston (1995)
6. Gholibeigi, M., Heijenk, G.: Analysis of multi-hop broadcast in vehicular ad hoc networks: a reliability perspective. In: Wireless Days, pp. 1–8. IEEE (2016)

7. Hafner, M.R., Cunningham, D., Caminiti, L., Vecchio, D.D.: Cooperative collision avoidance at intersections: algorithms and experiments. IEEE Trans. Intell. Transp. Syst. **14**(3), 1162–1175 (2013)
8. Khamespanah, E., Khosravi, R., Sirjani, M.: An efficient TCTL model checking algorithm and a reduction technique for verification of timed actor models. Sci. Comput. Program. **153**, 1–29 (2018)
9. Khamespanah, E., Sirjani, M., Viswanathan, M., Khosravi, R.: Floating time transition system: more efficient analysis of timed actors. In: Braga, C., Ölveczky, P.C. (eds.) FACS 2015. LNCS, vol. 9539, pp. 237–255. Springer, Cham (2016). https://doi.org/10.1007/978-3-319-28934-2_13
10. Lin, S., Maxemchuk, N.F.: The fail-safe operation of collaborative driving systems. J. Intell. Transport. Syst. **20**(1), 88–101 (2016)
11. Saeed, T., Mylonas, Y., Pitsillides, A., Papadopoulou, V., Lestas, M.: Modeling probabilistic flooding in vanets for optimal rebroadcast probabilities. IEEE Trans. Intell. Transp. Syst. **20**(2), 556–570 (2019)
12. Sanguesa, J.A., et al.: On the selection of optimal broadcast schemes in VANETs. In: MSWiM, pp. 411–418. ACM (2013)
13. Sanguesa, J.A., et al.: RTAD: a real-time adaptive dissemination system for vanets. Comput. Commun. **60**, 53–70 (2015)
14. Sanguesa, J.A., Fogue, M., Garrido, P., Martinez, F.J., Cano, J., Calafate, C.T.: A survey and comparative study of broadcast warning message dissemination schemes for vanets. Mob. Inf. Syst. **2016**, 8714142:1–8714142:18 (2016)
15. Sirjani, M., Movaghar, A., Shali, A., De Boer, F.S.: Modeling and verification of reactive systems using Rebeca. Fundam. Informaticae **63**(4), 385–410 (2004)
16. Suriyapaibonwattana, K., Pomavalai, C.: An effective safety alert broadcast algorithm for VANET. In: 2008 International Symposium on Communications and Information Technologies, pp. 247–250. IEEE, October 2008
17. Tseng, Y., Ni, S., Chen, Y., Sheu, J.: The broadcast storm problem in a mobile ad hoc network. Wireless Netw. **8**(2–3), 153–167 (2002)
18. Yousefi, B., Ghassemi, F., Khosravi, R.: Modeling and efficient verification of broadcasting actors. In: Dastani, M., Sirjani, M. (eds.) FSEN 2015. LNCS, vol. 9392, pp. 69–83. Springer, Cham (2015). https://doi.org/10.1007/978-3-319-24644-4_5
19. Yousefi, B., Ghassemi, F., Khosravi, R.: Modeling and efficient verification of wireless ad hoc networks. Formal Aspects Comput. **29**(6), 1051–1086 (2017)
20. Zeadally, S., Hunt, R., Chen, Y., Irwin, A., Hassan, A.: Vehicular ad hoc networks (VANETS): status, results, and challenges. Telecommun. Syst. **50**(4), 217–241 (2012)

Author Index

Printed in the United States
By Bookmasters